TOURISM IN EUROPE

TOURISM IN EUROPE
Structures and Developments

Edited by

W. Pompl

Fachhochschule Heilbronn
Germany

and

P. Lavery

University of Humberside
UK

CAB INTERNATIONAL

CAB INTERNATIONAL
Wallingford
Oxon OX10 8DE
UK

Tel: Wallingford (0491) 832111
Telex: 847964 (COMAGG G)
Telecom Gold/Dialcom: 84: CAU001
Fax: (0491) 833508

A catalogue entry for this book is available from the British Library.

ISBN 0 85198 852 0

Typeset by Solidus (Bristol) Limited
Printed and bound in Great Britain at the University Press, Cambridge

CONTENTS

CONTRIBUTORS

Peter Aderhold: Institute for Transport, Tourism and Regional Economics, Copenhagen Business School, Blaagaardsgade 23B, DK-2200 Copenhagen N., Denmark.

Isabel Albert-Piñole: Escuela Oficial de Tourismo, Plaza de Manuel Becerra 14, 28028 Madrid, Spain.

Gregory Ashworth: Department of Physical Planning and Demography, Faculty of Spatial Sciences, University of Groningen, P.O. Box 800, 9700 AV Groningen, The Netherlands.

Ian Barnes: Humberside Business School, University of Humberside, Cottingham Road, Hull HU6 7RT, UK.

Pamela Barnes: Humberside Business School, University of Humberside, Cottingham Road, Hull HU6 7RT, UK.

Michel Bauer: Faculté de Langues Appliquées, Tourisme et Affaires Internationales, Université de Savoie, BP 1104, 73011 Chambery Cedex, France.

Jan R. Bergsma: Netherlands Institute of Tourism and Transport Studies, Department of Tourism and Recreation, Sibeliuslaan 13, 4837 CA Breda, The Netherlands.

Aureliano Bonini: Trademark Italia, Via Gambalunga 56, 47037 Rimini, Italy.

Helen Briassoulis: National Centre for Scientific Research 'Demokritos', P.O. Box 60228, Ag. Paraskevi 15310, Athens, Greece.

Jonathan Edwards: School of Tourism, Department of Service Industries, Bournemouth University, Dorset House, Talbot Campus, Fern Barrow, Poole, Dorset BH12 5BB, UK.

Desmond A. Gillmor: Geography Department, Trinity College, Dublin 2, Ireland.

Derek R. Hall: Department of Geography, University of Sunderland, Forster Building, Chester Road, Sunderland SR1 3SD, UK.

Richard Hill: Fachhochschule Heilbronn, Fachbereich Touristikbetriebs-wirtschaft, Max-Planck-Strasse 39, 74081 Heilbronn, Germany.

Chris Holloway: Bristol Business School, University of the West of England, Coldharbour Lane, Bristol BS16 1QY, UK.

Claude Kaspar: Institut fur Tourismus und Verkehrswirtschaft an der Hochschule St Gallen für Wirtschafts-, Rechts- und Sozialwissen-schaften, Varnbüelstrasse 19, CH-9000 St Gallen, Switzerland.

Jan Koskinen: Oesterbottens Hoegskola, Vasaesplanen 15B, 65101 Vasa, Finland.

Christian Laesser: Institut fur Tourismus und Verkehrswirtschaft an der Hochschule St Gallen für Wirtschafts-, Rechts- und Sozialwissen-schaften, Varnbüelstrasse 19, CH-9000 St Gallen, Switzerland.

Patrick Lavery: Pro Vice Chancellor, University of Humberside, Cottingham Road, Hull HU6 7RT, UK.

Wilhelm Pompl: Fachhochschule Heilbronn, Fachbereich Touristikbe-triebswirtschaft, Max-Planck-Strasse 39, 74081 Heilbronn, Germany.

Peter Roth: Deutsche Zentrale für Tourismus, Beethovenstrasse 69, 6000 Frankfurt 1, Germany.

Francisco Sampaio: Tourism Division, School of Tourism, Technology and Management, Polytechnic of Viana do Castelo, Viana do Castelo, Portugal.

Anders Steene: Kalmar University College, Hoegskolan i Kalmar, ITEF, Box 905, IS 391 29 Kalmar, Sweden.

Albrecht Steinecke: Europäisches Tourismus Institut GmbH an der Universitat Trier, Bruchhausenstrasse 1, 5500 Trier, Germany.

Jon Teigland: Telemarkforskning, Postboks 3025, Roterud, 2600 Lillehammer, Norway.

PREFACE

Europe and tourism are closely linked for many reasons, although three are prominent. First, it was in Europe, particularly in Great Britain, that the tourist industry was invented, refined and developed. Second, Europe dominates world tourism with two out of every three tourist arrivals worldwide. For the past 40 years Europe has been the world's leading tourist destination receiving over two thirds of all international tourist arrivals and over half of all tourist receipts. The European tourist industry employs over 35 million people, representing over 8% of the workforce and receives over $66 billion a year from tourism receipts.

The third reason for the significance of tourism in Europe lies in the consequences of the establishment of the Single European Market. The aim of the Single European Act, which came into effect on 1 January 1993, is to encourage economic integration not least in the tourist industry of Europe. The full endorsement of the Maastrict Treaty will continue the process towards a unified Europe and will impact on decision-making processes, practices and policy formulation at national, regional and local levels as tourism policy is given a 'European' dimension. The Commission of the European Communities prepared a community policy on tourism in July 1982 and updated it in July 1985. This has greatly strengthened tourism in Europe and will continue to do so after 1992 and will enhance its attractiveness as a tourist destination. The Single European Act of 1992 emphasized the integration of tourism in Europe by setting the seal on measures designed to provide freedom of movement and protection of tourists, freedom of movement of the workforce and mutual recognition of qualifications. It has encouraged the integration of tourism in Europe by measures designed to provide freedom of movement and the protection of tourists. Before the Treaty of Rome was passed establishing the EC, the many national frontiers represented a very real barrier to the movement of travellers from one country to another. Since 1958, frontier formalities have been steadily relaxed and liberalized.

Customs duties between the member states have gone, as has much of the paperwork and the long queues at customs posts. There are no major problems concerning the personal effects that tourists bring with them and most formalities have been relaxed concerning cars, caravans and boats. All EC nationals are entitled to the medical services of the host country if they are so entitled under their domestic health insurance. The Commission is also seeking to harmonize car insurance and tourist assistance. All of these measures put tourism within the Community at a greater advantage over other regions in the world.

This book is seen as essential reading to all students on degree level courses throughout the European Community and indeed will appeal to those in other parts of the world who wish to be informed about developments in the European tourist industry.

The book is divided into two parts. The first has a series of thematic chapters covering the impact of the Single European Act on the tourist industry in Europe and covers topics such as transport, tourism policy, education and training and the social and cultural impacts of tourism.

The second part considers the structure of the tourist industry and trends in each Member State of the European Community, and each chapter has been written, where possible, by a native of that country to provide a national perspective. There is also discussion of tourism in the non-EC countries of Scandinavia and in Austria and Switzerland, the latter being taken as a case study of a non-EC country. Given the dramatic developments in Eastern Europe since 1989 the final chapter examines the issues facing tourism in Eastern Europe.

On a final and more personal note, together we formed part of a larger group of academics who produced the first Masters Programme in European Tourism in the mid 1980s when 1992 was a far off date on the calendar. This book is another result of that earlier joint venture, and perhaps it is fitting that it should be published in the year when a unified Europe becomes a reality.

Wilhelm Pompl
Patrick Lavery
January 1993

I

DEVELOPMENTS IN TOURISM IN EUROPE

1

THE HISTORICAL DEVELOPMENT OF TOURISM IN EUROPE

Albrecht Steinecke

Travelling, defined as overcoming geographical distances, is inseparably connected with the history of mankind, and is time-less. The Pilgrimages, trading-caravans, the Crusades and expeditions all originally had a religious, political or economic impetus. The journeys taken in these ancient times were generally unavoidable and may not have always been comfortable, but were a means of achieving a certain objective.

THE 'GRAND TOUR'

PC .2

Tourism differentiates itself from these types of journeys as it is travelling for pleasure. In ancient Rome such travel was a significant feature, for example to second homes at seaside resorts, such as Baiae on the Bay of Naples (Casson, 1974). Some of the earliest evidence of modern tourism is to be found in Europe in the 17th and 18th centuries. The young aristocracy undertook extended journeys through Europe for educational purposes, which saw the first form of diplomacy and foreign affairs. Sometimes these educational journeys could last several years. The main objective of the journey was to teach the young members of the nobility foreign languages, fencing, riding, dancing, the art of establishing connections of political or economic interest and manners befitting their rank. Accordingly, the journey led them to the centres of cultural, political, economic and religious life: London, Paris, Amsterdam, The Hague, Rome, Venice, Turin and Madrid.

Western and southern regions of Europe were the most frequented. This was otherwerwise known as the 'Grand Tour', which for British travellers commenced in Britain, passed through France (with a longer stay in Paris) to Italy, where travellers would spend about one year visiting the different cities. Italy was the most popular destination not only because of its cultural and artistic background, but also for its links with the cultural and scientific world of the Orient. The return journey would take them through Switzerland, Germany and The Netherlands.

The travellers' conduct during their journey was influenced by their elitist status, as members of the landed classes (i.e. aristocracy and gentry). A company of servants, tutors, mentors and a marshall (who administered the journey) had to assure a smooth journey. At the same time they also provided protection and loyalty to their aristocratic employer. These journeys had to be carefully planned and prepared for, often adopting the same 'Grand Tour' as that taken by the father or other relative. Letters of recommendation facilitated access to the local nobility in order to make sure that all the requirements of the journey were met.

As such large amounts of money and long periods of time were necessary for these journeys, it was a privilege that only the rich could afford, with the intention of increasing their influence and securing their status. It is important to understand that the relation of work to leisure time as we know it today did not exist for the majority of the population at this time. This makes it much easier to understand the elitist nature of such a 'Grand Tour'.

Life in pre-industrial society was determined by nature. Following the ever repeating pattern of seasonal changes, agricultural working activities depended on the whole on nature's seasonal demands. As a result there was little geographical mobility. People were bound to the village, living usually with several generations together. The longest possible journey would lead them to the nearest market place, where they sold their products and bought goods they could not produce themselves. All in all the rural population did not have the freedom of living or profession that we have today.

It was merely the aristocracy and gentry who had the necessary financial means, available free time and legal privileges to undertake a journey. The dictums of work and leisure did not exist for them; this therefore enabled them to spend an almost unlimited time travelling.

Due to the structural changes in Middle and Western Europe at the end of the 18th century, the exclusivity of travelling altered to a certain extent. Merchants and others with urban or trading occupations gained economic influence and status due to the increased ownership of factories and the expansion of national and international trade. By imitating the behaviour of the former noble elite, the bourgeoisie tried to increase their status.

This also influenced travelling behaviour. The 'Grand Tour' destinations also became popular destinations for the travelling bourgeoisie (Table 1.1). According to an investigation by Stadler (1975), who analysed a visiting register of a salt mine in Dürnberg near Salzburg (Austria) dating from 1778, 80% of all visitors were members of the secular and religious

Table 1.1. Periods of development of tourism.

Class	17/18th century	18th century	18th century/ beginning 19th century	Middle 19th century	End 19th century	Beginning 20th century
Landed classes (Aristocracy and gentry)	Grand Tour	Spa	Seaside resort	Mediterranean sea in winter/ Rhine Tour	Alpinism/ Mediterranean in summer	World Tour
Bourgeoisie		Grand Tour/ Educational journey	Spa	Seaside resort	Rhine Tour/ Mediterranean in winter	Alpinism/ Mediterranean in summer
Lower class				Excursion trains	Seaside resort	Seaside resort/ Spa

aristocracy. This pattern altered between 1778 and 1792, when the proportion of bourgeoisie, professors and students exceeded 60% of all visitors. This social advancement led to an expansion in tourism. For example, the number of people crossing the Channel at Dover doubled from 20,000 per year in the middle of the 18th century to 40,000 in 1785 (Robinson, 1976). At the same time the character of the journey changed. The bourgeoisie, as opposed to the aristocracy, had more limited financial resources and therefore the journeys were made shorter and activities during the journey had to be intensified. Sightseeing became a much more important part, with the developing of social contacts and obligations less so.

INLAND SPAS

In reaction to the bourgeoisie imitating the nobility's travel behaviour, the latter tried to widen the choice of destinations available to them, away from the majority of travellers. This constituted the same sort of travelling behaviour patterns of different social classes as can be observed today.

In their efforts to exclude themselves from the lower classes the nobility rediscovered inland spas. Mineral springs were again seen as popular resorts due to their healing effects for certain illnesses. However, the medical reasons for visiting a spa were soon to give way to reasons of entertainment. The characteristics of spas such as Bath or Tunbridge Wells in Great Britain and Baden-Baden, Aix-Les-Bains or Marienbad on the Continent reflect the demands of their aristocratic guests. Apart from bathing houses and swimming baths there were also large parks, concert halls and casinos. Due to this change in travelling behaviour, the second half of the 18th century witnessed the development of more and more spas, with more than one hundred in Great Britain and similar numbers on the Continent. Soon the bourgeoisie also discovered the inland spas and as before the same imitation-and-segregation-process between bourgeoisie and aristocracy took place (see Table 1.1).

SEASIDE RESORTS

This process of geographical segregation resulted in the aristocracy discovering the seaside as a part of nature, whereas up to that time it had been regarded as hostile, unhealthy and inhospitable. From the middle of the 18th century the coast became the nobility's favourite destination. The expansion of seaside tourism partly resulted from medical publications emphasizing the benefits of sea bathing. The bathing in and the drinking of sea water under medical supervision was considered to be a means of combating various diseases or disorders, for example deafness, cancer, leprosy and venereal diseases. In addition to medical reasons, entertainment soon became more and more important.

As with the spas, a specific seaside resort infrastructure was developed, the fundamental elements being bathing facilities, promenades, reading and conversation rooms, concert halls and theatres. Former fishing villages were confronted by the booming tourist industry, which in turn resulted in a change in the structure of the settlements and architecture. They no longer constructed their houses in such a way as to protect themselves from the weather elements. Instead the houses were built to face the sea, facilitated with new materials to protect the bricks against erosion. From now on, the view to the sea constituted the main factor of location. These seaside resorts, which quickly grew up at the beginning of the 19th century, especially along the south coast of England, are characterized by the line of settlements which were built along the coastline.

The sea also experienced a total revaluation in art and poetry, moving away from the image of a wild uncultivated landscape to a magnificent and powerful part of nature (Howell, 1974). Changes in perception of the relationship to nature, the trend of the lower social classes following in the footsteps of the upper classes, and the efforts of the elite to stand apart from the rest were factors which determined the development of tourism in the 19th and 20th centuries. From the middle of the 19th century the increasing number of middle-class tourists – mainly families with children – visiting seaside resorts, indirectly caused more and more of the French and Italian coasts to be developed for the tourist industry.

ALPINE RESORTS

Similar developments took place in the Alps in the middle of the 19th century, initiated by new attitudes and ideas contrasting with the negative image of the mountains in the 17th century. During the latter, the natural landscape, in the eyes of the average person, had no aesthetic value. The perception people had of nature was what mankind could create from nature, for example buildings and landscaped gardens. Nature was negatively associated with belief in witchcraft, evil ghosts and the supernatural. However, in contrast, the later literary works of Haller, Gessner, Saussure, Goethe, Schiller, Rousseau and Byron described the mountains as places where man and nature live in harmony. The later phases of the Grand Tour in the 18th and early 19th centuries also contributed to the 'discovery' of the Alps and other romantic aspects of nature (Nicolson, 1959).

The 19th century also brought forth a scientific interest in the mountains. For the well-educated members of the nobility the Alps became an interesting region for exploring. With their mineralogical, geological and geomorphological discoveries they broadened their knowledge of the nature and culture of this specific region. Then they made their discoveries known to the general public through lectures and publications in scientific journals and general educational periodicals. Sporting challenges were another reason for the surge in new interest in the Alps. Although the early mountaineers had their scientific reasons, in the middle of the 19th century mountaineering became a sporting activity in itself. Members of the British nobility were the trendsetters for this type of sport and hence in 1857 founded the first mountaineering club, the 'Alpine Club' in London. Soon other equivalent clubs followed in Austria (1862) as well as in Germany and Switzerland (1863). As with the seaside resorts, the Alps also bene- fited from a revaluation in social and economic attitudes initiated by members of the upper class from other regions.

It is only since the middle of the 19th century that the Alps have attracted tourists during the winter. In 1853 a Davos clinic began to specialize in the treatment of tuberculosis. The treatment would last a whole year and thereby changed the seasonal tourist's demands. A whole range of leisure activities also had to be offered to the friends and relatives of the patient during the winter months. In 1868 in Switzerland skiing started to be recognized as an alpine sport, although it took another twenty years for it to become popular.

THE TECHNOLOGY OF TRANSPORT PC·2

In general, up to the middle of the 19th century the demand for tourism was low. On the one hand the majority of the population suffered great economic, legal and time restrictions which gave them little opportunity to travel. On the other hand ancient means of transport meant that travelling was far less comfortable than it is today. The commencement of tourism was not initiated by revolutionary progress in methods of transport, nor did tourism itself induce developments in improved means of transport. Chronicles of travellers, which are documented in well-kept records dating back to the 17th century, testify to the danger and arduousness of travelling in these times. Road networks were sparse and the streets were in poor condition, causing travellers to have regular accidents and long delays. Mail coaches, which were of limited capacity, were unreliable and often robbed. Transport fares together with tolls and taxes made travelling very expensive (especially in Germany). The travelling speed never exceeded 7 km (four miles) per hour. To cover a distance such as from Berlin to Rome would have taken a person travelling in the 18th century more than two months.

This explains the time needed for the journey and the longer stays at the destinations during a 'Grand Tour' (Löschburg, 1977).

A revolutionary change took place when during the 19th century the steamboat and the railway were developed. They offered high transport capacities, low costs and a high speed of travelling. As a consequence of this, travellers developed a completely new understanding of space and time. The reduced efforts and costs not only extended the radius in which they travelled, but also allowed greater numbers of the population to participate in travel. From this time onwards not only the rich elite, but also the bourgeoisie in general contributed to the demand of tourism. The seaside resort, Brighton for example, experienced an increase in tourists from 50,000 to 360,000 (per year) after the London to Brighton railway was opened.

The increase in demand for tourism influenced urban development in tourist resorts. Between 1801 and 1851 British seaside resorts experienced the highest rate of growth compared with other cities (Cosgrove and Jackson, 1972; Lickorish and Kershaw, 1975a,b).

In Germany the extension of the rail network progressed slowly compared to that in Great Britain. However, between 1835 and 1860 the length of the track increased fivefold (1860: 11,600 km). Even before the beginning of the Second World War the rail network had expanded to a high density everywhere. From everywhere in Germany it was only a couple of hours' walk to the nearest railway station. Similar developments occurred with the road networks, increasing from 25,000 km in 1835 to 115,000 km in 1873 (Henning, 1973).

By the middle of the 19th century the fundamentals of tourism had been established, covering all the important features, i.e. sightseeing, education, health, bathing, alpine resorts and skiing. All the basic types of natural landscape had been developed to cater for the tourist industry. Attitudes and perceptions changed due to a new understanding of distance and nature and a generally positive attitude towards travel.

PUSH FACTORS

The development of the early form of tourism into mass market tourism was caused by various socioeconomic factors:

- increase in leisure time;
- increase in income;
- introduction of legally constituted holiday regulations;
- population growth;
- technological progress in general, including increasing motorization, in particular;

- changes in the occupational structure;
- urbanization.

The reduction in working hours has played a vital role within this process. During the early period of the Industrial Revolution in Germany, industrial workers had an average of 80–90 working hours per week. Up to the First World War the number of working hours had decreased to 60 per week due to several factors, e.g. mechanization, technological progress, sociopolitical reforms, union activities and legal regulations. In 1975, in Germany a 40-hour-working-week was introduced. Presently, trade unions are fighting for further reductions within the European Community.

For the first time the Federal Holiday Law (1963) set holiday regulations for the whole of the German population across the country. The number of holidays a person received increased from 16 days in 1960 to 30 days in 1990.

Reductions in working hours and new holiday regulations constituted changes which were necessary to enable growth in the tourist industry. Without increased non-working time it would have been impossible for an individual to make use of the leisure and tourism facilities.

Another important element in the development of the tourist industry is the increased involvement of the lower classes, leading to a steady increase in demand. In 1841 in Great Britain, Thomas Cook organized day-trips by train for members of the lower class. These trips to the seaside served the purpose of taking the workers' minds off their miserable living and working conditions, familiarizing them with middle-class habits as well as fighting alcohol abuse.

Especially after the Second World War a rise in real incomes also enabled the lower social classes to participate in tourism. A rise in income positively correlates with demand for holidays, as opposed to the erratic rise in the purchase of other goods. In addition, factors such as population growth, urbanization and changes in occupational structures were also important. The expansion of the industrial and service sectors, together with that of governmental bodies, resulted in an increase in bureaucracy and consequently more and more white collar workers and civil servants. These occupational groups represent an over-proportional share within the tourist industry.

An increasing number of people in Middle Europe were affected by urbanization. This in turn had a negative effect on the environment in which they lived. To combat this problem they tried to get away from it all and decided to spend their spare time going away on holiday.

Greater mobility, as a result of technological progress in the field of transport, enabled members of the lower classes to participate in tourism. In this context the growth in the ownership of cars is particularly important. Between 1951 and 1990, the number of cars per hundred inhabitants in

West Germany rose from 1.6 to 50.3 (Statistisches Bundesamt, 1952, 1991).

The increase in private car ownership caused the travelling demands of the tourist to be revolutionized. While the extension of railways resulted in a linear development of new tourist resorts, individual transport by car opened up almost unlimited spatial opportunities.

The widespread adoption of aircraft as a means of mass transportation (especially charter flights) had a similar revolutionary impact on the demands of the international tourist to that of the railway in the 19th century. Since the 1960s holiday destinations all over the world have been in reach due to carriers using large aircraft. With this more recent development the expansion of tourism – in spatial terms – has come to a standstill. There are no untouched natural landscape regions left to be discovered by tourists. However, tourism is still developing in other ways, such as the development of industrial heritage sites as tourist attractions, as well as other aspects of heritage and cultural tourism (see Chapter 2).

BIBLIOGRAPHY

Anderson, J. and Swinglehurst, J. (1978) *The Victorian and Edwardian Seaside.* Hamlyn, London.

Bausinger, H., Beyrer, K. and Korff, G. (eds) (1991) *Reisekultur. Von der Pilgerfahrt zum modernen Tourismus.* C.H. Beck, München.

Brendon, P. (1991) *Thomas Cook.* Secker and Warburg, London.

Burkart, A.J. and Medlik, S. (1976) *Tourism. Past, Present and Future.* Heinemann, London.

Casson, L. (1974) *Travel in the Ancient World.* George Allen and Unwin, London.

Cosgrove, I. and Jackson, R. (1972) *The Geography of Recreation and Leisure.* Hutchinson, London.

Henning, F.-W. (1973) *Die Industrialisierung in Deutschland 1800 bis 1914.* Teubner/UTB, Paderborn.

Hofmeister, B. and Steinecke, A. (eds) (1984) *Geographie des Freizeit- und Fremdenverkehrs.* Wege der Forschung, Bd. 592. Wissenschaftliche Buchgesellschaft, Darmstadt.

Howell, S. (1974) *The Seaside.* Studio Vista, London.

Hyde, W.W. (1917) The development of the appreciation of mountain scenery in modern times. *The Geographical Review* 3(2), 107–118.

Jackson, R. and Hudman, L. (1990) *Geography of Travel and Tourism.* Delmar, London.

Kulinat, K. and Steinecke, A. (1984) *Geographie des Freizeit- und Fremdenverkehrs.* Erträge der Forschung, Bd. 212. Wissenschaftliche Buchgesellschaft, Darmstadt.

Lavery, P. (1991) *Travel and Tourism*, 2nd edn. Elm, Huntingdon.

Lickorish, L.J. and Kershaw, A.G. (1975a) Tourism before 1840. In: Burkart, A.J.

and Medlik, S. (eds) *The Management of Tourism*. Heinemann, London, pp. 3–10.

Lickorish, L.J. and Kershaw, A.G. (1975b) Tourism between 1840–1940. In: Burkart, A.J. and Medlik, S. (eds) *The Management of Tourism*. Heinemann, London, pp. 11–24.

Löschburg, W. (1977) *Von Reiselust und Reiseleid*. Insel, Frankfurt-am-Maine.

Lowenthal, D. (1962) Tourists and thermalists. In: *The Geographical Review*, 52(1), 124–127.

Nicolson, M.H. (1959) *Mountain Gloom and Mountain Glory*. Cornell University Press, Ithaca.

Pimlott, J.A.R. (1947) *The Englishman's Holiday*. Faber and Faber, London.

Prahl, H.-W. and Steinecke, A. (1989) *Der Millionen-Urlaub. Von der Bildungs-reise zur totalen Freizeit*. IFKA-Faksimile. Institut für Freizeitwissenschaft und Kulturarbeit, Bielefeld.

Robinson, H. (1976) *A Geography of Tourism*. MacDonald and Evans, London.

Spode, H. (1987) *Zur Geschichte des Tourismus. Eine Skizze der Entwicklung der touristischen Reise in der Moderne*. Studienkreis für Tourismus, Starnberg.

Stadler, G. (1975) *Von der Kavalierstour zum Sozialtourismus. Kulturgeschichte des Salzburger Fremdenverkehrs*. Universitätsverlag Anton Pustet, Salzburg.

Statistisches Bundesamt (ed.) (1952) *Statistisches Jahrbuch 1952 für die Bundes-republik Deutschland*. Stuttgart and Köln.

Statistisches Bundesamt (ed.) (1991) *Statistisches Jahrbuch 1991 für die Bundes-republik Deutschland*. Stuttgart and Mainz.

Steinecke, A. (1983) Gesellschaftliche Grundlagen der Fremdenverkehrsentwick-lung. In: Haedrich, G., Kaspar, C., Kleinert, H. and Klemm, K. (eds) *Tourismus-Management, Tourismus-Marketing und Fremdenverkehrs-planung*. Marketing-Management, Bd. 8. De Gruyter, Berlin and New York, pp. 37–55.

Towner, J. (1985) The Grand Tour: a key phase in the history of tourism. *Annals of Tourism Research* 12(3), 297–333.

Towner, J. (1988) Approaches to Tourism History. *Annals of Tourism Research*, 15(1), 47–62.

Turner, L. and Ash, J. (1975) *The Golden Hordes. International Tourism and the Pleasure Periphery*. Constable, London.

Walton, J.K. (1983) *The English Seaside Resort: A Social History 1750–1914*. Leicester University Press, Leicester.

2

CULTURE AND TOURISM: CONFLICT OR SYMBIOSIS IN EUROPE?

Gregory Ashworth

THE ARGUMENT

A basic problem faced by this chapter is that although what can be broadly termed 'cultural tourism' is a major and growing form of tourism, the study of cultural tourism has for various reasons been relatively neglected. The first statement justifies the inclusion of a chapter on this form of tourism, whereas the second renders it peculiarly difficult to approach.

The argument of this chapter will proceed by an elaboration of the following assertions:

1. The cultural artefacts and expressions of people, whether past or present, provide a set of resources upon which a major European tourism industry has been constructed.

2. Although it is undeniable that tourism based upon cultural resources is an activity that has conveyed demonstrable economic and social values, its very success has generated costs that can no longer be dismissed as a marginal and acceptable inconvenience. The point has been reached in the development of this form of tourism where continued success threatens the quality and even continued existence of the resources upon which this and other uses of them depend.

3. The problem of reconciling these two assertions is compounded by a third namely, that the tourism industry has developed in such a way as to divorce consideration of the resources from the tourism product. In addition academic observers have had difficulty in applying the dominant paradigms of tourism studies to cultural tourism. This dual neglect is having increasingly serious practical consequences.

The field of enquiry enveloped by these three assertions is clearly beyond the scope of one chapter. Therefore one aspect of human culture has been selected to stand as an example of many more, namely the deliberate use of history as an economic resource in the production of the commodity 'heritage' for sale on tourism markets. The selection of the product heritage as well as the implied strongly economic approach drastically narrows the field of investigation while still allowing the critical question of the relationship between tourism and culture to be posed, and hopefully answered in a way that has a much wider relevance to policy.

The basic assertions will now be elaborated. The importance of heritage tourism within tourism will be demonstrated, or rather reasserted, not least because without this importance the further development of the argument would lose much of its sense and its urgency. Some of the wide ranging criticisms of the expansion of heritage tourism, particularly in Europe, will be briefly mentioned so that the extent of the increasing misgivings about further expansion can be appreciated. The paradoxical neglect of cultural tourism and the consequent failure of both the tourism industry and tourism studies to even recognize the existence of a growing resource problem will then be argued and a selection of recent European policy responses reviewed. If current approaches fail to appreciate and confront the real threats posed by success then a different structure of understanding must be constructed which does offer this hope. To this end some explanations of what is occurring will be offered in the very economic, and specifically marketing, terms which defined the problem in the first instance. Only then will the possibility of applying a model of sustainable development be explored so that conclusions can be drawn that will form the preconditions for its application in planning policies.

Each of these discussions needs exemplification but heritage tourism is such a pervasive phenomenon that illustrations of it can be found in every city and almost every village in Europe. The selection of cases therefore is somewhat arbitrary and Venice, Norwich and Bruges have been chosen for regular reference because they represent extreme cases which pose the problem in urgent terms and therefore have recently received the attention of both academics and policy makers. Not all or even most cities in Europe experience the problem with the same intensity but the lessons of the extreme case may well be more starkly put.

THE IMPORTANCE OF HERITAGE TO TOURISM

Historic resources, whether the conserved built environment of historic architecture and urban morphology, associations with historical events and personalities and the accumulations of past cultural artefacts, artistic achievements and individuals, taken together comprise the single most important primary attraction for tourists and thus heritage tourism sites and cities are the world's most important tourism resorts (Ashworth and

Tunbridge, 1990). This contention is difficult to demonstrate with a few general statistics because of the difficulties of definition argued below: However, a sampling of almost any detailed set of available statistics demonstrates the dimensions of the phenomenon. A number of European national studies, such as in Britain (English Tourist Board, 1981, 1991), Belgium (de Groote, 1987), France (Garay, 1980) and The Netherlands (Ministry of Economic Affairs, 1990) have placed heritage, variously defined, as the main motive for incoming foreign tourists. History, marketed as 'tradition', is a predominant element in the national tourism promotional images of most European countries (Ashworth and Voogd, 1986; Dilley 1986). Studies of domestic holidaymaking and day excursions place historical attractions among the top three types of destination sought in most European countries. The size of the foreign and domestic market available for heritage attractions is indicated by such randomly available statistics as, for example, that more than half the French population make at least one annual visit to an historic monument (Busson and Everard, 1987); or the predominance of heritage among the top 50 most visited attractions in England (Townsend, 1992). The sales of the heritage oriented 'Michelins' or 'Baedeckers', the subscriptions to heritage trusts and museum associations are evidence enough of the mass interest, if not obsession, in the recreational consumption of heritage.

The acceptance of the overwhelming evidence of this importance should not be allowed to conceal two cautionary caveats. First, historical resources are used in distinctly different ways by different types of tourist. They may form the primary motive for the holiday determining the itinerary, pattern of behaviour and satisfaction, or frequently be used as secondary or ancillary resources within quite differently motivated tourism trips, such as business and conference visitors (Labasse, 1984; Law, 1988), or seaside holidaymakers (Ashworth and de Haan, 1987). Culture is rapidly consumed. Even the major European concentrations of aesthetic masterpieces can rarely hold the attention of tourists for more than a few days or more usually hours (see Burtenshaw *et al.*, 1991 for a description of the characteristics of the European urban tourism visit). Consequently heritage tourism facilities tend to be highly clustered. This occurs both within cities, as demonstrated for example by Dietvorst's (1993) spatial product clusters for cultural tourism in the historic town of Enkhuizen, and also on a wider scale between cities which will form networks of similar cultural attractions from which the tourist composes the cultural tourism experience.

Secondly, it is salutary to remember that numerically the most important visitors to historical resources are local residents on repeat visits. Historical attractions are not only serving these demands for local recreation but increasingly are being used to shape a general ambiance of high amenity as an important factor in attracting the location of new commercial and governmental investment. There is a recent awareness of an increasing competition between cities, publicized in a growing number of league tables of the 'New Europe of the cities' (DATAR, 1989) and a growing use of culture in general, and historicity in particular, as an important element in shaping urban images for use in this competitive struggle (see the many examples in Ashworth and Voogd, 1990).

This multi-use of the same heritage attractions for different purposes may lead to a mutual reinforcement or to conflict in the use of resources. The main task of management will be to achieve the former and mitigate the latter.

THE COSTS OF HERITAGE TOURISM

The realization that the simple spatial coexistence of large numbers of tourists and the historic resources they have come to enjoy may lead to damage is as old as tourism itself. The recent spectacular success of heritage tourism has only made this problem more obvious and more serious. The feet, breath, and even digestion of visitors are now seen as posing a serious threat to the physical survival of Stonehenge, Lascaux cave paintings and the Sistine chapel respectively. More subtly tourists en masse destroy the ambiance of monuments, buildings and historic towns (see the many cases in Binney and Hanna, 1978). Indirectly, but probably even more important, are the costs imposed by secondary support facilities. However attractive the past may be to tourists, they remain citizens of the present and thus demand modern transport, accommodation and catering services. The cost in terms of visual intrusion and competition with other land uses serving local needs is most obvious in the case of tourism transport and accommodation. (The case of the dilemma posed by modern hotels built to house the visitors to historic cities and thereby damaging the attractive historic cityscapes that motivated the visit, is discussed and exemplified in various European cities in Ashworth (1988).)

In addition warnings about the damaging impacts of heritage tourism are being sounded from many quite different directions. The literature of cultural anthropology is increasingly a litany of complaint about the effects of tourism on vulnerable local cultures (see the many examples of tourism's alleged destruction of the vernacular included by contributors to Smith, 1977). Historians show a growing concern about tourism's bland bowdler-ization and simplification of Europe's rich and complex past which becomes reduced to a few marketable cliches: even more seriously they deplore the inherent distortion of what they regard as authenticity in the sale of a selective sanitized past to tourists. (Horne (1984) gives an impassioned complaint about the conversion of Europe's diverse and exciting historical experience into what he calls 'The Great Museum'.)

Even tourism's claim to further economic development is being challenged. Hewison (1987) apportioned blame to the 'heritage industry' for encouraging Britain's economic 'climate of decline' by its encouragement of an obsession with a comforting past rather than meeting the challenge of an exciting future. In a much more closely argued series of economic models Mossetto (1991) has demonstrated for the art cities of Europe that although trade originally produced art, art cannot in turn result in profitable trade. Therefore, tourism is intrinsically parasitical upon culture, contributing nothing to it and ultimately, through its failure to reinvest in culture, destroying it. Such arguments may not represent the majority of economists concerned with tourism but they are increasingly being voiced especially in the major tourist–historic cities of Europe.

From time to time such complaints have received a weak response from within tourism studies which more usually echo the 'boosterism and hype' (Cheng, 1990; Hughes, 1991) that is the dominating ethos of the tourism industry. The threat of Turner and Ash's (1976) 'Golden Horde' leaving a trail of 'cultural prostitution' (Pfafflin, 1987) is increasingly heard. In short, there is a widespread and growing feeling that cultural tourism is depleting and damaging the resources upon which it, and other important activities, depend both now and in the future. An examination, by those responsible for managing cultural resources, sites and places, of the justice of these charges that a serious resource problem exists is thus an urgent necessity. For if it is correct, or even if it is believed to be substantially correct by decision makers, then the further development of heritage tourism is likely to evoke stiffening resistance from many quarters. This argument is thus rendered of immediate practical relevance for the shaping of policy.

THE NEGLECT OF THE RESOURCE PROBLEM IN HERITAGE TOURISM

If heritage tourism is so demonstrably important and yet is subject to increasing misgivings about its use of resources, then why have these criticisms, if unfounded, not been refuted or if, at least in part, well founded not resulted in new approaches. The answer lies in two sets of failures.

The Failure of Analysis

The study of tourism has evolved as the study of an economic service activity. To some this sentence is a tautology and its accuracy is confirmed by the contents, approaches and assumptions of most texts on tourism. Historically what has occurred (as Hughes, 1991, has argued) is that the academic study of tourism has developed as a minor intellectual ancillary to a large and successful commercial activity. It has been concerned mainly with monitoring and measuring the economic impacts of this activity, suggesting policy strategies to maximize the economic gains to places, or at a humbler level staffing the industry with trained personnel.

The answer to the question about neglect is implicit in the above cursory description of the evolution and continuing survival of the academic discipline. Although many individual studies of tourism sites and towns have adopted a stance critical of the dominant approach (many of which have been referred to earlier), the economic paradigms, and their operationalization through what has been termed 'the industrial approach' (see the recent structuring use of this approach in Sinclair and Stabler, 1991), prevail.

Analytical studies of the relationship of heritage tourism to its local resources have generally been confounded by three fundamental difficulties; first, identification of specifically heritage tourism, second, extraction of it from the wider context of tourism as a whole or from other aspects of society in which it is inextricably imbedded, and third, measurement and description in some way of its incidence. Solution to these difficulties must be sought by bypassing them with a significantly different working definition, explanation and thus analysis of what is occurring.

What cannot easily be described or defined cannot easily be subject to investigation and therefore has tended to be ignored in favour of those elements that can. If, in addition, cultural resources are regarded as being largely in free and inexhaustible supply then the industry itself has little reason to encourage their study. Thus solutions to the resource crisis are unlikely to be found or even actively sought for, within the present dominant paradigms of tourism study.

Failure of Policy

The organizations responsible for managing the resources, shaping and promoting the product, and servicing the consumer are many, diverse and fragmented. This fragmentation is both horizontal, that is between suppliers, and vertical, that is between stages in the production process. This is the case in all tourism but is likely to be especially apparent in heritage tourism where many of the resource management agencies responsible for historic objects, sites and towns are either unaware of their role in tourism or discount its importance to them. Certainly no organization is in a position to exercise overall control, which in any event would be difficult as there is little consensus between different resource users about objectives.

Despite these intrinsic difficulties and resulting lack of a broad vision national tourism agencies in a number of European countries have recently demonstrated an awareness of the growing critical atmosphere within which tourism operates. The response has been a growing pile of official reports and public relations brochures, not least from Britain, the country generally agreed to be Europe's most successful seller of heritage to tourists. Typical of such documents is *The Green Light* produced by a consortium of the English Tourist Board, Rural Development Commission and Countryside Commission in 1991. Although it claims to be 'a guide to sustainable tourism' and recognizes the problems of damage, congestion and local negative reactions at historic sites and towns, its only 'policy' suggestions are more sensitive local site management, traffic routing and community participation and, if all else fails, then 'site hardening'. A more serious study is that of the official 'Task Force', established by the Secretary of State for Employment, which includes separate reports on tourism at historic monuments and in historic towns (Tourism and the Environment Task Force, 1992). These include a mass of fascinating detailed case studies describing best planning practice in heritage tourism in Britain and overseas. However, it totally fails to confront the general problem of demand and resources and thus arrives at no general solutions or even directions in which such solutions might be found. What is happening (Wheeller, 1991) is that the tourism industry is tackling the criticisms being made of it, not the problems that cause such criticisms. If there is no resource or environmental problem then it does not need to be defined nor do solutions need to be found. The problem is thus seen as one of promotion and public relations not resource use.

CULTURAL RESOURCES AND TOURISM PRODUCTS: THE COMMODIFICATION MODEL OF HERITAGE

The way in which history, that is those aspects of culture relating to the record of the past, is transformed into heritage, a commodity created to satisfy modern consumption demands and traded on modern markets including tourism, is a commodification process. This is by no means unique to this topic but has been applied to other areas of cultural endeavour, such as music (Whitt, 1987), the arts generally (Snedcof, 1985) or local cultures (Greenwood, 1977). Commodification can be approached through a simple analogy with other assembly industries (Fig. 2.1) which allows the various stages of such a process to be examined in the case of heritage products and in particular the relationship between resources and products to be described. The main elements are as follows.

Gregory Ashworth

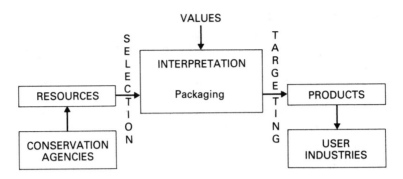

Fig. 2.1. Commodification of the past.

The Cultural Resources

These are drawn from the wide and varied selection of possibilities comprising the remembered events, personalities, mythologies and symbols of the past, often expressed through the surviving objects, buildings and sites. Two points need stressing. First, all resources are by definition only latent until activated by a use and in this case historic resources are in a very real sense created as much as activated by the conservation process. Tourism, therefore, can in one sense be credited logically with creating culture. Second, selection occurs, partly as a result of the vagaries of time and memory, but more importantly as an outcome of deliberate decisions about what is to be preserved or remembered.

Assembly

Historic resources become heritage products by a process of interpretation, which includes both selection and packaging. Packaging is not a marginal cosmetic enhancement intended to aid popularization or simplification; the interpretation is itself the 'core' product that is traded (Ashworth and Goodall, 1988). MacCannell's (1976) stress on the use of what he termed the 'marking' of sites as the essential process in 'sacralisation' expresses a very similar idea: the resource, in this case the 'site', remains dormant until 'marked' in some way as of tourist interest. This converts it into a heritage tourism product and the process becomes cumulative as the presence of visitors itself further 'marks' the site as significant, thus accounting at least in part for a tendency towards concentration.

The Heritage Product

Interpretation thus produces a range of heritage products according to the demands of the various markets for them. Although the range of product possibilities is not limitless, the nature of the final heritage products is rarely determined by the resource endowment and equally these do not, and are not intended to, reflect any supposedly accurate factual record of a past.

The Heritage Market

The existence of a tourism heritage market and concomitant exchange mechanism does not imply a direct pricing system still less any specific political policy of commercialization or privatization (despite Greenwood's, 1977, complaint). The practical difficulty is that not only can the same resources be used within differently interpreted heritage products, the heritage industry can supply the same products to quite different markets. Tourism is only one, and frequently not the largest, user of heritage. The multi-selling of the same product at the same time to quite different consumers for quite different reasons raises all sorts of potential conflicts: some of these are local and specific, such as land use conflict, whereas others are broader and more fundamental, such as resulting from the use of heritage simultaneously in support of local political state identities and as foreign tourism attractions (see the many examples in Ashworth and Tunbridge, 1990).

The Heritage Consumer

A major difference between the heritage product and the conserved relict historical resources is that heritage is only definable in terms of a legatee. It is someone's heritage and that 'someone' defines what is, and is not, heritage in that individual case. This reliance on valuation criteria extrinsic to the resource itself has numerous and fascinating social and political implications (some of which are pursued initially by Tunbridge, 1984) which are not directly relevant to tourism except that they underlie intrinsic tensions in the heritage market. Implicit in the way historic resources are used is that heritage is demand derived whereas historic conservation of buildings or museum exhibits purports to be supply derived. Thus the providers of the historic resources and the creators of the tourism heritage product are quite differently motivated and their attitudes towards the historic resources are thus quite different.

HERITAGE TOURISM PRODUCTS AND SUSTAINABLE HISTORIC RESOURCES

The commodification process model gives a simple description of what is happening within a closed production system but is inadequate for the resolution of the central resource/product dilemma of cultural tourism which results from that very closure. The problem of the threat of success to the resource base itself requires the placing of this micro industrial system within its macro context, thereby dispensing with the assumptions that the resources are inexhaustible and remain unchanged by the interpretation procedure, and that the production of tourism heritage has no impact outside the closed system. A model is thus sought that incorporates three sets of effects that are excluded from the commodification model, namely the effect that successful heritage tourism is likely to have upon other uses of heritage; the likely effects upon the production and maintenance of the historical resources upon which it is based; and the effect of current success upon the future continued long-term production of quality tourism heritage products.

The problem posed in this way has many similarities with the exploitation of a natural resource and thus suggests that sustainable development models may be appropriate if they can be suitably transposed.

Sustainable development has been defined as, 'a process of change in which the exploitation of resources, the direction of investments, the orientation of technical development and institutional change are all in harmony and enhance both current and future potential to meet human needs' (Opschoor and van Straaten, 1991). Figure 2.2 attempts to place the tourism heritage 'industrial' system described earlier within a broader context of a 'total heritage system', which traces the flows of costs and incomes. Such a model allows attention to be focused on three problem areas and their consequences, that all stem from the location of the resources used within heritage tourism outside the tourism system, as was apparant from the commodification model. The historic resources are preserved, maintained and managed, and notable here particularly financed, largely by agencies other than the producers of the tourism product. Such resources are for various reasons usually freely accessible without charge (such as historic cities) or sold well below cost (as with most museums and historic sites). This results in three potential difficulties, namely:

1. As heritage tourism exercises no monopoly in the use of its resources, it is in competition for these resources with other heritage users. Although unlike many exhaustible resources the same history, as argued above, can be used to produce quite different heritage for different users, this multi-use of resources can cause numerous difficulties. Actual physical land-use conflict is the most obvious but perhaps the least important and the most

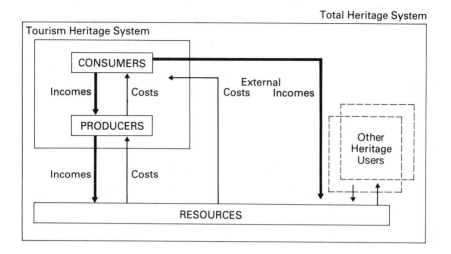

Fig. 2.2. Heritage sustainability model.

amenable to solution through the exercise of existing planning controls. More subtle but pervasive is when heritage used to support local cultural identities or local regional or national political images, is so different from that saleable to tourists that market segmentation is not practical. It is evident from the numerous cases of such conflicts discussed by Ashworth and Tunbridge (1990) that such problems are intrinsic to tourism because of the obvious different relationship to local history that exists between tourists and local residents. The most obvious current examples of this occur within Central and Eastern Europe where history is being used to satisfy the quite different requirements of both foreign tourism and the support of new ethnic and regional political identities. The conflict is not, as argued above, that heritage tourism distorts resources through the offence given by Boorstin's (1963) 'pseudo-event' to any abstract tenets of comprehensiveness or authenticity, merely that conflicting 'pasts' are being marketed from the same resources and often by the same agencies.

2. The position of the resource base outside the system of tourism accounts between tourism producers and consumers leads to an external set of costs and incomes. The difficulty lies in the likelihood of imbalance between the two. It is precisely this imbalance that powers most of the complaints in the British official reports discussed earlier. The costs imposed by tourism producers upon resources are likely to be more direct than the compensating flow of incomes from taxation back to resource maintaining agencies.

3. It is the second set of external costs, namely those of the tourists as consumers of historical resources, that is the most obvious to many observers and which has received the most attention. Compensating flows of incomes from heritage tourists to historic resources are again likely to be indirect. The most valuable, but elusive, income may stem from the increased consciousness of visitors of the value of preserving and enhancing historic resources. However, such psychic gains from the visitor as taxpayer and voter are particularly indirect in tourism when the visitor comes by definition from another place, and in heritage tourism frequently from another country or even continent.

TOWARDS SYMBIOSIS THROUGH SUSTAINABLE DEVELOPMENT: SOME APPLICATIONS

These general ideas can now be applied in some specified areas of policy and exemplification sought in some European cases.

Resource Revaluation

Central to both this argument and to ideas about sustainable development is the way resources are valued. In recreation studies the distinction between participatory demand and various forms of option demands has long been drawn: cultural resources in particular are likely to be valued other than for their immediate use by tourists. Such 'option', or 'deferred' demands (i.e. the value of maintaining a choice in the future) may be a 'bequest' demand (the satisfaction of leaving to future generations) or just an 'existence demand' (i.e. the satisfaction of knowing the resource exists) (Ryan, 1991). These types of demand frequently predominate in motives for the conservation and assembly of historical sites and artefacts. In particular the valuation of the artefacts and associations of the past as a heritage tourism resource has a number of potential points of conflict with the option or latent valuation of the same resources.

An advantage of heritage resources is that they are not in fixed supply in quite the same way as many natural resources. In purely practical conservation terms historic resources, including buildings and ships as well as smaller objects, can be moved, rearranged and even duplicated. Buildings from Venetian palazzi to British telephone boxes have been moved to new settings and open-air museums throughout Europe now house collections of rescued or even facsimile historic buildings that have become major tourism sites. It has already been argued that the conservation movement can be credited with creating the resources it conserves, in so far as its stimulation of an awareness of historicity endows value on objects or buildings which previously had no such value. (The history of interest in industrial archaeology in Western European countries since the 1950s for

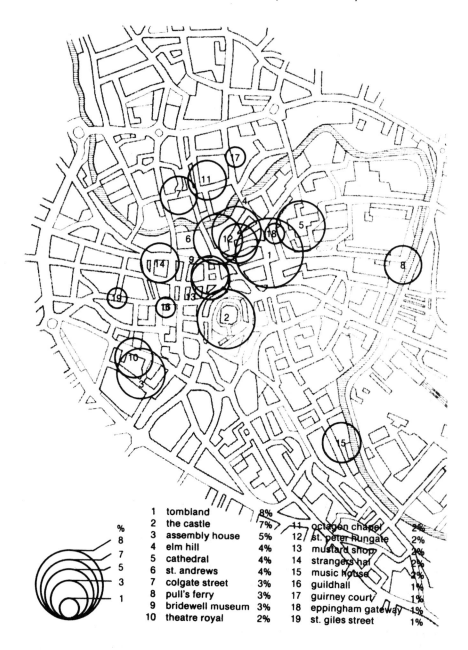

		%
1	tombland	8%
2	the castle	7%
3	assembly house	5%
4	elm hill	4%
5	cathedral	4%
6	st. andrews	4%
7	colgate street	3%
8	pull's ferry	3%
9	bridewell museum	3%
10	theatre royal	2%
11	octagon chapel	2%
12	st. peter hungate	2%
13	mustard shop	2%
14	strangers hall	2%
15	music house	2%
16	guildhall	1%
17	guirney court	1%
18	eppingham gateway	1%
19	st. giles street	1%

Fig. 2.3. Norwich: tourist–historic city.

example created in this sense historic resources from previously unvalued artefacts, buildings and indeed whole major cities such as Bradford or Halifax which have been developed into tourism products.) There has never been a clear demarcation between the preservation of what remains, the restoration back to what was but has since disappeared, and the replication of what could have been but never was.

There are numerous examples of the existence of a worldwide option demand for historical and cultural artefacts. The reaction to such events as the destruction of artistic treasures in the flooding of the Arno and upper Adriatic in 1966 was a torrent of money and concern to save a Florence or a Venice that most donors had never visited. The rescue work of UNESCO or more recently world concern about the shelling of Dubrovnik or the destruction of the Bosnian national library in Sarajevo demonstrates that the concept of a European or even world heritage is not confined to actual tourism visits. Indeed tourism may be seen as being as much a threat to this valuation of historical resources as natural disasters and warfare: sustainable tourism development will thus have to accommodate a range of different types of valuation of the resources it wishes to use.

A major difficulty with urban heritage resources is that they are spatially concentrated and occupy, often to the near exclusion of other functions, a compact area of the inner city. This is the 'tourist–historic' city described and delineated by Ashworth and Tunbridge (1990) which can be illustrated by the clustering of tourist interest in Norwich (Fig. 2.3). Dietvorst's Enkhuizen study (1993) went further by combining spatial clustering and functional association through 'portfolio' analysis thus demonstrating a complex use of varied resources for equally varied markets.

These two studies demonstrate something of the complexity in the way resources are used and recent work in Bruges and Venice also considers local planning responses. The historic centre of Bruges is a small portion of the total agglomeration but accommodates effectively all of the city attractive to heritage tourists, and similarly the 700 ha of the Venice lagoon city is in addition physically isolated from the city-region of which it is a part by water. In such cases it is nearly impossible to expand the resource base *in situ* with new attractions, and in both cities heritage tourism competes with other city centre functions, frequently effectively displacing them. The same historic resources that are valued by the commercial tourism industry also have values for other local purposes: tourism in both Venice and Bruges is credited, not always fairly, with furthering the expulsion or flight of other commercial and even residential activities that find it difficult to compete for the same resources (Page, 1992). In addition both cities have an enormous worldwide option demand for their cultural treasures and can do little to deflect a worldwide market exercising its option to visit its heritage.

Output Revaluation

There is again a consensus when considering the output side of the sustainable model that sustainable development strives to satisfy a series of equity goals often expressed in terms of balance or harmony. This may be an 'intersectoral equity' where the continued existence of the heritage tourism industry is secured by what amounts to a 'harvesting' policy that does not permanently deplete the resource upon which it depends. In the longer term the goal may be an 'intergenerational equity' which assumes the existence of a concierge function for the benefit of a future legatee encompassing notions of equity between past and present in such a way that present users do not 'borrow' from the potential users of the future.

In cities such as Venice and Bruges the contrast in objectives between heritage as a tourism resource for an export market and as a major component in local place identity and civic consciousness is so sharp that it leads to conflict which is expressed politically and even on occasion physically. For the Venice case, van der Borg (1992) introduces a time dimension to this conflict seeing it as the contrast between the immediate consumption of heritage by foreigners and the long-term continued existence of the relics of that history, undamaged by visitors, or by their transport and accommodation facilities, for local use in support of social and political urban identity.

Tourism Carrying Capacities

Unlike some of the other concepts discussed here the possibility that there is a discoverable carrying capacity for any particular site or place is such an attractively simple idea that tourism planners have long sought applications of it (Wall, 1983; Graefe *et al.*, 1984; Westover and Collins, 1987). The idea of capacity was particularly developed as a part of the product life cycle concept transformed to tourism places: here such terms as 'saturation' were applied to particular stages in a resort's development. Thus if pastoral agriculture could maximize its long-term profits by a fine calculation of livestock numbers and land areas, then sustainable heritage tourism can attempt the same, replacing animals by tourists, and pastures by historical resources.

The main difficulty with the application of this simple alluring idea, which promises to provide the tourism place manager with an exact set of figures which will maximize tourism yet sustain the resource base, is that it cannot be achieved by a consideration of the resource base alone. Commentators have long pointed out (Mathieson and Wall, 1982) that carrying capacity is an optimizing model that depends for its outcome on what is to be optimized. The above discussion of resources made clear that historical resources are valued in such different ways that a single tourist would be one too many for some preservational users, whereas for the tourist on the same site many thousands would not detract from the quality of the individual experience.

Secondly, and particularly apposite for cultural tourism where the resources are in almost all cases strictly managed, the capacity of the site is not only capable of being influenced by its management but is in practice largely determined by that management. Heritage is in many respects much more amenable to management than the exploitation of natural resources upon which the carrying capacity concept was evolved. The historical resources themselves can be moved, extended, and replicated, whereas tourist behaviour is capable of being influenced to a high degree and the heritage tourism experience is particularly tolerant of high densities and active management. Similarly the places where heritage tourism occurs, mainly multifunctional cities, are extremely physically robust and characterized by a varied economic base as well as an existing dense and socially diverse population capable of absorbing large tourist influxes.

Although general statements of carrying capacity therefore have little logical foundation and are of limited value in most heritage tourism situations, tourism is frequently confronted by specific problems of congestion. These occur in particular components of the tourism package at specific points in space and time. The physical capacity of an historic city is thus usually determined by the capacity of its hotels or its car parks rather than its museums, historical buildings or districts. Similarly other types of capacity, such as the limits of existing cultures and societies to absorb the demands of tourism without incurring damage or provoking negative reactions, may not in general terms be reached whereas at quite specific times and locations capacity may be exceeded and such damage result. Italian culture and history, and the cities that express these, are hardly threatened by tourists, and even on an August weekend, 90% of the historic lagoon city of Venice remains unexplored by tourists. But at particular times, specific places and for defined activities capacity is so exceeded as to provoke a negative reaction from both Venetians and tourists against heritage tourism in general in that city.

Thus carrying capacity is a specific not general management tool and is dependent upon the prior establishment of objectives.

As a result perhaps of the peculiar physical setting of lagoon Venice, carrying capacity has long been an attractive potential management tool and physical capacities seem particularly apposite (Canestrelli and Costa, 1990; van den Borg, 1992), not least because road access across the causeway and vehicle parking at Piazzale Roma presents an opportunity for the imposition of physical controls (so-called 'hard' measures as opposed to 'soft' measures of selective demarketing and influencing tourist behaviour). The difficulty was to calculate a maximum figure. Daily capacities are clearly more useful in this respect than annual ones and the local police have established 100,000 visitors as a maximum for public security (a figure exceeded on seven occasions in 1990): the capacity of public transport and parking suggests a figure of 25,000 (exceeded on no less than 187 days in 1990).

Bruges has no such natural barriers to aid the monitoring of such capacities or in practice to impose such hard controls. Jansen-Verbeke's definition of carrying capacity was in any event quite different, namely the negative reaction of local residents and organizations to the tourist. Capacity in any district was reached when negative reactions exceeded positive ones, and such a level clearly depends on more than just a crude total number of visitors, but also their distribution in space and time, their behaviour as well as the capacity of a specific district to absorb them without conflicts arising.

Homeostasis

The argument thus has to be clearly made why a heritage tourism product operating within a highly competitive market, which in general is more afflicted by over-supply of possibilities rather than shortage, should not automatically adjust supply and demand through the market. If this were so then the preceding discussion of resources, outputs and capacities would have little relevance to planning.

A problem with any system that treats environmental resources as factors of production is that the feedback may occur too late to prevent irretrievable damage to the resource. Tourism is especially prone to this time delay in adjustment because, unlike the purchase of many other consumer items, the holiday is a relatively rare event, purchased in advance on the basis of extremely indirect information about the product, and once purchased there is little the dissatisfied customer can do to adjust behaviour until the next such decision is to be made. Secondly, as argued above, the many different types of valuation of historical resources and thus different users of heritage derive quite different satisfactions from particular densities of visitors. The visitor to an historic site or town may thus experience no diminution of the quality of the tourism experience while simultaneously causing long-term damage to the resources being enjoyed.

A self-adjusting market system will use pricing mechanisms to keep demand and supply in equilibrium but in heritage tourism much of the supply is either not priced at all or is inadequately priced. The difficulty is that although the internal costs and benefits of the heritage tourism industry system may well be maintained in equilibrium, the resources lie outside such a system and are therefore subject to the classical problem of externalities.

Heritage tourism of course endows historic sites and cities with external benefits as well as imposing external costs. The tourism industry is quick to point out that it generates indirect employment and incomes as well as contributing to national and local taxes. In the field of heritage tourism an indirect benefit of crucial long-term significance to historic resources is the stimulation of interest in heritage and an awareness of the historicity of places. The growth of the movement for the conservation of the relics of the past and the growth in tourism to experience these have not merely always been associated, they exist in a mutually symbiotic relationship.

Thus it is not necessary to argue that the total costs exceed the total benefits, only that the relationship between the costs and benefits is necessarily far too indirect to keep the system in equilibrium. The solution is to internalize the externalities so as 'to close the substance cycle'. The difficulties in applying this idea to heritage tourism lie in its detailed operationalization rather than its logic. The heritage tourism industry must take more financial responsibility for the long-term maintainance of the resources upon which it depends, either directly and voluntarily through substantial subsidies to historic resource agencies (effectively sponsorship) or failing that indirectly and compulsorily through place specific, or user specific, taxation.

The difficulty with this is not as the industry always argues that it imposes a competitive disadvantage upon particular places, as this may be precisely one of the objectives, but that the difficulties of definition of both 'tourism industry' and 'tourist' mentioned earlier makes the allocation of costs to either intrinsically imprecise.

The links between the tourism industry and other aspects of the local economy have been examined in both Bruges and Venice. In Bruges the difficulty is defined by Jansen-Verbeke (1990) as the relative isolation of the local tourism industry from most other local commercial activities, whereas in Venice van der Borg (1992) has focused on the increasingly 'foreign' ownership of tourism facilities, especially hotels, which removes much of the profit and the sense of responsibility for, and sensitivity to, local problems from the city. Equally, however, there is a clear bias in the reactions of Venetian authorities to tourism in favour of particular types of tourism. Hotel-based staying visitors (about 13% of the total) are seen as imposing fewer costs and generating higher benefits; thus it is day excursionists (especially low spending visitors from Central Europe) that create the problem of mismatch that must be corrected. Local tourism 'bed taxation' has recently been abolished in Italy but municipal controls of parking offer some possibilities for recouping some of these costs.

In both cities there is agreement that faster feedback of information would ease entropy problems. At the simplest level information about the level of use of facilities in comparison to their capacity can be conveyed electronically and thus rapidly to booking agents who can advise potential customers accordingly thus encouraging a self-regulating system of adjustment of supply and demand.

CITIES, CULTURE AND TOURISTS

The resource problem, as argued above, and the solutions to it through the devising of sustainable management strategies for heritage tourism are both predominantly local. It is in the 'Europe of the cities' that the conflicts are most apparant but equally the opportunities most obvious, and where are to be found, in most countries, the management instruments and controls over land-use and transport which can be exercised to implement either hard constraints or soft promotional policies. Equally, however, it is the very distinctiveness of individual cities that is their attraction and the uniqueness of each case makes general prescription difficult.

There are numerous examples of such local policies aimed at more equitable distribution of visitors over space or through time. The very tendency towards concentration of heritage tourists in space as a consequence of their limited spatial range and local knowledge, together with their limited expectations of particular sites presents opportunities as much as problems. New heritage place product development in areas currently underused is a solution attempted in many cities, including Bruges where deconcentration strategies are considered by Jansen-Verbeke (1990), through manipulating the flow of information in the form of printed 'trails' and on site signposting. The partial success of Norwich in developing the relatively neglected historic city north of the river Wensum through 'marking' policies is discussed in Berkers *et al.* (1986).

However, local policies have a number of intrinsic disadvantages. In effect they are only able to manage the local consequences of the tourist flows rather than influence them more fundamentally and thus such strategies are often just short-term defensive reactions and at worst may just shift the problem elsewhere.

In organizational terms it is unreal to conceive of a single local policy for heritage tourism being implemented by a single responsible authority in a particular city. There are many different organizations, firms and agencies operating on various elements in the system each with its own policy. The strategies being pursued by the historic conservation agencies, local tourism operators, public service providers and many others may or may not reinforce each other and support the strategy being favoured by the local city government. Equally, as Burtenshaw *et al.* (1991) have argued in the case of a number of European cities including Venice, different governmental levels from the local to the international perceive the problem in quite different ways and are likely to pursue different and in this case contradictory strategies.

It is at the national level that the general mismatch of costs and benefits can be reconciled through fiscal and subsidy strategies. Equally the place product as assembled by the heritage visitor is unlikely to correspond spatially to a single city, however renowned or important such a city may be, but is most likely to be a network or circuit of such cities. Thus the manipulation of the urban network as a whole, or that part of it which constitutes the heritage place product of the consumer is an important management strategy. Capacity, for example, should not be considered in one city alone but in the context of its network of complementary and even competing heritage places.

Such observations apply equally at the international level where the intrinsic internationalism of heritage tourism, as argued earlier, together with the spatial distribution of the heritage cities of Europe in particular, has encouraged the development of international networks of one sort or another. European cities exist within both mutually supporting sets of heritage sites as well as competitive arenas of cities offering similar heritage products. Strategies applied in one city will have repercussions on others in quite different national jurisdictions. A further international dimension stems from the possibility of exporting external costs. The nature of the tourist transaction and frequently also the structure of the tourism industry raises the possibility of a national imbalance between benefits and costs. If as frequently occurs there is also a difference in the level of economic development between tourist generating and receiving areas then there is a clear case of exploitation of poor by richer regions. This problem is endemic of course to all types of tourism but the addition of the heritage element adds an extra piquancy as the history of poorer people is distorted, trivialized or ignored.

The difficulty with reconciling these potential conflicts at the international scale is that the organizational structures, and legislative and financial instruments are particularly undeveloped and ineffective at this scale. The idea of a common 'European heritage' is an abstraction and despite the efforts of the Council of Europe and 'Europa Nostra' to popularize 'best practice' there is only a minimal reflection in planning and management.

Ultimately as with all such sustainability issues more general social attitudes are involved. Sustainability is a 'normative idea involving perceived values and rights over resources' (Opschoor and van der Straaten, 1991) and thus over how such resources should be used. The rich and varied culture of Europe is the 'cultural capital' of the continent as a whole. Its development for tourism not only can occur, to the considerable profit of many, but must occur as, by the previous definition, Europeans cannot in logic be denied access to their own heritage. The issue is not, in almost all cases except the most extreme, whether heritage tourism should be tolerated or excluded. It is how can a particular set of cultural resources be used to satisfy a number of different demands being made upon them both now and in an unpredictable future. Sustainability is thus an issue in development not in preservation. It is a complex set of choices about what form of tourism, at what intensity, at which specific times and locations, and with what set of objectives in mind, that will be relevant to a particular city at a particular time.

The task of devising and implementing such sustainable policies for heritage tourism seems formidable, especially in the face of an industry that must first be convinced that a problem exists and the reactions of many local authorities in the economically disadvantaged regions of Europe to grasp eagerly at any proffered opportunity for immediate profits without too much concern for long-term costs. The philosophical and practical obstacles must be considered against the importance and urgency of the task. A continuance of the present unresolved crisis, multiplied by the expanding tourism demands of an increasingly prosperous, educated and mobile European population making effective, for the first time in European history, its claim to its cultural heritage, will lead to a threefold disaster. There will be irretrievable damage to irreplaceable cultural goods, a failure to exploit the unique economic potential of what promises to become Europe's largest commercial opportunity, and an impoverishment of the cultural experience for tourist and resident alike. In other words the alternative to the sustainable development of European cultural tourism will be increasingly unsustainable.

REFERENCES

Ashworth, G.J. (1988) Tourism accommodation and the historic city. *Built Environment* 15(2), 92–100.

Ashworth, G.J. and Goodall, B. (1988) Tourism images; marketing considerations. In: Goodall, B. and Ashworth, G.J. (eds) *Marketing in the Tourism Industry*. Croom Helm, Beckenham.

Ashworth, G.J. and de Haan, T.Z. (1987) *Uses and Users of the Tourist–Historic City*. Field Studies 10 GIRUG, Groningen.

Ashworth, G.J. and Tunbridge, J.E. (1990) *The Tourist–Historic City*. Belhaven, London.

Ashworth, G.J. and Voogd, H. (1986) Marketing van het Europees Erfgoed: een ondergewaarderde stedelijk-economisch hulpbron. *Plan* 9, 28–34.

Ashworth, G.J. and Voogd, H. (1990) *Selling the City*. Bellhaven, London.

Berkers, M., de Boer, G. and van Doorn, G. (1986) *Norwich: Policy in a Tourist–Historic City*, GIRUG, Groningen.

Binney, M. and Hanna, M. (1978) *Preservation Pays*. SAVE, London.

Boorstin, D.J. (1963) *The Image: or What Happened to the American Dream*. Penguin, Harmondsworth.

Burtenshaw, D., Bateman, M. and Ashworth, G.J. (1991) *The European City: Western Perspectives.* Fulton, London, Chapter 7.

Busson, A. and Everard, Y. (1987) *Portraits Economique de la Culture.* Notes et Etudes documentaires 4846, Paris.

Canestrelli, E. and Costa, P. (1990) *Determining Tourist Carrying Capacity: a Fuzzy Approach.* Dipartimento di Scienza Economica, Univ. degli studi de Venezia.

Cheng, J.R. (1990) Tourism, how much is too much? *Canadian Geographer* 24(1), 8–12.

DATAR (1989) *Les Villes Européennes.* La Documentation Française, Paris.

Decker, P. de (1991) Stad op stelten. *Planologisch Nieuws* 11(3), 220–234.

de Groote, P. (1987) *De Belgische Hotelsector: een Economisch-Geographische Analyse.* Universitaire Pers, Leuven.

Dietvorst, A. (1993) Planning for tourism and recreation: a market oriented approach. In: Van Lier, H.N. and Taylor, P.D. (eds) *New Challenges in Recreation and Tourism Planning.* Elsevier, Amsterdam.

Dilley, R.S. (1986) Tourist brochures and tourist images. *Canadian Geographer* 30, 59–65.

English Tourist Board (1981) *Planning for Tourism in England*, London.

English Tourist Board/Countryside Commission/Rural Development Commission (1991) *The Green Light: a Guide to Sustainable Tourism.* London.

Garay, M. (1980) Le tourisme culturel en France. *Notes et Etudes Documentaires.* Direction de documentation Francaise, Paris.

Graefe, A.R., Vaske, J.J. and Kuss, F.R. (1984) Social carrying capacity: an integration and synthesis of 20 years research. *Leisure Science* 6(4), 121–126.

Greenwood, D.J. (1977) Culture by the pound: an anthropological perspective on tourism as cultural commoditization. In: Smith, V.L. (ed.) *Hosts and Guests: the Anthropology of Tourism.* Blackwell, Oxford, pp. 129–138.

Hewison, R. (1987) *The Heritage Industry: Britain in a Climate of Decline.* Methuen, London.

Horne, D. (1984) *The Great Museum: the Re-presentation of History.* Pluto Press, London.

Hughes, G. (1991) Tourism; a comment. *Area* 23(3), 263–267.

Jansen-Verbeke, M.C. (1990) Toerisme in de binnenstad van Brugge: een planologsiche visie. *Nijmegse Planologische Cahiers* 35.

Labasse, J. (1984) Les congres activites tertiare de villes priviliges. *Annales de Geographie* 520, 687–703.

Law, C.M. (1988) Congress Tourism. *Built Environment* 13(2), 85–95.

MacCannell, D. (1976) *The Tourist: a New Theory of the Leisure Class.* Schoken Books, New York.

Mathieson, A. and Wall, G. (1982) *Tourism: Economic, Physical and Social Impacts.* Longmans, London.

Ministerie van Economische Zaken (Dutch Ministry of Economic Affairs) (1990) *Ondernemen in Toerisme.* SDU, The Hague.

Ministry of Housing and Physical Planning (1989) *National Environment Policy Plan: to Choose or to Loose.* SDU, The Hague.

Mossetto, G. (1991) The Economics of the cities of art: a tale of two cities. *Nota di Lavoro* 91.10 Dept of Economics, University of Venice.

Nijkamp, P. (ed.) (1990) *Sustainability of Urban Systems: a Cross-national Evolutionary Analysis of Urban Innovation.* Avebury, Aldershot.

Opschoor, H. and van Straaten, J. (1991) Sustainable development: an industrial approach. Paper to European Association of Environmental Economists. Stockholm.

Page, S. (1992) Managing tourism in a small historic city. *Town and Country Planning* 61(7/8), 208–211.

Pfafflin, G. (1987) Concern for tourism. *Annals of Tourism Research* 9, 576–588.

Ryan, C. (1991) *Recreational Tourism: a Social Science Perspective.* Routledge, London.

Sinclair, T. and Stabler, M. (1991) *The Tourism Industry: an International Analysis.* CAB International, Wallingford, UK.

Smith, V.L. (ed.) (1977) *Hosts and Guests: the Anthropology of Tourism.* Blackwell, Oxford.

Snedcof, H. (1985) Cultural facilities in multi-use developments. *Urban Land.* Washington.

Tourism and the Environment Task Force (1992) *Tourism and the Environment: Maintaining the Balance.* Report of the historic towns working group. Report of the heritage sites working group. London.

Townsend, D. (1992) Tourism attractiveness of cities. *Tourism and Recreation Research* 2.

Tunbridge, J.E. (1984) Whose heritage to conserve: cross cultural reflections on political dominance. *Canadian Geographer* 26, 171–180.

Turner, L.J. and Ash, J. (1976) *The Golden Horde: International Tourism and the Pleasure Periphery.* Constable, London.

Van der Borg, J. (1992) *Tourism and Urban Development: the Case of Venice.* Tourism Recreation Research.

Wall, G. (1983) Tourism cycles and capacity. *Annals of Tourism Research* 10, 268–270.

Westover, J. and Collins, G. (1987) Perceived crowding in recreation settings. *Leisure Sciences,* 9(2).

Wheeller, B. (1991) Tourism's troubled times. *Tourism Management* 12(2), 42–50.

Whitt, J.A. (1987) Mozart in the metropolis. *Urban Affairs Quarterly* (1), 15–36.

3

TOURISM POLICY IN THE EUROPEAN COMMUNITY

Ian Barnes and Pamela Barnes

INTRODUCTION

The purpose of this chapter is to look at the development of EC Tourism Policy in a period of rapid change, both within the Community and the context of the wider process of integration taking place across Europe. It will take particular account of likely developments in the post-Maastricht period, and the possible expansion of the Community to include new members to the South and East.

In the Maastricht package agreed by the European Council in December 1992, Article 2 of the Treaty on European Union calls for the implementation of common policies throughout the Community, which lead to the promotion of '... harmonious and balanced development of economic activities' (Council of the EC, 1991). These activities should take into account the need for growth which respects the environment, and offer a high level of employment, as well as raising the standard of living and social and economic cohesion. Article 3 of the Treaty lays down a list of policy areas, many of which impact directly on the industry; these include the removal of barriers to trade, the free movement of people, agriculture, transport, social and economic cohesion, environment, health, training, consumer protection and 'measures in the spheres of energy, civil protection and tourism'. This wide diversity of policy areas indicates the cross-sectorial nature of tourism.

The growing importance of the tourist industry to the European Community is reflected by the fact that it merits its first mention in the Treaties as part of the Maastricht agreement. The intention was that Community action in the fields mentioned in Article 3(t), such as tourism, should be pursued on the basis of the existing provisions of the Treaty.

Tourism is a horizontally structured activity, which concerns a number of EC policy areas. Virtually all initiatives will have some effect, although

36

the EC has initiatives which are headlined under the title of Tourism Policy. The most important developments relating to tourism within the EC have always had their origins in the major policy initiatives of the Community. Aspects such as transport policy (dealt with by Pompl in Chapter 4) and the Single Market initiative (dealt with by Lavery in Chapter 5), will only be lightly touched upon here. More emphasis will therefore be placed upon consumer policy, regional and social policy and the all-embracing importance of the European Monetary System (EMS) and the move toward the European Monetary Union (EMU).

The tourist industry has grown rapidly in recent years, building upon rising income levels and the movement of people across borders. In this sense, it is the essence of what the Community wishes to be. Fortunately it is an industry which is located in many areas which the EC Community would like to see further developed, because of long-standing problems of poverty, and high levels of unemployment. That is, it frequently works against the tide of development, which draws labour and investment towards the established centres for manufacturing industry, and financial services. In this respect it is an industry which is particularly important to the new member states in the South of the Community.

THE RATIONALE FOR AN EC POLICY ON TOURISM

In the early years of the Community's development, the tourist industry was seen as being something which was primarily the responsibility of the member states, and of little direct concern to the EC. Part of the reason for this was that a number of the major beneficiaries from international tourism were outside the Community. This situation changed in the 1980s, when the EC expanded to include first Greece in 1981, and then Spain and Portugal in 1986. In all these states, the tourist industry was a major part of their development.

Tourism generates 5.5% of the Community's national income, and accounts for 8% of end-user consumption. It employs 7.5 million full-time workers and 10 million if secondary activities are taken into account. The size of the industry, and the dependence of certain states upon it are an adequate justification for Community interest in it. In addition to this, however, it is the fact that it is an industry which offers huge potential for development and job creation. This is often in areas which find it difficult to find alternative sources of economic stimulus (Commission of the EC, 1992b).

When 1990 was designated the European Year of Tourism, the industry was firmly placed within the ambit of the Community's responsibilities. It was a recognition of the fact that the European tourist industry can only operate effectively within the market, if states are prepared to cooperate, and recognize that there is a high degree of interdependence within major policy areas affecting the industry. This is particularly important in regions such as the Mediterranean, which transcend national boundaries, and joint action is essential in areas such as the environment.

National tourist organizations often see themselves in competition with one another, taking the view that they are participating in a 'zero sum game'. That is, that if one country gains tourists, it will always be at the expense of others who would lose. However, there will be significant gains in terms of the quality of provision, if a variety of tourist activity can be promoted throughout the Community. It will benefit the industry in terms of reducing the over exploitation of certain tourist destinations. Also European tourism may well gain new customers, both from within the Community and from areas like North America and Japan.

The national provision of many of the services which tourists enjoy needs a mechanism for coordination. Although this can be left to market forces in many cases, there are a number of examples where this is inadequate because of differing modes of regulation. The growth of cross-border services makes the EC an ideal institution to provide a policy framework for development. However, this should only be in those areas where international rules and coordination would be appropriate. The European Community tries to ensure that the principle of subsidiarity applies, which means that intervention should not interfere with decisions best made at the local, regional or national level.

Finally, whilst the rationale for EC intervention in tourism is essentially driven by economic considerations, the industry does contribute towards the integration of people in a much deeper sense than a number of other industries. It involves contact between people and cultures. This can assist understanding and create a stronger feeling of European identity and citizenship.

DECISION MAKING

The primary responsibility for decision taking within the EC is shared between the institutions. The Commission has the responsibility for proposing new policy initiatives and in the implementation of policy. The Council of Ministers has the major say in what is finally acceptable. However, since the adoption of the Single European Act in 1987, the European Parliament (EP) has had an increasingly important role in decision making. The powers of the Parliament will have been further enhanced as a result of the ratification of the Maastricht Agreement. The EP also contributes actively towards the discussion of tourism issues in its

Committee on Travel and Tourism. Finally, of lesser significance, is the EC's Economic and Social Committee, which also discusses issues that relate to the industry, although it is regarded as being of less importance.

The Commission is divided into a number of departments called Directorate Generals (DG), which have specific responsibilities for areas of activity. In order to provide clarity of focus, the overall coordination role lies within DG XXIII, with DG III dealing with Internal Market Issues and Industrial Affairs, DG IV with Competition, DG V with Employment, Social Affairs and Education, DG VII with Transport, DG XI Environment, Consumer Protection and Nuclear Safety, XVI with Regional Policy, DG XXI with Customs Union and Indirect Taxation and DG XXII Coordination of Structural Instruments.

THE WIDER PROCESS OF ECONOMIC INTEGRATION

In the period after the Second World War until the late 1980s, it was possible to identify contrasting economic systems within Europe. In the East, there were command economies, where there were only limited possibilities for the operation of market forces. In the west of Europe, two trading blocs developed. At the centre of things there was the EC, whose membership grew in the period from six to its current twelve member status, and a population in excess of 330 million. The European Free Trade Area (EFTA) made up of relatively smaller states existed at the fringes of the EC. This was made up of countries who had political objections to EC membership. Finally, a small number of peripheral states existed in the Mediterranean region. These were characterized by low standards of living and generally backward economies.

The collapse of the command economies in the East, and the speed at which the Single European Market (SEM) has gone ahead has led to a very fundamental change in the organization of the European economy. We can no longer view the EC as 12 states in isolation, because of a strong possibility of expansion of the Community, with the creation of new, although possibly transient, trading blocs along the borders.

The EFTA states and the EC came to a basis of agreement to create the European Economic Area (EEA) in October 1991. This expanded the scope of the single market. However, in 1992 as a result of a referendum, Switzerland decided not to pursue its membership of the EEA. The EFTA states are characterized by high income levels and demands for consumer products, although numerically small, with a total population of 40 million. The relative wealth of the EFTA states meant that they were expected to help the poorer EC states. As part of the EEA package, they agreed to supply ECU 2 billion in soft loans at 3% interest and ECU

425 million in grants to the Structural funds to help the poorer states, particularly Greece and Portugal (*Financial Times*, 1991).

The EEA will spread the four freedoms, including the free movement of workers, throughout the geographical area covered by the 18 states. By the Spring of 1992, Austria, Sweden and Finland had already applied for membership of the Community, perhaps making the EEA a short-lived experiment. This would not add significantly to the supply of tourist destinations. These states have high wage costs, which limits their impact to the quality end of the market. Indeed, they will be net contributors to Europe's supply of tourists. However, Austria's membership of the EEA, and projected membership of the Community, does assist in the transit problems to Italy from Germany. Both Switzerland and Austria have tried to limit road traffic passing through their states, for environmental reasons. Being tied into a treaty with the EC should ensure that any future restrictions are not made more restrictive.

The break up of the command economies in the East posed problems for the Community, in the fragmentation that took place in Yugoslavia, which was accompanied by a civil war. Although this removed an important competitor in the Mediterranean tourist market, it also made unsafe the main land bridge between Greece and the Community. The alternative land route to Greece goes via Hungary, which is now part of the Central European Co-operation Committee (CECC). The other members are Poland and Czechoslovakia. The CECC states benefit in terms of trade and assistance from an Association agreement with the EC, which came into effect in March 1992. The CECC states aspire to eventual membership of the EC, and as such their citizens may well become more mobile, and seek jobs in the tourist industry. In the early 1990s only about 40% of their economies was service sector orientated, compared to the with over 60% for the EC. The development of these economies more strongly into tourism will come about, as they become more service sector orientated.

The applications of Cyprus, Turkey and Malta, as Mediterranean states, poses a much more direct challenge to the Community's tourism strategy. These states compete in the volume tourism market, and have similar climatic advantages to the other EC Mediterranean states. They are also providers of cheap mobile labour; if tourism does not lock their workers into their local economies they will increasingly participate in the traditional flows from South to the North of Europe. This is a particular fear in the case of Turkey, simply because of the size of its population.

The Mediterranean applicants do carry with them political problems, but have shown themselves to be aggressive and dynamic in the tourist market. Tourism grew at an average rate of 3.5% in the period between 1980 and 1990, and in Cyprus it grew at a rate 16% over the same period. In addition to this, it has an industry which is well placed to diversify towards the upper end of the market (*Financial Times*, 1992).

EC TOURISM POLICY

The Commission set out its main objectives for the EC's policy towards tourism in 1986 in the document 'First Guidelines Concerning a Community Policy Towards Tourism' (JUSLetter Bulletin, 1989). These objectives were:

1. Facilitating and promoting tourism in the Community.
2. Improving the seasonal geographical distribution of tourism.
3. Providing better information and protection.
4. Improving working conditions in the tourist industry.
5. Increasing the awareness of the problems of tourism particularly as concerns statistics and better use of Community financial instruments (Commission of the EC, 1988).

Following this in December 1986, the Council of Ministers adopted Resolutions concerning better geographical and distribution of tourists, and establishing consultation and cooperation procedures in the field of tourism. Tourism has had a heading in the EC budget since 1986, which has enabled the Commission to do studies and surveys on the tourist trade and tourist policies of member states. Also the EC Commission has collaborated with the European Commission of Tourists, an organization representing the national tourist organizations of 23 Western European Countries in the promotion of Europe as a tourist destination in the United States of America and Japan.

There were two informal meetings of Ministers of Tourism in 1988, and at the first meeting of the Council of Ministers of Tourism on 14 December 1988, 1990 was declared to be 'European Year of Tourism' (Commission of the EC, 1990a). The six countries comprising EFTA were also included as active and complete participants. The themes for the Year of Tourism included: promoting greater knowledge among citizens of the culture and life styles of the participating states; encouraging the staggering of holidays; encouraging the development of new tourist destinations; encouraging the development of new forms of tourism and of alternatives to mass tourism; promoting tourism from third countries to Europe. Finally, the promotion of intra-European tourism was to be promoted, particularly by facilitating the free movement of people (Council of the EC, 1989a).

Many of the actions put in place as part of the year were essentially of a voluntary nature, for example attempts to extend the tourist season. Others amounted to token gestures, such as displaying the Year of Tourism logo in tourist facilities. Where Community money was on offer, it tended to be in limited amounts, and inadequate for the purpose for which it was intended. In total ECU 5 billion had to be shared among the various schemes, half of which was to be devoted to administration, information and publicity campaigns. With a reliance on exhortation, and the lack of funding, it is no wonder that little was heard of the campaign outside the limited number of professionals working in the industry.

The achievements of the European Year of Tourism were said by the Commission to be the improved exchange of information, and the development of closer links between local national administrations, the Commission and trade associations. Useful projects were put forward in the areas of rural tourism, environmental tourism and cultural tourism. Also there were initiatives in the area of promoting tourism in relatively underdeveloped areas such as urban tourism (Commission of the EC, 1991).

The European Parliament believed that measures to promote tourism should not be limited to a 'European Year' (European Parliament, 1991). In 1991, following on from the Year of Tourism, the Commission of the EC proposed the 'Community Action Plan to Assist Tourism'. This set out a number of initiatives which were directly targeted at the industry (Commission of the EC, 1991). The plan was designed to achieve an all-round improvement in the quality and competitiveness of tourism facilities and services. Two broad categories of action were considered:

1. Strengthening the horizontal approach to tourism.
In order to ensure greater consistency and a greater impact from initiatives, it was felt that there needed to be improved statistical and detailed knowledge of the industry, including the impact of tourism. There needed to be more coordination of community and national policies, greater consultation with the industry, improved staggering of holidays and dispersion of tourism, and improved consumer protection (Commission of the EC, 1991, p. 19).
2. Support for specific measures to assist tourism.
Although there was a wide range of possibilities in terms of areas of support, the Commission selected a number of initiatives which they felt contributed most in terms of added value to Community objectives. These included cultural tourism, tourism and the environment, rural tourism, social tourism and vocational training (Commission of the EC, 1991, p. 22).

In February 1992, the European Parliament agreed with the plan, but insisted that the principle of subsidiarity be respected, so that the initiatives were taken at the local, regional, national or Community level as appropriate. They also called for support for the tourism sector in the former socialist countries. Other ideas were for an annual European Cultural Festival, and more extensive environmental initiatives. Finally, it suggested that more help be given to the travel facilities for young people and the aged (Europe, 1992a).

Much of the Action Plan was simply restating ideas and initiatives that had been in place for some time. The Community Action to promote rural tourism (Commission of the EC, 1990b) is an example of an initiative which resulted from the Year of Tourism. The aim of this was to improve information on rural tourism, help to create rural tourism products, and to encourage an improvement in the identification of quality of rural tourism. This was essentially a marketing exercise which was to be funded to a total of ECU 5.8 million until 1994. Although perhaps an important signal in terms of general priorities, it could be argued that such initiatives are just a token, given that Community funding for these purposes is available via the Regional Development Fund, the Common Agricultural Policy and via programmes like LEADER and FORCE. (LEADER is designed to promote information about sources of funding, and FORCE will help with vocational training.)

CONSUMER POLICY

The SEM is designed to promote the interest of the consumer by offering greater choice of products available. This should be the case with regard to the tourist industry, as the Community wishes to encourage the movement of tourists across borders, in order to promote development. The Community has found that it has needed to have a view on consumer protection, if for no other reason than that there is a real danger that national policies can act as non-tariff barriers, and so hinder the free movement of goods and services. In addition, this free movement can expose the consumer to a weaker form of consumer protection in some states. The SEM does not aim to raise all standards of protection to the highest level, but to provide a minimum standard. It is important, therefore, for the development of consumer confidence that this minimum standard is adequate to protect basic interests and to maintain confidence.

At a general level, tourism falls under the broad area of the EC's Consumer Policy, as well as being a policy area in its own right. The Community has long recognized that there is a need to think in terms of policies which take into account more than the requirements of just producers. A Consumer Consultative Committee was established by the Commission as early as 1973. In 1975, the first consumer programme was adopted, and in 1981 there was a second consumer programme. In 1989, a three-year action programme was adopted to cover the period 1990–1992 (Commission of the EC, 1990c). This programme identified four main areas which are important to build consumer confidence in the SEM: consumer representation, consumer information, consumer safety and most importantly, consumer transactions.

For the consumer, the purchase of a service, such as a holiday in another member state, raises problems because of the differing conditions applying to contracts, the problems of understanding other legal systems should things go wrong, the difficulty of complaining, the absence of legal aid if cases are fought in other states, the problems of dealing with civil law cases, the inability of consumer organizations to operate effectively across borders and language problems. This is exactly the kind of consumer problem that the EC is best designed to deal with. Taking action at the Community level helps to overcome the complexity of consumers having to protect their individual rights in different states.

The majority of consumers enjoy their holidays, but a significant proportion, perhaps as high as a third, consider that they have had a less than satisfactory experience (*Holiday Which*, 1985, 1987). In 1982, as a recognition of the fact that there were problems, the Commission produced guidelines for Community tourism, which included proposals for the protection of those taking package tours. In 1984 the scheme was adopted in principle by the Council of Ministers, but the Directive on Package Travel, including Package Holidays and Package Tours, was not adopted until June 1990. It was required to become part of the law of the member states by 31 December 1992. In the UK it will become part of national law as a result of a statutory instrument, which has as its basis the European Communities Act of 1972. The instrument will be subject to the agreement of both Houses of Parliament.

The Directive is designed to protect consumers whether travelling for business or private purposes. It lays down the rules governing the liability of tour operators and retailers, who will have to accept the legal responsibility for the service they offer. The only exceptions to this are in cases of 'force majeure' or in cases which cannot be foreseen or overcome. The Directive establishes the principle of compensation, subject to certain limits, some of which have their origins in international conventions. These are: The Warsaw Convention on the International Carriage by Air, as amended by the Hague Protocol of 1955; The Berne Convention of 1961 on the Carriage by Rail; The Athens Convention on Carriage by Sea; The Paris Convention of 1962 on the Liability of Hotel Keepers.

There is an acceptance within the Directive that national markets for package travel do vary considerably, both in terms of practice and tradition. The main features of the Directive are as follows.

1. The brochure must indicate clearly the price and other key information about the package offered.
2. Prices cannot be revised later than 20 days prior to departure. Also the way that prices are revised should be clearly indicated.
3. The organizer is responsible to the consumer for any failure to deliver the package described, even if it is related to a service provided by a third party.

4. There has to be adequate provision in the case of insolvency of a travel company (Commission of the EC, 1990).

It remains to be seen if the above requirements have a significant effect on the practical aspects of the industry, given attempts to improve codes of practice within the nation states, prior to the introduction of the Directive. If standards have to be raised, then there will be costs involved, which will be passed on to the consumer. Although increased costs will deter some consumers, the industry could well gain due to increased confidence in the quality of product offered.

The success of the Directive, however, depends on a number of factors. Although the EC has many legislative successes, there have been problems at a practical level in terms of implementation. Harmonization via the use of directives means that legislation throughout the Community should display the same characteristics, but the detail is frequently different. The Directive lays down minimum standards, but does not prevent higher standards of protection, so for example the UK insists on a 30 day limit on informing of any increase in prices, whereas the Directive only requires 20 days. This may mean that consumers are still confused as to their rights. Enforcement of legislation is the responsibility of the member state, and only where there is clearly a significant disregard of Community law will the Commission take action, ultimately by taking the case to the European Court of Justice. This means that a great deal depends upon the performance of the agencies involved at the national level.

Another aspect of Consumer Policy which has come increasingly to the fore is that of making cross border payments. The Commission wishes to pressurize banks within the EC to stop profiteering at the expense of the consumer and small business. There are only 200 million retail cross border payments every year within the EC, which is small in relation to domestic transactions. Cross border payments amount to only 0.8% of domestic business in the UK, and even in an open economy like Belgium, they amount to only 4%. The Commission blames this on the high level of charges, which can be 20 times the equivalent national rates. An example cited by Leon Brittan is of a British company charging ECU 42 to collect a French cheque to the value of ECU 67, also of a Belgian who was charged ECU 12.5 handling charges for a book costing only ECU 5 in Luxembourg. As tourism is an industry which is heavily dependent upon cross border retail payments, it is important for the development of the industry that this aspect is improved (Europe, 1992c).

The Commission wishes to ensure that such payments are both as rapid, reliable and inexpensive as payments made within the domestic economy. In March 1992, the Commission put forward an initiative, which, although not included in the Single Market programme, was seen as being indispensable to its success. They proposed that there be closer cooperation between the banks and their customers. The Commission proposes the first

European-wide 'Users Charter', which would set out customer service targets. This would give customers the right to have full information about the cost of services in advance, a breakdown of charges, the right to legal protection. It was also proposed that payments should take no more than 6 days. If the cost of payments can be cut by half, it was estimated that those savings would be ECU 1 billion per year, a benefit which would go predominantly to small and medium sized enterprises (Europe, 1992c).

ENVIRONMENTAL POLICY

The European Community's Environmental Policy was launched in 1972. It is a socioeconomic policy which touches on a wide range of concerns aimed predominantly at improving the living and working conditions of all the citizens of all the Member States. Since 1972, there has been a series of action programmes on the environment, which have identified the main aims of the policy for given periods.

The Fifth Environmental Action Programme, designed to start in 1993, is somewhat different in emphasis from its predecessors. Prior to this, the main thrust of the EC's environmental policy was by increasing the amount of legislation. However, passing legislation without ensuring implementation is not an effective way of conducting policy. In the Fifth Action Programme the Commission has turned towards a three-stranded approach to protecting the environment. This combines legislation with greater encouragement of the use of economic instruments, such as taxation and tradeable permits. In addition, more funding was to be made available for environmental projects.

Of the 400 pieces of legislation which the Community has enacted on the environment very few have been specifically related to tourism (although an improved environment in any region can assist tourism development). However, one of the earliest of the Community directives was enacted in 1976 to improve the quality of the water used for bathing (Council of the EC, 1975). The impetus for this directive came from tourist authorities in Italy and France, who were concerned that during the height of every summer tourist season, the industry suffered from the closure of beaches because of sewage pollution. The aim of the bathing water directive was therefore to set a standard for water and encourage a programme of monitoring of beaches which were used by large numbers of bathers. The general public within the EC has accepted this standard and it is recognized in the major tourist areas of the EC as part of the criterion used by the Member States in their 'blue flag' awards to resorts. The way to achieve the standards set by the bathing water directive is to reduce the amount of sewage that finds its way into the water. This means that tourist authorities have been in the forefront in putting pressure on both local and national government to invest in better means of disposing of sewage.

Although there have been few pieces of legislation directly relating to tourist activities, any action to prevent damage to the environment is ultimately going to be an advantage to areas which are trying to develop a tourist industry. Many environmental problems are not confined to any one national area and the Community is able to act in an international context on cleaning the environment in a way which other organizations are not able to work. The EC is backed by a Treaty, it has supranational institutions which can work on behalf of all the states and this makes it an effective organization when dealing with cross frontier pollution problems. This is particularly true with efforts to control the pollution problems of the Mediterranean. The EC has five member states with Mediterranean coastlines, and action by these states together will not only help to clear away the polluted industrial areas but also give the opportunity for help in the protection of the areas of coastline which are under threat from development. Joint action in the Mediterranean area will also ensure that those regions which rely on their natural advantages to attract tourists have extra protection.

The EC has developed a number of initiatives to assist the protection of the environment in particular regions, one example of which is the Mediterranean Special Programme of Action (MEDSPA). This is specifically concerned with protecting and improving the quality of the environment in the Mediterranean region. It is in initiatives of this type that advantages are apparent for tourism. Again though not specifically aimed to assist the development of tourism actions as part of this Programme will assist the tourist industry.

The Community is anxious to support the developing economies which are emerging as a result of the disintegration of the Eastern bloc and the Soviet Union. It has been recognized that there are possibilities of development in the service sector which would assist the economic development of the former Eastern bloc states. In order to assist tourism in Budapest £18 million has been granted to the city authorities to clean up the polluted stonework of the city's historic buildings.

The sums of money available through environmental grants in the EC are small but the greatest impact is from the presence of the legislation which is not specifically related to tourist developments, but will have a more wide-ranging impact on the environment and therefore improve the attractions upon which the industry depends.

FREE MOVEMENT OF PEOPLE

The measures within the ambit of the drive to complete the single market include measures to reduce the problems that Community nationals face when they cross borders, such as the adoption of the standard style of European passport and driving licences. Both these initiatives date back to well before the formal adoption of a tourism policy. The removal of fiscal barriers and the abolition of duty-free provisions within the Community should help further the free movement of people. The harmonization of access to health care can also be seen as being beneficial in building confidence to travel, although the gap between the standard of provision between the member states is still considerable.

Although the Single European Act confirmed the date of 31 December 1992 for the completion of the Single European Market, a number of states wished to take the process further. In 1985, the first Schengen Agreement (named after the place where the agreement was signed) involved France, Germany and the Benelux countries. From 1987 onward there have been only spot checks on the borders between the Schengen countries, where 400 million people cross in the course of a year. Travellers were required to indicate to the customs officials, by the means of a green sticker, if they had no goods to declare as they crossed frontiers.

Along with the opening of the borders, there was recognition that there was a need to coordinate features like policing, visa policies, firearms regulations, asylum laws and the registration of travellers in hotels. A second Schengen Agreement was therefore signed in 1990, with Italy joining the pact in December 1990, and Portugal and Spain joining in June 1991. The EC has been an enthusiastic observer of the process, and sees many of the Schengen initiatives as the basis of Community policy, once all member states are prepared to move forward with it. The Schengen Agreements have undoubtedly had a major impact on the free movement of tourists, and will also impact on workers in the industry, if it can be made to work. However, in April 1992 Schengen II was still not accepted at the national level, because of German sensitivity about asylum issues (Europe, 1992d).

SOCIAL POLICY

Social Policy at the EC level has tended to emphasize free movement of workers, which is an important aspect of the tourist industry, and frequently relies upon importing particularly seasonal workers. Since the start of the Single Market campaign, there has been concern that the Social dimension of the market is not neglected, and that groups of workers are not disadvantaged by the effects of greater economic integration. None of the single market measures are specifically social measures, so that recent Community action such as the Social Charter and the Social Chapter of the Maastricht agreement are aimed at redressing this imbalance. There is

concern over the treatment of workers, not only for social reasons, but because of the implications that lower standards offer unfair competition between the member states. Although Britain opted to stay out of the Social Chapter of the Maastricht Agreement, it is still bound by its obligations under the original Treaties and the Single European Act.

Specific Social Policy measures of importance to the tourist industry include:

1. The rights of migrant workers. They must must be treated equally, not only in their search for work, but in their treatment at work. If they become unemployed they also have the right to search for alternative employment, and the right to welfare payments if they fulfil the requirements of the country they are staying in.

2. The imposition of Community standards on, for example, the right to equal pay for equal work of equal value. This is an aspect of the Treaty of Rome which is yet to be fully implemented in all member states, despite the existence of rulings by the European Court of Justice. Initiatives launched in the 1990s include the Directive on the Protection of Pregnant Women on Maternity leave. Also the Community Action Programme on Equal Opportunity for Men and Women, which provides for a number of training programmes. Finally, as part of the Maastricht debate, there was an active discussion of issues such as the maximum hours spent at work.

3. The mutual recognition of qualifications across the Community (Council of the EC, 1989b). Considerable success has been achieved with regard to the recognition of professional qualifications, and those spending three years in higher education. There is now a movement to recognize vocational qualifications, with the issue of a European vocational training card, which would affect workers in the hotel and catering sectors.

There needs to be much more progress with regard to the effective implementation of legislation. Additionally the Commission feels that not sufficient is being done to protect workers in the black economy.

THE STRUCTURAL FUNDS AND REGIONAL POLICY

There are three major structural funds within the Community, with the possibility of a fourth being added as a result of the Delors II Package. Two of these were established as a result of the European Economic Community (EEC) Treaty of 1958: (i) the European Social Fund (ESF) was created to support the training and retraining of workers and support some job-creation measures; (ii) the Guidance Section of the European Agricultural and Guidance and Guarantee Fund (EAGGF) is used to modernize farming and related areas (iii) the European Regional Development Fund (ERDF) was established in 1975, to promote economic activities and to finance infrastructure projects in disadvantaged regions of the Community. In addition to this, the Community has the European Investment Bank, which takes an active role in lending money for development projects.

The Single European Act sets out the Community's regional development strategy in Article 130a, which states that the Community;

> ... shall develop and pursue its actions leading to a strengthening of its economic and social cohesion. In particular the Community shall aim at reducing disparities between the various regions and the backwardness of least favoured regions.

In 1988 the way that the structural funds operated was changed. Not only was the size of the funds doubled in real terms, but there was an attempt to coordinate the funds into a developed programme over a period of years rather than relying on specific one off projects. The planning was to be via negotiation of the Community Support Frameworks (CSF). These seek to lay out plans for the optimum deployment of the resources of the structural funds and other Community financial instruments including lending from the European Investment Bank (EIB). The aim is to speed up the process of social and economic cohesion by increasing the level of both private and public investment. The plan indicates how the providers of EC funding will participate via part funding on a multi-regional and on a single regional basis. The Commission then examines these plans in order to ensure that joint action is taken, and that priorities are chosen.

There is a wide range of examples of how Structural Funds are used to promote the tourist industry, either directly or indirectly. In Campania in Italy, the CSF proposed that funds be used to exploit architectural, historical and natural resources for tourism purposes, in Sicily, that subsidies be given to investment in holiday cottages in rural areas, and finally, that help be given to vocational training (Commission of the EC, 1990e).

At Maastricht, Economic and Social Cohesion was stressed as being one of the pillars upon which the Community was built, and the structural funds were a vital part of this process. The Commission believed that there was a need to improve and simplify the decision-making process associated with the structural funds. Also there should be a systematic evaluation of the results, based upon clear objectives. It was also suggested that Community initiative programmes be given greater prominence, with 15% of funds being devoted to them.

It was proposed that the amount devoted to Economic and Social Cohesion would rise by ECU 11.0 billion in the period to 1997. Some areas would benefit considerably more than others. Those regions which were regarded as lagging behind the Community would benefit to the extent of a two-thirds increase in allocation, whereas those eligible for a new Cohesion Fund would benefit by a 100% increase.

The new Cohesion Fund, which was to be set up by the end of 1993, was constructed to help those states whose GNP is less than 90% of the Community average (Spain, Portugal, Ireland and Greece). Its purpose was first of all to assist with the process of economic and social cohesion, but at a state level rather than at a regional level as is the case with the Regional Development Fund. The second purpose of the fund was to help the four states meet the convergence criteria in order that they might move to stage three of EMU. The Fund was designed to assist with investment to ensure effective application of environmental policy. Also trans-European networks were to be financed, entailing significant investment in transport infrastructure. Both of these areas are of benefit to the tourist industry.

Little progress had been made concerning the detail of the Cohesion Fund, apart from stating the policy sectors likely to benefit. However, the proposed Fund presupposed a high level of Community intervention at between 85 and 90% of the cost of projects, as against the usual 50% or less. This would reduce the burden on the member states (Commission of the EC, 1992a), and as such could be seen as a side payment for acceptance of the new treaty. This was very much in line with the demands of the Spanish government prior to the Maastricht Summit. The Cohesion Fund should therefore be regarded as a classic example of an expenditure side solution to a Community budgetary issue. Instead of making a direct payment to a member state, the money will be used to advance a policy area which the Community wishes to pursue. The amount allocated to the fund in Delors II was (from Europe, 1992b):

Year	1993	1994	1995	1996	1997
ECU millions	1500	1750	2000	2250	2500

THE EUROPEAN MONETARY SYSTEM

Two elements of the EMS are directly important for EC Tourism Policy:

1. The European Currency Unit (ECU), which is made up of the trade-weighted average of the EC's currencies. Although it is an artificial currency, it is the basis of the Community's transactions, so that funds paid to assist the industry's development are made in ECU.
2. The Exchange Rate Mechanism (ERM), which is the device used to maintain the stability of currencies within the EC. All currencies had become members of this element of the EMS by the spring of 1992, with the exception of Greece. Currencies can in most cases only fluctuate within a narrow band of a maximum of 2.25% either side of ECU. In the case of

the Pound, Peseta and Escudo, a 6% band operated as a transition measure.

From the mid-1980s to the 1990s, members of the ERM benefited from a long period of nominal stability of exchange rates. Between 1988 and the end of 1990, the Spanish peseta rose in value by 20% against the pound; this raised the prices of holidays, and was one of the factors leading to a decline in tourism flows between the two countries. The fact that both then became members of the ERM should have assisted tourism flows, although it is very difficult to calculate the extent of this, given the existence of other factors, such as the Gulf War and concerns about the physical environment.

Of greater importance, would be the move to monetary union, with the creation of a single currency. The transaction cost for large businesses of changing from one currency to another is between 0.5–1%, with tourists paying 2–3% and at times as much as 6%. The Commission estimates that if a single currency was adopted for the EC, then there would be a likely saving of ECU 15–20 billion per year (*Financial Times*, 1990). The tourist industry would be a substantial beneficiary from this process, as the cost of changing currency would disappear, and business and the consumer would be easily able to understand the relative prices. This should lead to member states' comparative advantage in particular tourism products being more fully exploited.

The movement to EMU involves three stages:

- Stage 1: The first stage involves the completion of the single market with freedom to move goods and capital by 1 January 1993.
- Stage 2: The second stage will commence on 1 January 1994. It is designed to prepare the ground for the establishment of the single currency. Member states will move to the narrow band of the EMS in this stage.
- Stage 3: This third stage will commence either in 1997 or 1999, depending on the degree of convergence between the EC economies. For this stage to commence, inflation rates will have to be harmonized, and budget deficits brought under control. All this depends upon the state of the European economy in the late 1990s, and the will of the member states to participate fully in the process.

The EMS became unstable in the period from September 1992 onward. Not only were there devaluations of the peseta, punt and escudo, but membership of the ERM was suspended for the lira and pound. The consequence was that the stronger currencies drifted upward in value. Overall this caused doubts about EMU being in place for the target date.

CONCLUSION

Policy towards tourism in the EC has been based on promoting the free flow of market forces. This has been beneficial for the growth of the industry, and further moves towards the completion of the internal market, plus specific measures such as the package tour directive will no doubt assist this process. The era of rapid overall expansion of the industry seems now to be past, but the trend does vary depending on the sector concerned. Beneath the overall trend, there are areas of considerable growth and those of real decline. As long as goods and services are sold into the market, there can be changes in fashion which result in decline taking place. However, many tourist facilities, particularly those in the Mediterranean could maintain their comparative advantage in the market, if care was taken in the pace and quality of their development. Once decline is allowed to set in, it is difficult to reverse, because the environment which is attractive to tourism tends to deteriorate. In areas where there is rapid expansion, there are difficult choices to make. If development goes ahead quickly in order to ride the tide of popularity, many of the natural features of resort areas may be destroyed.

There is no realistic alternative to a policy which promotes mass tourism, in part because of the need to offer the consumer what he wants. What is required within the EC is a policy for balanced tourism expansion. This implies a shift in the policy emphasis. There is a need to promote the permanent tourist potential of resorts, and to avoid the shifting patterns of development which is now apparent. Good quality development which avoids the problem of overexpansion in the future needs more from the EC than just the encouragement of greater tourist flows. It needs the EC to involve itself in a closer partnership with local and regional authorities. Although there have been considerable increases in the level of the structural funds, even greater resources are needed if we are to avoid the mistakes of regions like the Costa Brava and the Italian Adriatic. There also needs to be even greater emphasis on environmental policy, especially in areas close to tourist development, and of course in the resorts themselves.

REFERENCES

Commission of the EC (1988) *Package Travel: Protection for the Consumer*. Background Report ISEC/B11/88, London.
Commission of the EC (1990a) COM(90=) 803 final.
Commission of the EC (1990b) COM(90) 438.
Commission of the EC (1990c) *Three Year Action Plan of Consumer Policy in the EC (1990 1992)*. COM(90) 98 Final.

Commission of the EC (1990d) COM (90) 232 Final SYN 122 30 May.
Commission of the EC (1990e) *Community Support Framework 1989–93.*
   Objective 1: Italy.
Commission of the EC (1991) *Community Action Plan to Assist Tourism* COM
   (91) 97 final 1991.
Commission of the EC (1992a) *From the Single Act to Maastricht and Beyond –*
   The means to Match our Ambitions in Europe. Document No 1762/63 19
   February.
Commission of the EC (1992b) *Panorama of EC Industry 1991–92*, Chapter 24.
Council of the EC (1975) Directive 7/8/12 1975 '... Concerning the quality of
   bathing water ...' EC 76/160.
Council of the EC (1989a) Council Decision of 21st December 1988 on an Action
   Programme for European Tourism Year (1990), *Official Journal of the*
   EC. 21. 1 89. No. L 17/54.
Council of the EC (1989b) Directive 89/48/EEC; OJL19, 24.1.89.
Council of the EC (1991) *Treaty on European Union.*
Europe (1992a) 19 February 5671 (new series), p. 11.
Europe (1992b) 11 March 5686 (new series), p. 13.
Europe (1992c) 26 March 5697 (new series), p. 8.
Europe (1992d) 15 April 5712 (new series), p. 4.
European Parliament (1991) *Report of the Committee on Transport and Tourism.*
   A3–0155/91/Part A.
Financial Times (1990) 21 March, p. 2.
Financial Times (1991) 23 October, p. 2.
Financial Times (1992) *Survey of the Republic of Cyprus.* 23 March, p. 1.
Holiday Which (1985, 1987) January editions.
JUSLetter Bulletin (1989) *Tourism within the European Community*, No 10/89,
   Association pour la Diffusion de l'Information Juridique, Brussels, p. 4.

FURTHER READING

Butler, M. (1986) *Europe: More than a Continent.* Heineman, London.
Commission of the European Communities (1992) *From Single Market to*
   European Union. Luxemburg.
Euroconfidential (ed.) (1992) *1992 Directory of EEC Information Sources.*
   Belgium.
Euromonitor (1992) *Travel and Tourism Data: A Comprehensive Research Hand-*
   book of the World Travel Industry. Luxemburg.
European Parliament (1982) *Collection of the Institutional Documents of the*
   Community, 1950–1982. Committee on Institutional Affairs, Luxemburg.
European Parliament (1991) *Report on European Union.* Luxemburg EP Doc C3–
   97/91.
Lodge, J. (ed.) (1989) *The European Community and the Challenge of the Future.*
   Francis Pinter, London.
Pinder, J. (1991) *European Community. The Building of a Union.* Oxford
   University Press, Oxford.

4

THE LIBERALIZATION OF EUROPEAN
TRANSPORT MARKETS

Wilhelm Pompl

INTRODUCTION

The removal of physical, technical and fiscal barriers to free trade within the EC from 1993 will open new markets, reinforce the division of labour between the regions and bring a higher level of income resulting in higher tourism expenditures. One effect of all these benefits will be more traffic. In Eastern Europe the six former Comecon countries have initiated a process of change away from central planning and restrictive social and political conditions, which previously had imposed an iron curtain hindering East to West trade and tourism. Even if the realization of the full travel potential in Eastern Europe is retarded by economic austerity and the lack of hard currency, the development of the infrastructure will lag behind the growth of traffic volume in both directions. Yet even today the carrying capacity of Europe's transport systems already seems to be over-burdened, at least in certain geographical areas where freight and passenger transport coincide and where local, regional, transit and incoming traffic meet.

However, for the tourism industry growth per force means growing traffic volume. So the habitual congestion on motorways and at major traffic intersections, delayed flights, lack of car parks in the destination areas at home and abroad cause vital problems for the whole tourism system. Besides this, transport-related environmental consequences endanger this leisure and pleasure industry: visual and auditory pollution, the destruction of natural beauty spots, biological diversity and man-made cultural heritage, as well as climatic changes due to the greenhouse effect, resulting from carbon dioxide emissions.

These global problems and the international character of the tourism industry beg for pan-European transport policies and action. But even within the EC this goal is still remote. The Treaty of Rome (Art. 3; Art. 74 to 84,

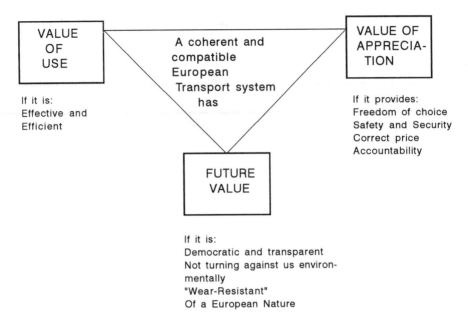

Fig. 4.1. Values of a European transport system. Source: Group Transport 2000 Plus (1990).

1957), on which the European Community is founded, envisaged the adoption of a common transport policy by the end of 1965. Nearly 30 years later the Single European Act (1986) was still urging the completion of the European Community in the field of transport as one of the priorities. (Since then the problems with the opening up of the Eastern European states with their internal problems – witness the former Yugoslavia and the Soviet Union – have increased still further.) The transport industry remained highly protected till the early 1980s. Only judgements by the European Court of Law, especially in Case 13/83, where the court ruled that the Council had infringed the Treaty of Rome by 'failing to ensure freedom to provide services in the sphere of international transport' and finally the Single Act of 1986 brought the necessary pressure to move towards a common transport policy.

The Group Transport 2000 Plus (1990), set up by the European Commission, has formulated the desired quality characteristics of a European transport system by clearly stipulating the 'values of use, appreciation and future' (Fig. 4.1).

The 'value of use' implies an efficient and effective transport system. Efficiency requires that all costs of a specific means of transport (operational, infrastructural and external costs) are charged to the users and not in part to the general public or to future generations. Fair competition is maintained between modes of transport and no one is protected or privileged; so that at the end each mode of transport fulfils the task it is best suited for. Effectivity demands that all resources (capital, energy, space and subsidies) are used cost-effectively and the transport system contributes to the achievement of a free internal market in Europe.

The 'value of appreciation' responds to the market and consumer needs. Safety and security are prime aims. Freedom of choice guarantees that the user is free to find the mode of transport most suitable to his needs and preferences as well as a proper selection between price and quality from a wide range of products.

The 'value of the future' is met when decision-making practices are democratic, transparent and flexible, the environmental damage is reduced to the absolute minimum level, the transport system can absorb wear and tear over a long period, and when there is an added 'European value whereby an idea is out of order unless placed in a European context'.

REGULATION OF EUROPEAN TRANSPORT MARKETS

It is generally agreed that the real reason for the regulation of transport markets lies in the public service nature of the industry. Transport is a public utility like water supply or communications and it is one of the prime responsibilities of the state to secure the provision of these pre-quisites of any modern economic and social system. The proper func-tioning of a national and international transport network includes services to particular destinations and at particular times even when they are – seen from the purely economic view – not profitable. These non-profitable services can be offered either by government or by private enterprises when they are compensated directly in cash or indirectly by regulations that allow a profitable fare structure for cross subsidization and reduce competition by regulating market access and capacities. Throughout Europe a high involvement of government enterprises in this sector can be found (Sánchez-Neyra, 1986; Wackermann, 1987, Becheri, 1989; OECD, 1990). Rail transport, regional and local bus transport are, and air transport has been, largely state monopolies.

Apart from the public service argument, governments have vital interests in the transport sector. For a long time national transport autarky had been the undoubted doctrine: each state must be in a position to provide and control the transport needed by producing these services through national companies. Furthermore, transport demand is an econ-omic asset to be exploited by the national companies only. Economic theory argues that transport is a kind of natural monopoly, as it is more effective to have single-operator services only; the lost benefits of com-petition are compensated by economies of infrastructure (only one rail network) and economies of scale and scope. These arguments had been widely adopted as long as the different modes of transport were infant industries. But with their maturing in economic and technical terms, increasing criticism demanded a liberalization of the tight regulations.

Transport policy in Europe is like a multidimensional patchwork as it has to consider different vertical levels, different areas of policy and different policies for each mode of transport. The different levels are:

- The local/regional transport policy of local/regional authorities;
- The national transport policy of the member states, highly regulated, often protectionistic and more often non-compatible due to their own historic roots, procedures, regulations and 'rights';
- The common transport policy of the EC bodies, following the subsidiarity principle, but nevertheless as a result of setting standards and implementing EC laws becoming increasingly the decision-making supranational bureaucracy;
- The policy between the EC and the non-EC world. These external relations become more important the more the EC acts as a single entity against third countries.

Transport is related to different areas of policy. As transport is not just another sector of the economy even if its 7% of EC Gross Product shows it to be an important part of it but a *conditio sine qua non* of any economic system, there exists a close interrelationship between transport policy and other fields of policy like regional development policy, economics, energy, defence, social and environmental policy. The different policies for each mode of transport have to take into consideration their special characteristics as well as their competitive and complementary relationship.

A European transport policy must integrate these multifarious factors in order to contribute to improving transport conditions and the EC undoubtedly has to play the leading role, due to its economic power, geographical location and political *raison d'être*. But it can not reach its aims without cooperation with the rest of Europe, some of them being important transit countries between the EC Member States. The principal tasks are (Commission of the EC, 1991):

- Setting up transport networks to provide effective links within the EC as well as between member states and non-Community countries;
- Harmonizing standards and national legislation in the operational, fiscal, social and environmental fields;
- Fostering fair competition between the various modes of transport and between their operators;
- Encouraging regional economic and social balance, so that disadvantaged or peripheral regions do not remain cut off from the rest of the Community.

AIR TRANSPORT

Changes in the Regulatory Framework

The entire European air transport system is currently in a phase of radical policy reorganization and at the same time Europe's airlines face the biggest crisis in their history. Already in 1990 a slowdown in demand due to the weak economic situation and an increasing proportion of low fare passengers in the traffic mix had brought yields down at a time when operational costs were increasing. For the 22 major European carriers, grouped in the Association of European Airlines (AEA), this meant an operational loss of US$2.5 billion. The situation deteriorated dramatically in early 1991. In a three-month period during and after the Gulf War as much as one quarter of the market chose not to travel and load factors on intra-European services reached a level of around 35%. It will take the airlines years to recover from this recession. In 1991 the number of passengers fell by 8% (instead of an expected rise of 6%) and even capacity cut-backs could not avoid a 3 point drop in load factor. The financial result was a disaster for an industry whose profits have always been marginal: more than US$1.5 billion loss in 1991 (AEA, 1992) (Fig. 4.2).

Until the mid-1980s international air transport was characterized by state-owned national flag carriers operating their scheduled services in the regulatory framework of the multilateral Chicago Convention and the bilateral air service agreements. According to de facto monopolistic practices, market entries, traffic rights and capacities were commonly shared between the respective national airlines on the basis of reciprocity, tariffs co-ordinated via the IATA price cartel and subject to approval by the two governments concerned (double approval system). Charter carriers operated in their own separate markets under fairly liberal conditions but gradually came under attack from scheduled carriers who wanted a share in the growing holiday travel market. This non-scheduled traffic – more than 90% being Inclusive Tour Charter – accounts in terms of passenger kilometres (PKM) for 50% of total intra-European passenger traffic and as much as 65% of international passenger traffic within Europe (AEA, 1991b).

Little of this regulatory system will survive in the Single Market. The liberalization policy of the EC prohibits price-fixing agreements, opens new access to routes and provides free capacity offers; more and more state-owned airlines are going to be privatized, new carriers will emerge, co-operations and joint ventures are new options in the process of strategic management. Reasons for this radical overhaul are not only to be found in the decision of the EC to accomplish the Single Market. Other factors were

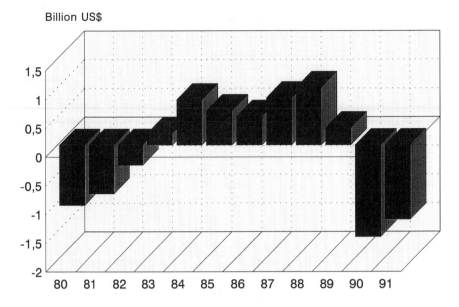

Billion US$

Fig. 4.2. Financial results of AEA Airlines 1980–1991. Source: AEA (1991, 1992).

the deregulation of the US national and partly-international air transport system and the rising number of non-European carriers from socialist and third world countries. These carriers have obtained reciprocally based traffic rights to Europe and so helped to increase the already existing excess capacity, resulting in the establishment of a so-called grey market, where tickets are sold below the government approved prices (Pompl, 1991). This 'liberalization' of tariffs, illegal but no longer the subject of prosecutions, led to a two-level price system: one with legal tariffs and the other with bucket shop prices.

The activities of the different EC bodies, especially the Commission, were and are nevertheless the driving forces behind the liberalization process in European air transport. In the opinion of the Commission European air transport showed a tendency to excessive fares, lack of regional services and general contempt for the passenger, sheltered by a regulatory system which prevents competition from new and more innovative airlines. Rejecting US-style deregulation, the Commission proposed an evolutionary approach to liberalization and it took in fact almost a decade with delays and dilutions to implement this process. Occasionally it needed even the help of the European Law Court for the enforcement of the competition rules provided by the Treaty of Rome. The first real step to liberalize the European air transport system was the EC Directive on Inter-Regional Air services (416/83/EEC). But only when the council had adopted the so-called liberalization packages (the First Package 1987, Official Journal 1987 L374; the Second Package 1990, Official Journal 1990 L217) did the common air transport policy come into effect. The main aspects of the packages are:

- Market access: Each Member State now has the right of multiple designation allowing it to establish more than one airline to operate on intra-European routes with passenger traffic of more than 100,000 pax per year.
- Capacity control: Carriers authorized to operate bilateral services between Member States on any route had formerly to split their capacities on strictly equal terms. Step by step this equal ratio was changed to a 75 : 25 ratio in 1992 and is intended to be completely free in 1995.
- Traffic rights: Designated carriers are now allowed to establish services between the main airports in their own country and regional airports in other Member States with no limits on distance or size of aircraft. The 1989 package also provides, within certain limits, fifth-freedom rights, i.e. to load and unload passengers in an intermediate country on a flight to a destination country.
- Fare control: Airlines are no longer allowed to align their fares with those charged by their competitors. The governments of the two states concerned still have the right to approve the fares on intra-European routes, but a wide range of special fares get automatic approval already when they lay in commission defined fare zones.

The final 'Third Package' (1990 L240) passed in July 1992, providing free market access and unrestricted traffic rights for community airlines (full cabotage rights, however, will be granted by 1997 only) and the abolishing of the double approval system in favour of a double dis-approval system under which any filed tariff becomes automatically authorized unless both governments object within 14 days. The Commission itself will ensure that the Community's competition rules are not violated.

In the process of creating a single European market, the Commission sees the adoption of a common approach to external relationships with third countries in matters of commercial air policy as absolutely essential. This concerns the network of more than 600 bilateral air service agreements based on the Chicago Convention and would mean transfering the competence of the Member States to the EC. It is, however, doubtful whether the Community would obtain significant additional benefits for its airlines. In pursuit of the global plan agreed by the EC and the six EFTA countries to establish a European Economic Area, the Council has opened negotiations to extend the Community air policy to the EFTA countries; a separate provisional agreement has been concluded exclusively with Norway and Sweden (Euroconfidentiel, 1991).

The Airlines' Reactions

The airlines responded to this gradual but continuous modification of their market environment not only with new products and innovative fares, but also with new corporate strategies that will definitely change the structure of the whole air transport industry. Financial participation, mergers and cooperations are the key words.

Since 1985 many airlines have progressively strengthened their national position by mergers or financial participation in order to improve their international competitive strength: British Airways (BA) acquired British Caledonian (1988), Air France took over UTA and Air Inter (1991), just as Swissair did Balair and Crossair. Lufthansa, prevented by national law from taking over the former GDR's Interflug, nevertheless got most of the routes after Interflug closed; in 1992 Lufthansa bought an option for a majority stake from 1993 in AeroLloyd to use it as a low cost supplementary to its quality charter carrier Condor. In addition, most of the national flag carriers use the acquisition of regional and feeder services as well as the extension of their charter operations to round off their home market domination.

The predicted emergence of European mega-carriers is not yet in sight. As any merger resulting in the disappearance of a national carrier – and most national carriers are still at least partially government owned – would have national implications for the government, some kind of joint owner-ship of a merged operation seems more likely (Gialloreto, 1988). Since the failure of the BA/KLM merger, transnational financial participation is as yet only on a limited scale: BA and KLM with 20% each of Sabena (Belgium), Air France and Swissair with 2% each of Austrian Airlines, Air France with 37% of Sabena and 40% of Czechoslovakia Airlines (CSA), Lufthansa with 26% of Lauda Air (Austria). Spain's Iberia acquired 40% of Aerolineas Argentinas, 35% of Ladeca (Chile) and 45% of Viasa (Venezuela) to secure its leadership on the Europe–South America market. But with the ongoing process of privatization of national airlines, mergers seem to be more likely in the future. The most successful joint ventures are certainly the computer reservation systems Amadeus and Galileo (see below). Jointly owned new airlines are mostly found in the holiday market: SunExpress by Lufthansa and Turkish Hava Yollary, Air Russia by BA and Aeroflot, LTE-Espana by LTU (Germany) and investors from Spain. BA's 49% participation in the former regional German carrier Delta, now Deutsche BA, is the first attempt to invade a foreign national market.

Cooperations and strategic alliances without integration of capital interest seem still to be in the greatest interest of the airlines. The globalization of the markets requires intercontinental presence and access. On the marketing side combined networks and hubs, a joint fares policy and pooling of intercontinental routes strengthen the market position; sharing of terminal facilities, maintenance equipment, spare parts, stocks and common training facilities reduce costs.

Infrastructure Problems

The anticipated growth of European air transport (6–7% per year) is seriously endangered by the present inadequate infrastructure, mainly airway and airport capacity. The results of these shortages are congestion and delays, higher costs for airlines, passengers and the environment by producing a high level of unnecessary pollution, noise and energy consumption. An estimated 5 billion US$ total annual loss is due to delays, inefficient routings, non-optimal flight profiles, unnecessary holding patterns and low Air Traffic Control (ATC) productivity (Table 4.1). This figure will rise to US$10 billion annually by the year 2000 unless major improvements are undertaken immediately (ATAG, 1992). In 1990, more than 20% of all European flights were delayed more than 15 min. In Western Europe ATC is operated by 30 control centres using 22 different ATC-systems with very low compatibility – and in Eastern Europe the standard is even lower. The problem of limited airspace has to be solved by a single Europe-wide air-control system at ECAC-level (European Civil Aviation Conference of 28 European states), as this intergovernmental organization includes almost all European countries. As this means relinquishing some national sovereignty in that field, some states prefer an interconnection of national ATC systems without transferring power to a new supranational body. ECAC's 'Strategy for the 90s for European Airspace' gradually moves from the implementation of the Central Air Flow Management under the coordination of Eurocontrol which will be operational in 1993 to a harmonized and finally integrated ATC system; this Enhanced Air Traffic Management and Mode S Implication in Europe (EASIE) should be in operation by the year 2001.

According to an AEA statement, '22 out of 46 international airports in Europe will run out of runway capacity before the mid nineties and another 11 airports will face similar problems between 1996 and the year 2000, if no means are taken' (AEA, 1991). This shortfall will not only fail to meet the future demand for air services, but is also restricting competition. In Europe, allocation of landing and take-off times (slots) is regulated by agreement between airlines following guidelines issued by IATA. According to this system, airlines having a slot in a given period can keep it

Table 4.1. Penalties of inadequate infrastructure.

Affected group	Nature of impact on affected group	Economic cost to affected group	Economic benefits (to others)
1. Airlines	Delays	Higher operating costs	
	Curtailed growth	Loss of business (revenues, profit, employment)	Gains by substitutes to air travel
2. Airports	Curtailed growth	Loss of revenues	
3. Air travellers	Delays	Loss of productivity, especially to business people	
		Higher costs passed on by airlines (loss in real income)	
4. Tourist industry	Loss of revenue due to curtailed growth	Loss of inbound business	Increased revenue for other national economies when tourists change country of destination
5. Labour pool	Fewer jobs due to curtailed growth	Loss of income; concomitant personal social disruptions	
6. Business and industry	Loss of revenue	Loss of profit to businesses	Increased business activity elsewhere when businesses relocate
	Higher operating costs		
7. Governments	Decreased tax and fee income	Loss of revenues	
8. Aircraft manufacturers	Decreased passenger demand resulting from congestion	Loss of production as fewer aircraft are required in a severely constrained environment	Gain as more aircraft needed to offset moderate congestion

Source: ATAG (1992).

indefinitely as long as they operate ('grandfather rights'); they can use this slot for any route from this airport or even swap it with other airlines. Because slots are airline specific, 'at an airport that is working at full capacity for any length of time a prospective new entrant airline can effectively be excluded from most of the routes using this airport' (OECD, 1988). As this certainly favours established carriers and discriminates against new entrants, the Commission has proposed a regulation for a Code of Conduct (Official Journal 1991 C 43). Newly created, unused slots or slots that have not been used during the previous flight plan period should be placed in a pool and then distributed among the applicant airlines with at least half of these slots going to new entrants; slots may even be reclaimed from carriers that operate more than six daily flights on a route. This, however, limits the established airlines' scope for expansion since most of the actually or potentially congested airports are their principal hubs; they are indeed important economic assets which enable them to compete effectively on a worldwide basis against the powerful US-mega carriers and the fast-growing airlines from Asia (AEA, 1991).

Tax Harmonization

The Commission's proposals on the harmonization of taxes will have important consequences for tourism passenger transport, as they intend to make cross-border journeys subject to Value Added Tax (VAT). Since air transport has not been liable to VAT as yet in most EC countries this implies, together with the abolition of duty-free sales at airports and on board, both increased costs and lost revenues for the airlines and will certainly tend to cause price increases.

INFORMATION TRANSFER: COMPUTER RESERVATION SYSTEMS

The development of Computer Reservation Systems (CRS) from simple inventories of available seats to global travel management systems for the whole tourism industry was more than just a mere adaptation of general databank technology to meet the needs of the airlines; it has indeed been both a stipulation and a consequence of deregulation and liberalization. To benefit from the competitive opportunities, tariffs, routes and products had to be changed quickly and often in order to react immediately to fluctuations in demand and the activities of other airlines (Bennett and Radburn, 1991). This means that new tariffs and their conditions, new routes, their frequencies and changing seat availability have to be communicated without delay to the points of sale. Relying on phone calls and printed

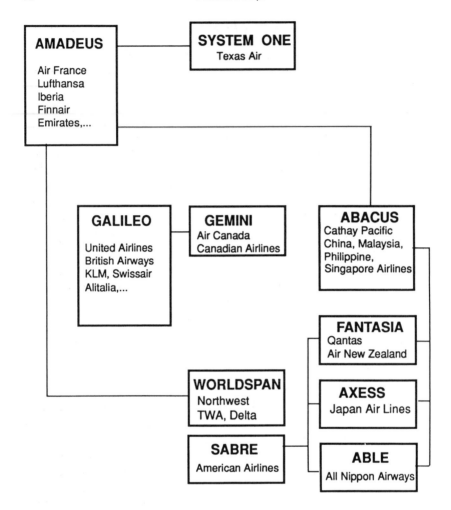

Fig. 4.3. Global network of computer reservation systems.

guides no longer met the requirements of a competitive sales management. Additionally the CRS produce the necessary data for yield management programmes that allow effective control of the passenger mix for each single flight as a new management tool.

The outcome of US deregulation has been the emergence of a few dominant airline CRSs controlling the market and giving their owners enormous competitive advantages over their 'have not' competitors. In the mid-1980s the US-based CRS started to establish a foothold in Europe. The European airlines in turn, seeing the enormous potential profit and the threat of US control of European distribution channels, tried to set up a single joint European-wide CRS. However, as they failed to agree, two consortia were established in 1987 to develop their own CRSs: Amadeus as a joint venture of Air France, Iberia, Lufthansa and SAS, and Galileo with British Airways, Alitalia, KLM, Swissair and Sabena as principal members.

Both systems on the one hand integrate the already existing national reservation system like START in Germany, ESTEREL in France, SIGMA in Italy or SMART in Scandinavia and on the other hand reach for global presence through links with CRSs in other continents (Fig. 4.3).

The range of functions of the new CRSs not only includes the airline mode with information on tariff and seat availability, reservations, automatic pricing, ticketing, accounting, travel information (like health and vaccination requirements, travel documents, foreign exchange rates and meteorological information) and internal links with the airline's flight operations, but also provides the agencies and tourism intermediaries with:

- Booking facilities for tour operators for the whole range of tourism products like hotels, rail travel, car ferries, cruises, travel insurance, car rentals and tickets for cultural and sport events.
- Office automation functions like accounting, pay roll, sales and profitability analysis, customer profiles.
- In combination with personal computers (instead of simple display screens) the implementation of in-house management information and operation systems.

The EC Commission, having carefully studied the US deregulation process and its results, became concerned about possible abuses of CRS harming consumers and air transport competition. As cooperations the size of Amadeus and Galileo may restrict competition in various manners it can only be established by block exemption on anticompetition agreements (Art. 85 (1), Treaty of Rome). This exemption has been granted for carriers who want to develop, purchase or operate a CRS jointly (Regulation 83/91 EEC). But a Code of Conduct for CRS was adopted in July 1989 (Regulation 2299/89 EEC) to ensure fair and equal competition. The most important of those regulations are:

- Any carrier is allowed to participate and any subscriber to use the system on equal and non-discriminating conditions.
- Any participant can withdraw from the system without penalty on giving reasonable notice.
- The system vendor must provide a neutral display which lists the data given by currently participating airlines in a comprehensive, accurate, transparent and unbiased manner – ranking of this information is set out in annexes to the Regulation.
- Fees charged have to be non-discriminatory and reasonably related to the costs of the services.

Complaints from participating airlines or subscribers will be investigated by the Commission, which may impose fines or even withdraw the exemption from the anticompetitive law.

RAILWAY TRANSPORT

Europe's national railways, once the pride and most important public transport mode of their states, are suffering from more or less the same problems: poor financial performance, loss of market shares in the freight, commuter and tourist sectors, and a lack of financial capital as well as political and public support to place the necessary investments for new infrastructures and product improvements. In the past the benefits of railway traffic – low energy and space consumption, high security, less effect on the environment – could not be turned to competitive advantage over other modes of transport. The liberalization of the transport markets even seems to worsen the existing poor situation: more city-to-city and long distance coach services together with lower promotional air fares and more intensive interregional air transport will entice passengers away and force the railways into competitive price cuts.

The national governments and the EC have done very little to change the frame of action of the state-owned railway companies. A retrospective evaluation of the development of European railway policy shows that the cooperation in international organizations like UIC (Union International des Chemins de Fer, since 1945) and UCE (Union des Chemins de Fer Européenes, since 1991) had only limited results like the coordination of timetables and tariffs; the European Conference of Ministers of Transport (ECMT) never progressed beyond the status of being an advisory body and the EC's numerous proposals, recommendations and communications had only declamatory value. So Whitelegg (1988) draws the following conclusion: 'The situation of railways remains relatively untouched by the activities of the Common Transport Policy. The scale of subsidy is still larger than the EC would prefer, the pursuit of national goals and investment strategies is still very much outside a European framework, and there has been very little progress in getting states to agree on any form of equal treatment of rail and road.'

However, in July 1991 the Council of Ministers adopted two directives which might be an important breakthrough for the railway companies enabling them to play a more important role in the European traffic market. The Directive on the Development of the Community's railways (440/91/EEC) intends to ensure the following four main principles:

1. Greater autonomy for railway administrations of Member States to be managed on normal business principles with the companies having complete responsibility for their own commercial operations.

2. Normalization of accounts by compulsory separation of costs for infrastructure and transport operations.

3. Financial reconstruction of the railway companies.

4. Access to the network of the 12 European railway systems for international groupings of railway undertakings to loosen control of the state-owned monopolies and increase competition.

In addition, Directive 1893/91/EEC limited the public service obligations to urban, suburban or regional services only. In all other cases, where a public organization wants transport from the railways the prices are subject to individually negotiated contracts.

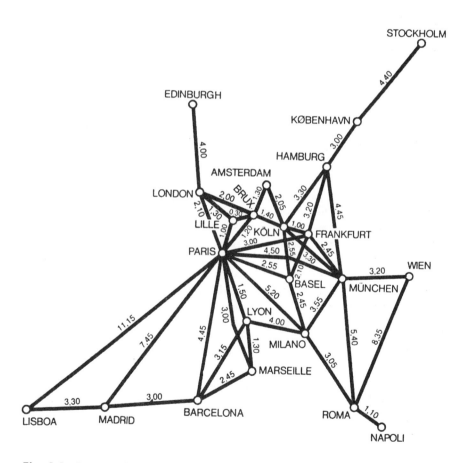

Fig. 4.4. European high speed train network. Figures indicate travelling times (hours). Source: Deutsche Bundesbahn.

The new strategies of the railways lie especially in the fields of product improvements and innovative pricing policies. Belgium, France, Germany, the Netherlands and the UK in 1987 agreed on a 'North western' high-speed rail network linking London (via the Channel Tunnel), Brussels, Amsterdam, Paris and Cologne (Fig. 4.4). In 1989 the railway companies of the EC Member States along with Austria and Switzerland proposed the development of a European high-speed rail network which by the year 2015 should consist of 35,000 km of network at costs of 200 billion ECU (at 1989 prices). This new transport system will connect the most important urban centres not only in the EC but in the whole of western Europe including expansions to the East and enabling present journey times to be reduced by half. The operating surplus of high-speed trains in respect of demand and financial profitability shows that railways can regain market shares from the airlines, especially at distances between 300 and 1000 km, where the train is twice as fast as the car and half as fast as the plane. AEA (1991) estimates that 110 city pairs will be affected by the new high-speed trains and that about 20% of the airline passengers on these routes will be diverted. To realize this, the existing national high speed networks like TGV in France, ICE in Germany, AVE in Spain or IC 250 in Britain will have to be extended and integrated. Apart from the legal framework, compatibility problems of infrastructure and equipment have to be solved: track gauge, line profiles, electric power supply systems, braking and signalling systems. Due to the close relationships between national railways and manufacturers of trains and railway infrastructure considerable vested interests are involved. And the lack of cooperation between the national railway companies still remains a crucial point.

Marketing specialists make it quite clear that for too long the corporate mission of the railway companies was dominated by the concept of being a transport provider only (Levitt, 1986). Their company philosophy has been production-oriented instead of customer oriented. The difficult financial situation forced almost all of the national railways to reduce their route operations and service standards considerably with negative consequences for the holiday traveller. As many unprofitable branch lines were closed, access to the departure stations of trunk routes became difficult and many smaller destinations were no longer served. Travel times increased, travelling became inconvenient (having to change trains with heavy luggage) especially for the elderly and families travelling with children, the rolling stock became defunct and obsolete. In their efforts to win back the tourist traffic the rail companies are gradually improving the quality of their services, introducing new rolling stock (air-conditioned trains with hostess service, restaurant cars, service in the compartments, luggage lockers, video entertainment), touristic trains and through coaches to tourist resorts with coach links and luggage service to smaller destinations, and international car-sleeper trains.

As in the tourism sector railways are mostly used for domestic travelling, the cross-border oriented high speed trains will have their main importance for city tours – the trains becoming an attraction in themselves like the TGV already is – and feeder services to international airports. Integrated rail and fly systems connect the international airports with the rail trunk routes including complete check-in for the flight at the train stations and promotional fares. For the railway companies this is an opportunity to generate new traffic, the airlines can attract passengers living far away from airports more easily and can substitute unprofitable short-haul air traffic, and the airports themselves are relieved of private car traffic.

Furthermore, special products have been discovered for railway enthusiasts and nostalgic travellers enjoying the romance, luxury and service of the grand old days of railway traffic: the legendary Orient Express from London to Venice, the Al Andalus in Spain or the scenic Glacier Express in Switzerland. In addition there is the re-emergence of numerous steam railways on disused tracks, privately restored and operated, which have become tourist attractions (for examples in Britain see Holloway, 1986).

With the growing charter flight traffic at reasonable prices to tourist destinations, fare levels and fare structures were no longer competitive. During the last decade railroad prices have gone up by 50% which is double the rate of air transport or the costs for private car transport. So groups and families with children prefer the private car as a cheaper mode of transport. In an effort not to lose even more market share the railway companies have introduced and are still developing innovative fares for different touristic target groups like Interrail and BIJ (Billet individuel pour des groupes des jeunes = individual group ticket for young people), Family Cards, Regional Rovers or Senior Savers. As some of these promotional tariffs for individual travellers are lower than the fares quoted to tour operators for Rail Inclusive Tours, a new pricing structure for the professional tourism industry must be developed. Especially inclusive prices for rail packages, be it real package holidays as for example 'Golden Rail' in Britain or rail packages only including fares and excess fares, home-to-home luggage transport, sleeping car and meals. And the system of differential pricing and yield management successfully operated by the airline industry has still to be adopted by the railway corporations.

The future of Europe's railways will not only be influenced by these new product and pricing strategies, but primarily by the infrastructure costing. During the last decades the railway companies have not been in a position to finance the rail infrastructure without subsidies and ever increasing loans and there is no chance of them being able to do so in the years to come. But with the new regulatory framework the Member States have the chances and obligations to restructure their railway systems in

order to stop the decline; it gives the railway undertakings the entrepreneurial freedom and true management responsibility to transform the
image of a permanent loss-maker running into billions. It may also focus
the interest of the public and the political institutions on the economic,
safety and ecological advantages of rail traffic against the other modes of
travelling.

COACH TRAVEL

Coach operators offer a wide range of services both directly to the tourist
and to the package tour operators. Holloway (1986) categorizes these
services under the following general headings:

- Scheduled coach routes, both domestic and international;
- Hire services for groups and tour operators;
- Tour and excursion operating;
- Transfer services.

Apart from the transfer and excursion business, the coach is an important
mode of transport for package tours, be it singular trips or long-distance
shuttle service (pendular traffic). In the past a number of multilateral
agreements within Europe have been negotiated to faciliate the organization and operation of coach tourism in Europe (regulations 117/66/
EEC, 516/72/EEC, ASOR 1983; see Euroconfidentiel, 1991).
Nevertheless the progress towards the completion of the Single Market will
bring some serious changes for coach operators as indicated by the Council
Regulation on common rules for the international carriage of passengers by
coach and bus (684/92/EEC):

1. Licensing of international coach package tours (shuttle and occasional
services) will be almost abolished. In connection with the freedom to
provide services a coach operator can offer his international services at any
place throughout the EC. Tour operators offering their services in low
price markets can take the advantages of cooperating with foreign low-cost
companies to the disadvantage of national bus companies.
2. Operators from one country will be allowed to offer their services on a
route between two Member States, enabling them to pick up passengers
from the foreign country crossed on the way to the destination area.
3. On shuttle services up to 20% of the passengers can be accepted on a
transport-only formula to obtain a better rentability by higher load factors.
4. The permission to carry out local excursions in connection with international transport allows a foreign coach operator to offer day trips in the
destination area for his clients.
5. Any carrier for hire or reward will be permitted to undertake carriage

by means of shuttle services or occasional services in any Member State if he is authorized in his State of establishment to carry out these transport services.

The implementation of these liberalized rules faces strong opposition from those countries that see their own operators in a position of competitive disadvantage due to high costs and disadvantages of location. There are enormous differences in automobile, value added and petrol taxes between the EC Member States, quite apart from differences in insurance, wage levels and social expenditures. A model calculation comparing costs in Germany and Spain for two identical coach operators shows a difference of almost 20,000 ECU per coach and year (Table 4.2). The allowance to pick up passengers en route in other Member States brings disadvantages for operators in those countries that could only be passed in transit up till now, but will be additional markets in the future. An English or Dutch coach operator can then pick up clients in France on his way to the Spanish coast – a chance French operators will not have due to their geographical location. The economic outcome of a licence-free coach shuttle service will be influenced by the imbalances in the tourist flows with their traditional north–south routings. The chances for operators in Belgium or Germany to compensate for the loss in business due to the penetration of Southern European companies in their home markets by additional efforts abroad are very limited, as only a small number of

Table 4.2. Costs of coach operations in Germany and Spain.

Cost	Germany (ECU)	Spain (ECU)
Wages	21,000	16,000
Vehicle tax	217	63
VAT on turnover	9,514	–
Fuel tax	4,505	3,050
Total	35,236	19,113
Difference		16,123

Source: Mörl (1991.
Calculated with an average operation of 200 days per year, the advantage to the Spanish operator is 92.50 ECU per day of operation.
Calculated with an average fleet of eight buses per operator, the advantage to the Spanish operator is 162,854 ECU per year.

tourists from the destination countries can or will book coach trips to Middle or Northern Europe.

As it seems to be very unlikely that the harmonization of costs will be achieved before the liberalization of transport rights, the additional competition will bring fares down further. Against the background of the already existing cut-throat competition, in the aftermath of deregulation the collapse of many smaller, less efficient and less experienced companies can be expected unless they develop new marketing strategies. Responses to this challenge lie in:

1. Cooperation between coach operators for a better penetration of their markets and a more efficient operation;
2. Positioning of their products in the high quality sector, using coaches with enhanced comfort, on-board entertainment, upgraded food and beverage service, experienced drivers and well-trained guides, and by appealing to people's predilection for nationally renowned products ('Made in Britain', 'German Quality Product');
3. Innovative specialized products, relying on the specific advantages of coach travel: comparatively low fares, door-to-door travelling without luggage and transfer problems, continuous guide assistance, tailor-made itineraries for groups or and an adventure-orientated product concept.

PRIVATE CAR TRANSPORT

The car is by far the most popular means of transport for leisure purposes both for day excursions and holiday trips. Its advantages lie in flexibility and mobility (the user can decide when and where to go, has his own vehicle at the destination), its convenience (door to door transport, luggage) and its cost advantages when travelling as a family or in small groups. The cost advantages are individual ones only, as usually the external costs of car transport are not taken into account.

Automobility will increase further. Even moderate forecasts based on extrapolation of the 1975 to 1988 average rate of road transport growth assume that the volume of transport at the end of the millennium will be 43% higher than in 1990 and 74% up in the year 2010 (European Parliament, 1991). The completion of the single market and the long depressed demand in East Europe (where a rise of 1000% in car ownership is expected) will certainly lead to even higher increases in traffic flow. The existing situation for travellers is already problematical enough: high death toll and casualty rates (50,000 persons killed and 1.5 million injured annually), time-consuming and stressful trips due to traffic jams and lack of parking space, and for the transit and destination areas there are noise, air pollution and congestion. A European-wide systematic and forward-looking approach is needed, taking into account that road traffic-related decisions are made at local, regional, national and international level. Here again the EC must accept its leading role by coordinating the necessary infrastructural developments to overcome the problems of missing links, black spots, bottlenecks and insufficient capacity, even in negotiations with third states as far as they are important transit countries (Austria, Switzerland or the former Yugoslavia). Concerning environmental issues a balance needs to be struck between environmental imperatives and economic growth by setting standards for tolerable levels of speed, safety, capacity and environmental nuisance.

Yet these measures, as important as they are, will not prevent the impending collapse of road transport.

- Growth rates would be reduced if road transport were charged with the full costs caused (i.e. including external costs) by environmental taxes or road pricing, where the traveller is charged for road use depending on distance, time of day, number of occupants and type of road.
- To improve efficiency and use of the existing infrastructure the member states should coordinate their holiday spreading schemes (better staggering of school holidays) in order to achieve a more equal seasonal distribution of the holiday traffic flows.
- Better traffic management. The already positive experiences with traffic forecasts and their publication as early as the holiday decision making periods can be enforced in order to reach a better weekly and daytime distribution. Adequate travel and routing information for people on the move helps to avoid traffic jams at bottle necks or tailbacks.
- The geographical distribution of tourist activities could be promoted by the development of areas or sites whose tourist potential has not yet been adequately exploited (Commission, 1986).

Facilitating international tourism is another field of action. The elimination of all obstacles to crossing frontiers – customs controls, frontier checks on passports, driving licences and insurance cards – is only a natural consequence of the completion of the Single Market. But with the easing of intra-EC border controls we must contend with the problem of free movement of terrorists, drug dealers and illegal immigrants. The Schengen agreement between Belgium, France, Germany, Luxembourg and The Netherlands provides for the elimination of frontier controls on the identity of persons travelling from one of these countries to another. This measure will be implemented Community wide with the completion of the European Union as envisaged in Maastrich 1991.

THE CHANNEL TUNNEL

The inauguration of the Eurotunnel in 1993 will for the first time in history connect England with a fixed transport link to the Continent. This will not only facilitate travelling and generate additional traffic, but also be an important step for the political and social integration of Europe. That is why

> the Channel Tunnel is probably the single most important
> development in European Transport this century. Its significance is
> as symbolic as it is practical, but in a growing European Community
> seeking to become more unified and economically successful, symbol
> and reality are not easily disentangled.
>
> (Whitelegg, 1988)

In the Anglo-French Treaty of 1987 the Eurotunnel company was granted the concession to develop, finance, construct and operate a tunnel under the Channel connecting England and France according to its own commercial policies until the year 2042. Eurotunnel is a private sector organization, consisting of two separate companies (Eurotunnel PLC Britain and Eurotunnel SA France), built by a consortium including five leading banks and ten major construction companies in both countries. The prospected costs of £8.1 billion are, therefore, financed without Government funding. The tunnel system incorporates two tunnels for trains only and runs 40–100 m below the bed of the Channel. The overall length of the tunnel is about 50 km, with an entrance at the English side at Farthingloe near Folkstone and on the French side at Sangatte near Calais. Road vehicles carrying passengers and freight will travel between the terminals on specially designed piggy-back shuttle services operated by Eurotunnel itself. Through trains between Britain and destinations on the Continent will be run jointly by British Rail and the respective other national railway companies under Eurotunnel's operational control. The journey times on the train will be 30 min with an additional 20 min for immigration, customs control and loading time, resulting in a time advantage of approximately one hour against the ferry.

With the opening of the tunnel, transport capacity across the Channel will be doubled overnight. Eurotunnel estimate that during the first year of operation about 14.6 million passengers on the shuttle and 14 million on through trains will use the tunnel. According to forecasts (BTA, 1988) this new mode of transport will divert all the present rail-linked traffic on to the through trains, carry two-thirds of all car traffic between the UK and the Continent, capture more than 80% of current cross-Channel coach passengers and take three-quarters of the day excursion traffic.

Among the current transport operators the ferries and hovercraft will be hit hardest by the new competitor. But with streamlined on-shore and loading operations, improved access to ports and faster crossing times the time disadvantage will be reduced and costs cut. There is also a fair chance that for many travellers the time spent at sea will be regarded as a pleasant break of the journey and can become a highlight when the ferry operators upgrade their services (general refurbishing, multilingual staff, restaurants) and offer additional attractions like shopping malls, cinemas, entertainment complexes and children's play areas. The seaport-towns are also trying to compensate for the reduced ferry operations by changing from transit spots to tourist destinations. Dover for example has built the heritage centre 'White Cliffs Experience', developed Dover Castle as a tourist attraction and plans to use its harbour as a centre for sports and leisure sailing. Nevertheless the lower number of passengers, price competition and loss of yield due to the abolition of the duty-free shops will entail a rationaliz-ation of the ferry operations and the two major companies, P&O and Sealink Stena, have already asked for government approval for joint services. The hovercraft are most threatened by the new competition, as their time advantage against the ferries is absorbed by the tunnel connec-tions and their current operation revenues allow little space for price incentives.

Air transport will in general be less affected as travel time by train to destinations that are not reached by through trains increases significantly. Forecasts assume that about 16% of all UK–Continent air traffic will switch to the train, most of it from the routes London–Paris and London–Brussels.

The economic and tourism benefits of the tunnel can only be fully realized when major improvements allow the existing infrastructure – roads, rail, stations – to accommodate the increase in traffic and link the tunnel to other parts of the countries. Whereas on the Continent the railway companies of Belgium, France, Germany and The Netherlands have decided to install a tunnel-linked high speed train network, the lack of high speed lines on the British side limits the scope for the full exploitation of these new opportunities there.

CONCLUSION

The realization of the Treaty of Rome is progressively leading to a liberaliz-ation of the European transport markets with free pricing systems, unrestricted market access and unlimited capacity offers. More and more state-owned enterprises are going to be privatized. The resulting stronger competition will certainly affect smaller operators, especially when they cannot find gaps in the markets, whereas the real big undertakings strengthen their competitive position by acquisitions, mergers and strategic alliances.

Facilitating of travelling and enhanced prosperity, both expected outcomes of the Single market, will result in growing tourism and thus in growing mobility. The objective of a European policy which includes the Member States and the other European countries can not only lie in the harmonization of national rules and the elimination of bottlenecks in the infrastructure. Apart from the problems of financing, the impacts on the environment would be irresponsible and an unlimited growth of motorways and airports is already no longer socially accepted. An integrated transport policy demands the implementation of other strategic options like regional and social distribution, a new traffic management in order to achieve an optimum use of existing capacity and even the deliberate slow down of growth rates by an appropriate and non-discriminatory allocation of costs. Otherwise the expanding mobility will unavoidably end in temporary immobility due to traffic infarcts.

REFERENCES

Air Transport Action Group (ATAG) (1992) *The Economic Benefits of Air Transport.* IATA, Geneva.

Association of European Airlines (AEA) (1991) White Paper on Air Transport and the Internal Market. Brussels.

Association of European Airlines (AEA) (1991a, 1992) *Annual Reports.* Brussels.

Becheri, E. (1989) *Il ruolo dei trasporti e le attività turistiche in Politica del Tourismo*, 2/3, Maggioli Editore, Milano, 243 pp.

Bennett, M. and Radburn, M. (1991) Information technology in tourism: the impact on the industry and supply of holidays. In: Sinclair, M.T. and Stabler, M.J. (eds) *The Tourism Industry: An International Analysis.* CAB International, Wallingford, UK.

British Tourist Authority (BTA) (1988) *The Channel Tunnel – An opportunity and a challenge for British Tourism.* London.

Cecchini, P. (ed.) (1988) *Research on the Costs of Non-Europe.* EC Commission, Brussels.

Commission of the European Communities (1991) *Transport in Europe.* Brussels.

Commission of the European Communities (1985) Completing the Internal Market. White Paper from the Commission to the European Council. Brussels.

Commission of the European Communities (1986) The Single European Act. Supplement to the Bulletin of the EC, 2. Brussels.

Conseil National du Tourisme (1991) *Le tourisme et le transport par autocar et l'Europe.* Paris.

Euroconfidential (ed.) (1991) *European Transport Policy for the 1990s.* Rixensart, Belgique.

European Parliament (1991) Report of the Committee on Transport and Tourism on Community policy on transport infrastructure (DOC EN/RR/110880).

Fitzpatrick, J. and associates (1989) *Travel and Tourism in the Single European Market*. Economist Intelligence Unit Special Report No 2014, London.

Gialloreto, L. (1988) *Strategic Airline Management*. Pitman, London.

Group Transport 2000 Plus (1990) *Transport in a Fast Changing Europe*. Brussels.

Holloway, C. (1986) *The Business of Tourism*. Pitman, London.

Levitt, T. (1986) *The Marketing Imagination*. Macmillan, New York.

Mörl, G. (1991) Ungleiche Kosten bevorteilen Wettbewerber. Internationales Verkehrswesen, 6 pp.

Organization for Economic Cooperation and Development (OECD) (1990) *Competition Policy and the Deregulation of Road Transport*. Paris.

Organization for Economic Cooperation and Development (OECD) (1988) *Deregulation and Airline Competition*. Paris.

Pompl, W. (1991) *Luftverkehr – Eine Ökonomische Analyse*. Springer Verlag, Heidelberg and New York.

Savage, I. (1985) *The Deregulation of Bus Services*. Gower, Aldershot.

Sánchez-Neyra, S. *et al.* (1986) *La política de transportes en la Communidad Económica Europea*. Madrid.

Wackermann, G. (1987) Acte unique et transports touristiques. *ESPACES*, 88, 15–18.

Whitelegg, J. (1988) *Transport Policy in the EEC*. Routledge, London.

5

A SINGLE EUROPEAN MARKET FOR THE TOURIST INDUSTRY

Patrick Lavery

INTRODUCTION

Although the creation of a Single European Market (SEM) from January 1993 will have an impact on the European Tourist Industry, for some years now the European Commission has been developing policies on Tourism. The importance of Community policies on Tourism are that they will help to underpin the overall significance of tourism as a phenomenon in Europe and support the predominance of European tourism on the world scene.

It is because of Europe's prevailing position in the world tourism economy that the Single European Act is so important. Already Europe receives two out of every three tourist arrivals worldwide. For the past 40 years it has been the world's leading tourist destination, receiving 67% of all international tourist arrivals and 57% of tourist receipts. Within the European Community the tourist industry employs 35 million people representing over 8% of the total workforce. Europe receives $66 billion a year from tourism receipts out of a world wide total of $120 billion (World Tourism Organization, 1992).

The importance of tourism both as a phenomenon and as a contributor to the national economy varies throughout the 12 member states of the European Community. One issue, therefore, is whether the creation of a single market will benefit the Community as a whole or only those countries which are the main tourist destinations. The question is what will the SEM mean to the individual countries and to the Community as a whole?

It is probably best to clarify what we mean by the Single Market and what it will do, so that any discussion on tourism can be set out against this policy context. The aim of the SEM is to bring about a profound restructuring of the economic and political life of Europe. The move towards the Single European Act in December 1992 was influenced by the view that until it is in place the European economy would continue to lag behind that of Japan and the United States. A report to the European Parliament in 1981 referred to the inefficiencies of the fragmented European economy and said that corrective action needed a unified internal market. The publication of a White Paper in 1985 (Commission of the European Community, 1985) and finally the Cecchini report in March 1988 helped to continue the impetus of a SEM policy. The Cecchini report quantified the benefits to the economy of the European Community by a SEM. Cecchini argued that within 5–6 years of the creation of a SEM:

• 2 million additional jobs would be created within the EC;
• The GDP of the European Community would rise by 2.5–7.0% over and above the growth rates the community would otherwise achieve;
• the inflation rate would be lower (by 6 percentage points) than it would otherwise have been.

Cecchini argued that by removing physical barriers to the movement of goods and people, firms would be able to move to locations within the EC where they could operate most efficiently. By being able to sell to a larger unified market firms would achieve increased economies of scale. The removal of technical barriers to trade would also produce more intense levels of competition.

However, the distribution of benefits arising from the SEM within Europe may be unequal and may emphasize the dominant position of the larger countries with more advanced economies.

TOURISM EXPENDITURE AND INCOME FLOWS WITHIN THE EUROPEAN COMMUNITY

Table 5.1 shows the distribution of tourism receipts and expenditure for the Member States of the EC and highlights the countries in Europe. Four countries – Germany, UK, France and The Netherlands – account for over three-quarters of international tourist expenditure by EC countries. Germany dominates as the main net exporter of tourists accounting for 36% of the total in 1990. This represents an expenditure of £23.6 billion which accounts for 7.4% of all imports to Germany (OECD, 1988). The United Kingdom accounts for just over 18% of EC tourist expenditure and although it is a major tourist destination, UK nationals spend more in other parts of the EC than is received from visitors to the UK, leaving a net deficit on the balance of trade of over £1.6 billion.

At the same time five countries – Spain, France, Italy, Germany and the UK – account for three-quarters of all tourist receipts in the EC. Tourism is particularly important in the UK and Germany because both

Table 5.1. European Community Countries: international tourism receipts and expenditure, 1987.

	% shares	
	Receipts	Expenditure
Belgium-Luxembourg	4.3	6.0
Denmark	3.2	4.4
France	17.1	13.1
West Germany	11.1	36.0
Greece	3.3	0.8
Irish Republic	1.2	1.2
Italy	17.3	6.9
The Netherlands	3.9	9.8
Portugal	3.1	0.6
Spain	21.1	3.0
UK	14.5	18.1
Total	100.0	100.0

Source: OECD (1988).

incoming and outgoing tourist flows are among the most significant in the EC. Spain, Italy and France are the three most important destinations for Community tourism. However, Portugal and Greece have shown the most rapid growth in international tourism income (Table 5.2) during the 1980s.

Although Portugal and Greece have a smaller share of the total EC tourist market the income they receive from tourism is of more importance to their national economies than it is in the other EC countries. For example, in Portugal income from tourism accounts for 5.4% of the country's GDP compared with 1.5% for the UK or 0.7% for Germany. Tourism income represents 5.2% of the GDP in Spain and 4.6% in Greece. The picture thus emerges of a group of southern European states, mainly around the shores of the Mediterranean, where tourism has grown rapidly and where it is a major part of the local economy.

The most recent study of the importance of tourism to the generation of jobs (O'Hagan *et al.*, 1986) is somewhat dated but the ratio between tourism expenditure and job equivalent is not expected to have changed significantly over the past 6 years. The UK, Germany and France, together with Italy account for 71% of tourism employment in the Community (Table 5.3). The UK and Germany, as large exporters of tourists, provide employment in the travel agency and tour operations sectors although as major destinations they also provide significant jobs in the accommodation and retail sectors.

Table 5.2. Trend in real international tourism receipts, 1983–1987 (1982 = 100).

	1983	1984	1985	1986	1987	1983–87 % change
Belgium-Luxembourg	113.2	116.6	114.3	112.1	125.7	11.0
Denmark	102.8	108.2	108.3	105.9	108.5	5.5
France	109.1	122.4	124.4	114.6	118.9	9.0
West Germany	102.8	111.0	98.8	97.2	99.0	−3.7
Greece	84.6	101.7	114.3	121.6	126.6	49.6
Irish Republic	101.2	104.8	117.5	107.8	120.8	19.4
Italy	105.8	104.6	101.0	87.7	89.8	−15.1
The Netherlands	98.9	124.8	123.3	122.1	123.0	24.4
Portugal	106.5	125.7	144.3	157.5	185.5	74.2
Spain	111.9	127.5	129.7	144.9	150.2	34.2
UK	120.3	132.3	148.4	146.1	159.5	32.6

Source: OECD (1988).

One consequence of the SEM is that in absolute terms these countries will continue to dominate tourism employment in the Community, although the economies of Portugal, Spain and Greece will continue to grow. However, tourism-based employment is not evenly distributed across the different sectors of the tourist industry, and the accommodation sector

Table 5.3. Full time job equivalents generated by tourism expenditure, 1985.

	Tourism employment ('000)	Tourism employment as % of total employment
Belgium-Luxembourg	180	4.7
Denmark	114	4.4
France	1487	6.9
West Germany	1300	5.1
Greece	260	6.9
Irish Republic	62	5.8
Italy	1405	6.7
The Netherlands	172	3.3
Portugal	355	8.6
Spain	980	9.1
UK	1081	4.4
EC-12	7396	6.0

Source: O'Hagan *et al.* (1986).

accounts for over half of all employment because it is a very labour intensive area of activity and often consists of small family-run businesses.

In part, the impact of the SEM on each Member State's tourist industry will depend on the potential market size in that country and its existing and potential share of intracommunity tourism. The remainder of this chapter examines the impact of the Single Market on the individual sectors of the tourism industry and the forecasted benefits arriving out of EC tourism policy in the 1990s.

AIR TRANSPORT AND THE AIRPORT SECTOR

By the late 1990s problems of congestion of the air routes and peak season passenger congestion at the main airports handling charter traffic will not be alleviated by particular EC developments. On the contrary two possible developments (the abolition of duty-free concessions and immigration controls for intra-EC air traffic) would mean on the one hand a significant loss of revenue and on the other high investment costs in redesigning the terminal buildings to allow these passengers to be dealt with as domestic rather than international passengers.

Although the Council of Ministers accepted a package of air transport liberalization measures in 1987, the European civil aviation industry has in reality made very slow progress towards freer market access and increased competition (see Chapter 4). However, it is expected that during the 1990s more routes will be opened up to competition and more competitive prices across Europe. One measure would involve market access where a greater number of airlines are allowed to compete on certain routes, and the right to stop off and pick up passengers at points along certain routes would be granted to European Community airlines.

However, despite EC policies aimed at liberalizing air services, any Member State can still refuse services from a regional airport if it is indirectly served by existing routes. This is important because although traffic at all major European airports grew during the 1980s the highest growth routes were at the major secondary regional airports such as Manchester or Gatwick – as the major airports become heavily overloaded. Much charter traffic in particular uses these regional centres (Table 5.4).

The main growth in the air transport sector has arisen from a series of bilateral agreements between Member States such as the UK and Eire and the UK and Holland. The growth in traffic that resulted from these agreements emphasizes the underlying latent demand. Between 1976 and 1983 there was no growth in traffic between the UK and Holland. By 1987, two years after the agreement, total UK–Holland traffic had grown by over 20%.

Table 5.4. Growth in numbers of passengers at selected EC airports 1980–1987.

Airport	Country	Annual average growth 1980–87 (%)
London Heathrow	UK	3.6
Frankfurt	Germany	4.7
Paris Orly	France	4.0
London Gatwick	UK	10.5
Paris (Ch. de Gaulle)	France	7.2
Rome	Italy	4.7
Amsterdam	Holland	5.4
Madrid	Spain	2.8
Copenhagen	Denmark	4.1
Athens	Greece	2.1
Manchester	UK	10.5
Cologne	Germany	2.2

Sources: IATA, Association of European Airlines, International Civil Airports Association.

The emergence of major hub airports and regional hubs and feeder routes that occurred in the United States (Lavery and Van Doren, 1990) has also been taking place in Europe with a marked increase in services between the smaller regional airports and the key hub airports during the 1980s. Collaborative ventures between the larger carriers such as British Airways and KLM will strengthen this trend. At the same time the growth in long-haul traffic and the increased use of larger aircraft has encouraged the growth of the major airports and main regional centres. The growth of air/charter traffic during the 1980s also saw an increasing switch to larger aircraft, seeking better load factors and reduced operating costs. This led to the rapid growth of airports such as Gatwick and Manchester at the expense of the smaller provincial airports.

Most of these trends have occurred in spite of, rather than because of, EC Single Market legislation. However, if the EC liberalization of air travel does take effect with deregulated fares and access to markets it could lead to an even more rapid growth than forecast, with all the attendant problems of congestion of the skies, peak season ground congestion and demands for even greater airport expansion at the major hubs.

TOUR OPERATORS

The Single Market is likely to affect tour operators in terms of (i) operating costs; (ii) cross border expansion.

Although the Treaty of Rome allows for the right of business to set up anywhere in the European Community and in theory allows for the free movement of people and jobs, tour operators still have to comply with the statutory and other regulations laid down by the Member State concerned. The abolition of exchange controls and the move towards a single European currency will slightly improve the ability of firms to trade across borders. Also recent experience has deterred UK tour operators from trying to break into other European markets. For example, Intasun (part of the former International Leisure Group) in 1986 tried to establish a presence in the West German market, but found the German market leader TUI had a contractual deal with 2600 travel agents prohibiting even other German operators selling through these retail outlets. The arrangement was approved by the German Federal anti-trust office. After 2 years Intasun closed its German office.

The most likely trend is for the larger tour operators to establish pan-European activities through mergers, acquisitions and joint ventures. For example, the Thomas Cook chain has negotiated an association with Wagon Lits (which it once owned); the German operator NUR owns firms in Belgium and Holland, and TUI, the German market leader, is a shareholder in Touropa Austria and has a 30% share in a French tour operator. In the United Kingdom and Germany a small number of large tour operators control a majority of the market, and if EC Competition policy places limits on the market share that firms such as Horizon or TUI can hold, they may seek more joint ventures as they seek to expand.

Part of the Community's tourism policy is aimed to provide better information and protection for tourists, and part of the drive is for pan-European consumer protection. The Council has issued a directive on package travel, including package holidays and package tours and tour operators are faced with the prospect of increased costs and liabilities which has become Law. It seeks to impose strict liability on tour operators for the contents of the holidays they promote, so that, for example, it would be the tour operator who would be liable for any damages incurred by the traveller regardless of where the complaint/injury occurred. In addition, limitations may be imposed on an operator's ability to change departure dates, impose surcharges or otherwise alter the original package and provide the client with a clearly understandable written contract at the time of purchase. Tour operators regard all of these measures as an imposition that will push up operating costs.

THE ACCOMMODATION SECTOR

This is probably the one sector of the tourism industry where the completion of the Single Market will not alter significant trends in the hotel sector that have continued during the 1980s. This area has seen the emergence of a number of very large hotel chains. Three of the top ten hotel chains in the EC, including the Forte group the largest, are UK owned (Table 5.5). However, several of these EC-based companies have a worldwide presence and in recent years their investment has been more evident outside the EC. The number one group Trusthouse Forte has 16 hotels in EC countries (excluding the UK) and 650 in the rest of the world. The Accor group has 15 establishments in other EC countries but 104 outside of Europe. The major hotel chains in the EC have concentrated on market segmentation and moving into expanding destinations in the international market rather than seeking greater EC expansion outside their 'home' country.

What is more likely is that the European Community will seek to encourage non-hotel accommodation and farm tourism as part of a broader policy supporting the less prosperous parts of the EC. This is also in keeping with EC policies to encourage social tourism and encourage

Table 5.5. Major EC hotel chains, 1989.

Rank	Company	Country	Rooms	Units
1	Trusthouse Forte	UK	74,800	793
2	Accor	France	62,410	534
3	Club Mediterranée	France	53,733	212
4	Sols	Spain	29,450	110
5	Ladbroke	UK	26,379	208
6	Wagons Lits	France	24,540	187
7	Grupo Unidos	Spain	22,000	125
8	Meridien	France	18,000	53
9	Societe du Louvre	France	15,876	164
10	Crest	UK	9,758	79
11	Iberotel	Spain	7,900	37
12	Queens Moat Houses	UK	7,749	87
13	Mount Charlotte	UK	6,935	58
14	Penta	UK	6,893	15
15	Lonrho	UK	6,120	12
16	Ciga	Italy	5,451	33
17	Melia	Spain	5,340	17
18	Climat de France	France	5,024	124
19	Steigenberger	West Germany	5,000	30
20	Maritim	West Germany	4,980	23
	Total		398,338	2,901

Source: DAFSA in Panorama of EC Industry (1989).

participation by less prosperous members of the population. However, even if these types of accommodation are encouraged, and provided with special incentives, they are unlikely to remain more than a small part of the accommodation sector.

EC policies to encourage the freedom of movement of people and jobs may well encourage the large and growing hotel chains of the UK and France to recruit southern European hotel staff at relatively low wages. The signing of the Social Charter at the Maastrict meeting of EC Heads of State in December 1991 may well limit their ability to discriminate against lower paid staff.

The Single Market and EC policies are likely to benefit the consumer using the accommodation sector, because there will be a move towards harmonization of professional training standards across the EC and also a move towards health and safety legislation. Health and safety legislation, if implemented at Member State level, will have a much greater impact on the small family run hotel and it may well have an effect similar to the introduction of fire regulations in the UK in the early 1970s when many small hotels closed down.

THE RETAIL TRAVEL SECTOR

The retail travel sector, in the form of the high street travel agent, is the one activity most clearly recognized by the general public to represent the tourist industry. It is also one sector where the advent of the Single Market has given rise to concern rather than optimism about the development of the sector.

Four factors will affect the future of the high street retail travel market, particularly the smaller independent concerns.

1. Increased liability for the contents of holiday packages sold.
2. A trend towards concentration.
3. Increased use of computerized reservation systems (CRS) and polarization of CRS.
4. Deregulation of air travel.

If the new legislation on package holidays puts the liability on the tour operator, travel agents will not be affected. However, the legislation leaves open the liability and it may be shared between the retailer and the producer of the holiday package. Given the already extremely slim profit margins for retail travel agents any increased costs could mean more smaller firms going out of business.

The emergence of a small group of very large tour operators and the growth of direct sell operations and a much more complex market may work against the smaller independent holiday retailer. The emergence of Computer Reservation Systems may help the smaller independent retailers, but if experience in the USA is a guide, the impact of both deregulation (of air travel) and CRSs on travel agents has been considerable. In Europe the position is complicated by the emergence of two systems – Galileo and Amadeus – rather than a single European CRS. Galileo with British Airways as a major partner is likely to become the major distribution network in the UK, Holland and Italy. Amadeus with its linkup with Lufthansa and Air France will predominate in France and Germany (see chapter 4).

Vast sums of money are involved in setting up CRS and they are now a major feature of airline strategic planning. American and United have spent about $750 million on Sabre and Apollo development and United has talked about £1 billion worth of new investment in computer systems and personnel. Texas Air is spending $200–400 million to make the System 1 CRS more competitive. In fact System 1 has been selected by the AMADEUS Consortium in Europe as the basis for their CRS. Each of the other main CRSs is investing heavily in order to increase or at least maintain their market share.

The impact of both deregulation and CRSs on travel agents in the US has been considerable. The major CRSs are looking for retail outlets who can bring them a large amount of business in the fastest possible time and that often means agents producing a lot of business travel. However, although there are over 29,000 travel agents in the US, only 7% of these accounted for 28% of agency sales and the picture has been one of fewer agents doing more business. In many cases dwindling profits have led to consolidation, and many agents have joined or formed chains that are able to offer good national coverage and the kinds of discounts on air tickets, hotel rooms and car rentals that come with volume of business. All CRS vendors are now offering agents personal computers and three offer IBM's new PS/2 standard. These smart terminals offer a variety of accounting and administrative backup as well as the reservations systems.

THE CONSEQUENCES OF EC POLICY OBJECTIVES FOR THE EUROPEAN TOURIST INDUSTRY

The development of the European Tourism industry is influenced by two sets of factors:

1. The explicit EC policies on tourism.
2. Factors arising from completion of the single market.

The EC Commission's policy on tourism is based on a communication

submitted to the Council of Ministers of the Community in January 1986
and the main themes are:

1. Facilitating tourism in the Community.
2. Improving the geographical and seasonal distribution of tourism.
3. Better use of financial aid.
4. Better information and protection for tourists.
5. Improvement of working conditions.
6. Improved knowledge of the tourist sector and increased cooperation
among member countries.

This topic is addressed more fully in Chapter 3 and therefore only covered
briefly here.

Facilitating Tourism

Since 1988 most of the policy measures, such as the introduction of a single
European Community passport, have been introduced. Other obstacles to
the crossing of internal borders are gradually being removed, such as the
abolition of internal customs controls, duty-free allowances. Visa and
residence permit systems will also be integrated on a Community basis.
Standardization of assistance on health and legal matters will also give EC
Nationals the same rights as those available to the nationals of the country
they are visiting.

Improving the Geographical and Seasonal Distribution of Tourism

Almost two-thirds of EC tourists go on holiday in July or August and over
half go to a seaside location. This leads to acute peak season congestion,
not only on the coastline but on the roads leading to it. Moreover, if
enough resources are diverted to providing an infrastructure that meets this
peak season demand, then they will be greatly under-used for the rest of
the year.

The Commission of the EC has therefore prepared directives to
counter these problems. These relate to:

• *Reducing seasonal and local concentration*: The EC directive making
  major tourism-related projects subject to environmental impact
  analysis will address this issue. Also Member States have been asked to
  consider the staggering of holidays, to ensure the fuller use of under-
  used locations, to improve road traffic information and generally
  cooperate to encourage a better spread of tourist activity. The
  Commission has jointly financed two studies to look at various
  approaches to staggering school and industrial holidays.

- *Social tourism*: aimed at helping the less well off in the Community to take maximum advantage of the possibilities available in the various Member States. The Commission is keen to produce a guide to social tourism and to finance projects that would assist in this area.
- *Rural tourism*: the Commission is actively seeking to promote farm tourism and tourism generally in rural areas. Allied to this is the view of tourism as a means of regeneration of the local economy especially in the economically marginal and less developed regions of the EC.
- *Cultural tourism*: this is important because it generally relates to events and facilities that are not dependent on the prevailing weather and which are available on a year round basis. It also brings in many international tourists such as the Japanese or North Americans with their high per capita spending. A concern for the richness of the EC cultural heritage has already led to finance for restoration work on the Doge's Palace in Venice and the Parthenon in Athens.

Community Financial Aid

After the signing of the Single European Act in 1987 the EC member governments committed themselves to a doubling of the structural fund budget between 1987 and 1993. There was also a commitment to discriminate in favour of the least prosperous regions of the Community, including Eire, Greece, Spain and Portugal. The enlargement and reform of the structural funds includes measures which will assist in the development of Europe's tourist industry, not least in the poorest regions of the EC.

There are three structural funds:

1. **The European Agricultural Guidance and Guarantee Fund**, which although primarily aimed at improving agricultural productivity, has also supported the promotion of many tourist activities that supplement farmer's incomes.

2. **The European Social Fund** which concentrates on employment training, especially for young people and the long-term unemployed.

3. **The European Regional Development Fund** which assists infrastructure developments in deprived regions in the Community. Between 1980 and 1986 the European Regional Development Fund provided 326 million ECU in aid of 660 tourist projects including hotels, conference centres, sports centres, museums, archaeological sites and other similar initiatives (EC Commission, 1987).

Another source of EC finance is the European Investment Bank which between 1980 and 1986 gave 350 million ECU, in the form of low interest loans, for more than 1000 tourism projects including holiday villages, marinas, ski lifts and many small and medium-sized tourism enterprises.

Table 5.6. EC structural fund payments to 1993 (million ECU).

	European Regional Development Fund	European Social Fund	European Agricultural Guidance Fund	Total
Greece	294	152	78	524
Portugal	223	191	28	442
Spain	345	312	21	678
Italy	564	539	146	1249
Irish Republic	135	247	87	469

Source: *Official Journal of the European Communities* (December 1988).

The European Investment Bank and the European Regional Development Fund have also financed under other headings, infrastructural developments that have a direct impact on the growth of the tourist industry. For example, they have provided funding for over 2000 km of motorways in Europe including a permanent link between France and the UK, and a motorway linking Germany with Greece via Austria and Yugoslavia.

One priority attached to the increased structural fund monies is to compensate the less-developed regions in the Community for the impact of the Single Market on their local economy. The Official Journal of the European Communities (1988) indicates that five countries stand to gain significantly from the increased allocation of structural funds (Table 5.6). However, it remains to be seen whether these additional monies will adequately compensate or protect these parts of the Community from the full impact of the Single European Market.

Other Tourism Initiatives

Tourism policies are also seen as a means of implementing some of the measures contained in the Social Charter, including improved working conditions, better information and protection for tourists and increased awareness of the specific problems of tourism in the European Community.

Working conditions

In order to improve working conditions in the tourist industry the EC has financed a study to examine the employment situation in hotels, restaurants and cafes. It has also sought to standardize computer vocabularies and provide access to the data banks of all Member States in order to standardize and improve reservation systems. The Commission has also issued a directive to ensure that occupations in restaurants, public houses, furnished hotels and camp sites can be practised by Community citizens in the Member States of their choice.

Better information and protection

Another Commission priority in the late 1980s was to provide better information and protection for tourists. The EC information services produced a brochure *Travelling in Europe* which contains information on crossing borders, duty-free allowances, health care and so on, and a phone service to provide a more complete guide on all Member States.

Standardizing hotel information

The Council of Ministers of the Community has also approved a recommendation drawn up by the Commission in consultation with the hotel industry, for standardizing the main information about hotels (Commission of the EC, 1988). Although a complete classification of hotels covering all Member States would be difficult to achieve it is a long-term aim of the Commission. This resolution recommends that:

1. Member States ask national tourist organizations, in collaboration with the hotel sector, to assume responsibility for collecting, checking and publishing information on hotels based on a standardized information system.
2. This information be published in official guides.
3. Hotels display the prices of rooms at the hotel entrance and in each room.
4. Within two years Member States make every effort to bring into force a standardized information system.
5. Member States send to the Commission each year the official hotel guides published in accordance with this recommendation.

Finally, the Council of Ministers invited the Commission to make an analysis, in cooperation with Member States, of their tourist bodies and for representatives of their hotel industries, of their existing hotel grading systems and to examine the practicality and desirability of producing a Communitywide grading system for hotels.

PROMOTING TOURISM IN THE SINGLE EUROPEAN MARKET

Promotion of tourism in the EC takes two forms. First, there is the internal role that tourism as a phenomenon can play. Secondly, the advent of the Single European Market provides a great opportunity to promote Europe in the world market as a single destination.

Internal Promotion of Tourism

This is seen as a means of combining the efforts of the Member States and the Commission to achieve a better distribution of tourism. Moreover, by reducing the problems of seasonality and congestion it will help to ease pressure on the natural and cultural resources of Europe. In order to relieve the peak summer concentration of people and traffic on the coastal regions and the roads leading to them the Commission are seeking to encourage the development of alternative tourist destinations and new forms of tourism. The European Regional Development Fund is being used to assist tourism projects in less developed regions, and the reform of the Common Agricultural Policy will affect tourism in rural areas. Actions using monies from the Agricultural Guidance and Guarantee Fund should help to stimulate secondary activities, such as tourism, in rural areas. Certainly, studies have shown that Farm Tourism can provide a significant input to the individual farm income and can make farming viable in situations where it would normally be economically marginal.

Marketing Europe as a Single Destination

This will be easier to achieve once the Single European Market is in place. In preparing a marketing strategy it is worthwhile 'regionalizing' Europe to put together different types of holiday destination based on social, cultural and other characterisitics. For example Austria, West Germany and Switzerland have similar culture and language and are linked by a modern rail and motorway network. Similarly, the three Scandinavian countries Denmark, Norway and Sweden have a distinctive culture and close association. In fact the tourist boards of these Nordic countries jointly promote inter-Scandinavian travel, although this may be done through the rest of Europe rather than in the long-haul markets. For example, France, Italy, West Germany and Switzerland can promote the Alpine region, although this is unlikely to attract North American visitors for winter sports as they have comparable facilities. Belgium, The Netherlands and Luxembourg could also engage in joint promotions stressing their close proximity and varied cultural heritage. However, the predominant trend is for individual countries to market their country as a single tourist destination, when it is clear that the majority of long-haul tourists wish to maximize their visit because of the time and cost of travelling to Europe, and wish to visit as many countries as possible during their visit. Events in 1986 showed the wisdom of adopting a marketing strategy that seeks to diversify into as many long-haul markets as possible. One immediate repercussion of the Libyan bombing raid in April 1986 was a dramatic decline in the number of Americans travelling to Europe because they feared terrorist reprisals. In May 1986 there were 40% fewer American visitors to the United Kingdom than in the same period in 1985. In Greece and France there were 60% fewer US tourists and 50% fewer in Italy.

Australia, southeast Asia and Japan are growing in importance as generators of tourism to Europe and have considerable scope for expansion despite the great distances involved. Europe accounts for about 12% of the Japanese overseas visitors (over 350,000 tourists) and they are among the highest spending tourists in Europe. Despite the distance and the high air fare, Europe has steadily increased in importance as a destination for Japanese tourists since 1964. It is also the destination where they stay longest. Since the 1970s the European Travel Commission (who comprise representatives of all the European national tourist organizations [NTOs]) have been very successful in promoting Europe as a whole, and supplementing the individual efforts of each national tourist office. Their main efforts are targeted at travel agents, who handle 92% of the overseas market in Japan. A small group of companies associated with major finance houses are often wholesalers and retailers selling package tours to Europe. The future for this market is likely to be less emphasis on a packaged tour (particularly for the 20% of the Japanese who are on repeat visits) and more emphasis on special interest travel opportunities. What Europe is selling to Japan is a small size continent with 23 different countries, cultures and an endless variety of both historical and natural environments. It is destination that can be visited several times without repeating previous experiences.

The initiative of designating a European Year of Tourism was an early example of what might be achieved following the SEM in January 1993. The main objectives of the European Year of Tourism were:

1. To promote the establishment of a large area without frontiers.
2. To develop the role of tourism as a means of creating a 'people's Europe'.
3. To stress the economic and social role of tourism in regional development and employment creation.

Under these three broad headings there were several themes that formed part of the programme of events and initiatives during 1990. These included the development of new tourist destinations and the development of new forms of tourism, in particular alternatives to existing mass tourism.

The year's events were also designed to encourage greater knowledge among European citizens, especially young people, of the cultures and life styles of other European countries.

THE GROWTH OF EUROPEAN TOURISM IN THE SINGLE MARKET

It is possible to produce forecasts of the growth in the European tourism industry in the 1990s, using two major sources, the Cecchini report (Cecchini, 1988) and the work of Edwards (1988).

The Cecchini report forecast that the completion of the Single Market by the end of 1992 is expected to provide approximately 200 billion ECU in cost savings to firms and in the medium term the creation of over 2 million additional jobs as real economic growth is boosted by between 3 and 7%. These forecasts are based on the premise that much of the improved economic performance will come about through the removal of barriers which directly restrict intra-Community trade. Also firms will make significant cost savings through exploiting the increased economies of scale in a single enlarged market.

The growth of the tourist industry in Europe stems in part from its strength as a generator and receiver of tourists. This is due to a number of factors, for example:

- More than half of the population takes a period of paid holidays every year.
- European incomes are higher than comparable incomes in many other regions of the world.
- There is a large and well established tourist industry and infrastructure.
- The geography of Europe means that distances between countries are relatively small, Europeans are highly mobile with higher than average levels of car ownership, and there is a good road, rail and air network which makes travel quick and easy.

Evidence shows that even where economies are stagnating or growing slowly, where relative prices remain unchanged a 2% real growth rate in private consumption is associated with a 4% growth rate in travel spending. For example, despite the recessions of the early and late 1980s the rate of growth in travel spending showed an upward trend.

Caution needs to be used in applying the forecasts of Cecchini and Edwards to tourism trends in the Single Market for two reasons. First, the Cecchini report did not calculate the variation in benefits of the SEM between Member States, but rather focused on macroeconomic projections. Secondly, Edwards in his forecasts of growth in real expenditure on international travel and tourism did not make any allowance for the impact of the Single Market.

Several internal and external factors will affect the growth of tourism in the EC during the 1990s. These are based on a number of forecast trends over the next decade:

- In the European Community moves towards a single currency and the strengthening of the European Monetary System will ensure a period of balanced non-inflationary growth.
- Most EC countries will record rises in real private consumption expenditure.
- The Japanese yen will remain strong, and Japanese trade surpluses will continue. The portion of outward tourism from Japan will help offset these surpluses.
- The value of the US dollar will fall as it attempts to deal with its budget and balance of payments deficits.

A consequence of these various forecasts is that most experts predict that spending on tourism will grow at a faster rate than it would otherwise have done, as a consequence of the Single Market. Moreover, 80% of international travel in Europe is in fact intra-European travel. Forecasts of growth in the EC indicate that tourism spending will grow at a faster rate than it would otherwise have done, particularly in countries such as Italy and Spain. Intraregional arrivals accounted for 91% of international arrivals in Italy and 95% in Spain, so the major tourism destinations (see Table 5.1 above) are likely to see their position reinforced after 1992.

Conclusions

It is clear that the policies of the EC to encourage the freedom of movement of people and jobs and the promotion of tourism within the Community, for economic and social reasons, will encourage more Europeans to travel between Member States. Developments such as the Channel Tunnel and extended TGV rail network, and motorway construction will make more of Europe more accessible. Attractions such as EuroDisney, near Paris, will encourage more travel between EC countries. Underpinning these developments are generally favourable forecasts for a period of stable, non-inflationary growth, with increases in tourist spending running at roughly double the rate of private personal consumption expenditure.

However, the SEM will have a variable impact on the individual sectors of the tourist industry. In the case of the hotel sector it is likely to have a limited impact because the bulk of existing establishments are controlled by a relatively small number of very large hotel chains and they increasingly take a world perspective on market opportunities. Measures to implement fire safety standards and social and employment conditions are more likely to affect the small hotel sector.

In the case of tour operators and retail travel agents pressures for firms to become increasingly competitive and flexible may well lead to greater concentration of activity at the expense of the smaller independent agency. The introduction of stricter Community-wide consumer protection laws may have a significant impact on both of these sectors of the industry – particularly tour operators. The new laws will impose a strict liability on tour operators for the contents of the holidays they promote. Any claims for damages will be based on their responsibility for the tour package regardless of where the fault or injury occurred.

Air travel is expected to continue to grow with the consolidation of a number of hubs such as London (Heathrow) and Amsterdam (Schipol) and more joint agreements between large carriers and smaller carriers based on major hubs. The traffic from regional centres is expected to grow but it is likely to be in the links between the larger regional airports and the major hub airports. Peak season congestion, on the ground and in the air, will continue to be a problem through the 1990s.

The overall conclusion is that the Single Market will reinforce Europe's position as the world's leading tourist destination although its impact on the individual sectors of the tourist industry will be to underline trends of concentration and market segmentation already established by the early 1990s.

REFERENCES

Cecchini, P. (1988) *Research on the Costs of Non-Europe.* EC Commission.

Commission of the European Community (1985) *Completing the Internal Market.* White Paper from the Commission to the European Council, Brussels.

Commission of the European Community (1987) *The European Community and Tourism.* 9/87. Brussels.

Commission of the European Community (1988) *The European Community and Tourism.* Brussels.

Commission of the European Community (1989) *Panorama of the EC Industry.* Brussels.

Edwards, A. (1988) *International Tourism Forecasts to 1999.* Economist Intelligence Unit, special report no 1142.

Lavery, P. and Van Doren, C. (1990) *Travel and Tourism: A North American–European Perspective.* Elm Publications, Huntingdon, pp. 100–2.

Official Journal of the European Communities (1988) Brussels.

O'Hagan, J.W., Scott, Y. and Waldron, P. (1986) *The Tourism Industry and the Tourism Policies of the Twelve Member States of the Community.* Brussels.

Organisation for Economic Cooperation and Development (1988) *Tourism Policy and International Tourism.* Paris.

World Tourism Organization (1992) *Yearbook of Tourism Statistics.* Madrid.

6

LABOUR, VOCATIONAL EDUCATION AND TRAINING

Chris Holloway

VOCATIONAL EDUCATION, TRAINING AND THE TOURISM INDUSTRY'S NEEDS

The travel and tourism industry is of immense economic importance to most European countries, employing some 35 million people, some 8.5% of the European workforce, and representing over 5% of the wage and salary income (American Express/EIESP, 1991). Employment in 1991, as estimated by the World Travel and Tourism Council, is shown in Table 6.1.

The travel and tourism industry is the largest employer by far in Germany, France and the UK, and in many countries the growth in employment in this sector is outstripping that of other fields of employment. One worker in seven in the Mediterranean countries is directly dependent upon tourism. In Britain, it has been estimated by the National Economic Development Council (NEDC) (1991) that some 1.5 million people are employed in the sectors embracing accommodation, non-institutional catering, tourist attractions and services, sports and leisure, with a further half million employed in passenger transport, travel organizations and services.

In recent years, the European travel and tourism industry has been undergoing a transformation, a process which promises little respite in the 1990s, with the advent of harmonization among European Community members post-1992. The accelerating pattern of change is caused partly by the economic swings which all the European economies have experienced during the 1980s, and in part by developments occurring within the travel industry itself, which has become increasingly competitive as it approaches maturity. These are characteristics that are common, to a greater or lesser extent, to all Europe's tourism-generating countries.

Integration and concentration of firms within the industry, brought about by, and partly resulting from, the computer revolution, is causing

Table 6.1. Employment in travel and tourism, Europe.

Area	Jobs (000s)	% all service jobs	% total employed
Western Europe	18,267	18.2	8.4
Eastern Europe	16,623	20.9	8.5
Total	34,890	19.3	8.5

Source: *WTTC Report*: Travel and Tourism in the World Economy (1991).

profound changes in the way products are marketed, affecting firms both large and small. In most European countries, a handful of large tour operators – typically between four and six – have become responsible for four out of five of the outbound package holidays sold. Retail travel agents in these countries are now similarly dominated by a small number of major chains, sometimes as a result of take-overs or mergers, sometimes through franchise agreements, although this trend appears to be flattening out in the early 1990s. The balance of the outbound market, and virtually the entire domestic and in-coming markets to these countries, continue to be served by many small businesses.

The industry is still seen as offering an attractive career for many young people. However, the glamour image soon palls for these once employed in the travel business, and there is a high turnover of staff in most sectors, especially in hotels, catering and retail travel. Half of London's hotels experience annual labour turnovers in excess of 100% (American Express/EIESP, 1991), and the average length of service in Dutch travel agencies is less than three years. This high turnover is partly due to conditions of work, including long hours, high pressure and significant peaks and troughs in the workloads, but a more important reason is the relatively poor salaries compared to other industries, which tend to encourage young employees to leave the travel business altogether. Average wages are lower than either the service sector itself, or those found in the economy generally.

In most European countries, these low salaries have led to a situation where female employment is dominant, at least in subordinate roles (although this is less true of Spain), and the industry, notwithstanding its glamour image among the young, is held in generally low esteem. This is a problem compounded in the UK by the fact that service industries enjoy lower status than they do on the Continent. The reputation of the industry as an employer of part-time, seasonal workers in 'Mickey Mouse' jobs is a further hindrance to recruitment, although this reputation is seldom well founded; one study in Britain has found that less than one job in 20 is subject to seasonal lay-offs (Battersby *et al.*, quoted in NEDC, 1991). There is a high dependence on foreign labour, especially within the hotel and catering sector (11% of the French hotel industry are foreign workers, compared with only 6% in the economy as a whole (Brygoo, quoted in American Express/EIESP, 1991).

The recent maturation of the industry, and the large number of small firms of which it is composed, result in relatively poor human resources management. Recruitment and training for the industry still tends to be largely *ad hoc*; few employers concern themselves with the long-term career aspirations of their staff, focusing instead on their own immediate need for staff with job-specific skills and competences. This focus has particular implications for recruitment and training, and for the development of vocational curricula. An example of the problems that this can give rise to is the shortage of good management ability among staff promoted from counter clerks in retail travel and similar sectors. It may not be purely coincidental that the job of retail travel managers has become downgraded in recent years, with the growth of the multiples and the centralization of management functions, and this has helped to overcome some of the earlier problems of poor management in the sector.

Finally, it must be recognized that the nature of the tourist market itself is changing. The overseas traveller is becoming increasingly sophisticated in both travel knowledge and choice. This development is forcing tourism managers to focus on product quality and value for money, rather than price alone.

All these developments help to shape the provision of training and education of those who work, or plan to work, in the industry. In this chapter, this provision is examined by drawing upon the experience of a number of European countries, in particular those of Germany, France, Italy, The Netherlands, Norway and the UK.

VOCATIONAL EDUCATION FOR WHAT?

Perhaps before turning to an examination of vocational education and training, mention should be made of the difficulty of defining what is meant by the 'travel and tourism industry' in a European context. Tourism-related labour can spread across sectors ranging from hotels and catering, transport, retailing and other business services, to agriculture and local and central government. The variety of definitions within Europe leads to different approaches to course curriculum design which add to the difficulties in seeking mutual recognition of qualifications between the European partners. For example, in The Netherlands recreation is seen as integral with travel and tourism, and in France, too, the terms 'leisure' and 'tourism' are used synonymously – at least, in terms of curriculum development. Germany has not yet recognized the need for vocational education or training for leisure and recreation, and Britain has chosen to develop distinct curricula for leisure and tourism, despite significant areas of overlap in knowledge and skills. Similar problems arise in considering the role of hotel and catering, which is considered in some countries, such as France and Holland, to lie outside the field of travel and tourism, whereas in others it is integral. This has resulted in an almost total separation in the curricula of hotel and catering courses and tourism courses in the former countries. One must also appreciate that the distinction between tour operating and travel agencies, so notable in the industry in Britain, is far less evident in most Continental countries. Travel agencies in Italy, for example, will commonly form an in-coming tour operating division, a rare event in Britain.

As the characteristics of tourism in each country differ, so will knowledge and competence differ; Germany, for example, lays stress on a knowledge of spa tourism, whereas an understanding of farm or rural tourism would be an essential prerequisite in Norway or Denmark. Water recreation plays a prominent role in tourism in Holland, while in the Southern European countries the role of 'animateur', linking tourism and entertainment, is an important one, but one that has so far not been widely recognized or adopted in Northern Europe.

PLANNING FOR VOCATIONAL EDUCATION

Little, if any, attempt is made in most European countries to plan vocational courses in travel and tourism to meet the manpower needs of the industry. The result is a mismatch between provision and demand which is often astonishing. For example, in The Netherlands, the industry employs some 62,000 people, at last half of whom are undertaking full-time vocational courses; some 10,000 trained people each year are entering a job market which at best can assimilate a tenth of that number.

There are a number of reasons for this over-supply. In The Netherlands, as in Belgium, one dimension is the influence of denominational colleges, through which the churches jealously guard their traditional autonomy in the provision of education. Another factor, common to a number of European countries, is the parallel systems of private and public education, with private colleges often duplicating the courses provided in the state sector. Private colleges are commercially orientated, interested predominantly in recruitment, and seldom showing concern as to whether or not their courses lead to employment in the industry.

The perceived attraction of work in the tourism industry accounts for the very high levels of demand in all countries. In Britain, ratios of 20:1

are not uncommon in applications for a tourism course compared with the number of places available, and ratios of 10:1 are typical for applications to hospitality courses (NEDC, 1991). Similar figures are experienced on the Continent, and for prestigious courses such as that offered in tourism management at the Oppland Regional College at Lillehammer, Norway, this figure will be many times higher. This will often result in the colleges in question seeking not only higher academic qualifications, but imposing additional entry requirements such as, in the case of Lillehammer, some years of practical experience in the industry, before applicants will be considered.

Where vocational education is broadly based, encompassing a sound liberal education or a broad knowledge of the business world, and producing an all-rounder capable of functioning effectively in any area of business, this over-supply may not be a major cause for concern, providing that the qualification achieved is widely recognized outside the travel industry. However, where curricula are narrowly defined and there is a growing tendency to specialize in increasingly specific sectoral skills and competences, as is the case in the UK, this over-supply can be more worrying. Drop-out rates from courses are low in the UK, compared to other European countries such as Holland, but a smaller proportion of British students – as few as 60% – actually enter the industry, compared with typical European figures of 75–90%, although it must be said that many European schools and colleges are poor at maintaining records of their former students' employment. Little research is available on the difficulties experienced by students with tourism qualifications seeking to enter other industries, but clearly an increasingly narrow curriculum will be likely to hamper their job and career prospects.

All EC members with the exception of Ireland are anticipating a drop in the number of 15–24-year-olds between 1990 and 1995 – Britain alone is forecasting a drop of 200,000 school-leavers in that period (Messenger, 1991). Germany anticipates a drop of 40%, and this may account for the generally relaxed attitude shown by governments towards the current over-supply of qualified staff. Germany has also benefited from an influx of former East German and other Eastern European labour since unification, which will help to overcome a labour shortfall, although much of this labour is unskilled and without the work ethos shared by the former West Germans. This is a reminder that the question of quality as well as quantity of labour must be addressed, and effective marketing by educationalists for other courses may tempt applicants away from travel-related curricula, particularly if it can be shown – as is the case in many European countries, among them Germany and France – that a broader-based business education appears to be equally attractive to employers recruiting staff for the travel industry.

Provision for formal vocational courses in travel and tourism has arisen in most European countries not so much in response to the expressed demand of industry, as through the general expansion of education, and specifically vocational education, within these countries, following the perceived need by the governments concerned for a better educated workforce to compete economically with other countries. Thus, course development in Britain and elsewhere was institutionally led, developing within departments having some peripheral interest in this field of study, such as Departments of Hotel and Catering, Geography or Business Studies. However, in Britain, unlike its Continental neighbours (and unlike the USA and Japan), employers have been slow to recognize any relationship between vocational education and training and economic success (Institute of Manpower Studies, quoted in Messenger, 1991).

In most European countries, even in the otherwise highly efficient Germany, the process of educational planning is centralized and bureaucratic, and in consequence, reform of the curriculum is a slow and lengthy practice, with inadequate emphasis given to meeting regional needs. By contrast with other European countries, Britain has shown how fast – some would say too fast – change can occur, having within a five-year period seen changes in curriculum design, the introduction of competence-based learning, new modes of delivery and new forms of access to national qualifications.

Although efforts have been made in the past to solicit industry's views on the development of new curricula, most employers have had no experience of post-compulsory education, and had neither the knowledge, time nor interest to devote themselves to educational issues. An example of the extent of this apathy is the response of travel industry employers in France to an invitation to help plan the new tourism curriculum; of 40 firms invited, six replied, and just four eventually participated in the planning process. Those firms which do participate tend to be the larger corporations, whereas the small companies making up the bulk of the travel industry achieve no voice in the planning process.

Among those employers who have been willing to collaborate in planning vocational courses, common patterns emerge in all countries; little consensus as to what is needed, and conflicting views both about the benefits of 'liberal' versus 'vocational' education, and broad-based 'general' tourism qualifications versus 'specific' job-skills training. All too often, where industry has become involved, employers representatives have called for a 'better educated workforce' while still pressing for job-specific skills teaching in the curriculum at the expense of time devoted to broader education, which they criticize as being too 'academic' and theory-based. However, confusion about what specific skills should be covered has forced planners to fall back on providing more general courses with the provision for specialist skills options where there is a clearly identified need for these locally. This has been the case in France, where Government pressure to raise standards generally, coupled with a demand for better educated staff at all levels in the travel industry, has led the Government to abandon the (French level 4) Brevet de Technicien in Tourism (a further education course comparable in level to the Baccalaureat) in favour of a new Brevet de Technicien Superieur Tourisme-Loisirs, a two-year higher education course for which the Baccalaureat or equivalent is the normal entry requirement. While this may be leading to a better educated workforce, the jobs for which these students are destined in the first instance are frequently routine and repetitive, unlikely to absorb the interest of diplomates. The problem faced by the industry of meeting the job and career expectations of an educated workforce remains a real one, in respect of both work conditions and salary levels, and it is one which so far is not being addressed.

WORKPLACE DELIVERY OF VOCATIONAL EDUCATION AND THE APPRENTICESHIP SCHEME

Industry's suspicion of academic qualifications has made the formal in-house training programme a respectable alternative in theory, though not yet in practice, for most European countries. There is a growing consensus on the value of the workplace as a centre of learning, but with training delivered in a more formal manner than the traditional 'Sitting by Nellie' technique. Although the concept of an 'apprenticeship' system is welcomed, and this has been implemented in some European countries, the travel and tourism industry has been largely excluded from these plans, apart from the hotel and catering sectors, due to the small size of most firms, who feel they cannot spare staff to devote to individual training.

Certainly, in spite of differing traditions of education among the European partners, most recognize that workplace experience offers benefits which cannot be achieved in any educational institution, such as facing the pressures which are a normal feature of real-life jobs, and learning at first hand the sheer variety of different work situations that are encountered. For this reason, most European countries attempt to ensure that tourism courses have an element of work placement – ranging from as little as a few days, to as much as 40 weeks – to reinforce the theoretical learning achieved in college. This mix of theory and practice is laudatory, and provides opportunities to apply skills, such as hands-on computer work, which may be difficult to experience within college, but the quality of work placement is variable, and too often, employers treat it as no more than a means of recruiting poorly paid seasonal staff, rather than of providing a formally supervised and structured training period.

However, Germany offers what is in effect a system of apprenticeship that is greatly admired by its European partners. This is the so-called 'Dual System', which requires all young people leaving school upon completion of their sixteenth year to continue their education through a combination of work-based training and part-time attendance at a local Berufsschule, or training college. The content of the work-based training is determined by a complex set of national training regulations, which are drawn up in close collaboration between educationalists, employers and employees' representatives. The educational curriculum is based on a national framework, again following consultation with industry, which can be locally interpreted within each 'Land', or individual German state. Patterns of attendance differ, but typically the trainee will study for three years, attending college for two days a week, with the remaining three days spent in the workplace.

It is essentially the existence or absence of a set of training regulations that places an occupation within or outside of the Dual System. There are some 400 recognized training occupations, including several within the hotel and catering sector (cook, receptionist, etc.). As yet, there are none within the leisure sector, and only one, the Reiseverkehrskaufmann (female: -kauffrau), or travel business specialist, within the travel and tourism industry.

Perhaps this lack of tourism qualifications is also a reflection of the apathy towards formal education so commonly found among members of this industry even in Germany, when compared with those from other industries who have participated so enthusiastically in the preparation of curricula.

The German 'Dual System' apprenticeship scheme has much to commend it. It is distinguished by the extent to which it is employer led, employer controlled (through the Chambers of Commerce, who oversee in-company assessment) and in part employer delivered by staff trained and qualified to do so. However, it has the added advantage of drawing not only those who have left school before the age of 18, but also many in their late teens and twenties, who wish to top up their formal education with vocational training for specific jobs. Over 50% of those entering the Dual System are older than 16 when starting their programme, and have therefore spent longer in general education, and many will have achieved their 'Abitur', or school-leaving qualification at age 18/19. This is particularly true of those entering the travel industry and similar vocational areas. This combination of a good general education, maturity and experience of the Dual System training programme is rightly envied by educationalists in other countries, and reflects the strong commitment not only to general education in Germany, but also to a first class system of 'end-on' training to complement it. However, it is debatable to what extent this system could or should be transferable to other countries, without an accompanying change in underlying attitudes towards training and education in those countries.

This is not to say that the German system is without fault. Certainly, the quality of delivery is not uniform throughout the Länder, and there are significant weaknesses in some of the institutions delivering the formal input; for example, in some colleges, staff teaching the travel course have little or no direct knowledge of the industry, and insufficient scope or desire to gain such experience through staff development programmes. Furthermore, some of the confusion found among employers in other countries with respect to education is also prevalent in Germany. Tourism employers, for instance, seldom give the Reiseverkehrskaufmann qualification, which is one of six business and commercial qualifications, any preference over other, more general qualifications, even in those sectors of industry where the job-specific skills it offers are most in demand. Nor does the qualification appear to have any quality of transferability for other areas of business, even for the hotel and catering sector. This must be of concern for a vocational education qualification currently qualifying some 6000 people each year.

INDUSTRY-LINKED TRAINING SCHOOLS

It remains true that many of the larger individual firms in European tourism, and even some trade sectors, prefer to provide their own training outside the formal educational systems, whether in-house or in associated private colleges. This has always been true of the aviation industry, but is common in most sectors of the travel business. In Germany, for instance, the retail chain Hapag Lloyd maintains a training school in Bremen, whereas in France, large organizations such as Club Méditerranée prefer to provide their own in-house training. The retail travel sector has always been suspicious of externally directed training for the skills and competences they seek, instead forming links with private training colleges to deliver approved courses. Unlike similar training in the UK, where approved courses in retail travel practice are delivered in a number of public colleges throughout the country, it is more common for travel agencies in other European countries, through their trade body, to support a course at a specific institution. In France, for example, SNAV, the official travel agents' organization, jointly operates its own private college outside Paris, l'Ecole Pratique du Tourisme, together with the professional transport organization, l'Association pour le Developpement de la Formation Professionelle dans les Transports. In Norway, DNR, the Norwegian travel agents' body, supports a course developed at a private business college in Oslo, the Merkantilt Institutt, because in its view the state sector could not provide the kind of qualification sought. The Institute itself is now seeking national recognition for the course from the Norwegian Department of Education. In Germany, however, the DRV, the equivalent trade body, plays no part in operating or supporting courses, Germany being virtually alone in lacking formal tourism education provision at further education ('technician') level, outside of the Dual System.

VOCATIONAL EDUCATION FOR MANAGEMENT

Vocationally oriented university level courses in travel and tourism are a relatively recent development in most European countries, although post-graduate courses in tourism have been available for many years in countries such as Britain and Switzerland. Once again, debate is centred on the provision of a broad education in management vis-à-vis an education aimed specifically at the management of travel and tourism services. There are strongly held views on both sides, and those responsible for educational planning in most countries have resisted the concept of studying tourism at first degree level until quite recently. Tourism options have been available for somewhat longer on economics, geography or business studies degree courses and on shorter courses of higher education such as the two year Higher National Diploma in Business and Finance in Britain, but the explosion in higher education during the 1980s has led to many of the shorter courses being upgraded to degree status (as in Britain and Norway) and the development of purpose-designed first degrees in tourism (as in Britain, France and Germany). Courses have also been lengthened to accommodate the specialist options demanded by industry. Discussion is now centring on whether to provide a common curriculum during the foundation year, to develop a modular approach to business studies at degree level which would allow a 'pick and mix' approach to the tourism syllabus, or to provide a dedicated tourism course which, although reflecting the views of an influential section of travel employers, may prove too narrow in scope for long-term career development. It is perhaps too early to pronounce judgement on this issue, with graduates only coming on-stream from many of these new courses during the 1990s, but it is the British educationalists alone, responding to pressure from employers, who have chosen the narrow path, providing entire courses for increasingly specific sectors of the industry, and applying all broad business skills teaching to the travel industry. As just one example of this development, Britain chose in 1991 to pilot an HND in Travel and Tourism, breaking away from the more traditional approach of teaching tourism as options on Business and Finance HND courses. This approach has been paralleled in France, with the development of the new BTS in which all modules are travel and tourism related.

In Germany, the recent introduction of travel and tourism degrees at the technical universities (Fachhochschulen) is a departure from the broader-based academic qualifications so long admired in the country.

These, too, have yet to prove themselves, although they have qualities which are less common in other countries. For example, in contrast to the Dual System of further education, tourism teaching is often delivered by practitioners still employed in industry, who have not only valuable current experience, but also the necessary academic qualifications to teach at university level; industry managers with PhDs are not unusual in Germany, even within the travel and tourism sector.

Perhaps it is the respect for academic learning which is found widely on the Continent that sets Britain apart from its neighbours. As one member of the Berlin Chamber of Commerce was heard to quote in a recent address, 'top management today is so complex, and requires so broad an overview, only an academic is capable of fulfilling the role'. This is a view that would be shared by very few managers in British industry, let alone in the travel industry, where on-the-job experience is still rated as the main ingredient for progression into management posts.

EDUCATIONAL INNOVATIONS AND CURRICULUM DEVELOPMENT

Like the travel industry itself, education all over Europe, and at all levels, is in a state of major upheaval. Even in countries where change in education has traditionally taken place very slowly, such as Norway, approaches to education are being re-evaluated, curricula redesigned, consideration being given to new modes of access and delivery. Vocational education has been affected as much as any other sector in this upheaval.

In the 20 years up to the end of the 1980s, European labour policies were focused on trying to hold down unemployment, whereas in the 1990s the emphasis has shifted to work creation and the removal of artificial barriers to employment, especially for older workers requiring retraining for new jobs, and for women returning to work after raising families.

Curiously, there is little evidence that these issues, which figure prominently in current British educational planning, are being adequately addressed on the Continent, nor is any provision being made for these educational markets within travel and tourism education. There is little parallel on the Continent to the UK's efforts to attract the mature student to full-time courses, or to attract the older woman back into industry through the provision of specialized refresher courses. One exception to this rule is Norway where it is common for mature adults in to return to education throughout their working life. However, since all vocational education at technician level is conducted in schools rather than colleges, no separate provision is made for the adult seeking retraining. Although the attempts in Britain to attract the older female worker back into the travel industry have been commendable, if this is seen by employers merely as a means of replacing declining numbers of cheap young female staff by equally ill-paid older female labour, it will again reflect a failure to come to terms with the underlying problems of poor salaries in the industry. None the less recruiting such staff, and providing them with appropriate training, will aid the growth of part-time and flexitime working in those sectors of industry noted for their peaks and troughs.

Similarly, the concept of accreditation for prior experience and learning (APEL), currently the focus of much attention in Britain, plays no part in the educational reforms taking place in the European partners. A traditional view is taken that qualifications should be the outcome of a recognized period of study and standard assessment through examination. This tends to preclude exemptions from any of these examinations for alternative forms of study. Modularization of curricula, and opportunities for the transfer of credits achieved to other courses, are also developments largely limited at present to the UK.

The curriculum for travel and tourism studies at all vocational levels was initially broadly based, as we have seen, and focused on the acquisition of knowledge and understanding rather than skills and competence. This practice is still to a large extent true of the Continental countries, but Britain, influenced by developments in competence-based education and training in the USA originating in the 1960s, recommended in a 1985 Government review of vocational qualifications that vocational qualifications should relate more clearly to workplace competence.

Since the establishment in Britain of the National Council for Vocational Qualifications (NCVQ), which has been charged with the development of a national framework of vocational qualifications, substantial progress has been made towards accrediting courses at initially four levels of competence (later this will be extended to higher levels of vocational education also).

Among these, accreditation has been achieved for BTEC (Business and Technology Education Council) courses in travel and tourism at National Diploma level (equivalent to the school leaving A levels, or a vocational Baccalaureat). Here, educationalists and industrialists have collaborated closely in defining the standards of competence required for each industry, through the establishment of Industry and Lead Bodies (ILBs). The Association of British Travel Agents (ABTA) is the major trade body for the travel and tourism industry in the UK, and their National Training Board was appointed to define these standards for the travel industry.

To achieve recognition for a course as an NVQ, there must be evidence of a substantial industry input, and agreement on the competences needed to make up the required number of units within the course. These units may also be acquired individually, in a process of credit accumulation leading towards the achievement of an eventual award when sufficient units have been completed. This will undoubtedly be a boost for those working in the travel industry, and others who seek to gain formal qualifications by part-time study.

From a position where, a few years ago, collaboration had been limited between educationalists and industry, these recent developments have begun to alter the picture significantly. ILBs are employer-led, and these employers are exerting considerable influence within the area of travel education, while the governing bodies of the colleges themselves are today increasingly dominated by representatives from industry. However, this trend is leading some educationalists to fear that the drive towards competence and skills testing will be at the expense of the necessary knowledge and understanding of the travel industry. There is less concern about transferable general and social skills than with the job-specific skills serving the technical needs of individual travel sectors, which some argue are best taught end-on, and complementary to, broader-based vocational education.

Apart from the 'knowledge versus skills' issue, there is a wide variety of approaches taken towards the design of tourism curricula in the different European countries. At one extreme, the German approach tends to be highly prescriptive, setting out in great detail the nature and content of its vocational education and training programmes, whereas in Britain there is still a wide margin of flexibility within guidelines, based on validation of courses through a number of professional bodies (such as the Institute of Leisure and Amenity Management or the Hotel, Catering and Institutional Management Association) as well as through the public sector. Even in a centralized bureaucracy such as France, with a national curriculum for tourism, in practice there is still sufficient flexibility to offer regionally appropriate travel courses, which are organized under the auspices of bodies other than the Department of Education; for example, farm tourism or tourist guide courses offered under the jurisdiction of the Department of Agriculture in the Rhône-Alpes region.

What constitutes the 'body of knowledge' for a travel and tourism course at any level can be debated endlessly. A number of attempts have been made to define it – notably by the Tourism Society in the UK in 1980 (Nightingale, 1980, 1981) – but the end result can best be described as an economic overview of the component sectors of the industry, allied to a mixture of knowledge and skills drawing on such disparate disciplines as history, geography, law, economics, sociology and marketing applied to the industry.

However, any acquired body of knowledge will inevitably be greater in Continental countries than in Britain, simply through the amount of time devoted to each subject. Formal delivery of teacher-centred knowledge, often theory-based, amounts to an input of typically 30 to nearly 40 hours a week of class contact, compared with a more typical 15–22 hours in

Britain. Part of this differential is explained by the relatively high amount of teaching time devoted to the study of modern languages on the Continent, but in addition to this class contact, students are also expected to undertake substantial work on their own outside of class hours.

Another notable distinction between the British and Continental approaches to curriculum content is the Continental emphasis on classical and liberal studies which would be judged as peripheral in a British context. The French BTS, for example, includes study of the history of civilizations and the history of art, as well as three to four hours a week devoted to the study of the mother language. It was pointed out earlier that in this curriculum, all modules were related to tourism, but clearly, determining what constitutes tourism is interpreted far more liberally than would be the case in Britain. The importance attached to such liberal studies is interesting and would be incomprehensible to British employers; however, its relevance to Continental employers can be judged from a German entry test for counter staff in a major travel agency chain, which includes a requirement that applicants distinguish between different types of classical Greek architecture.

Employers' main criticisms of the Continental curriculum tend to focus on weaknesses in certain areas of skills teaching in particular, the lack of sufficient information technology, and in the acquisition of interpersonal and behavioural skills. The importance attached to the latter is increasing as the emphasis shifts to teaching sales techniques as a vital component of any service industry course, while the relevance of the former becomes daily more significant as computer reservations systems come to dominate operations in all sectors of the travel industry. CRSs are accessible in colleges, at a price, either live or in training mode, and educationalists in most countries recognize the need to provide better computer skills training, but the quality of input is variable, and often depends on the form of educational provision. In France, for instance, the state sector has access to resources, including IT, which the private colleges simply cannot match, whereas the reverse is true in other European countries, and in some cases, such as Italy and The Netherlands, both the private and public sector are deficient, although it must be added that it is not uncommon for standards between colleges in both sectors to differ markedly, making comparisons and generalizations difficult.

THE ROLE OF LANGUAGES IN VOCATIONAL TOURISM EDUCATION

It is in the teaching of foreign languages that Britain is seen to be at its weakest compared with its neighbours. All the Continental countries place great emphasis on learning foreign languages, but it must be stressed that most vocational students will have a strong foundation of at least one foreign language, and often two, based on their years of compulsory schooling. In countries like The Netherlands, Flemish Belgium and Norway, where the mother language is rarely spoken abroad, this can lead to as many as four foreign languages being taught simultaneously on vocational tourism courses. There are also examples in The Netherlands of some modules in travel and tourism courses being taught in a foreign language, thus reinforcing the teaching within the language module. Even in France, which is commonly pictured as antipathetic to speaking foreign languages, the BTS curriculum includes at least one compulsory foreign language, and students have a choice of two further languages. These countries also benefit from having television channels broadcasting in anything up to five foreign languages, and films in English are seldom dubbed, so that children accommodate to learning languages from a very early age. Languages are seen as immensely important in these societies, and the philosophy of educationalists is to teach language in use, so that the emphasis is on everyday speech. Many young people in these countries also seek to travel or work abroad to improve their language skills.

Language, alongside interpersonal and technical skills, is the requirement most often demanded by employers in the tourism industry, especially in fields such as tourist information centres, hotels and catering, tourist attractions and public sector tourist boards, but it is also viewed as very useful by many employers in travel agencies and tour operating. This contrasts with the views of employers in Britain, where languages are seldom demanded outside of those posts where frequent contact with foreign tourists is likely, such as the TICs and guiding. Unexpectedly, Britain's attitude appears to be shared by a substantial number of travel agency employers in Germany, who feel that language skills have been over-rated; and in that country, languages do not form part of the Dual System tourism curriculum. The assumption appears to be that those following a vocational course will have achieved a sufficient level of ability through the compulsory schooling system – and there is considerable evidence to justify this belief, at least in the more common languages of English and French.

CHALLENGES FOR THE FUTURE

It is not only the travel and tourism industry itself which faces great challenges in the coming decade, but the vocational education and training that supports it. It is therefore vital that the industry and educationalists come to a common understanding about the role of vocational education, and learn to work closer together in planning courses that are appropriate, not just in the short term, but to meet the needs of future management in the industry.

In the short term, the industry must be attractive enough to recruit staff with the intelligence and competence to adjust to rapidly changing circumstances. It must be a matter of concern that, at a time when there is significant over-supply of qualified tourism students in most of the countries examined, the industry nevertheless still suffers a serious shortfall in the number and quality of applicants it attracts. The mobility of labour within the Community may compound this problem. 1993 and its aftermath provide both opportunities and challenges. Not only will individual firms have greater freedom and incentive to operate within each other's borders, but the move to inter-European recognition of qualifications will encourage qualified staff to widen their own horizons when job-seeking. For the most part, young Britons do not share the insularity of their elders, and are showing interest in Continental Europe as a first destination for work in the travel industry (although many lack the language skills they will require to compete effectively with nationals in their home countries). Britain in turn provides an attraction, at least in the short term, for European workers seeking to improve their language skills, who can bring to the travel industry qualities of dedication and interpersonal skills not easily found among British job applicants. This trans-border mobility will affect tourism employees to a greater extent than others, by nature of the personalities the industry attracts, and those responsible for human resources planning in the industry must come to terms with the problems this will pose, not least in providing appropriate in-house training.

Where Britain still lags is in developing the genuinely European outlook which is shared by its partners. It is true that many of these nations share advantages denied to Britain: of being at the crossroads of Europe, and linked geographically, socially and economically to a far greater degree than is the UK. Dutch officials, asked about their preparations for the post-1992 era, reply that they have been ready since the 1960s! Linguistically and attitudinally, they are ready to cope. Their attitude is shared by other European nations, but commitment itself is not enough. In tourism vocational education, there is little evidence of planning for the post-1992 era, even in such an ostensibly committed nation as The Netherlands (although once again this is a generalization, and isolated examples exist to disprove the rule). Curricula in all the countries examined seldom provide a genuinely international perspective, and the massive resourcing that will be required in order to retrain staff to gain this knowledge is simply not available.

Work placements, now an accepted feature of travel and tourism courses in all countries, have remained difficult to find abroad, due to the travel industry's resistance to the recruitment of foreign students, although this situation is now improving. In France, however, the French 'stages' which are a required feature of the tourism courses are unpaid, thus penalizing applicants from other countries who are seeking paid placements.

In the post-1992 era, British vocational education faces many challenges, but it offers some strengths which its neighbours cannot easily match. Innovation, progressive methods of delivery, especially in part-time and distance learning techniques, effective monitoring and quality control and new methods of assessment are all strong features of the British educational scene. Most of these benefits are the outcome of the country's ability to respond rapidly to change. But further changes are now needed, not just within education, but throughout society.

An examination of vocational education and training outside of the social context within which it operates is clearly inadequate. Britain compares unfavourably with its neighbours when one takes into consideration the regard that employers, parents and students themselves have, not simply for vocational education, but for education in general. What is clear is that good resources, appropriate curricula and innovative delivery count for little without a positive commitment to learning on the part of students. Throughout the Continent, the quality of students themselves, in terms of their commitment to work, their interpersonal skills, and in particular their attitudes towards work in service industries, is on balance superior to that of British students. Whether this is in spite of, or due to, their general education, and whether there is the will and means to change this, are matters of great import for British society.

BIBLIOGRAPHY

Airey, D. and Middleton, V.T. (1984) *Tourism Education: Course Syllabi in the UK – a Review.* Tourism Management, March, 57–62.

American Express/European Institute of Education and Social Policy (1991) *Education for Careers in European Travel and Tourism.* Summary published in Ritchie, J.R.B. and Hawkins, D.E. (eds) (1992) *World Travel and Tourism Review,* Volume 2. CAB International, Wallingford, pp. 207–217.

APC International (1989) *VET for the Single European Market.* APC, Middlesex Polytechnic, UK.

Association Française des Administrateurs de l'Education (1990) *The French Education System and its Administration.*

Bundesanzeiger Herausgegeben vom Bundesminister der Justiz (1980) *Bekanntmachung der Verordnung ueber die Berufsaufbildung zum Reiseverkehrskaufmann/Frau nebst Rahmenlehrplan* 25/80.

Bundesinstitut fuer Berufsbildung (BIBB) Berlin (1989) *The Federal Institute for Vocational Education and Training.*

CEDEFOP (European Centre for the Development of Vocational Training) (1990)

Tourism and Vocational Qualifications CEDEFOP NEWS no. 3 August, Berlin.

CEREQ (Centre d'Etudes et de Recherches sur les Qualifications) (1989) *The System of Vocational Training in France.* Paris.

Department of Education and Science (1990) *What 1992 means for Education.* DES, London.

European Institute of Education and Social Policy (EIESP) Paris (1990) *1992 and Beyond: France, Germany, Italy, Netherlands.* no. 1, June.

European Institute of Education and Social Policy (EIESP) Paris (1989) *Strategies for Vocational Education and Training Project: Travel and Tourism Group's Report on the Visit to The Netherlands.* Oct/Nov.

European Institute of Education and Social Policy (EIESP) Paris (1990) *Strategies for Vocational Education and Training Project: Travel and Tourism Group's Report on the Visit to The Federal Republic of Germany.* May.

European Institute of Education and Social Policy (EIESP) Paris (1991) *Strategies for Vocational Education and Training Project: Travel and Tourism Group's Report on the Visit to France.* Nov 1990.

European Institute of Education and Social Policy (EIESP) Paris (1991) *Strategies for Vocational Education and Training Project: Travel and Tourism Group's Report on the Visit to Italy.* May.

European Institute of Education and Social Policy (EIESP) Paris (1992) *Strategies for Vocational Education and Training Project: Travel and Tourism Group's Report on the Visit to Norway.* Nov/Dec 1991.

EURYDICE Brussels (1989) *Guide to European Community Programmes in the Field of Education Training and Youth.*

Focus Consultancy Ltd, London (N/D) *Working with Europe: an FEU Handbook.*

Foster, H. (1989) *Qualifications in Tourism.* BIBB, Berlin.

Holloway, J.C. (1991) 1992 and All That: some reflections on comparative vocational education and training for travel and tourism among European Community members. In: *New Horizons in Tourism and Hospitality Education, Training and Research.* Conference Proceedings, University of Calgary.

Jallade, J.-P. (1989) *Recent Trends in Vocational Education and Training: an Overview, European Journal of Education 24/2.*

Karbowski, J. (1989) *Initial and Further Vocational Education in the Area of Tourism in the Federal Republic of Germany.* BIBB, Berlin.

Kirsch, J.-L. (1989) *The Educational System in France.* CEREQ, Brussels.

Leveneu, C. and Bigazzi, P. (1989) *Travel and Tourist Agencies – Training and Structure of the Sector and Key Characteristics.* CEREQ, Brussels, July.

Maas, J.C.A.M. (1989) *The Dutch Education System: a Summary.* Holland, July.

Messenger, S. (1991) The UK hospitality and tourism industry: an overview of the issues affecting the supply of education and training in the 1990s. In: Cooper, C. (ed.) *Progress in Tourism, Recreation and Hospitality Management*, Vol 3. Belhaven Press, London.

Ministere de l'Education Nationale de la Jeunesse et des Sports, Commission Professionelles Consultatives, Paris (1990) *Documents Methodologiques.* March.

Ministere de l'Education Nationale de la Jeunesse et des Sports (1989) *Brevet de Technicien Superieur Tourisme-Loisirs.*

Ministere du Tourisme, Direction de l'Industrie Touristique (N/D) *Note sur les Differentes Titres de Guides-Interpretes delivré par le Ministre chargé du Tourisme.*

National Economic Development Council (1991) *Developing Managers for Tourism.* NEDC, London.

Nightingale, M.A. (1980) *Tourism Occupations, Career Profiles and Knowledge.* Tourism Society, London.

Nightingale, M.A. (1981) Tourism occupations, career profiles and knowledge. *Annals of Tourism Research*, 8(1), 52–68.

Parsons, D.J. (1986) *Jobs in Tourism and Leisure.* English Tourist Board, London.

Tilkin, J.W.M.J. (1989) *Labour and Education in the Sector Tourism and Recreation.* Holland, July.

Uthman, K-J. (1989) *Procedures for Curriculum Development for Vocational Training in the Federal Republic of Germany.* BIBB, Berlin.

World Travel and Tourism Council (1991) *Travel and Tourism in the World Economy.* WTTC, New York.

7

TRAVELFLOWS IN EUROPE: A STATISTICAL SUMMARY

Peter Roth

INTRODUCTION

Until some years ago the volume and the direction of travelflows in Europe were not completely unknown but were nevertheless unclear, indeed obscure. There was no doubt that a high percentage of all trips and a much higher percentage of European holiday trips were spent in the Mediterranean. But these assumptions could not be supported scientifically.

Beyond that, information about other European regions was rare, and even if any existed, it would not have fit into a common context, because there was no common framework or unified basis. Therefore the data could not be evaluated or compared. An overall picture could only be constructed or drawn with the help of different indicators, for example on the one hand the volume of inclusive trips or on the other hand the official national statistics and holiday analyses. But this could provide only a partial answer because of the nature of the basic data. Because of methodological shortcomings and differences in the offical national statistics and native analyses of holiday trips, the European travel picture could not be described sufficiently. For that reason one was dependent on the booking figures of the larger travel agencies to obtain current information about the development of travelflows in Europe.

It is to be assumed that many tourism researchers realized that such information was incomplete because it restricted itself mostly to inclusive trips. But in the absence of data on trends in the important segment of individual trips, data on inclusive trips had to represent the total volume of travel activities. This was an unsatisfactory situation especially as conclusions were often drawn about the whole holiday sector (and sometimes even about the development of all transport) from the developments in the package business of large tour operators and travel agents.

THE ORIGIN OF THE TRAVEL MONITOR

At the beginning of the 1980s some private European tourism market researchers came together and tried to build up a common European database for solving this problem. The result was called the European Travel Monitor – a representative study about the European travel market. The European Travel Monitor is organized as a participation study. Those firms and organizations which have taken part in the study and support it have its results exclusively at their disposal. The producer of the European Travel Monitor is the European Travel Data Center in Luxembourg.

*   The European Travel Monitor covers the following European states: Austria, Belgium, Denmark, Finland, France, Germany, Great Britain, Greece, Iceland, Italy, Ireland, Luxembourg, The Netherlands, Norway, Portugal, Spain, Sweden, Switzerland, Poland, Hungary, Czech and Slovak Federal Republic and The Baltic States.
*   It registers all segments of the travel market, the private travel market and the business travel market.
*   All trips with at least one overnight stay are recorded.
*   Every second month across Europe 36,000 interviews are conducted, giving 200,000 interviews per year. This random sample is representative of 280 million Europeans over 15 years of age.
*   The information is recorded through a standardized questionnaire.

The European Travel Monitor was started in 1988. We now know that in 1988 Europeans undertook nearly one billion trips with overnight stays. For the first time a baseline quantity of the total volume of European travel was established, which can validly be compared for example with the 1.1 billion trips with overnight stays of the Americans. Other comparisons are now also possible. Whereas the share of overseas trips by US-Americans amounts to 1%, the share of overseas trips by Europeans in relation to the total volume of trips with overnight stays is much higher and accounts for 7%.

All information about travelflows in the European travel market in this chapter is presented with the kind permission of the European Travel Data Center in Luxembourg.

TRAVEL DESTINATION

The two most important foreign travel destinations (whether for holidays or not) for Europeans in 1989 were France and Spain: 14% of all trips made by Europeans had their destination in France and 13% in Spain (Table 7.1).

Table 7.1. Travel destination.

Rank	Market of destination	All trips (millions)	1989 (%)
1	France	28	14
2	Spain	27	13
3	Austria	19	10
4	Germany	19	9
5	Italy	18	9
6	Outside Europe	14	7
7	Switzerland	9	5
8	Eastern Europe	9	5
9	Belgium/Luxembourg	9	4
10	Great Britain	8	4

Source: European Travel Monitor (1989).

Holiday Trips

In 1989 the most important destination for holiday trips for Europeans was Spain which accounted for 16% of all European holiday trips. However, contrary to 1988 the volume of holiday trips of Europeans to Spain decreased from 24 millions to 22 millions. After Spain the most popular destinations of holiday trips in 1989 were France (13%), Austria (12%) and Italy (10%) (Table 7.2).

Table 7.2. Travel destinations – holiday trips.

Rank	Market of destination	Holiday trips (millions)	1989 (%)
1	Spain	22	16
2	France	18	13
3	Austria	16	12
4	Italy	13	10
5	Germany	9	6
6	Yugoslavia	6	5
7	Greece	6	5
8	Switzerland	6	4
9	The Netherlands	5	4
10	Belgium/Luxembourg	5	4

Source: European Travel Monitor (1989).

Business Trips

The most important destination for business trips of Europeans in 1989 was Germany: 18% (5 million) of all European business travellers came to Germany, followed by France with a share of 14% (4 million), then Great Britain, Spain, Belgium/Luxembourg, Italy and Switzerland follow with about 2 million business trips in each case (Table 7.3).

Table 7.3. Travel destinations – business trips.

Rank	Market of destination	Business trips (millions)	1989 (%)
1	Germany	5	18
2	France	4	14
3	Great Britain	2	8
4	Spain	2	7
5	Belgium/Luxembourg	2	7
6	Italy	2	6
7	Switzerland	2	6
8	USA	1	5
9	The Netherlands	1	4
10	Sweden	1	4

Source: European Travel Monitor (1989).

Table 7.4. Travel destinations – VFR trips.

Rank	Market of destination	VFR trips (millions)	1989 (%)
1	France	2.6	13
2	Germany	2.6	12
3	Italy	1.7	8
4	Austria	1.3	6
5	Spain	1.2	6
6	Switzerland	1.1	5
7	Belgium/Luxembourg	1.0	5
8	The Netherlands	1.0	5
9	Great Britain	0.9	5
10	Yugoslavia	0.5	3

Source: European Travel Monitor (1989).

VFR (Visiting Friends and Relatives) Trips

The most important destinations for VFR trips of Europeans (without holidays) are France and Germany. In each case about 2.6 million of the international trips were spent by Europeans in France or in Germany. After them come Italy with 1.7 million trips to friends and relatives, Austria (1.3 million), Spain (1.2 million) and Switzerland (1.1 million) (Table 7.4).

MARKET OF ORIGIN

All Trips

With a share of 31% of all international trips the people of Germany made the most trips abroad. In 1989 this amounted to about 63 million, about 5 million less than in 1988. The other main international European travel markets were Great Britain (14% of all European trips abroad), The Netherlands and France (8% each), Belgium/Luxembourg and Italy (7% each) (Table 7.5).

Table 7.5. Markets of origin.

Rank	Market of origin	All trips (millions)	1989 (%)
1	Germany	63	31
2	Great Britain	28	14
3	The Netherlands	17	8
4	France	15	8
5	Belgium/Luxembourg	15	7
6	Italy	14	7
7	Sweden	10	5
8	Switzerland	8	4
9	Austria	7	3
10	Denmark	6	3

Source: European Travel Monitor (1989).

Holiday Trips

The major European travel markets are also the main holiday markets. A total of 37% (50 million) of all international holiday trips were made by people from Germany (in 1989), although compared with 1988 this was about 4 million trips fewer. The other important countries of origin for holidays abroad are again Great Britain (19%), The Netherlands (9%), Belgium/Luxembourg and France (in each case 7%) (Table 7.6).

Table 7.6. Markets of origin – holiday trips.

Rank	Market of origin	Holiday trips (millions)	1989 (%)
1	Germany	50	37
2	Great Britain	18	13
3	The Netherlands	12	9
4	Belgium/Luxembourg	10	7
5	France	10	7
6	Italy	8	6
7	Sweden	6	5
8	Switzerland	5	4
9	Austria	4	3
10	Denmark	3	2

Source: European Travel Monitor (1989).

Business Trips

The biggest countries of origin for foreign business trips in Europe are Great Britain and Germany (in each case 4 million trips) (Table 7.7).

Table 7.7. Markets of origin – business trips.

Rank	Market of origin	Business trips (millions)	1989 (%)
1	Great Britain	4.4	15
2	Germany	4.3	14
3	The Netherlands	3.0	10
4	France	2.9	10
5	Sweden	2.9	10

Source: European Travel Monitor (1989).

VFR (Visiting Friends and Relatives) Trips

The biggest countries of origin for international VFR trips (withouth holidays) is Germany. About every third European trip to friends and relatives is made by Germans (Table 7.8).

Table 7.8. Markets of origin – VFR trips.

Rank	Market of origin	VFR trips (millions)	1989 (%)
1	Germany	7.3	35
2	Great Britain	3.1	15
3	Switzerland	1.7	8
4	Italy	1.5	7
5	Belgium/Luxembourg	1.4	7

Source: European Travel Monitor (1989).

THE PURPOSE OF TRIPS

In 1989 68% (135 million) of all international European trips were holiday trips, 15% (30 million) were business trips, 11% represented trips to friends and relatives and the remaining 6% other trips (health, religion, for example).

Table 7.9. Means of transport.

Transport used	All trips (millions)	1989 (%)
Private car	86	43
Plane – scheduled	40	20
Plane – charter	31	16
Bus	29	14
Train	17	8
Ship – ferry	13	7
Rental car	4	2
Ship – cruise	2	1
Other	5	2

Source: European Travel Monitor (1989), two answers possible

TRANSPORT

In 1989, the car was the favourite means of transport for Europeans' trips abroad. It accounted 43% or 86 million. 36% of all European trips and even 55% of all business trips were made by aeroplane (Table 7.9).

TRIP ORGANIZATION

In 1989, 28% of all European trips were inclusive trips (55 million), giving an increase in volume between 1988 and 1989 of about 2 million.

In 1989, 31% of overseas trips (62 million) involved some form of booking prior to the journey, and 41% of overseas trips (80 million) were undertaken without any prior booking whatsoever. In Western Europe 117 million trips were exclusively or in part booked through the travel trade, an increase of about 7 million over 1988.

LENGTH OF TRIPS

Of all foreign European trips 74% (149 million) were of four nights and more and were called long trips. The rest, about a quarter (52 million), were short trips with a length of 1–3 nights. Compared with 1988 the volume of short trips to foreign countries increased by about 5 million, the volume of international long trips decreased by about 3 million. Long trips dominated, 41% of all international holiday trips having a length of 11 nights and more; as far as business trips are concerned shorter stays of 1–3 nights (48%) predominate (Table 7.10).

Table 7.10. Length of trip.

Length of trip	All trips (millions)	1989 (%)
1–3 nights	52	26
4–7 nights	56	28
8–10 nights	24	12
11–14 nights	34	17
15 nights or more	35	17
Mean length (nights)	9.6 nights	

Source: European Travel Monitor (1989).

TRAVEL SEASON

In 1989, nearly 40% of Europeans travelled in the third quarter of the year (July–September). In comparison with 1988 (39%) this is a small decline in summertime international trips. The lowest volume of international trips was made in the first quarter of the year (19%) (Table 7.11).

Holiday trips were characterized by extremely high seasonality. The month of August represented the high season (about 23 million international holiday trips); and there were nearly 20 million international trips in July. The best months for international business trips on the other hand were April and October.

Table 7.11. Travel season.

Travel season	All trips (millions)	1989 (%)
January – March	38	19
April – June	51	26
July – September	72	36
October – December	38	19

Source: European Travel Monitor (1989).

II

STRUCTURES AND TRENDS IN DIFFERENT EUROPEAN COUNTRIES

8

TOURISM IN THE UNITED KINGDOM

Patrick Lavery

INTRODUCTION

Tourism in the United Kingdom consists of two main elements, holidays by the British within their own country and overseas tourists visiting the UK. These two facets of the domestic market have quite different holiday preferences and patterns of behaviour, and are therefore covered separately in this chapter. It is also necessary to take account of worldwide, especially European, developments, influencing the post 1945 domestic tourist industry in the United Kingdom.

During the 1920s and 1930s holidays with pay in the UK became more common and in 1925 the Ministry of Labour estimated that 1.5 million manual workers received holidays with pay. In 1938 the Holidays with Pay Act gave a new stimulus to mass tourism, and by June 1939 over 11 million workers received holidays with pay (Brunner, 1945) and almost one person in three went away from home for a holiday. By 1945 80% of the work-force received holidays with pay (Patmore, 1972).

The years following the Second World War saw a gradual growth in tourist activity. The geographic scale of the War had broken down international barriers and introduced great social changes. Those returning from the War expected greater opportunities, better living standards and more activity in their lives. This was to affect the scale of both domestic and international tourism. There was no sudden dramatic change in the pattern of domestic tourism, although the numbers spending a holiday away from home continued to grow as the population of Britain grew and more of the workforce had holidays with pay.

There was little change in the pattern of tourist destinations. More than two-thirds of all main holidays were taken at the seaside. Holiday camps were replacing the traditional resort as a basis for a self-contained 'package' catering for all the visitor's needs. Billy Butlin pioneered the first such camp at Skegness in 1937 and by 1939 there were 200 such camps around the British coast catering for 30,000 people a week. Public transport was still popular in 1951 and only 25% travelled by car. The Festival

129

Patrick Lavery

Millions of Visits

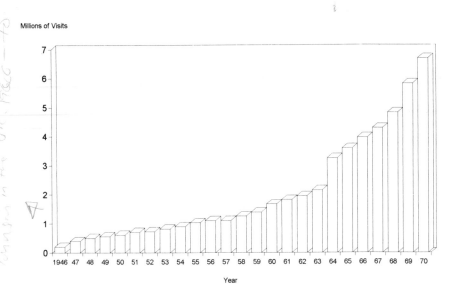

Fig. 8.1. Overseas visitors to the United Kingdom, 1946–1970.

of Britain in 1951 and the Coronation of Elizabeth II in 1953 gave an impetus to the development of new tourist facilities. The Government introduced a limited grant scheme to provide financial help (albeit limited) to hotels catering for overseas visitors and in the 1956 Distribution of Industry Act, which gave the Treasury powers to make loans or grants in areas of high unemployment, hotels were included for the first time. It was during this period of the mid to late 1950s that the then British Travel Association attempted to encourage holidays in Britain with a cooperative scheme in which the British resorts and industry took part. This was designed to extend the holiday season and to encourage more people to visit Britain's holiday resorts.

The number of visitors to Britain from overseas also grew rapidly during the 1950s from 203,000 in 1946 to 6.7 million in 1970 (Fig. 8.1). Initially 69% of these foreign visitors arrived by sea and 31% by air. But the dramatic growth in air travel during the 1960s reversed these figures. From the development of holidays with pay in the 1930s to the growth of overseas visitors during the 1950s and 1960s the domestic tourist industry came of age. Within the space of 30 years there emerged a major industry employing hundreds of thousands of people and producing many millions of pounds for the national economy. It is a very large and complex industry often with linkages between hotel groups, travel companies, transport operators, promotional agencies and tourist boards. Later in this chapter the structure of the industry and the problems and challenges facing domestic resorts and firms are discussed.

TOURISM ARRIVALS IN BRITAIN

In 1989 over 17 million overseas visitors came to the United Kingdom spending almost £7 billions. Table 8.1 shows that, despite the recession of the early 1980s and the downturn in the world economy in the late 1980s the number of overseas visitors and the United Kingdom's income from overseas visitors continued to grow.

In 1989 visitors from European Community Countries represented the

Table 8.1. Overseas visitors to UK: numbers and expenditure 1964 to 1989.

Year	Number of all overseas visitors ('000)	Expenditure of all overseas visitors £m
1964	3,257	190
1965	3,597	193
1966	3,967	219
1967	4,289	236
1968	4,828	282
1969	5,821	359
1970	6,692	432
1971	7,131	500
1972	7,459	576
1973	8,167	726
1974	8,543	898
1975	9,490	1,218*
1976	10,808	1,768*
1977	12,281	2,352*
1978	12,646	2,507*
1979	12,486	2,797*
1980	12,421	2,961*
1981	11,452	2,970*
1982	11,636	3,188*
1983	12,464	4,003*
1984	13,644	4,614*
1985	14,449	5,442*
1986	13,897	5,553*
1987	15,566	6,260*
1988	15,799	6,184*
1989	17,338	6,945*

*Tourism expenditure includes expenditure of overseas visitors in the Channel Islands.
Source: Department of Employment. International Passenger Survey: Business Monitors MA 6 and MQ 6 'Overseas Travel and Tourism' (HMSO) (Annually since 1964).

Table 8.2. Overseas visitors to UK: numbers (by market countries/areas) 1979 to 1989.

Country of permanent residence	1979 ('000)	1989 ('000)	Change 1979/89 (%)	Share of market 1989 (%)
USA	1719	2842	+65	16
Canada	477	639	+34	4
North America	2196	3481	+59	20
Belgium/Luxembourg	629	618	−2	4
France	1377	2261	+64	13
West Germany	1547	2027	+31	12
Italy	408	708	+74	4
The Netherlands	976	940	−4	5
Denmark	292	259	−11	1
Irish Republic	923	1302	+41	8
Greece	97	128	+32	1
Spain	312	622	+99	4
Portugal	44	95	+116	1
Western Europe EEC	6605	8960	+36	52
Yugoslavia	50	31	−38	–
Austria	50	148	+34	1
Switzerland	305	424	+39	2
Norway	231	287	+24	2
Sweden	419	481	+15	3

Finland	52	166	+219	1
Gibraltar/Malta/Cyprus	57	111	+95	1
Others	43	81	+89	–
Western Europe Non-EEC	1268	1728	+36	10
Middle East	579	457	–21	3
North Africa	156	93	–40	1
South Africa	149	145	–3	1
Rest of Africa	279	310	+11	2
Eastern Europe	64	165	+157	1
Japan	140	505	+261	3
Australia	406	535	+32	3
New Zealand	91	123	+35	1
Commonwealth Caribbean	46	70	+53	–
Latin America	227	179	–21	1
Others	280	586	+109	3
Rest of World	2417	3168	+31	18
All Countries	12,486	17,338	+39	100

Note: Figures are rounded, so that component figures may not add up to totals.
Source: BTA Digest of Statistics – International Passenger Survey: Visits to the United Kingdom by Overseas Residents.

largest market share (52%) followed by North America (20%), the rest of the world (18%) and non-EC Western Europe (10%).

Table 8.2 shows the numbers of overseas visitors to the United Kingdom in 1979 and 1989, and indicates several interesting trends. The number of visitors to the UK from the United States grew by 65% between 1979 and 1989 to a total of 2.8 million in 1989. These United States tourists spent £1.7 billion – almost one-quarter of the total income from overseas visitors. The next main market is the European Community Countries, who in volume terms provide over half of all overseas visitors to the UK (British Tourist Authority, 1990). Italy, France, Spain and Portugal have all been fast-growing markets for UK inbound tourism during the 1980s. Visitors from Belgium and The Netherlands showed a slight decline over the same period.

In volume terms Switzerland (424 million) and Sweden (481 million) provide the greatest number of non-EC overseas visitors from other European countries, and both showed a steady growth in numbers during the 1980s.

The picture was less favourable from some medium and long-haul markets during the 1980s. Political and economic crises during the 1980s including the Libyan bombing and its aftermath and events leading up to the Gulf War, were responsible for a marked decline in numbers of visitors from the Middle East (down 20%) and North Africa (down 40%). However, this decline was offset by significant increases in visitors from Japan (261%), Eastern Europe (157%), Australia, New Zealand and Commonwealth Caribbean countries (all over 30%).

Some of the long- and medium-haul markets (USA, Japan, Middle East) are particularly important for the United Kingdom tourist industry because they spend more per head and stay longer than visitors from other countries. These points are discussed in more detail later in this chapter.

The main gateways for overseas visitors are the two airports close to London – Heathrow and Gatwick – and the Channel ports of Dover and Folkestone. The concentration of these gateways around London helps to enhance its position as the United Kingdom's main tourist destination for overseas visitors. In 1989 9.2 million overseas visitors spent part of their stay in London and 14 million UK residents had holidays in the city. Together they produced an income of almost £4 billion and tourism generated an estimated one in ten jobs in Greater London (BTA, 1990).

The overseas visitors and UK domestic visitors complement each other. The overseas visitors concentrate on London and several historic towns and cities, whereas the UK domestic market is still focused on seaside holidays. However, UK holidaymakers since the 1960s have increasingly favoured foreign destinations and this has exacerbated the long-term decline of UK seaside resorts – an issue discussed later in this chapter.

Outside of London and the south east, Scotland attracts more overseas visitors than any other part of the UK, particularly North American tourists who account for about 40% of overseas visitors to Scotland. The typical overseas tourist will aim to visit several major cities, and about one-third come on inclusive tours which invariably take in London followed by a 'milk run' which takes in Bath, Stratford, Edinburgh and possibly York or Cambridge.

FORECASTS FOR OVERSEAS VISITOR MARKET

By 1995 the British Tourist Authority expects that over 22 million foreign tourists will visit the UK (British Tourist Authority, 1991). About 60% are forecast to come from Western Europe and 20% from North America. This represents a slight increase in transatlantic traffic and a maintenance of the present market share in other world markets (Table 8.3). The average annual rate of growth is expected to be between 4% and 5% with the Japanese market growing at up to three times this rate.

By 1995 the British Tourism Authority expects that overseas visitors will be spending more than £11 billion on visits to the UK. With income from overseas tourists forecast to increase at an annual average growth rate of 8% between 1990 and 1995 tourism is likely to grow faster than any other domestic economic activity. Holiday traffic continues to be the main market segment, but it is declining slightly in importance due to the increase in the business travel market.

It is expected that Europe will continue to be the predominant source of visitors to Britain, for several reasons. Western Europe enjoys higher than average living standards, most of the population have holidays with pay and are highly mobile, assisted by a modern integrated transport network. Eastern Europe is emerging from decades of communism and as its economy develops, has potential for international travel.

The opening of the Channel Tunnel in 1993 (subject to delay) and the extension of the TGV high speed rail link will mean that the UK is perceived to be closer and more accessible to the continent. Whilst this may encourage more outbound traffic it could also attract more inbound tourists especially from Italy and Spain, which were two of the fastest growing markets in the 1980s.

TOURISM IN THE UK BY UK RESIDENTS

Several features characterize the UK domestic tourist market. First, it has been static, if not in long-term decline since the 1960s. Secondly, it has

Table 8.3. Forecast overseas visitors' spending in UK.

	1990		1995		Average annual growth (%) 1989–1995
	£m	% Share of World Total	£m	% Market Share	
France	450	5.8	688	5.9	9
Germany	471	6.1	649	5.6	7
The Netherlands	197	2.6	244	2.1	4
Belgium/Lux.	109	1.4	162	1.4	8
Italy	337	4.4	589	5.1	12
Spain	298	3.9	482	4.2	10
Denmark	66	0.9	86	0.7	5
Total EC	2447	31.7	3681	31.7	9
Switzerland	175	2.3	239	2.1	6
Norway	109	1.4	149	1.3	6
Sweden	192	2.5	305	2.6	10
Total W. Europe (Non-EC)	792	10.3	1243	10.7	9
USA	1685	21.8	2121	18.3	5
Canada	273	3.5	355	3.1	5
North America	1958	25.3	2477	21.3	5
Australia	423	5.5	612	5.3	8
Japan	298	3.9	776	6.7	21
Rest of World	2528	32.7	4206	36.2	11
Total World	7725	100.0	11,600	100.0	8

Source: International Passenger Survey/BTA.

been slow to respond to the challenge of alternative destinations overseas. Investment is urgently needed to improve transport links, especially connecting the road and rail infrastructure, and to alleviate airport and airspace congestion as well as surface links to airports.

Over 90% of the United Kingdom resorts have a coastal location and their townscape and infrastructure were developed to cater for the needs of a type of tourist who has all but disappeared. The townscape of most resorts reflects their history of rapid development during the 19th century with a great influx of capital investment in the form of hotels, entertainment complexes, amusement parks, promenades and piers – all of which are so familiar to us today.

In Britain most resorts were well established by the late 19th century. For most tourists up to the 1960s the most popular form of travel was by rail, and having arrived by train the resort was a self-contained provider of all the visitor's needs from accommodation to entertainment because the tourist was not mobile and spent most of his holiday within the resort. This is reflected in the layout of the seaside resorts, with the railway station, the main shopping and tourist streets leading to or along the sea-front, which usually had a promenade and pier. Along this sea-front area are grouped the hotels and boarding houses, shops and entertainment areas.

Although this range of land uses persists, the types of tourist and patterns of tourism are quite different from those that contributed to the original growth and wealth of resorts in Britain. Today's tourists, if they are from overseas, will be visiting several resorts perhaps staying a short time in each and will be highly mobile. Most domestic holidaymakers arrive by car and more often tend to use resorts for short-break holidays in spring or autumn as a supplement to an annual holiday abroad. They have quite different wants and objectives compared with their predecessors. They are much more mobile – most arrive by car, much more curious about the surrounding area, and more affluent and discriminating. Seaside resorts have had to adapt to this new kind of tourist, and to more fierce competition from abroad or alternative forms of tourist destination. For example, groups of resorts have formed consortia to market their product more effectively and one of the best known of these is the Torbay area which uses the slogan 'The English Riviera'.

There are also two other types of established tourist resorts in the UK: (i) the capital cities such as London and Edinburgh whose positions as centres of business and culture make them attractions in their own right; (ii) towns with historic and cultural associations such as Stratford, Bath, York or Oxford.

New types of tourist destinations have also emerged. Some are industrial towns that have cleverly packaged their surrounding hinterland often exploiting historical or literary associations. For example, Bradford stresses its links with the Bronte sisters, whilst South Tyneside promotes itself as 'Catherine Cookson Country'. Other attractions are based on Britain's rich and pioneering industrial heritage such as the Ironbridge Museum at Coalbrookdale which traces the story of iron and steel-making, or the North of England Open Air Museum at Beamish. The Beamish Museum, which covers over 300 acres, has recreated a microcosm of industrial life in North-East England as it was in the early years of the 20th century.

Since their creation in the late 1940s the 10 national parks of England and Wales have attracted growing numbers of tourists – although they often contained long-established resorts such as Keswick (Lake District), Buxton (Peak District) or Tenby (Pembrokeshire). More recently, some of the national parks have seen the growth of time-sharing developments.

Since the 1960s the UK seaside resorts have seen a decline in their share of the long-stay holiday market due to the growth of competitive package holidays to the Mediterranean. One of the overriding issues facing many traditional resorts is that of adapting the resort amenities and infrastructure to meet the changing needs of tourists in the 1990s and beyond. The resort authorities need to identify development opportunities, they need to consider ways and means of increasing their share of the tourist market, of attracting commercial investment, and of promoting the resort development package. A key element in their development strategy is the provision of all-weather leisure attractions in the form of indoor resort complexes, such as the multi-million pound Sandcastle Development opened in Blackpool in 1986.

A Profile of Domestic Tourism in the UK

The most popular domestic destination for UK visitors is the West Country accounting for 22% of domestic spending (£1.8 billion) and 22% of all bed-nights (Fig. 8.2). The North West (including the Lake District) and Yorkshire and Humberside (including the Dales and North York Moors) are the next most popular destinations (British Tourist Authority, 1990). London is the next, although visitors to London spend fewer nights there – no doubt a reflection of the higher cost of accommodation in the capital.

The most frequent type of accommodation used (Table 8.4) is visiting friends or relatives. VFR accounts for 37% of all holiday trips in the UK, with hotel/motel or guest house accommodation accounting for 21%. Camping and caravaning accounts for a further 23%. The remaining 19% is fairly evenly distributed between second homes, timeshare and self-catering in rented accommodation. There have been some slight but subtle shifts in the pattern of accommodation use between 1971 and 1989. The proportion of holidaymakers using campsites has halved from 8% to 4%. There has been an even more dramatic decline in the use of the traditional boarding house from 18% (1971) to 6% (1989). The proportion using caravans has remained constant, and the number of VFR visitors has declined slightly. Licensed hotels/motels have gained slightly, as have holiday camp/villages. The recent success of Center Parcs has no doubt influenced the latter figures.

The picture thus emerges of a domestic holidaymaker who is seeking low cost holidays – given that accommodation is usually the largest single cost of a holiday. This is reinforced by the socioeconomic profile of UK holidaymakers (Table 8.5) which shows that social classes C, D and E account for 70% of all UK trips. This reflects the downmarket drift of UK resorts over the past 30 years, and represents a strong marketing challenge for the domestic tourist industry.

The method of transport used to reach the UK holiday destination has changed considerably over the last 40 years. As Table 8.6 shows, the numbers arriving by car and rail between 1951 and 1991 have been completely reversed, with three out of every four visitors now arriving by car. This has had a dramatic effect on the types of holiday people take as well as on the environment of the resorts and holiday regions in the UK. For example, the growth in car ownership has led to a growing preference

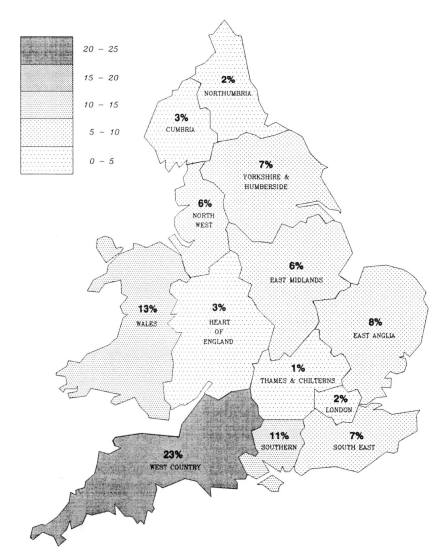

Fig. 8.2. Percentage of British tourist main holiday visits to the Tourist Board Regions, 1989. Note: visits to the regions will add to more than the total as some visitors frequented more than one region. Source: British Tourist Authority, British Tourism Survey Monthly.

Table 8.4. Accommodation used on holidays of four or more nights in Great Britain 1981–1989.

	All holidays (%)								
	1981	1982	1983	1984	1985	1986	1987	1988	1989
Licensed hotel/motel	17	19	17	21	19	20	19	20	20
Unlicensed hotel/boarding house, etc.	7	9	8	8	6	7	7	6	6
Friends'/relatives' home	26	26	25	24	23	23	23	22	22
Caravan	18	19	20	20	21	21	20	23	21
Rented accommodation	14	13	13	10	13	13	14	12	13
Holiday camp/village	6	6	7	7	7	9	8	8	8
Camping	7	5	6	6	5	3	3	4	4
Paying guest in private house	3	2	2	2	3	1	2	2	2
Other	5	5	6	5	6	5	6	7	6
Total	103	104	104	103	103	102	101	104	102

Source: BNTS/BTSY.

for touring holidays, where resorts are seen as a base from which to visit a much wider hinterland. Tourist businesses in the resorts now have to face competition from a wide range of attractions in the surrounding region and many resorts now market regional attractions as part of the overall appeal of the resort. In the UK as in Europe, there has been a corresponding growth in the ownership of touring caravans and campers and static caravan and camp sites, and this trend has affected the tourist resorts and holiday regions in two ways. First, the traditional forms of holiday accommodation have lost some of their market share to caravaning and camping. Secondly, the proliferation of caravans and tents has spread from the fringes of the traditional resort into the formerly less accessible parts of the tourist regions, creating significant planning problems.

The UK tourist industry has seen a slow, gradual but steady decline in the domestic market since the early 1970s, as the number of Britons taking holidays abroad has outstripped those taking holidays at home. Since 1972 the number of domestic trips made by British residents has declined slightly while the number of trips abroad has more than doubled (Fig. 8.3). This trend has occasionally been interrupted by a fine English summer or steep price rises for overseas holidays, but the long-term trend has remained constant. One further reason for the decline in the UK domestic market is

Table 8.5. Demographic profile of holidaytakers 1989.

Base	Adult population of GB[a] (%)	Holidays in Britain[b] (%)
Age (years)		
16–24	18	11
25–34	18	18
35–44	17	19
45–54	14	15
55–64	14	15
65+	19	21
Social class		
AB: professional/managerial	17	19
C1: clerical/supervisory	22	25
C2: skilled manual	29	30
DE: unskilled/pensioners etc.	32	27

Notes: Regions of residence are the Registrar General's regions.
[a]based on the characteristics of the British resident adults who formed the basis of the sample survey.
[b]holidays of 4+ nights.
Source: BNTS.

Patrick Lavery

Table 8.6. Main method of transport used by UK residents to reach the UK holiday destinations 1957 to 1991.

Mode of travel	1951	1961	1971	1981	1991
Car	28%	49%	63%	72%	76%
Rail	48%	28%	10%	12%	10%
Bus or coach	24%	23%	17%	12%	8%

Source: BTAS/ETB Annual Reports.

that for UK residents Britain was increasingly a destination for second or third short-break holidays, and as the recession developed in the early and late 1980s the short-break market went into decline.

There is still a marked seasonal concentration in the timing of tourist trips in Britain by residents. Almost two-thirds of all holiday trips are concentrated in the months between May and September. In some regions, notably Northern Ireland and Wales, between 40% and 50% of main holidays (i.e. 4 or more nights) are taken in July and August. Although there has been a slight decline in the proportion taking their main holidays in July during the 1980s the concentration of main holidays in July and August has remained constant since 1970. This brings with it problems of peak season congestion in the main resorts and holiday areas and the roads

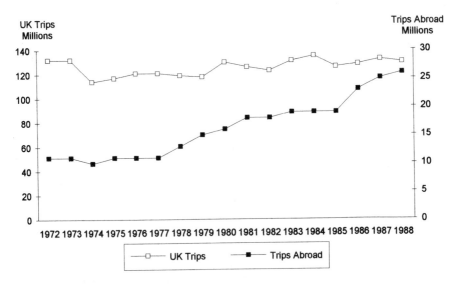

Fig. 8.3. Tourist trips by British residents, 1972–1988.

leading to them. Moreover, if this peak season demand is to be provided for, it means building in a level of capacity such that these resources will be under-used for the rest of the year.

PLANNING AND DEVELOPMENT OF TOURISM IN THE UK

Although the tourist industry in the UK is largely aimed and run by the private sector, an important part of the promotion and marketing of individual resorts and the UK as a tourist destination is done by public sector bodies such as the National, regional and local tourist boards. In 1969 the government issued the *Development of Tourism Act* which established a statutory British Tourist Authority and tourist boards for England, Scotland and Wales, with a responsibility for promoting the development of tourism to and within Britain and to encourage the provision and improvement of tourist amenities and facilities in Britain. The national tourist boards had similar functions including publicity, advisory and information services and research.

During the 1970s and 1980s the English, Scottish and Welsh tourist boards undertook a wide range of marketing and promotional activities, including ETB's 'operation off-peak' aimed at extending the holiday season by promoting spring and autumn holidays.

The English Tourist Board was empowered under Section 4 of the Development of Tourism Act to give financial assistance for tourism development projects and during the late 1970s and through to 1989 millions of pounds were invested in a wide range of schemes from upgrading small hotels to assisting in the development of Centre Parcs' first all weather holiday village in Sherwood Forest. Over £100 million was invested during this period largely in the form of grants to several thousand tourism projects.

Within England there are twelve regional tourist boards who, as well as marketing and promoting their own region as a tourist destination, provide development advice to commercial operators within their area and liaison and advice on tourism planning and management issues with local authorities. Much of the local administration of the Section 4 grants scheme for capital projects was administered by the regional tourist boards. Each Regional Board is also responsible for the preparation and development of tourism strategies for their respective regions.

At the most local level many local authorities are directly involved with the tourist industry in a variety of ways. Often they aim and manage facilities that are major tourist attractions such as museums, theatres, country parks or historic monuments. To give some indication of the scale of local authority involvement, in the early 1980s it was estimated that local authorities were responsible for over 500 art galleries and museums, 700 indoor swimming pools, 600 indoor sports centres and 200 golf courses. Between 1984 and 1987 district councils spent over £521 million on tourism-related projects and over 10,000 new jobs were created both directly and indirectly as a result of this investment. Over the past decade many local authorities, in association with Tourist Boards and various other agencies have developed tourist facilities based on their cultural, industrial or historic heritage. For example, Torfaen Borough Council in association with the Welsh Development Agency, the Wales Tourist Board and the National Coal Board developed the Big Pit Mining Museum. Portsmouth has developed a range of attractions based on the theme of maritime heritage with HMS Victory, HMS Warrior and the Tudor warship, Mary Rose, as the centre-pieces of a formal Royal Dockyard. The city is now embarking on a major development programme with a £5 million water recreation centre; a £100 million marina and a £100 million indoor shopping centre.

Local authorities have also begun to realize the advantages of coming together to establish marketing consortia with the common aim of increasing their region's share of the domestic and international tourist market. For example, Devon, Somerset, Torbay, Exeter and Plymouth have formed a consortium to attract more US visitors to the south west of England. Several local authorities combined to promote nationally the Great English City Break campaign.

Tourism Development Action Programmes

In the UK during the 1980s the English Tourist Board pioneered and developed a new approach towards achieving an effective partnership between the public and private sector to develop tourism at a local or subregional level and to maximize economic and social benefits for the whole community.

Earlier in this chapter reference was made to the steady long-term decline of many small seaside resorts in the UK, which have lost at least half of their staying visitor market since the early 1970s. This has led to a process of environmental degradation and undermining of the general environment of these resorts. What is at stake is not just a problem for tourism, the loss of a few hotels or attractions, but the whole character and attractiveness of these towns as places to live, work in and visit.

In response to these trends and the challenge they presented, the English Tourist Board recognized the need to secure confidence – both public and private sector – in the long-term development of these tourist resorts. In the 1980s the English Tourist Board introduced a practical experiment based on a series of Tourism Development Action Programmes (TDAP) eventually covering 20 different areas.

There are five types of TDAP location:

1. Traditional seaside resorts, for example Torquay.
2. 'Heritage' towns, for example Norwich, Lancaster.
3. Larger industrial and/or maritime centres such as Bristol or Portsmouth.
4. Rural areas, for example, Exmoor.
5. Rural resort areas such as Cornwall or the Isle of Wight.

Their size and scale varies widely. Some, like Lancaster, are based on part of a District Council area. Others like Exmoor or Cornwall involve several District and County Councils.

Tourism Development Action Programmes have six characteristics:

1. They are partnerships between the public and private sectors – close collaboration and cooperation is sought between a wide range of public and private sector organizations in the area.
2. They are area based – in other words, they draw on local knowledge and expertise and address local needs and opportunities.
3. They are action orientated. The emphasis is on implementing initiatives rather than prolonged research and strategy preparations.
4. They are comprehensive and integrated – i.e. they include information, environmental advice and training initiatives.
5. They are corporate in approach and involve the sharing of objectives and work programmes both within and between organizations.
6. They are of fixed duration, usually 3 years. The concept is based on kick-starting initiatives which will then acquire sufficient momentum for progress, based on local resources, to be sustained in the long term.

Typically partners in TDAP will include the District and County Councils, the regional and national Tourist Boards, Chambers of Commerce and other private sector associations, as well as government agencies such as the Countryside Commission, the Sports Council and the Rural Development Commission. They are usually managed with a Steering Group providing overall guidance and control and a working group which is responsible for the day to day implementation of the programme.

Portsmouth Harbour is one such TDAP. It was a joint venture between two local councils, the County Council and the regional and national tourist board, which began in 1985. Its primary focus was to stimulate and develop tourism in Portsmouth and Gosport. The plan focused on six key issues:

1. Raising the tourism profile of the area.
2. Identifying and developing the potential of the heritage attractions.
3. Improving the visitor's experience of the area.

4. Developing other attractions, events and activities.
5. Increasing the amount and improving the quality of accommodation.
6. Conducting targeted marketing campaigns.

The whole emphasis of the TDAP approach is to provide public sector funding as a catalyst for the encouragement of tourism developments and joint public and private sector planning. The different levels of investment between the public and private sector highlight this point. At the beginning of the TDAP the public sector allocated £50,000–60,000, whereas the private sector tourism-related development in Portsmouth amounted to over £50 million.

MARKETING THE UK AS A TOURIST DESTINATION

The UK has a number of strengths and opportunities as a tourist destination, but any marketing strategy needs to take account of threats and weaknesses in the UK market as well as social, economic, demographic and political trends in those countries which generate large numbers of visitors to the UK.

The strengths of the UK tourist product include a wealth of historic towns, cities and villages, a rich heritage of buildings, events and historic associations, attractive countryside and visual arts. Over one-quarter of all visitors' expenditure is on shopping which represents a further strong attraction. Research over many years shows that Britain's heritage, culture and countryside are the main reasons why foreign tourists come.

The weaknesses include a lack of foreign language skills in the domestic tourist industry, litter, restrictions on Sunday trading and on shopping hours generally, absence of a national coordinated accommodation reservation scheme, inconsistent opening hours of historic buildings and sites, problems with the transport infrastructure including peak season congestion and perceived high costs of accommodation.

The British Tourist Authority, which is responsible for marketing the UK as a tourist destination, has identified a wide range of product weaknesses and has attempted to advise and persuade government and industry to take specific action to counter them, but this is likely to be a slow and lengthy process.

Opportunities for the UK market are linked to the forecasts of continuing growth in demand for travel and tourism, and developments such as the Channel Tunnel will reduce journey times between the UK and mainland Europe. Improving links with Europe, either through the tunnel and rail network or improved air travel, are particularly important as Europe is likely to continue to be the main source of international travel over the foreseeable future. Moreover, the expansion of the European

Community through closer links with the EFTA countries, and the opening up of Eastern Europe, will provide a further impetus to inbound tourists to the UK.

One factor that may affect this scenario is that investment is needed urgently to alleviate airspace and airport congestion. The BTA have forecast that 16 key European airports will be capacity constrained by the year 2000. These include Heathrow, Frankfurt, Athens and Stockholm. Other threats include the reverse effect of the Channel Tunnel which may encourage more UK residents to take foreign rather than domestic holidays. Allied to this the opening of EuroDisney and a variety of other tourist attractions in Northern France will intensify competition with the domestic market. This outflow of UK tourists will be a target for many competing European national tourist boards which are investing greater resources in their own marketing campaigns.

Several long-haul markets offer increased potential for inbound tourism to the UK. For example, although the United States is a major market for UK tourism, only 1 in 10 of its citizens hold passports, so there is great potential for further growth. Many economies in southeast Asia and the Far East are expected to grow, and could be valuable sources of overseas tourists. Japan is particularly important as only about 12% of Japanese tourists visit Europe, but their numbers have grown steadily over the past 30 years despite the distance and high air fare. They are among the highest spending tourists and they tend to stay the longest.

FUTURE CHALLENGES FACING TOURISM IN THE UK

The creation of the Single Market in January 1993 will mean changes in several areas including frontier controls, the liberalization of air travel, harmonizing of VAT, new package travel regulations and movement towards a single European currency. The creation of the SEM will not bring a sudden and dramatic change to the UK tourist market. It will expose the domestic tourist industry to gradual change and increasing competitiveness from the tourist industry in other European countries. They too see the UK as a lucrative tourist market and will be seeking to encourage more UK residents to take holidays abroad.

The opening of the Channel Tunnel will provide an opportunity to increase the number of incoming tourists. Euro-tunnel forecasts that the majority of tunnel travellers will originate in France, Belgium, The Netherlands and Germany. They forecast 14 million through train journeys in the first year of operation. However, delays in the UK in developing a high-speed rail link between the Tunnel and London could lead to a reduction in this figure.

As more governments perceive tourism to be the solution to their economic problems, competition for the global market will continue to intensify. The opening up of Eastern Europe will provide a source of (relatively) low cost destinations for western tourists visiting the East and the UK as a destination will have to increase its competitiveness.

The current economic recession in Europe and North America and political instability in the Middle East caused tourism demand to slump in 1991 with some dramatic consequences, not least the failure of the International Leisure Group, formerly one of Britain's major tour operators.

REFERENCES

British Tourist Authority, Annual Reports.
British Tourist Authority (1990) *Digest of Tourist Statistics* No. 14. London.
British Tourist Authority (1991) 1993 *Cross-Channel Marketing Strategy.*
Brunner, E. (1945) *Holiday Making and the Holiday Trades.* Oxford University Press, Oxford.
Development of Tourism Act (1969) HMSO, London.
Patmore, A. (1972) *Land and Leisure.* David & Charles, Newton Abbot.
Yale, P. (1992) *Tourism in the UK.* Elm Publications, Huntington.

9

TOURISM IN THE REPUBLIC OF IRELAND

Desmond A. Gillmor

Within the context of European tourism, the industry of the Republic of Ireland is small but none the less distinctive. Its island location on the western periphery of the continent affects detrimentally the cost and ease of access to Ireland for tourists. The cloudy and moist nature of the cool temperate maritime climate of this position means that it lacks the appeal of the sun destinations on the southern fringe of Europe. However, this location has contributed to the landscape and cultural character which are important attractions of the country. The lower level of economic development associated in part with peripherality also contributes through the effect which past emigration has on the important ethnic sector in Irish tourism. Also, recognition of this development problem has led to substantial Structural Funds being made available by the EC for investment in Irish tourism.

TOURISM TRENDS

The tourist industry of the Irish Republic has expanded considerably since the Second World War but with some setbacks in the growth in visitor numbers (Fig. 9.1). Development has been associated principally with those factors which have contributed to the expansion of European tourism in general, including the growth in disposable income, improved transport, more leisure time and greater tourism organization and promotion (Gillmor, 1985). The introduction of car ferries in the 1960s was of significance not only in terms of visitor numbers but also in increasing the mobility of tourists within the island. Tourist numbers at particular times have been affected also by factors such as the general economic situation, currency exchange rates, development incentives, marketing strategies and changing fashions.

The major setback to growth was that of 1969–1972, when visitor

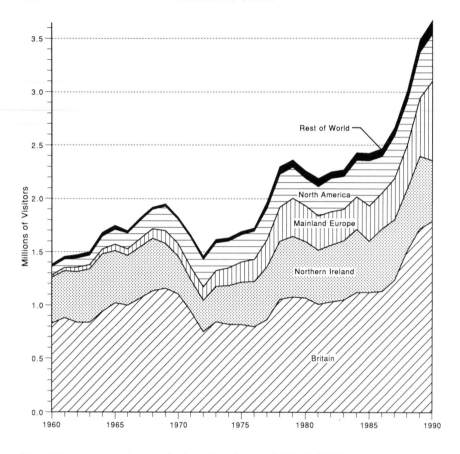

Fig. 9.1. Visitor numbers in the Republic of Ireland, 1960–1990.

numbers fell by 25%. This resulted mainly from the deterrent effect of
violence in and associated with Northern Ireland, with many potential
visitors not realizing that the Republic of Ireland was largely unaffected
(Pollard, 1989). The violence continues to be a great problem for Irish
tourism and an escalation in the early 1980s contributed to the difficulties
at that time. This setback, however, was related more to the international
recession and to the country's loss of competitiveness because of price
inflation in the 1970s and early 1980s, together with some deficiencies in
product development and weaknesses in overseas marketing. Ireland came
to be considered as an expensive destination but inflation has since fallen
below the European average. The subsequent rapid growth in tourist
numbers was related to active government promotion of the industry and
new investment in it, reduced access fares following some liberalization of
air transport, and greatly increased return visits by recent emigrants
following an escalation of emigration in the mid-1980s.

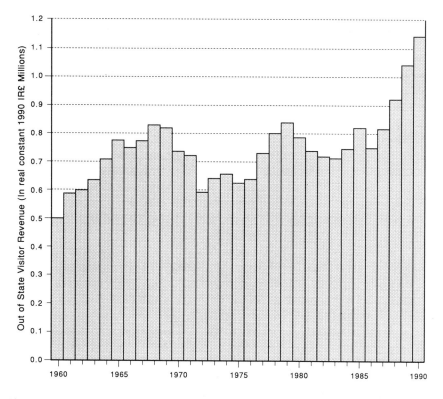

Fig. 9.2. Revenue in real terms from external tourism in the Republic of Ireland, 1960–1990.

The difficulties which Irish tourism has experienced are illustrated even more clearly by the trend in real income than by that in visitor numbers (Fig. 9.2), as the expenditure per tourist has declined. Earnings in the first half of the 1980s were less than those of the expansionary years of the late 1960s. The Republic of Ireland failed to keep pace with the growth of European and world tourism, its shares of both having fallen greatly from those of 1960. Although some of the reasons for this differential were specific to Ireland, others, such as the growth of Mediterranean tourism, were unrelated. Substantial growth occurred in the period 1985–1990, however, when there was an increase in real terms of 7% per annum.

In 1990, 3.67 million external or out-of-state tourists visited the Republic of Ireland and spent IR£866 million. The carrier receipts to Irish air and sea companies in transporting them were IR£263 million. To these values are added the IR£10 million spent by day excursionists, mainly from Northern Ireland, to give the total revenue of IR£1139 million from external tourism in 1990. The revenue from domestic tourists was IR£413 million, 27% of the total tourism revenue of IR£1552 million.

Desmond A. Gillmor

TOURISM MARKET

A distinctive feature of Irish tourism is the large ethnic component, visiting relatives and friends having been given as the reason for coming by 41% of overseas visitors in 1990. The other reasons were: holiday 47%, business 19%, any personal reason 12% and study 4%, with the percentages totalling more than 100 because of multipurpose trips. Holidaymakers are predominantly of higher socioeconomic status, reflecting the facts that Ireland is regarded as an expensive destination and that three-quarters of visitors come on independent holidays rather than package tours. There is a high proportion of older tourists, with nearly half of people travelling alone and only a tenth being families with children. The proportion of overseas visitors arriving by air is 60%. One-third are on their first visit to Ireland and tourists stay an average of 11 nights.

Significant changes have occurred in the nationality structure of the export tourist market (see Fig. 9.1 and Table 9.1). These changes resulted initially from trends which became evident in the 1960s but were accelerated by the recession of the early 1970s. The principal features were the diminished relative role of the UK market and the growth in continental European and North American traffic, leading to greater diversification. More recently, the North American market has stagnated while business from mainland Europe has continued to expand.

While the UK remains the mainstay of the Irish Republic's export tourism, its market predominance has diminished considerably, especially in terms of revenue. The Northern Irish sector had been static for some years prior to the outbreak of violence in 1969 but the number of tourists from there declined by 40% in 1968–1972. This reflected especially a greater reluctance on the part of Protestants to visit the Republic as attitudes hardened. A more general factor has been the increased tendency to holiday elsewhere in Europe, especially on packages to the Mediterranean region, and this has also affected traffic from Britain. British people who

Table 9.1. Percentage structure of external tourism revenue in the Republic of Ireland, 1960, 1970, 1980 and 1990.

Source area	1960	1970	1980	1990
Northern Ireland	21	11	12	8
Britain	58	47	43	39
Mainland Europe	3	8	21	29
North America	16	32	19	19
Rest of World	1	2	5	5

were not of Irish descent and connection were greatly deterred by the violence and associated political considerations, and still 55% of tourists come to visit relatives and friends. This, together with their lower income level and greater number of children which are also related to the large ethnic component, contribute to per capita spending by British visitors being less than that of other overseas tourists.

In contrast, North American visitors have a high spending level and they tend to be of older age structure and with a greater proportion of women. Visiting relatives and friends is the purpose of the trip for 26% of them. The eastern USA is the major source area, reflecting the distribution of population and Irish immigration together with the influence of distance. Over half of American tourists visit at least one other country and marketing has promoted Ireland as part of a European tour. The strength of the dollar contributed to an increase of one-third in North American visitors in the early 1980s. Traffic from other non-European sources is mainly from Australasia and resembles in some respects the North American market.

Mainland Europe has been the high-performance sector of the tourism market since 1960, starting from a very low base then. Growth was uninterrupted in the early 1970s, perhaps in part because the predominantly young visitors were less deterred by the violence. Also accession of Ireland to the EC led to greater awareness of it as a holiday destination and the inauguration of direct ferry sailings from France increased accessibility. France, Germany, Italy and The Netherlands are the sources of 70% of continental visitors. Only 17% of the tourists come for the purpose of visiting relatives and friends, reflecting the lesser amount of Irish migration to mainland Europe and its greater recency. There is also a striking predominance of young adults who belong to the higher socioeconomic groups among continental visitors.

Domestic tourism's share of consumer spending has increased. Half of the population takes a holiday away from home and 60% of main holidays are spent within the state. The 5.04 million domestic trips in 1990 comprised 33% long holidays (4+ nights), 38% short holidays (1–3 nights) and 29% trips for other purposes, with long holidays contributing half the revenue. Family groups with children comprise 40% of home holiday-makers, over three times the proportion among overseas visitors.

TOURISM ORGANIZATION

While the government Department of Tourism, Transport and Communications has primary overall control of tourism policy, responsibility for implementation of this policy and for general tourism development rests with the semi-state company Bord Fáilte (Irish Tourist Board). The

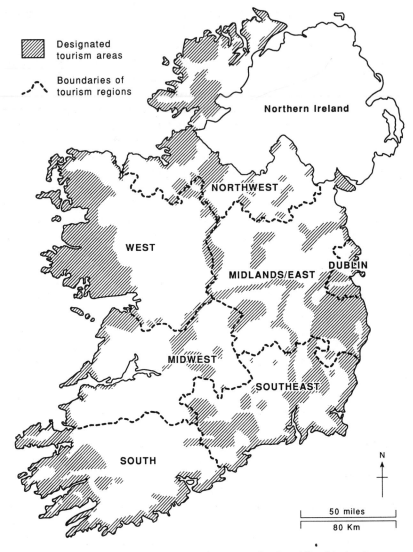

Fig. 9.3. Tourism regions and designated areas in the Republic of Ireland.

functions of Bord Fáilte are similar to those of other national tourism organizations and include promotion and marketing, which absorb the bulk of its expenditure, together with planning, development, research and regulation. A separate organization, CERT, has responsibility for training for tourism. The interests of the principal participants in the industry are represented at the national level mainly by the Irish Tourist Industry Confederation. Irish tourism is characterized by its small scale of enterprises and there has been only very limited penetration by international capital.

One of the most important developments in Irish tourism administration was the formation of a distinctive intermediate level of organization in 1964 through the establishment of eight regional tourism organizations (RTOs) by Bord Fáilte. The number was reduced to seven in 1984, through the merging of the Dublin and Eastern regions, and in 1988 responsibility for the Midwest was transferred to the multisectoral agency Shannon Development. There was some regional redefinition in 1989 to correspond to the regions delimited by the government for the purposes of planning for the use of EC Structural Funds (Fig. 9.3). The general functions of the RTOs have been to stimulate and coordinate local effort in the development of tourism, to service visitors through a countrywide network of information and reservation centres, to promote and market their regions, to maintain a watching brief on environmental matters and to implement national policies and plans at the regional level. Pearce (1990) identified cyclical swings in the centralization and devolution of function, with the RTOs having important roles at first and then Bord Fáilte almost turning its back on them in the late 1970s and early 1980s but with their recent greater integration into the national scheme.

Marketing is one sphere in which there has been some disagreement concerning relative national and regional roles. Bord Fáilte has always reserved responsibility for overseas marketing on the basis that promotion of the image of Ireland as a whole is the most cost-effective way of marketing a small country internationally. In order to do this, Bord Fáilte maintains a series of offices abroad in the major source countries and it has endeavoured to obtain greater participation in marketing by the commercial organizations. Some of the RTOs have undertaken limited overseas promotion and they have cooperated with Bord Fáilte in certain marketing programmes. Some local interests would like to see much greater efforts being made to attract visitors specifically to their regions.

Many plans for tourism have been produced since the 1960s. That which had the most specifically spatial dimension was the national development plan and associated eight regional plans for the period 1976–1980. Much of the planning and development effort was focused on certain designated areas, which comprise much of the coastline, uplands, major rivers and lakes (see Fig. 9.3). They were delimited on the basis of both their natural and human resources and also the existing use and potential for tourism. The designated areas are those parts of the country which are considered critical to the future growth of tourism and which must be safeguarded.

A new impetus to Irish tourism development began to emerge in the mid-1980s. This seems to have been stimulated by the difficulties being experienced by the industry at that time, the search by government for remedies for severe national economic and employment problems and the publication of a White Paper (Government of Ireland, 1985) and consultancy reports on tourism (Stokes Kennedy Crowley *et al.*, 1986; Price Waterhouse, 1987). A positive government attitude towards tourism was evident in its 1987 Programme for National Recovery. This outlined a strategy for the next five years whereby the number of foreign visitors would be doubled, an additional IR£500 million of foreign tourism revenue would be earned and an extra 25,000 jobs created. These ambitious targets were to be attained through lower access fares, the development of inward air charter traffic, better marketing and the aggressive promotion of investment in the industry. Investment was encouraged by the application to certain tourism enterprises over the period 1987–1991 of the Business Expansion Scheme, providing tax relief on venture capital.

Ireland's plans for tourism development were approved and adopted by the EC in 1989 as The Operational Programme for Tourism 1989–1993 (Department of Tourism and Transport, 1990). This involved essentially application of the earlier targets and policies to this period but provided for Community funding of almost half of the planned IR£300 million investment. This would come mainly from the European Regional Development Fund and also the European Social Fund and was made possible by the doubling of Structural Funds to promote cohesion associated with the Single European Act. The Operational Programme is designed to enable Irish tourism to compete successfully so that it might stimulate the economic growth needed to reduce unemployment and raise incomes towards EC levels, tourism having been identified as one major means of doing this.

Tourism Product

It is not easy to evaluate precisely the attractions which a country such as Ireland has for visitors, whose personal needs, preferences and experiences vary greatly. Market research suggests that the appeal revolves mainly around its scenery, people and culture. Attractive and varied countryside has been given by visitors as the main single reason for choosing Ireland. This image has ingredients of rugged mountains, coastal scenery, green luxuriance and a distinctive pattern of fields and rural houses. The reputation of the Irish people for friendliness and hospitality is an important asset. The relaxed atmosphere and the relatively unpolluted environment appeal to visitors who come mainly from urban–industrial places. The cultural character and heritage of the country, including its literature, music, monuments and historic buildings, comprise a major resource. For those visitors of Irish birth or ancestry, the ethnic connection and the opportunities to visit relatives and friends and to trace their roots are important considerations. The general use of the English language facilitates tourism, in addition to those students who come to learn it. The Operational Programme identified the strengths of Irish tourism as being friendly people, a vibrant folk tradition, a clean and unspoiled environment, a distinctive architectural and cultural heritage, a good accommodation base and a worldwide ethnic market.

Whereas opinion surveys indicate the appeal of the country, the activities in which visitors engage cast further light on the tourism product. Sightseeing and exploring the countryside comprise the leading category of activity, reflecting the importance of the landscape resource. This contributes to the significance of touring holidays in Irish tourism. Other important general activities include walking, picnicking, beach activities, visiting pubs, listening to traditional music and shopping.

Participation by overseas holidaymakers in the principal activities for which data are available is shown in Table 9.2. This is dominated by the passive pursuits of visiting historic sites and museums and stately houses and gardens, which thus constitute major tourism resources for all markets but especially mainland Europe and North America. More specialized interests are those of North Americans in genealogy and continental Europeans in language study. The active pursuits have grown considerably and are more important in holiday decision making than their relative participation levels would suggest, for instance half of those who play golf are influenced by its availability in choosing to visit Ireland. The country affords considerable scope for hillwalking or hiking, the many rivers and lakes provide a basis for widespread angling and the Irish reputation for horses is an asset in attracting people for equestrian activities. Many of those who engage in water-based activities have planned to go inland cruising, especially on the River Shannon. The level of participation in

Table 9.2. Pre-planned involvement of overseas holidaymakers in certain activities in the Republic of Ireland, 1990.

Activities	No. ('000)	%	Activities	No. ('000)	%
Historic visits	617	36	Genealogy	95	6
Museums/art galleries	349	20	Cycling	92	5
Gardens	337	20	Pilgrimages	81	5
Great houses	318	18	Horse racing	54	3
Walking	188	11	Water-based	51	3
Theatre/concerts	167	9	Language study	49	3
Angling	150	9	Equestrian	45	3
Golf	132	8	Bird watching	42	2

active pursuits is highest among mainland Europeans and lowest among North Americans.

Accommodation is an essential part of the tourism product and its supply has grown with the industry in quantity and quality. Although there has been a trend towards higher grade and increasing size of hotel, the predominant feature of accommodation provision is that of the small scale of enterprises. Most hotels are family-owned businesses and a substantial amount of other serviced accommodation is provided on a bed and breakfast basis. Hotels generate more employment than the other sectors but there has been a shift towards self-catering for reasons of cost and independence. A wide diversity of accommodation is available. One handicap in accommodation provision is the seasonality of business, 52% of overseas tourists arriving during the four months June to September, but holidaymaking is even more peaked.

The structure of accommodation use by overseas visitors in 1990 was: hotels 29%, guesthouses 6%, town and country homes 17%, farmhouses 3%, self-catering (rented, caravan, camping, youth hostels) 15%, unlisted 7% and with friends and relatives 43%, the percentages totalling more than 100 because of the use of more than one category by some tourists. The very high proportion of people who stay with friends and relatives results from the large ethnic element in Irish tourism. The proportion for British visitors was 59% as compared with 17% for those from mainland Europe, reflecting the different migration patterns. The use of serviced accommodation, especially hotels, is highest among North Americans. Visitors from continental Europe have diverse usage but are proportionately highest in self-catering accommodation, with many young people staying in youth hostels.

SPATIAL PATTERN OF TOURISM

It is difficult to examine the spatial distribution of tourism because of data deficiencies. Those available at the county level relate only to a small sample of overseas visitors and they must be treated with caution (Fig. 9.4). They relate to all visitors, including those coming for business or social reasons as well as holidaymakers. Even regional revenue data, which include domestic and Northern Irish visitors in addition to those from overseas, are derived from estimated regional allocations of national revenue rather than being precise figures (Fig. 9.5).

There is a distinct spatial pattern of tourism, as is indicated in the maps. The Dublin, Southwest and West regions accounted for 57% of national tourism revenue in 1990. The pattern would be even more uneven if it were not for the substantial ethnic element in Irish tourism, which is

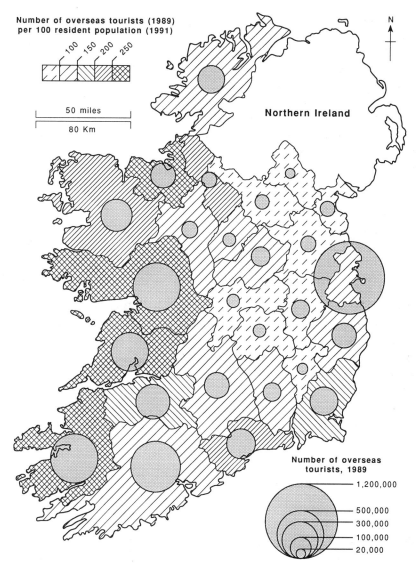

Number of overseas tourists (1989) per 100 resident population (1991)

100 150 200 250

50 miles

80 Km

Northern Ireland

N

Number of overseas tourists, 1989

1,200,000

500,000
300,000
100,000
20,000

Fig. 9.4. Overseas tourists by county in the Republic of Ireland, 1989.

related more to the distributions of migration sources and of relatives and friends than to normal tourist resources. The pattern of other holiday-making is shown more by relating visitor numbers to the resident population, though this does not allow for differential regional migration rates (Fig. 9.4).

The spatial distribution of tourism reflects the geographical patterns of the various tourist attractions, the regional levels of development, invest-

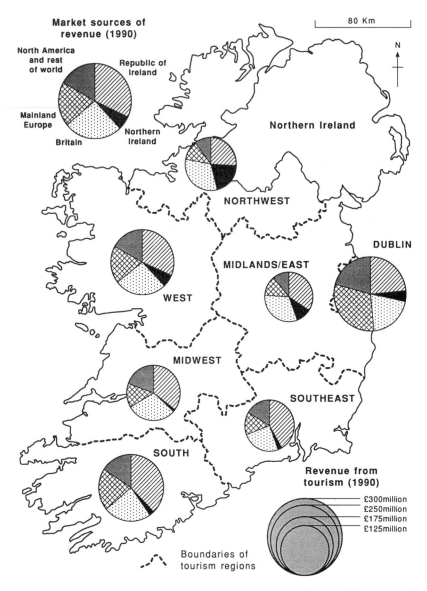

Fig. 9.5. Market structure of regional tourism revenue in the Republic of Ireland, 1990.

ment and promotion, and the location of tourist gateways. It is strongly oriented towards the coastal zone, with the maritime counties receiving most of the tourism revenue. This is partly because of the scenic attraction of the coast itself and the scope which it provides for beach and water-based activities. It follows also from the predominantly peripheral distribution of upland relief and of urban settlement, the latter having historical and cultural features and also accommodation and entertainment facilities. The western part of the country is that which has the greatest appeal to tourists. This results from a combination of its physical assets of a long attractive coastline and extensive upland scenery, together with the character of its human landscape, people and traditional culture. Major historic sites, great houses and gardens are more common in the east and south. Eastern regions get a higher proportion of the revenue than they would otherwise have because of their proximity to entry points for overseas visitors. Dublin is the single most important focus for tourists, having 22% of the national revenue and being visited by two-fifths of overseas tourists. This reflects the various attractions of the capital city in addition to it being the country's main international gateway and a centre for business travel. In the northern part of the state, proximity to the border with Northern Ireland has a deterrent influence, affecting especially the northwestern peripheral county of Donegal which otherwise has major tourist attraction.

There is some regional differentiation in the market sources of tourism revenue (Fig. 9.5). The facts that the British sector is the one in which variation is least and that it tends to be relatively most important in the least popular regions reflect the large ethnic element among British travellers which is drawn less than other tourists towards the main destinations. That the British role is proportionately greatest in the Midlands/East and Northwest regions is influenced by the attraction of the lakes of the northern midland area for British anglers and relative proximity to access routes from Britain. The Northern Irish component is the most localized, one-third being to the adjacent Northwest, especially Donegal, with the Midlands/East and West also popular. The North American contribution is highest in Dublin and the Midwest, related to air arrival and departure at Shannon and Dublin and to the attraction of the capital city. The appeal of Dublin is most marked with regard to visitors from continental Europe, accounting for nearly one-third of its revenue, and their contribution is high also in the Southwest and West. The proportion of revenue derived from domestic tourism is highest in the Southeast, reflecting its relative proximity to Dublin as the main source of Irish visitors and also the attraction of its beaches and relatively sunny climate. The Southwest and West are popular with Irish holidaymakers, accounting for two-fifths of the revenue from domestic tourism.

The location of tourist accommodation provides an alternative means of investigating the spatial pattern of tourism (O Cinnéide and Walsh, 1990–91). This permits mapping below the levels of the region and county but spatial variation in occupancy rates cannot be allowed for. The general distribution of bedrooms in hotels and guesthouses is indicated in Fig. 9.6; they account for two-thirds of the bed capacity in serviced accommodation

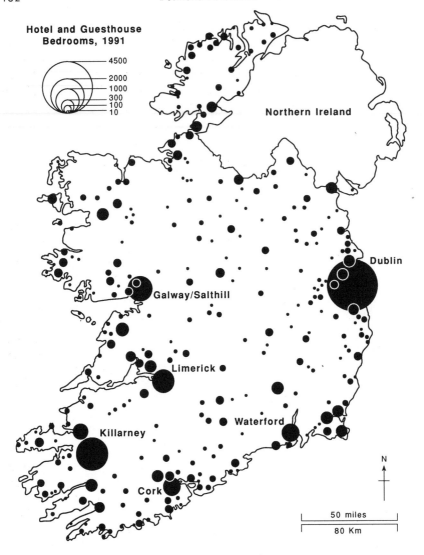

Fig. 9.6. Hotel and guesthouse bedrooms in the Republic of Ireland, 1991 (based on O Cinnéide and Walsh, 1990–91).

and more than that in terms of revenue. The map conveys an impression of somewhat greater concentration than exists because of the allocation of some establishments to the nearest town. The importance of Dublin as the leading centre of tourism is evident. It is followed by Killarney, where a long-established tourist industry has been based on the famed beauty of its lake and mountain scenery. It is unique as an inland resort, most concentrations of hotels and guesthouses being on the coast, either in urban centres or seaside resorts. Ranked third is Galway/Salthill, which is a city and seaside resort but serves also as a touring centre and the gateway to the beautiful area of Connemara to the west. Much more dispersed than hotels and guesthouses are the country homes, farmhouses and self-catering accommodation, thus greatly extending the locational choice available to the tourist and spreading the impacts of tourism, especially in the west.

IMPACTS OF TOURISM

The direct and indirect impacts of tourism on the Irish economy, society and landscape are diverse and far-reaching but they have been the subject of little research. As elsewhere, it is difficult to assess precisely tourism's economic impact because of the disparate nature of the industry, its inter-penetration with other activities and data deficiencies. The available sources were presented and evaluated by the consultants Tansey, Webster and Associates (1991) and their report is used in this section as the most comprehensive and recent assessment.

After earlier growth in its role, the significance of tourism in the national economy lessened from the late 1960s with the difficulties encountered by the industry and the greater expansion of other economic sectors but this trend was reversed in the late 1980s. In 1990 the contribution of tourism to GNP was 6.6%, 5.1% from the export sector and 1.5% from domestic tourism. Tourism was estimated to have a multiplier of 0.94 as spending filtered widely through the ecomony. There is a substantial yield to the exchequer through tax revenue, estimated to be 27% of tourist spending and equivalent to about 5% of total government receipts from taxes on income and expenditure and social insurance contributions. Total earnings from external tourism in the Irish Republic amounted to 7% of the value of all exports of goods and services in 1990. The beneficial contribution to the national balance of payments is greater than this suggests because the import content of tourist spending, estimated at 8%, is much lower than that of expenditure in the economy as a whole. Leakage of revenue out of the country is further reduced by the predominantly Irish ownership of tourist facilities. The net contribution of tourism to the balance of payments is a positive one, as the receipts from external visitors exceed by two-thirds the expenditure abroad by Irish residents.

The provision of employment is a particularly important consideration in a country where the national unemployment rate is 19%. It is estimated that there were about 80,000 full-time job equivalents in tourism in 1990, equivalent to 7.1% of total employment and to 12.6% of that in the service sector. Over 60% of this is direct employment, two-thirds of which is in the catering and transport industries, but many sectors of the economy benefit.

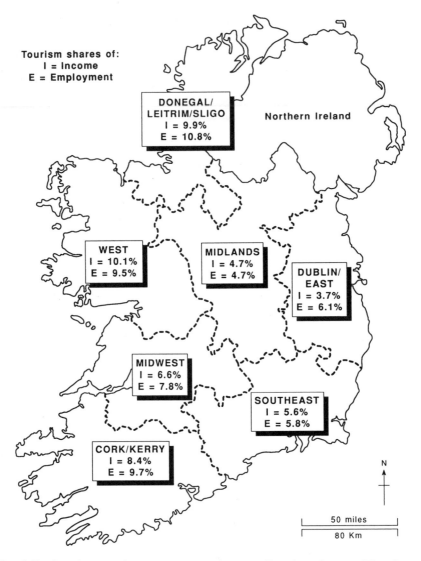

Fig. 9.7. Contributions of tourism to regional income (I) and employment (E) in the Republic of Ireland, 1990.

The substantial seasonal element in tourism employment may be seen to be a deficiency but many employed on this basis are students and housewives who would not be prepared to work full time and for whom tourism is a valuable income supplement.

    The impact of tourism has an important regional dimension. The regional contributions to income and employment are shown in Fig. 9.7, using the regional delimitation of 1988 because data for personal income are not available for the new tourist regional system. The values are lowest in the East and Midlands and tend to increase westwards, so that tourism's contributions are greatest in the less-developed west where they are needed most, though the benefits to midland districts are not commensurate with their needs. The combined regions of the West and Donegal/ Leitrim/Sligo had an estimated 12% of national personal income in 1990 and 22% of tourism revenue, though there may be some indeterminable leakage of revenue from these peripheral regional economies. Domestic tourism redistributes income and employment spatially within the state, as a high proportion of the holidaymakers come from the more developed regions and urban centres.

The social and environmental effects of tourism in the Republic of Ireland are varied and complex. It may be seen to contribute to a small extent to social disruption and diminution of cultural identity but it has added to the quality of life of local communities and stimulated greater awareness of heritage. Tourism revenue provides the economic rationale for the support of facilities which benefit local people also, including those relating to the arts, history, entertainment, recreation and dining. There are environmental costs of tourist development, including pressures on sand dune and upland environments and on historic sites, the effects of increased numbers of people on congestion and waste creation, and the impacts of poorly sited or designed camp and caravan sites, second homes and hotels. These are much less evident than in many other countries, however, because of the highly dispersed nature of Irish tourism. Also concern for the industry has been a vital force in promoting interest in environmental conservation in general and the protection of the landscape in particular, as maintenance of a high quality environment is seen as being essential to the welfare of Irish tourism.

CONCLUSION

Tourism is of major importance in the economy and life of the Republic of Ireland but considerable difficulties have been encountered in its development. The Operational Programme identified the weaknesses of the industry as comprising: deficiencies in the quality and range of important elements of the tourism product; lack of price competitiveness; difficulties in marketing, exacerbated by the negative image relating to the troubles in Northern Ireland; access difficulties and cost associated with the country's isolated location. The peripherality which hinders access has facilitated the retention of some of that Irish individuality appeal which should become even more significant in an increasingly unified Europe. Also its hindrance of many other economic sectors makes the need for tourism development to increase revenue and employment all the greater.

Present policy is to endeavour to counter the weaknesses in Irish tourism through a fourfold strategy. The primary component is a product strategy designed to provide a better and wider range of tourist attractions and facilities. This focuses on five product themes comprising: active pursuits; passive pursuits; cultural, heritage and entertainment interests; leisure, fitness and health facilities; business travel. It includes human resource training, efforts to reduce seasonality and the development of tourism centres, theme towns and traditional resorts. The other components are a competitiveness strategy to provide better value in terms of price and quality, a promotion strategy aimed at greater penetration of existing markets and entry to new ones, and a distribution strategy to ensure that the product is made readily available to the potential customer through an improved information and reservation network. This more vigorous and better coordinated approach on the part of government, Bord Fáilte and the industrial practitioners can do much to further the development of Irish tourism but also the future of the industry will be affected inevitably by influences beyond the control of any of these agents.

REFERENCES

Department of Tourism and Transport (1990) *Operational Programme for Tourism.* Stationery Office, Dublin.

Gillmor, D.A. (1985) *Economic Activities in the Republic of Ireland: a Geographical Perspective.* Gill and Macmillan, Dublin, pp. 302–37.

Government of Ireland (1985) *White Paper on Tourism Policy.* Stationery Office, Dublin.

O Cinnéide, M. and Walsh, J.A. (1990–91) Tourism and regional development in Ireland. *Geographical Viewpoint* 19, 47–68.

Pearce, D.G. (1990) Tourism in Ireland: questions of scale and organization. *Tourism Management* 11, 133–51.

Pollard, J. (1989) Patterns in Irish tourism. In: Carter, R.W.G. and Parker, A.J. (eds) *Ireland: a Contemporary Geographical Perspective.* Routledge, London and New York, 301–30.

Price Waterhouse (1987) *Improving the Performance of Irish Tourism.* Stationery Office, Dublin.

Stokes Kennedy Crowley *et al.* (1986) *Tourism Working for Ireland: a Plan for Growth.* Irish Hotels Federation, Dublin.

Tansey, Webster and Associates (1991) *Tourism and the Economy.* Irish Tourist Industry Confederation, Dún Laoghaire.

10

TOURISM IN BENELUX

Jan R. Bergsma

INTRODUCTION

Benelux functions as an economic and to some extent as a political entity, where customs formalities at the borders have almost completely disappeared long before 1993 and the Single European Market. With regard to tourism, however, natural features, traditions and the existing national administrations result in The Netherlands, Belgium and Luxemburg differing considerably from each other. Therefore the three countries will be described separately in this chapter. For each Benelux country a description will be given of the tourism product and tourist industry, the domestic as well as foreign travel behaviour of the inhabitants, the importance of incoming tourism and the tourism policies that have been formulated.

TOURISM IN THE NETHERLANDS

Dutch Tourism Product and Tourist Industry

The Netherlands are a relatively small country of about 41,000 km^2 with more than half lying below sea level. Almost one-fifth of the land area is called 'polder', which means land reclaimed from the sea. For these reasons The Netherlands are characterized by flatness – the highest mountain is no more than 300 m – and the abundant presence of water. The country has a great number of lakes and is crossed by many rivers and canals. Together with the well-known tourist attractions (like windmills, clogs, bulbfields and cheesefarms, which have become the stereotypes of Dutch tourism, numerous watersport opportunities, huge waterdefending constructions like the Deltaworks and the many historic cities appear to be

Table 10.1. Number and capacity of accommodation in The Netherlands (1990).

Type	Number of establishments	Capacity (in number of beds × 1000)
Hotels, pensions	3000	125
Campsites (> 20 places)	2700	1650
Second home and bungalow-parcs	570	130
Total	6270	1905

Source: Bergsma (1991).

main features of the Dutch tourism product. They are responsible for an ever-growing number of visitors each year.

In addition to the natural and cultural resources, a typical Dutch phenomenon is the great density and variety of leisure and theme parks. Apart from EuroDisney near Paris, The Netherlands have the biggest theme park in Europe, the Efteling, which has been receiving about 2.5 million visitors each year for many years. Besides the Efteling there is a great number of other theme parks, all of which have to invest continuously in new attractions in a highly competitive environment.

The accommodation industry in The Netherlands can be characterized by a relatively small number of hotel beds and the availability of many camp sites and bungalows (Table 10.1). In addition to the camping-facilities more and more farmers (in 1990: 1200) offer to supplement their decreasing agricultural income. The Netherlands rank number three in the world in total capacity of camping sites (1.7 million), only slightly behind France and the United States.

The luxury bungalow parks of Centre Parcs are well-known, offering not only overnight accommodation but also all kinds of all-weather leisure and sport facilities, like whirlpools, saunas, tennis courts and shopping facilities. The formula of Centre Parcs has been unexpectedly successful, realizing a 97% year-round occupancy rate. The eight Centre Parcs establishments in The Netherlands, with a total supply of 5000 bungalows (which is approximately 20% of the total bungalow capacity), offer accommodation for almost 40% of the total Dutch bungalow market (Bergsma, 1991). Since 1987 the expansion of Centre Parcs has taken place in surrounding countries like Belgium, Great Britain and France, since it was believed that the domestic Dutch market was saturated.

The travel industry in The Netherlands is characterized by the relatively low prices charged for package holidays on the price-sensitive Dutch market, resulting in small profit margins of less than 3% for most tour operators. The Dutch are independent travellers, so the number of holidays booked is traditionally low, although since 1988 there has been an increased tendency to book in advance.

International forces ensure that most of the Dutch tour operators feel it necessary to be linked one way or another to foreign tour operators. For example, giant German tour operators like TUI are shareholders in Dutch companies like ARKE. Still remarkable is the important role banks and some department stores play in the distribution and selling of travel products.

Tourist Behaviour of the Dutch

The Dutch are well known for their enthusiasm for travel and the long tradition they have in holidaymaking. In 1990 more than 25 million holidays were taken, of which roughly 16 million had at least four over-night stays. Despite the relatively small size of the Dutch population (14 million), Dutch holidaymakers can be found everywhere in the world. Less than 10% of the population never go on holiday, which is a lower percentage than in any other country. It is not only the wealthier sector of the population that likes to travel, lower income groups also show a high proportion of travellers. In a way holidaymaking can be considered a basic need for the Dutuch in the sense that demand increases more than proportionately with rises in income, but once acquired holidaymaking is not easily discarded when incomes go down.

Holiday intensity

In terms of holiday intensity, i.e. the proportion of the population that take a holiday at least once a year, The Netherlands rank very high in Europe showing a figure of 69.9% in 1990. If short-break holidays are also taken into account the percentage rises to 74.6% (NRIT, 1991). Although there has been a rapid growth over the last decades, during the last couple of years the intensity seems to have reached a certain saturation level. The absolute number of holidays is still growing because of the increasing average number of holidays per holidaymaker (Table 10.2).

The Dutch market is a major supplier market for the West European travel industry. The Dutch take a higher proportion of holidays abroad than most other nationalities. Of all 16 million holidays taken in 1990 55% were spent abroad. In number of overnight stays this rose to 63%.

Jan R. Bergsma

Table 10.2. Key figures Dutch holidays (> 4 nights).

	1966	1970	1975	1980	1985	1990
Holiday intensity	40.8	45.9	53.8	67.5	63.7	69.9
Total number of holidays (million)	6.1	7.3	9.2	13.2	12.8	16.3
Proportion domestic (%)	60	54	49	45	48	45
Proportion foreign (%)	40	46	51	55	52	55
Number of holidays per holidaymaker	1.24	1.24	1.29	1.44	1.45	1.67

Source: NRIT (1991).

Destinations

Although destinations on the Mediterranean coast offering sun, sea and sand are important, the Dutch also show preference for mountain areas and the countryside.

For domestic holidays the two most important destinations are the North Sea coast (receiving 14% of all domestic holidays) and the Veluwe, which is a forested area in central Holland (12%). For holidays abroad France is destination number one; 22% of all Dutch holidays abroad (i.e. 2 million) are spent in France, followed by Germany (14%), Austria (12%) and Spain (9%).

The continuing popularity of Austria as a holiday destination is partly a result of the growing number of winter holidays by the Dutch. Almost one-third of all holidays abroad are spent as winter holidays. For skiing, Austria is the most popular destination (Table 10.3)

Accommodation

It is clear from the accommodation used that the Dutch are lovers of campsites and have a long tradition in this respect. Domestically about 40% of all holidays are spent in tents or caravans; another 37% are in rented bungalows, of which a considerable proportion is offered on luxury five star bungalow parks. Hotels account for only 6% of all domestic holidays of a minimum of four nights; for short breaks this percentage is twice as high (12%). Second homes and 'visiting friends and relatives' are rather insignificant compared to most of the other European countries (4%).

Table 10.3. Outgoing tourism in The Netherlands: main destination countries (%).

Country	1988	1989	1990
Austria	14	13	12
Belgium	7	8	8
France	18	19	22
Germany	15	16	14
Great Britain	3	3	3
Greece	4	4	5
Italy	5	5	4
Luxembourg	3	3	2
Spain	12	10	9
Switzerland	4	4	4
Total (=100%) (million)	8.9	9.5	9.0

Source: NRIT (1991).

Abroad the Dutch tend to stay more in hotels (34%), but there campsites are also important (28%), especially on holidays in France. The third main category is formed by the self-catering apartment sector on which 17% of all holidays abroad are based (Table 10.4). Related to the popularity of camping is the fact that durable goods like caravans and tents are more widely owned in The Netherlands than in any other country in the world.

Table 10.4. Dutch holidays (> 4 nights): accommodation choice (%).

	Domestic			Foreign		
	1986	1988	1990	1986	1988	1990
Hotel, pension	7	6	6	34	34	34
Bungalow/2nd home	45	43	41	19	15	15
Tent/caravan	38	41	39	30	29	28
Boat	4	5	5	1	1	0
Apartment	1	2	3	12	19	17
Other	5	3	6	4	2	6
Total (=100%) (million)	6.0	6.5	7.3	7.3	8.9	9.0

Source: CVO/NRIT (1991).

Table 10.5. Dutch holidays (> 4 nights): means of transport (%).

	Domestic			Foreign		
	1986	1988	1990	1986	1988	1990
Private car	84	87	85	62	61	59
Train	6	5	5	3	3	5
Plane	0	0	0	16	19	19
Coach	2	3	2	15	14	13
Boat	3	1	1	1	1	1
Other	5	4	7	3	2	3
Total (=100%) (million)	6.0	6.5	7.3	7.3	8.9	9.0

Source: CVO/NRIT (1991).

Means of transport

Most holidays of the Dutch are taken with the private car. Of domestic holidays as much as 87% and of foreign holidays 62% are based on car transport, which is understandable considering the small size of The Netherlands, where public transport is not as efficient as private transport. Moreover, the car is the easiest way with which the popular caravan, tent or other camping equipment can be transported (Table 10.5).

Length of stay and expenditure

The average length of stay is gradually decreasing, and this is related to the increase in the number of holidays taken by each holidaymaker. Between 1985 and 1990 the average length of stay for domestic holidays decreased from 12.2 to 10.6 days and for foreign holidays from 15.2 to 14.6 days (NRIT, 1991); at the same time the average number of holidays increased from 1.45 to 1.67. In general holiday expenditure is increasing, with obviously, big differences between the type of accommodation chosen; costs vary from an average of DGL 628 for a holiday abroad in a hotel to an average of DGL 273 for a domestic holiday on a campsite. The total expenditure of the Dutch on holidays (of more than 4 nights) were about DGL 12.5 billion, which is 4.6% of the total private consumption. Domestically the Dutch spend DGL 2.3 billion and abroad DGL 10.2 billion (NRIT, 1991).

Incoming Tourism

Although growing, compared to the total number of Dutch holidaymakers, incoming tourism is relatively unimportant. Of the total number of overnight stays in The Netherlands only 18% are by foreigners, although in hotels this is 55%. In terms of revenues from tourism (including short breaks and day trips) only one-sixth results from incoming tourist spending.

The short average length of stay of approximately 2.5 days is a result of the relatively high proportion of day-travellers from Belgium and Germany, and in addition most overseas visitors visit The Netherlands only as part of a wider European tour. The most important nationalities to visit The Netherlands are Germans (responsible for 45% of all overnight stays by foreigners), British (12%) and Belgians and North Americans (both 7%). Looking at the types of accommodation chosen by incoming tourists, hotels account for just over 50% of all overnight stays; in particular the British and Americans prefer to stay in hotels, whereas more than 70% of the Germans sleep in bungalows or on campsites. The tendency over the last five years, however, has been an increasing popularity of camping and bungalow facilities.

Of the main destination areas the four big cities Amsterdam, Rotterdam, The Hague and Utrecht account for 28% of all overnight stays by foreigners, mainly accommodated in hotels. The second main area which foreigners head for is the North Sea coast (19%), the majority accommodated on campsites and in bungalows.

The main reasons for foreigners in general to visit The Netherlands are landscape (46%), the coast and sandy beaches (36%), the cosy atmosphere and friendly people (34%) and the museums and cultural life (33%) (NBT, 1988).

Tourism Policy and Promotion

The significance tourism has to the country's economy cannot be neglected. In 1990 total tourism expenditure (including short breaks and day trips) in The Netherlands by domestic and incoming tourists was about DGL 31 billion, resulting in 140,000 man years direct employment and another 38,500 man years indirect employment. Including part-time employees approx 230,000 people are employed as a result of tourist expenditure, which was over 10% of the total employment in the private sector. From 1982–1989 tourist expenditure increased by 33%; at the same time tourism employment increased by 10%.

It is estimated that the Dutch tourism–recreation and hospitality sector represents between 40,000 and 45,000 firms, of which the majority are

174   *Jan R. Bergsma*

Table 10.6. Balance of trade in travel in The Netherlands.

	1980	1982	1984	1986	1988	1990[a]
Receipts (DGL billion)	3.9	4.8	5.4	5.5	5.7	6.6
Expenditure (DGL billion)	9.8	9.6	10.5	12.0	13.3	13.3
Deficit (DGL billion)	5.9	4.8	5.1	6.5	7.6	6.7

Source: Nederlandse bank (1990).
[a]NRIT (1991).

very small-sized (Ministerie van Economische zaken, 1990). As already indicated the home market is the most important. Only DGL 6.6 billion derive from incoming tourist expenditure. The Dutch spend more on their foreign holidays abroad than foreign tourists do in The Netherlands. In 1989 the Dutch spend DGL 13.3 billion in other countries, which resulted in a deficit on the balance of trade in travel of DGL 6.7 billion (Table 10.6).

In the 1970s the government decided to pursue an active tourism policy aimed at narrowing the yearly increase in the gap between import and export in tourism. Since 1979 three tourism policy papers have been published, each covering a period of five years. Apart from measures for improving the quality of the tourism product, a considerable amount of money has been made available for promotion, especially on well-chosen specific foreign markets (like Italy and Spain).

In the third tourism policy paper for 1990–1994 each year DGL 75 million is made available by the Dutch Ministry of Economic Affairs to realize their policy of which 50% is for promotional activities of The Netherlands Bureau for Tourism (NBT). The NBT is acting increasingly as an enterprise-oriented organization, trying to encourage the private tourist industry to contribute financially. Nowadays the NBT is financed about 50% by government subsidies, the other 50% is funded by the private travel and tourist industry. For the promotion of the Dutch tourist product on the Dutch market there is also an extensive network of tourist offices (VVV's i.e. Verenigingen voor Vreemdelingen Verkeer) at provincial and local level.

Particularly in the last three years the Dutch tourism policy combined with the activities of the NBT has had the effect it was aiming for: as a result of a considerable growth in the number of incoming tourists and tourist expenditure the deficit on the balance of trade in travel has decreased and is now at the same level (DGL 6.7 billion) as in 1987, after having reached its highest level in 1988 (DGL 7.6 billion).

TOURISM IN BELGIUM

Belgian Tourism Product and Tourist Industry

Many people have been to Belgium, but only a few have actually stayed in what for many travellers is nothing more than a transit country. Many north European tourists heading for France or Spain cross the Belgian borders. The little awareness of being in Belgium makes the country not very well known. Nevertheless Belgium (30,519 km^2; 9.9 million inhabitants) has four main tourist regions. The most important in number of visitor nights is the coastal area with more than 60 km of sandy beaches and its traditionally famous seaside resorts like Blankenberge, Knokke and Ostend. The three other areas are the heritage towns and historic cities like Antwerp, Brugge, Brussels, Gent en Leuven, the hilly forested Ardennes-region with the river Maas and the Campine (Kempen) region. Brussels not only attracts holidaymakers, but as 'European capital' also a considerable number of business travellers.

The main types of accommodation available in Belgium are hotels, establishments for social tourism, spa centres, holiday centres mainly for children and – although much less than in The Netherlands – campsites. Almost two-thirds of all 3416 accommodation establishments are hotels; in terms of capacity the hotels represent 17% of the total. The only 725 campsites, however, offer over 65% of the total accommodation capacity. Most of the hotels – in particular the bigger ones – are concentrated in the historic cities (offering over 80% of all available accommodation in these cities and offering over 40% of all hotel capacity in Belgium). Another

Table 10.7. Number and capacity of accommodation in Belgium (1990).

	Number of establishments	Capacity (number of beds) × 1000
Hotels	2123	93.7
Establishments for social tourism	413	69.2
Spa centres	32	4.8
Children's holiday centres	123	22.7
Camping sites	725	373.2
Total	3416	563.6

Source: Nationaal Instituut voor de Statistiek. (1991).

25% of the total hotel capacity is located along the coast but this represents only 14% of the total accommodation capacity in this region, which is dominated by campsites (70%). Most establishments for social tourism can be found in the Ardennes and Campine region (Table 10.7).

Tourist Behaviour of the Belgians

Holiday intensity

Belgians traditionally have not been as enthusiastic travellers as their neighbours to the north. On the contrary: for many years the holiday intensity of the Belgians was only 40%. Only at the end of the 1980s did the intensity begin to grow rapidly to today's 56%. With this figure Belgium still shows one of the lowest propensities to travel in Europe. Only relatively poor EC countries like Portugal and Ireland have a population that travels less. For them the average standard of living forms an important explanation, but this is not the case for the Belgians with their comparatively high purchasing power. The Belgians simply seem to have a 'lack of tradition in travel' and travelling and holidaymaking are not perceived as being as important as they are in many other European countries. Age and education appear to be significant determinants in Belgian travel behaviour. Belgians under 24 years show a considerably higher intensity rate (approx. 65%) than the average. Of all Belgians who have completed university education even 75% take a holiday at least once a year.

Of the estimated 5.5 million Belgian holidaymakers each year little more than half spend their holiday abroad. This group is overrepresented by young singles and couples without children. About one-fifth of each holiday is spent during the winter, of which about one-third is for skiing. Here a difference can be noticed in destination preference between the Flemish and the Walloons. The Walloons tend to go to France and Italy, whereas the Flemish are more attracted by Britain and Austria.

Destinations

Table 10.8 shows that in number of overnight stays the coast is the most important destination for domestic tourism (accounting for almost 60% of all domestic tourist nights). Ranking as very unimportant as domestic tourist destination are the historic cities which only register 454,000 overnight stays by Belgians.

Belgian holidaymakers abroad can mostly be found in France (approx. 3 million visitors each year, which is just below 45% of all international

Table 10.8. Belgium: number of overnight stays in different tourist regions (million) (1990).

	Domestic tourists	Incoming tourists	Total
Coast	13.9	2.2	16.1
Historic cities	0.5	5.1	5.6
Ardennes	4.3	1.6	5.9
Campine region	3.0	2.6	5.6
Other	2.3	1.3	3.6
Total	24.0	12.8	36.8

Source: Nationaal Instituut voor de Statistiek (1990).

visits by the Belgians); both Italy and Spain have 15%, followed by the UK and Germany (both 6.5%). It is remarkable how few Belgian tourists go to the Netherlands for their holiday (4%).

Accommodation

Of almost 24 million domestic tourist nights, 38% are spent on campsites and 17% in social tourism accommodation. About 11% of all domestic tourist nights are in hotels, which almost is twice as much as the situation in The Netherlands. Based on figures of the Westvlaams Ekonomisch Studiebureau WES and the EC Omnibus Survey (conducted in 1985) it is estimated that 37% of all overnight stays on foreign holidays by Belgians are in hotels, followed by rented houses/apartments (17%), and holiday villages/holiday camps (16%). About 15% of all holiday nights abroad are spent on campsites.

Means of transport

As in The Netherlands, not quite as marked, is the dominance of private car use, both for domestic and for foreign holidays. It is estimated that about 65% of the domestic holidays are car based, whereas for approximately 55% of all foreign holidays the car is taken (European Omnibus Survey, 1986). The market share of the train (about 10%) is the same for domestic and foreign holidays. Obviously air travel is especially significant in international travel: around 15% of all foreign holidays by the Belgians are expected to be based on transport by plane. There are some fairly

Table 10.9. Balance of trade in travel in BLEU.

	1984	1985	1986	1987	1988	1989
Receipts (billion BFR)	96	98	98	106	118	113
Expenditure (billion BFR)	113	121	130	141	162	160
Deficit (billion BFR)	17	23	32	35	44	47

Source: Toerisme (1989), VCGT.

marked differences for particular destinations: for example, over three-quarters of all foreign holidays to number one destination, France, are by private car, whereas flights have a share of less than 4%. The plane in particular (especially for charter flights) is popular for holidays to Spain.

Expenditure

Statistics on the balance of trade in travel apply to the Belgian Luxemburg Economic Union (BLEU) as a whole. Travel between Luxemburg and Belgium is considered as 'domestic' travel and therefore has no influence on the figures in Table 10.9.

In 1989 the total travel receipts of the BLEU were about 113 billion Belgian (= Luxemburg) francs (BFR). Total expenditure by out-going travellers was approx. BFR 160 billion. The deficit therefore was 47 billion francs. The deficit in 1984 was only one-third of that in 1989, which means that the gap between travel expenditure and travel receipts is widening very fast.

Incoming tourism

Of the almost 13 million overnight stays by incoming tourists, which is about one-third of all overnight stays in Belgium (see Table 10.8), about 4.5 million are thanks to Dutch tourists. The second important group of incoming tourists is Germans (almost 2 million) followed by the French and the British (both 1.2 million). North American tourists take the fifth place being responsible each year for about 600,000 overnight stays.

With regard to the type of accommodation (Table 10.10) we see that almost 70% of the Dutch tourists stay on campsites and accommodation for social tourism, while for example the majority of the British tourists stay in hotels (90% of all their overnight stays in Belgium) and only 4% on campsites. A result of these marked national differences in accommodation preference is that for the hotels the British market is by far the most

important foreign market (responsible for about one-sixth of all overnight stays by foreigners and for over 10% of all overnight stays in hotels); for the Belgian campsites the Dutch represent 72% of all their foreign clients. Of all tourists staying on campsites in Belgium one out of six has Dutch nationality. With regard to the location of most accommodation types it is not surprising that most of the Dutch incoming tourists can be found in the Campine and Ardennes region, where they represent almost 80% of all foreign tourists. On the other hand, in the historic cities the British are the most important group of foreigners. On the coast the Germans are over-represented, many of them using apartments and rented villas. Incoming tourism in general is especially important in the historic cities, where over 90% of all tourist nights are by foreigners. Foreign tourists are not so important in the coastal area, where they represent only 14% of all over-night stays.

Tourism Policy and Promotion

Because Belgium is divided into two language areas: Flanders (Vlaan-deren) where people speak Dutch (Flemish) and Wallonia where French is spoken, 'there are different administrative regions. Some affairs like foreign trade and finance are handled at a national level, whereas responsibility for most aspects of tourism is divided into both a Flemish and a Wallonian Ministry. In Wallonia, tourism is the responsibility of the CGT (Commisariat General du Tourisme) focusing on legislation and invest-ment and the OPT (Office de Promotion de Tourisme) dealing with marketing and promotion. In Flanders, the VCGT (Vlaams Commissariaat Generaal voor Toerisme) is responsible for all aspects. Each province in Belgium finances its own Federation Touristique'. The tourism policy in Belgium, which does not have a long tradition and is not yet very well established, aims mainly for 'quality improvement of the tourism product' and 'promotion and publicity in order to encourage tourism activity' (VCGT, 1992). Of the total annual budget of the VCGT of BFR 609 million in 1990 about BFR 180 million was meant for promotion. More than BFR 200 million each year is used for investment in infrastructure and for subsidies of particular accommodation types.

TOURISM IN LUXEMBURG

Tourism Product and Tourist Industry

The very small Grand Duchy of Luxemburg (2,589 km^2; 380,000 inhabi-tants) is divided into four main tourist regions: the Central area in which

Table 10.10. Overnight stays in different types of accommodation in Belgium (in million) in 1990.

Type	Domestic tourists	Incoming tourists	Total
Hotels	2.7	6.8	9.5
Establishments for social tourism	4.1	2.5	6.6
Children's holiday centres	1.1	0.05	1.2
Camping sites	9.3	2.8	12.1
Other[a]	6.7	0.7	7.4
Total	23.9	12.9	36.8

Source: Nationaal Instituut voor de Statistiek, 1991.
[a]Rooms for rent, villas, apartments, spa centres.

the capital of Luxemburg is located; the Ardennes region continuing north west into the Belgian Ardennes; the Mullerdall with well-known tourist towns as Echternach and finally the Moselle area in the most eastern part of the country.

The capital is not only important for holidaymakers, but also attracts a considerable number of business travellers because of the many EC services located there. The Ardennes region offers not only attractive scenery in summertime but also cross country skiing facilities in winter.

The major types of accommodation found in Luxemburg are hotels (including pensions and so-called 'auberges') and camping sites, of which the latter account for 80% of the total capacity. Most hotel capacity can be found in the capital city of Luxemburg and its surroundings. Most camping sites are located in the Ardennes region. Both types of accommodation account for about half the total number of overnight stays (Table 10.11).

Tourist Behaviour of the Luxemburgers

Luxemburg has a very well-established travel market and the Luxemburgers show a higher propensity to travel abroad than anyone else in Europe. Of course the small size of the country is an important factor for explaining the dominance of international travel, but it is also important that one quarter of the 380,000 inhabitants are in fact foreigners.

If we look at domestic and international travel the overall holiday intensity of the Luxembourgers (60%) is a little higher than the European average. Of the total number of holidays almost 95% are spent abroad and only some 5% domestically. Despite the small population the Luxemburg

Table 10.11. Luxemburg: accommodation and number of overnight stays (1990).

	Number of establishments	Capacity (number of beds × 1000)	Overnight stays (million)
Hotels	401	7.9	1.2
Campsites	127	50.6	1.2
Other	43	2.8	0.3
Total	571	61.3	2.7

Source: Ministère des classes moyennes et du tourisme (1992).

travel market is still rather attractive for the travel industry, because around 10% of all international trips are to long-haul destinations. Futhermore, Luxemburgers tend to use the services of tour operators and travel agencies more than any other nationality in Europe. Domestically the favourite destination in number of arrivals is the centre region, although absolute numbers are very low. The Moselle region appears to be the most significant region in number of domestic tourist nights (60% of total). The average length of stay of domestic holidaymakers in hotels is about six nights; in the Moselle region, however, the average length of stay in hotels and pensions is over 15 days. On campsites the average length of stay of domestic holidaymakers is 14 nights.

Related to the high proportion of holidaymakers that go abroad, and the importance of far-away destinations, is the popularity of the plane as means of transport. Of all holidays by Luxemburgers about one-fifth are normally by plane. For the same reason road travel is less than the European average.

Incoming Tourism

Together with the dominance of outgoing tourism the importance of incoming tourism gives Luxemburg a very international character. Of all nights spent by tourists in Luxemburg 93% are by incoming tourists. In hotels this percentage is even higher (Table 10.12).

The most important incoming tourists are the Dutch, who account for almost half of the total number of foreigners. On campsites the Dutch account for over 70% of all overnight stays by incoming tourists. Overall incoming tourists have an equal preference for hotel accommodation and campsites.

Most incoming tourists go to the Centre region and the capital. In number of arrivals as well as in number of overnight stays this region

Table 10.12. Luxemburg: incoming tourists per type of accommodation° (% of overnight stays).

	Hotels	Camping sites	Total
Germans	11	3	7
Belgians	28	20	24
French	10	1	6
Italians	3	–	2
Dutch	20	72	48
British	6	2	4
North Americans	5	–	3
Others	17	2	6
Total (=100%)	1.1	1.1	2.2

Source: Ministère des classes moyennes et du tourisme (1992).
°Other types of accommodation have not been taken into account.

receives almost two-thirds of all incoming tourists. In hotels the average length of stay is about two nights; on campsites incoming tourists stay just over five nights.

Tourism Policy and Promotion

In Luxemburg tourism policy is the prime responsibility of the Ministry for Tourism. The national Tourist Office is particularly involved in tourism promotion and publicity. As in The Netherlands, the Ministry publishes five-year programmes in which the tourism policy is outlined. In the fourth five-year programme (1988–1992) a total budget of 650 million Luxemburg francs were made available mainly to be used for investment in tourist infrastructure and in the modernization of hotels. In the national tourism policy special attention is paid to the (further) development of congress tourism, principally in the capital.

CONCLUSION

Despite the fact that tourism statistics are not based on the same methodology and definitions it is easy to conclude that, from the point of view of the tourism product, the tourist industry, travel behaviour or tourism policy, the three Benelux countries show a great number of marked differences.

In The Netherlands and Luxemburg, where propensity to travel is high, tourism is a much more established phenomenon than in Belgium, where tourism is not perceived as being as important as in the other two countries. This is reflected in the as yet not very strongly developed travel and tourism industry in Belgium and the short tradition of tourism policy-making.

In The Netherlands domestic tourism compared to incoming tourism plays a more dominant role than in Belgium and Luxemburg. In Luxemburg, where tourism is more international than in any other European country, domestic tourism is very insignificant compared to the number of visitors from abroad and the number of outgoing tourists.

Because of the Dutch eagerness to travel abroad the deficit on the balance of trade in travel is considerably higher than it is for Belgium and Luxemburg. In Holland the receipts are less than half the total expenditure; although decreasing in the Belgian Luxemburg Economic Union (BLEU) receipts still account for over 70% of total travel expenditure.

Another significant difference is the accommodation profile. In The Netherlands, campsites represent almost 50% of the total number of accommodation establishments, whereas in Belgium and Luxemburg this figure is only just over 20%. The Dutch holidaymakers love camping, not only in their own country but also abroad. A considerable number of customers on campsites in Belgium and Luxemburg appear to be Dutch. It is remarkable that for Belgium and Luxemburg the Dutch belong to the most important incoming tourists in the number of overnight stays, whereas for the Belgians and Luxemburgers The Netherlands is not a very popular destination. Even in the area of promotion there is not much similarity between the three countries. The Benelux is not promoted as one destination; each country has its own promotion strategy and is carrying out its own activities.

After considering all the differences between the three countries, which in some respects are much bigger than between many other European countries, it is in fact very hard to find any common features. Maybe in an economic sense it is logical to deal with the Benelux as an entity; but regarding tourism it would be rather artificial, because in this perspective the Benelux is no more than the simple abbreviation of BElgium, The NEtherlands and LUXemburg, these being three very different nations.

BIBLIOGRAPHY

Anonymous (1988) *Belgium and Luxembourg*, International Tourism Reports, No 1. Economist Intelligence Unit, London, pp. 59–76.
Anonymous (1988) *The Netherlands*, International Tourism Reports, No. 2 Economist Intelligence Unit, London, pp. 5–20.

Ashworth, G.J. and Bergsma, J.R. (1988) New policies for tourism: opportunities or problems. *Journal of Economic and Social Geography*, KNAG, Amsterdam.

Bergsma, J.R. (1986) *Toeristische bedrijvigheid en de vestigingsplaats.* Serie onderzoekscerslagen GIRUG, Groningen.

Bergsma, J. (1991) *De verblijfsektor in Nederland.* Internal publication Netherlands Institute of Tourism and Transport Studies, Breda.

Cockerell, N. (1987) Netherlands outbound. *Travel and Tourism Analyst* November, 25–36.

Cockerell, N. (1988) Belgium and Luxembourg outbound. *Travel and Tourism Analyst* 2, 51–65.

European Omnibus Survey (1986) *European Holidays*, paper on conference of the International Geographical Union, Palma de Mallorca, pp. 25–31.

Ministère des classes moyennes et du tourisme (1992) *Rapport d'activité 1991.* Luxembourg.

Ministerie van Economische zaken (1990) *Ondernemen in Toerisme.* SDU Uitgeverij, 's Gravenhage.

Nationaal Instituut voor de Statistiek (1991) *Statistiek van het toerisme en het hotelwezen, jaar 1990.* Brussel.

NBT (Nationaal Bureau voor Toerisme) (1988) *Toerisme, trends en toekomst.* Leidschendam.

NRIT (Nederlands Research Instituut voor Recreatie en Toerisme) (1991) *Trendrapport 1990.* Breda.

Office National du tourisme (1990) *Orientations futures du tourisme luxembourgeois.* Luxemburg.

Pinder, D. (1988) The Netherlands: tourist development in a crowded society. In: Shaw, G. and Williams, A.M. (eds) *Tourism and Economic Development: Western European perspectives.* Belhaven Press, London, pp. 214–229.

VCGT (Vlaams Commissariaat Generaal voor Toerisme) (1990) *Toerisme 1989, jaarverslag.* Brussel.

11

TOURISM IN SCANDINAVIA

Peter Aderhold, Jon Teigland, Anders Steene and Jan Koskinen

INTRODUCTION

Scandinavia is normally regarded as one united, homogeneous region. This is especially true in countries located a long way from the area.

On one hand this view is correct. The Scandinavian countries are all 'at the top of Europe' and have a common history, cultural heritage and share a high standard of living.

On the other hand, there are important, fundamental differences between these countries including, for instance, the differences in size and the marked difference in their landscapes, scenery and wildlife. The Danish countryside is flat and 'cultivated', whereas Norway, Sweden and Finland have large areas of untouched natural countryside, fjords, mountains, lakes etc. Seen from a tourist's point of view, this makes each country an entirely separate 'tourist product', each with an entirely different scope of experience and different target groups.

So, from a marketing point of view, Scandinavia cannot be treated as one product or one tourist destination – at least not on the major tourist markets in central Europe. But on markets located a great distance from Scandinavia, such as North America or Japan for example, a joint marketing strategy would make sense. These tourists, who travel such long distances, are usually primarily interested in big cities, which can be treated as a more homogeneous product.

As a tourist-generating market for other tourist products and destinations, Scandinavia cannot be described as a single market area either. Of course, there are a number of similarities between the Scandinavian languages, but the differences are too great to talk of one common Scandinavian language which could be used as the basis for promotional material, for example. In terms of media, each country also has its own 'media landscape and culture', so implementing a united Scandinavian marketing and media strategy would be almost impossible.

The objective of this brief analysis of tourism in Scandinavia is to illuminate this dichotomy, by describing both the similarities and the differences between the countries comprising Scandinavia. This chapter is therefore designed to give a wide perspective of the four countries involved, in terms of their most relevant tourism data. It cannot be considered as a complete analysis. And when reading the tables shown in this chapter, it is worth bearing in mind that the statistical information from the different countries does not lend itself to direct comparison due to the different methods, definitions and time scales used.

This chapter was compiled by four researchers, each of whom obtained the respective data and future development trends from the country in which he lives.

The analysis focuses on three central aspects:

- The economic scope of tourism in Scandinavia and its implications.
- The Scandinavian countries as tourist-generating countries.
- Trends for future development in the four countries.

GENERAL BACKGROUND DATA

The region's geographical structure and the considerable differences in the sizes of the countries are shown clearly in Fig. 11.1 and Table 11.1. With only 43,000 km², Denmark is just a tenth the size of the other three countries, which are all between 300,000 and 500,000 km², making them among the geographically largest countries in Europe.

In terms of population, the countries are more similar. Sweden has a population of 8.6 million, while the other three countries have between 4 and 5 million inhabitants. A total of 23 million people inhabit the four Scandinavian countries.

Economic differences are also less apparent than the geographical points mentioned previously. Denmark, Norway and Finland all have a gross national product in the region of US$100 billion. However, Sweden's GNP is almost twice this amount.

THE DIMENSION OF TOURISM IN SCANDINAVIA, AND ITS ECONOMIC IMPORTANCE

The scope of tourism is usually defined as the number of tourists, and the overnight stays they make, combined with the income from travel currency generated by foreign tourists (see Table 11.2).

Scandinavia

Fig. 11.1. Map of Scandinavia.

These data, however, which are normally published in international tourism statistics, fall far short of giving a realistic view of the tourism industry, as the following comments will show:

• The number of nights spent in rented summerhouses accounts for a considerable proportion of tourism in Scandinavia – in Denmark, 58% of all nights spent by foreign tourists are spent in rented summerhouses. Unfortunately, this figure appears only in the Danish statistics.

Table 11.1. General data.

	Total	Denmark	Norway	Sweden	Finland
Size of country (1000 km^2)	1.255	43	387	487	338
Population (million)	23.0	5.1	4.3	8.6	5.0
Gross National Product 1991 (billion US$)	548	105	100	227	116

Table 11.2. Dimensions of tourism (1991).

	Denmark	Norway	Sweden	Finland
Nights spent by national and international tourists in registered accommodation (million)				
1. National (domestic)	46	18	28	11
	17	12	23	8
2. International				
Other Scandinavian countries	29	6	5	3
Other countries	6	2	2	1
	23	4	3	2
Nights after categories of accommodation (million)				
Hotel/holiday centre etc.	12	12	17	9
Camping	13	5	10	2
Summerhouse	18	n.a.	n.a.	n.a.
Others (youth hostel, etc.)	3	n.a.	1	n.a.
Tourism receipts/expenditures (billion US$)				
Tourism receipts	3.6	1.8	2.7	1.0
Tourism expenditures	3.5	3.5	6.2	2.5

Equivalent figures are not available for the other Scandinavian countries. Therefore, the figures in Table 11.2 give a rather misleading view of the volume of tourism in these countries, since one of the most important forms of overnight stay is not included.

- Summerhouse owners spending their holidays (of five days or more) in their own summerhouses are also not included. However, this form of holiday is very common throughout Scandinavia, especially in Sweden and Norway, where it plays an important role in the holiday cultures fo these countries and the very high holiday intensity.

- The income and expenses from travel currency are also distorted by a number of factors. This means that the figures can be used only in a very limited way to measure tourism. The figures also contain factors which have nothing to do with tourism (border trade, for example, which is an important factor for all four countries). The methods used for registration and calculation also vary somewhat from country to country.

The figures in Table 11.2, therefore, only go part of the way towards giving a complete description of the Scandinavian volume of tourism. As far as Denmark is concerned, the figures are very realistic, because all forms of overnight stay are either systematically registered or estimated on the basis of in-depth studies. The figures for the other three countries, however, represent only a proportion of the actual tourist volume.

Another way of describing the dimensions of tourism takes into account, in economic terms, various criteria, as shown in Table 11.3.

The capacity of overnight stays gives a certain picture of the size of the tourism sectors in each of the four countries:

- Sweden seems to have the greatest accommodation capacity of the four countries (measured as hotel capacity and camping sites), followed by Norway, with Denmark ranking third. Again, there is some uncertainty as to the capacity of summerhouses rented out to tourists. In Denmark about 35,000 summerhouses are officially registered for rent, yet careful estimations indicate a further 15,000 are unregistered but rented out regularly on a commercial basis. The situation in the other countries is somewhat similar, but no estimates concerning unregistered rented summerhouses are available.

  In other words, the figures for hotels and camping sites are very accurate, but the data concerning the important aspect of summerhouse capacity are very uncertain.

- The number of employees working in the tourist sector is estimated to be between 60,000 and 90,000 in Denmark, Norway and Finland, and about 120,000 in Sweden. In addition to this direct employment, there is also a substantial indirect employment effect to consider. Denmark, for example, has an estimated 30,000–40,000 people employed

Table 11.3. Economic dimensions of tourism industry 1990/91.

	Denmark	Norway	Sweden	Finland
Capacity of accommodation				
Number of hotels	950	1170	2337	762
Number of hotel rooms (1000)	35	56	75	42
Number of camping sites	521	800	700	348
Number of summerhouses (1000)	200	350	625	354
Number of summerhouses to rent (1000)	35	25	30	10
Number of (direct) employees in tourism (rough estimation only) (1000)	60–90	60–90	120	80
Percentage of total job market (rough estimation only)	3.5–4.0	3.0–4.0	4.5–5.0	3.2–3.5
Tourism-generated turnover (billion US$) (rough estimation only)	6.5	4.0	15.0	3.3
Estimation of economic importance of				
Domestic tourism (%)	50	70	85	78
Incoming tourism (%)	50	30	15	22

Table 11.4. Tourist market 1990/91.

	Total	Denmark	Norway	Sweden	Finland
Adult population (million)	18.0	4.2	3.3	6.5	4.0
Number of holidaymakers (million)[a]	12.3	2.8	2.4	5.0	2.1
Net holiday intensity (%)[b]	68	66	74	77	58
Number of holidays (million)	31.5	4.0	5.6	18.0	3.9
Domestic holiday trips (million)	18.7	1.5	4.3	10.0	2.3
Holidays abroad (million)	13.5	2.5	1.3	8.0	1.7

Sources:
Denmark: population 16 years +, Danish Travel Survey (1991).
Norway: population between 16–79 years, Norwegian Holiday Survey (1991).
Sweden: population 20 years +, Turistdata of Swedish Tourist Board (1991).
Finland: MEK, A: 68, Finnish Tourist Board (1990).
Notes:
[a]At least 1 holiday per year lasting at least 5 days (4 nights).
[b]Percentage of holiday makers in relation to adult population.

indirectly, as well as the 60,000–90,000 people employed directly in the tourist branch.

- Tourism's influence on the national job market of each country appears to be about equal, i.e. between 3.5% and 5%.
- Estimations of turnover generated by tourism in these four countries shows that Sweden has the largest turnover with approx. US$15 billion. The turnover in the other three countries is considerably lower.
- 'Domestic tourism' and 'incoming tourism' are also aspects in which the four countries differ. In Denmark these are of equal importance, yet in the other three countries, 'domestic tourism' is of greater importance, which follows, since these countries have an extensive share of domestic travel.

The figures stated above should also be treated with caution. They are, in some cases, rather general estimations based on studies which often differ greatly in purpose and methodological approach. Nevertheless, the figures give a wider perspective of the scope and impact of tourism in the four Scandinavian countries.

SCANDINAVIA AS A TOURIST-GENERATING MARKET

Due to their high standard of living, the people of Scandinavia are a good potential market for many other tourist countries. With 23 million inhabitants and a very high holiday intensity, Scandinavia is one of the most interesting tourist-generating regions for many countries both inside and outside Europe (Table 11.4).

About 68% of all adult Scandinavians (12.3 million of the total 18 million adults living in the four countries) take at least one holiday lasting a minimum of five days every year.

The four countries differ on some points as shown in Table 11.4.

- With 77% and 74% respectively, Sweden and Norway have the highest net holiday intensity in Europe except Switzerland.
- Denmark's holiday intensity (66%) is similar to that of Germany and England, whereas Finland's is a little lower.

These 12.3 million holidaymakers take a total of 31.5 million holidays, i.e. 2.6 holidays per holidaymaker (travel frequency).

This very high travel frequency must be seen in the context of the high number of private summerhouses in Scandinavia (more than 1.5 million private summerhouses, as shown in Table 11.3). These holidays (of at least five days) in private summerhouses are registered in the representative tourist surveys, but they are not registered in the official statistics of nights spent in the respective countries, as mentioned previously. The special

Table 11.5. Destinations 1990/91.

	Total	Denmark	Norway	Sweden	Finland
Number of holiday trips (million)	31.5	4.0	5.6	18.0	3.9
Domestic holiday trips (million)	18.7	1.5	4.3	10.0	2.3
Holidays abroad (million)	13.5	2.5	1.3	8.0	1.7
Other Scandinavian countries	6.3	0.5	0.5	5.0	0.3
Other European countries	6.4	1.7	0.7	2.7	1.3
Outside Europe	0.8	0.3	0.1	0.3	0.1

Sources:
Denmark: population 16 years +, Danish Travel Survey (1991).
Norway: population between 16–79 years, Norwegian Holiday Survey (1991).
Sweden: population 20 years +, Turistdata of Swedish Tourist Board (1991).
Finland: MEK, A: 68 Finnish Tourist Board (1990).

Scandinavian summerhouse culture means that it is common for most families to take one or more holidays (of more than four days) in their own or friends' summerhouses. Since this form of holiday is comparatively cheap, most families spend an additional one or two holidays in other Scandinavian or European countries. This is reflected in the ration of 'domestic holiday trips' and 'holidays abroad'. Denmark differs noticeably in comparison with the other three countries: while the majority of Danes (approx. two-thirds) spend holidays abroad, more than half the population of the other countries spend their holidays in their own country.

This trend is due to more than just the summerhouse culture mentioned previously, since this culture is less widespread in Denmark than it is in the other three northern Scandinavian countries. Size and location also play important roles. A comparatively short journey will take a Dane abroad, whereas inhabitants of the other three countries have to cover large distances to qualify for the same category. This also affects the travel destinations of the four nationalities, as shown in Table 11.5.

Nearly half of all holidays abroad made by Scandinavians were spent in Scandinavia. Again, marked differences are apparent. While only approx. 20% of all Danes and 17% of all Finnish holidaymakers spent their holidays in other Scandinavian countries, more than 60% of all Swedish holidaymakers went to a neighbouring Scandinavian country (5 million of a total 8 million holidaymakers). And almost 40% of Norwegians took inter-Scandinavian holidays.

As many holidaymakers spent their holidays in Europe (6.4 million) as those who spent their holidays in Scandinavia (6.3 million). Of holidays spent abroad, the proportion of holidaymakers travelling to the European countries south of Scandinavia is highest for Finns and Danes (76% and 68% respectively). For Norway this proportion is over 50%, though only about one-third of Swedish holidaymakers visit other European countries. In spite of this, since the population of Sweden is so large, this group, consisting of 2.7 million travellers, comprises by far the largest group of Scandinavian holidaymakers travelling to Europe.

A total of approximately 800,000 Scandinavians travel to countries outside Europe every year. With approx. 300,000 long-distance travellers each, Denmark and Sweden form the largest markets, whereas Norway and Finland each have a long-distance market volume of approximately 100,000 people.

FUTURE DEVELOPMENT TRENDS

The future development trends for these four Scandinavian countries over the next 5–10 years, will be described individually according to the following main perspectives:

- Development trends relating to the travel behaviour of the respective populations in terms of quantity and quality, e.g. outgoing tourism in the four respective countries.
- Expectations of the Scandinavian countries concerning tourism development from other markets to the respective Scandinavian countries, i.e. incoming tourism development in terms of quantity and quality.
- General trends concerning tourism development in the four countries (attitudes to tourism, the environment, etc.).

Denmark

The behaviour of Denmark's population is expected to develop in the following ways over the next 5–10 years.

- The net holiday intensity is expected to increase gradually from close to 66% to 70–75%.
- The travel frequency is expected to increase comparatively quickly from the present 1.4 to about 2.0 holidays per holidaymaker per year.
- This increase in frequency and consequent increase in the number of two and three-time travellers will benefit inland tourism, i.e. the number of inland travellers will increase, but the dominance of travellers heading abroad (1990: 63%) will continue, measured in market share.
- Danes are expected to become more critical of forms of mass tourism and certain destinations. They are likely to avoid regions of mass tourism in increasing numbers. (In just the past 3 years, the market shares of Spain, Greece and Italy have dropped from 40% of all foreign holidays to 26%.) Likewise, Danes will become increasingly aware of the environment, preferring holiday destinations with unspoiled environments.

The following trends are expected to affect the development of incoming tourism in Denmark:

- Generally speaking, interest from southern parts of Europe is expected to increase, which will benefit Denmark. One basis for this expectation is that the inhabitants of the south European countries will become progressively more experienced travellers and will expand their horizons towards the North. Another reason is that the Northern countries have a cleaner environment and are characterized to a greater extent by forms of free individual tourism, which are expected to become more sought after.
- The tourist product 'individual holiday cottage', which already comprises 58% of foreign demand in Denmark, is expected to

continue to be the most sought after tourist product in Denmark in the future.

- Efforts are underway to extend the season from the present 3–4 months to 6–8 months a year and are expected to be successful.

Generally speaking, during the past 3–5 years, Danes have become more aware of the economic opportunities tourism offers as a industry. This development is expected to continue in future years.

Recently, so-called 'networks' have been created and supported systematically, to develop and formalize cooperation between separate tourist attractions on a local and regional level. This development has just been started and is expected to remain a central subject for tourism politics at both a national and regional level.

Danes are generally very aware of their environment and consistently apply this awareness to tourist development, more than was previously the case.

During the past 3–5 years, a number of tourism training schemes have been started up. These are expected to develop as a result of the more professional approach being adopted in the tourist branch.

Norway

Change in supply

Norway experienced an economic boom during 1984–1986 resulting from high oil prices. This created a situation with a surplus of both accommodation facilities and some kinds of capital-intensive attractions, such as alpine ski areas. Only a proportion of the total accommodation capacity is being utilized. This figure has been decreasing for several years, and in 1990 was as little as 35% for tourist establishments with 20 beds or more. Only 20–30% of the hotels are therefore doing economically well. Most of the others have lost all their own capital, and bankruptcy has become a common occurrence.

Consequently, the building boom of new accommodation facilities has stopped, except in the region around Lillehammer, which is to host the Winter Olympic Games in 1994. The expected growth of tourism in the Olympic region is, however, not yet visible. If lasting growth is not generated, the existing surplus in the region of the capital and most other parts of Norway will simply be compounded by the substantial growth in facilities around Lillehammer.

Change in demand

The economic depression in Norway and increasing prices in Sweden have reduced the Norwegian tourist traffic abroad for the first time since 1970. The level of holiday-taking has, however, not changed, which means that there has been a slight increase in Norwegian demand for holidays in Norway. These economic problems have merely reduced people's ability to travel abroad, not their interest in doing so.

The Norwegian tourist demand is unlikely to increase significantly during the next 5–10 years. The net travel intensity is already high, problems of unemployment are growing and will probably last for several years and an increase in net income, because of changes in the tax system, will probably be used to reduce loans as well as promote travel abroad again.

The change in foreign demand has been closely connected with the increased holiday-taking in Germany and Denmark during the last half of the 1980s. In the next 5–10 years, this increase is likely to slow down, and the flow of tourists to Norway will be linked with changes in the economies of neighbouring countries and those in the EC.

If tourist demand for environmental quality continues to grow, foreign demand may also increase. The decision to stop tax-free shopping between the EC countries, and the proposed bridge connecting Denmark and Sweden may, on the other hand, reduce this demand and change the geographical pattern.

The Norwegian dependency on income from oil makes it very difficult to give accurate projections. Changes in oil prices because of increased oil production in Kuwait, Iraq and/or Russia may change the Norwegian economy both substantially and relatively quickly. This would also have an impact on domestic and foreign tourist demand.

Sweden

Until now, increased productivity in the industrial countries has resulted in increased leisure time. A sixth week has already been added to the existing five week holiday time in Sweden, so at least in the near future, time is unlikely to restrict the growth of Sweden's travel and tourism. Most of the more long-term prognoses have also supported the idea that the amount of leisure will continue to develop and increase. With more leisure time and above all longer holidays, people are choosing to divide their holiday allowance up, taking several shorter holidays at different times of the year. A great deal of evidence points to the fact that Swedes also prefer to split their holiday time into a greater number of shorter trips.

The new consumer is characterized as being highly educated, with international experience. In practical terms this means they are articulate and demanding, possessing a clear view of the choices available (including the international perspective) and are less fixed in their preferences. As pronounced individualists, these new consumers have a desire to mark their identity and individuality.

Retired people make up another, major group of tourists. These elderly people are now increasingly better off in terms of economic situation and health. This physical mobility means that they continue to travel until they reach much greater ages than was previously possible.

Vacation travel is bound to decrease to a certain extent in the near future because of the current economic recession. However, the cheaper holiday forms will probably not be affected. Coach travel will be perceived as an increasingly attractive means of transport in comparison with charter flights, which in future will be used to cover longer distances to Eastern destinations.

A study of future trends in development was completed in the autumn of 1991 at the Institute for Tourism-economic Research College in Kalmar. A summary of the main points likely to occur from now until the year 2000 is given below.

- The population will be older, in good health and with good economic resources to travel.
- Summerhouse stays, boating tourism, visiting relatives and friends, as well as one day trips, will all increase in popularity.
- Tourism by car will also continue to increase, especially in the 'new' Eastern Europe.
- Charter travel to distant destinations will also increase.
- Coach tourism will continue to increase and will be seen as a pleasant way to travel and socialize.
- The customer groups will be generally more geared toward activities. Shopping continues to be a popular activity.
- Demands for safety during the trip and at the destination will increase.
- Sweden's power of attraction as a destination in the year 2000 will be based on nature, culture, the environment, history, winter sports and different activity arrangements.
- The popular international destinations will continue to attract tourists, even in the future, since sunshine and swimming will continue to be popular products.
- The traveller of the future will demand products with higher standards of quality.
- Leisure travel nationally and internationally will be characterized by varied combinations of transport, i.e. tourists will fly long distances and then rent a car on reaching their destination.

Finland

During the past decade, the average growth rate of tourism in Finland was 5%, measured as nights spent in registered accommodation. The number of domestic tourists has grown from 5.2 million in 1980 to 8.2 million in 1990. At the same time, the number of tourists from abroad has grown from 1.8 to 2.7 million. The share of international tourists, however, has declined by 3% compared to the early 1980s, and in 1990 was 23%.

Large investments have been made in accommodation facilities, restaurants and other services throughout the tourist industry. The capacity of accommodation has increased by 55%, which translates as an additional 15,000 hotel rooms. Unfortunately, demand has not kept up with this investment rate – it has actually declined – resulting in a situation where utilization of accommodation facilities has dropped to 45% or even less in some hotels and areas.

The goals for future development of tourism in Finland are:

- Primarily to improve profitability of the tourist industry in order to safeguard the welfare of the industry and jobs of people employed in the branch.
- To increase net income from international tourism by 4% by the end of 1996 and by 7% by the end of the decade.
- To increase domestic tourists' use of tourist services by 3% annually.

Strategies to achieve these goals:

- Reinforce the competitiveness of the tourist industry.
- Enhance Finland's attractiveness and alter and promote Finland's profile as a tourist destination.
- Segment the marketing of tourist products and services.

SUMMARY

The aim of this chapter has been to provide a brief overview of the key figures characterizing the region in general and the four countries in particular in terms of various dimensions of tourism, and the structure of the tourist markets in Denmark, Norway, Sweden and Finland. Some development trends for these countries have also been outlined. As mentioned, some of the figures in this analysis have to be treated with caution because of different methods of measurement used or lack of data, especially regarding the registration of nights spent in summerhouses. However, it provides an overall idea of the scope and structure of tourism in Scandinavia.

SOURCES OF DATA

Denmark

Aderhold, P. and Merser, H. (1992) *The Danish Travel Survey 1991*. Main results published by the Danish Tourist Board, Research Department.

Danish Tourist Board, *Dansk Turisme 2/91*.

Danmarks Statistik, *Data on Denmark 1991*, Volume 11, August 1991.

Danmarks Statistik, *Statistical Yearbook*, 95th edn, September 1991.

Danmarks Statistik, *Statistical Ten-year Review*. 82nd edn, September 1991.

Reiseliv i Norden (1983) Udarbeidet pa opprdag av Nordisk Ministerrad København.

Norway

Central Bureau of Statistics of Norway (1991) *Statistical Yearbook*. Oslo.

Teigland, J. (1990) Nordmenns feriereiser i 1970 og 1980-arene. Norwegian Institute for Nature Research, Lillehammer.

Haukeland *et al.* (1991) Ferieundersøkelsen 1991. Norwegian Institute for Transportation Research, Oslo.

Sweden

Statens Industriverk (1987) Hotell och Restaurangnäringen – Probleminvertering. Stockholm.

Statistiska Centralbyrån (1991) Statistisk årsbok. Stockholm.

Swedish Tourist Board (1991) Tourist Data Base. Annual publication, Stockholm.

Finland

Finnish Tourist Board (1991) Tourism Statistics.

Finnish Tourist Board (1992) Finland Summerland.

Suomen Tiedostopalvelut Oy, *Reisen in Finnland.*

12

TOURISM IN FRANCE

Michel Bauer

SUBJECTIVE AND OBJECTIVE IMPORTANCE OF TOURISM IN FRANCE

Tourism is an old tradition in France. As early as the end of the 18th century, wealthy English people included in their 'Grand Tour' the countries of France and Italy. Therefore, the French style of tourism is different from those of the new tourism countries such as Spain, Greece or Tunisia. In France the tourist will find an old network of hotels and restaurants scattered around the country and sometimes this is old-fashioned. It provides customers with an older heritage of cathedrals, castles, spas or a newer one of seaside facilities or winter sport resorts. But all these components are not really a tourist product from the marketing point of view. These components are sold in most cases directly to the customer, on the spot, without being included in a package tour, without tour operators, without distributors or intermediaries. On the one hand, a good deal of tourism is made up of activities spread around the country, organized in very small or medium-sized enterprises. On the other hand, a large majority of French people are not interested in the development of mass tourism.

Until recently, the French considered tourism either as the rule of hospitality (in their second homes or in some relatives' houses), or as a social conquest against their employers (paid holidays from 1936). It was also considered as a very agreeable but not very serious activity (see pictures of Patrice Lécomte: 'les bronzés' and 'les bronzés font du ski'). In his speech of 15 January 1992, the French Minister of Tourism confirmed this opinion: 'In France, we have been considering tourism for too long a time as a simple leisure activity and a possible direction of development for a poor country'.

Nevertheless, the French are proud of their buildings, and 'the prince' may launch new 'cathedrals' to be shown to foreigners or to the masses: the Beaubourg centre built under President Pompidou receives 8 million people a year (more than the Eiffel Tower with 6 million), La Cité des Sciences 5 million, Le Musée du Louvre with its new pyramid 3.5 million, le musée d'Orsay 2 million, l'Arche de la Defense etc. built, restored or developed under President Mitterand. Visiting some of them was free.

A reluctance to commercialize systematically tourism activities is apparent in a special issue of the magazine *Autrement* on 'les vacances' (the holidays – Paris 1990). Initiated in 1936, 'the holidays for everyone' concept was further developed in the social sector after the Second World War. The sociologist Dumazedier (1962) and some former Youth Hostel members set up a joint group ('Peuple et Culture'). They presented a new approach to holidaymaking called the 3 D: 'Developpement' (cultural development), 'Délassement' (relaxation), 'Divertissement' (entertainment). Tourism development has been based in many countries on the 3 S (sea, sun, sand) concept. In France, on the contrary, the modern tourist industry finds its origins in the 3 D concept: for example the 'Club Med' which was initially a non-profit organization. The magazine *Les Vacances* summarizes: 'The objective is not commercial: the point is to enable those who have never been on holiday before to have one.'

In 1962 students of Hautes Etudes Commercials (HEC), the leading Business Administration School in France, wrote a book *The New Tourists*. They noticed that 'for many people, tourism is a second-rank phenomenon with no special solutions. Tourism is not a system different from its components. This is the real obstacle to a development of tourism'.

A generation later, French society is deeply transformed. Capitalism and the consumer society are embraced, at least in the media. Contemporary heroes include Tapie (the man in the Adidas take-over) in the

Table 12.1. Breakdown of consumption linked to stays in France (1990).

Consumption of	%
Paid accommodation	23.4
Free accommodation	13.8
Catering	19.5
Food and Beverage	20.4
Leisure services	9.6
Other services	9.7
Consumer durables	3.6

Source: Ministère du Tourisme (1991).

business world, or Trigano of Club Med and Jacques Maillot of Nouvelles
Frontieres in the tourism industry. After the current economic 'crisis',
electors and politicians wish to develop new jobs and export activities to
exploit the consumption of goods and services associated with tourism
(Table 12.1).

Progressively, the French have realized that tourism provides an
opportunity to create jobs and to develop exports even if the importance of
the tourism industry is proportionally less in France than for example in
Spain or Austria.

The leisure and tourism industry is faced with the difficulty of
operating independently and being considered as an autonomous industry.
Bernard Preel, director of an important consultancy organization, criticizes
those involved in tourism in France, whether local politicians or tourism
professionals (Credoc, 1992): '36,000 mayors and 500,000 people elected
in local authorities think and behave as managers in tourism, and the same
goes for the most important firms of the engineering and building sectors
which earn a lot of money with the works and facilities in tourism'. For
them leisure and tourism are considered merely as a by-product of town
and country planning, of the building industry and more recently of the
marketing of towns and regions. This harsh verdict, from one of the leading
specialists in tourism in France, is further proof that tourism is not
considered to be a serious and independent industry, but for reasons other
than those of 30 years ago. Why, in spite of this continuing attitude, has
France always been one of the leading countries for tourism in the world
and has been the leader in Europe for the last three years in terms of
incoming tourism?

STATISTICS

The statistics presented here are taken from the 1991 edition of the official
abridged book published annually by the Ministry of Tourism. Basic data
on geographical aspects of France are shown in Table 12.2.

International Flows

For a long time France has been the co-leader with Italy for incoming
tourism in Europe. In the early days of tourism the preeminence of the
French language and culture were key reasons for this; while this period is
now over, it still influences and attracts many tourists. French people were
astonished to see so many visitors arriving for the festivities to mark the
bicentennary of the French revolution. France again took first place in
Europe on this occasion.

Table 12.2. General geographical data on France.

A hexagon: length north/south and east/west: 900 km

Inhabitants: 56.3 million
Density of population: 102 inh/km^2

Surface: 551,000 km^2 (without overseas territories)
region Rhône-Alpes: surface of The Netherlands and 5.5 million inhabitants
Provence, Cote d'Azur: surface of Belgium and 4.1 million inhabitants

GNP: 6100 billion FF
GNP/inh (in SPA) = Germany, Italy, The Netherlands or UK +/− 5%

Highest mountain: Mont Blanc 4807 m (shared with Italy)
Length of the coasts: 3000–5500 km (depends on the sources)
Length of the frontiers: 3000 km
Navigable rivers and canals: 6400 km
Roads: 800,000 km

26 regional parks, 6 national parks (and one overseas)

Climates: oceanic, continental, alpine, Mediterranean
Languages and dialects: French, Occitan, Corsican, Alsacian, Flemish, Basque,
Catalan, Breton.

In the field of outgoing tourism the ranking of France is not as exceptional as in incoming. The expenditure of the French represents only 40% of the total amount spent by Germans, or two-thirds of that spent by the British. The first conclusion could be that France is a country of welcome, but also 'home, sweet home' for the French.

Tourism for French People

Over the last 30 years the vacation departure rate has increased (with some small exceptions). But in 1988/89 the rate reached a peak in a mature market: a smaller number of French people (60%) went for a holiday for a shorter period of time. Until the mid-1980s the general trend was based first on the extension of holidays: two weeks of compulsory 'paid holidays' in 1936, changed later into 3 weeks, 4 weeks in 1969 and 5 weeks in 1982.

The availability of these 'idle' days seems to contradict the recent stagnation of the departure rate. Preel gives an explanation of this new trend: 'The leisure times thread their way through the working time, occur in mid-week, develop all year round with the splitting up of holidays (short breaks). The flexibility asked by the executives and the pleasure in multiple doses shown by the yuppies speeds up the demand for short but intensive breaks' (Credoc, 1992). In other words, severe competition is developing

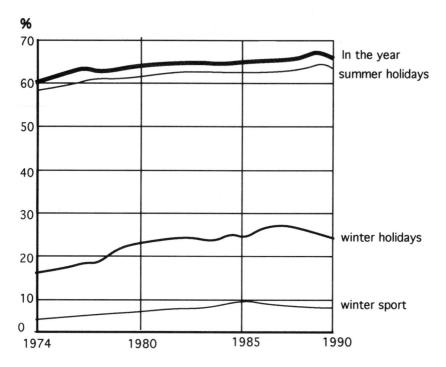

Fig. 12.1 Percentage of French population taking holidays. Source: Ministère du Tourisme.

between different expenditure possibilities and a slow increase in incomes. Therefore, there is now a stagnation of holiday numbers (Fig. 12.1).

The Real Importance of the Tourism Industry in France

The definition of the limits of the field of tourism is not clear. Cautiously, the Ministry of Tourism gives four definitions of tourist consumption: the smallest aggregate includes only the turnover of accommodation and catering enterprises (hotels, cafés, restaurants) with leisure and travel retailing; this aggregate represented 2.5% of the Gross National Product (GNP) in 1989. The biggest aggregate represented 9% of the GNP: in a systematic approach every product connected with the tourism industry was taken into account. This figure shows that tourism is one of the most important industries in France, even though it is often not highly regarded (Fig. 12.2).

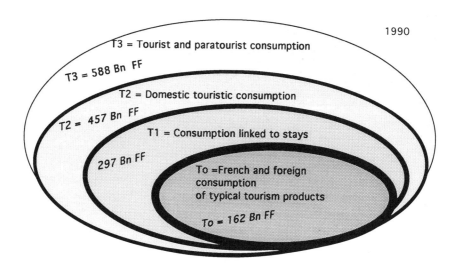

Fig. 12.2. The importance of tourism in the French economy (1990). Source: Ministère du Tourisme.

GEOGRAPHY AND HISTORY

The first feature striking a tourist travelling through France is the diversity of the landscapes and the size of the country, which is slightly larger than the UK and Italy combined (see Table 12.2). Such diversity can be found in many other European countries but not so strong in terms of life-styles, climates and landscapes. This unusual size in Western Europe certainly distorts the importance of the flows between France and other countries: first French people don't need to travel abroad to feel abroad. Second, foreigners have more opportunities to travel through France and find in some 'province' what they prefer.

A number of features of the French landscape include:

- The length and diversity of the shores of the North Sea, the Channel, the Atlantic Ocean, the Mediterranean Sea: rocks or sands, cold and tonic waters (Thalassothérapie) or warm and sunny beaches.
- The importance of the relief: the high northern Alps of Mont Blanc or the Mediterranean Alps, high snowy plateaux in the Jura mountains, volcanic hercynian mountains in the middle of France, moors and heaths in Brittany, extensive plains of the north-eastern region.
- The diversity of human surroundings, from the historical cities of Paris, Dijon or Toulouse to the villages of the Loire Valley or 'Guyenne', the

deserts of Limousin or Champagne, or the really touristic area on the 'Cote d'Azur' created by English people in the last century or the Languedoc shore and the wintersport resorts created by the French technocrats.

- These peculiarities are backed by a 'quality' very seldom found in the outgoing areas: a low density of population caused by centuries of birth control and recent rural migration. This 'desertification' of most of the territory has left a lot of space free or nearly free for leisure and holiday activities: second homes, golf courses, marinas and winter sports resorts.

France also lies between the most important European outgoing countries (Germany, UK, Benelux) and the most important incoming countries (Italy and Spain) – a position similar to that of Switzerland or Austria. This is a very considerable advantage for car, train or bus tourism where French people know how to keep in their resorts tourists en route for other countries. This advantage could be even greater with the development of short-break holidays in quiet spots not so far from home. But it is not always the case, and many northern tourists merely spend one or two days travelling through France on the way to other Mediterranean countries. This is why France ranks as is the first country in the world for the number of international tourists entering the country, but only the second after the United States for receipts!

It is also noteworthy that the whole of France is not used by the tourism industry. Although some rural districts have started extensive development, Corsica is not nearly as developed as Majorca or Sardinia, and the DOM/TOM (islands in the Caribbean, the Pacific Ocean or the Indian Ocean) are not as developed as the Canaries for Spain or Hawaii for the United States.

A historian, Fernand Braudel (1986), begins his book *The Identity of France* with these words: 'I put the History of France in its space, a space at the same time too large and too contrasted, and therefore many "Frances" had to live side by side'. So, the historian finds the same diversity as the geographer. In spite of the old tradition of centralism, 'Jacobinism' or 'parisianism', we find this diversity in the power of the local authorities reinforced by the 1982 law concerning decentralization. Investors in the tourism industry need to be aware of this, in order to penetrate the network of local and national decision makers with whom they have to work to be successful.

Taking into account the history, it should also be noted that France was until the 18th century the most populated country in Europe (before the early development of birth control), maybe with Russia. Therefore, it is not surprising that such a large heritage has been left by the numerous ancestors of the currently deserted country of France.

ACCOMMODATION AND CATERING

Hotels

The Ministry of Tourism gives statistics only for registered tourism hotels (starred). Recently Frangialli (1991) quoted 20,000 registered hotels with approximately one million beds and 700,000 non-registered beds. This means that in 1992 around 40% of the beds are non-registered (compared with approximately 50% 30 years ago). Briefly, in the accommodation field, it appears that France is preserving network of old-fashioned hotels, whilst also developing a brand new system of hotels: 2-, 3- and 4-star hotels were developed and built, whilst the number of one-star hotels was decreasing. Recently, investors decided to launch a new design for modern one-star hotels, which could modify the trend. The leader in this field is Formule 1 (Accor) which launched the new concept of very cheap modern hotels and in 1991 had more than 200 hotels.

In fact the hotels were modernized, but the owners often remain independent, and the chains are not developed to any high degree. The exception is, of course, Accor, the top European hotel group in terms of the number of beds they own (7 billion FF turnover in 1990 and 10 billion FF in 1991 with Pullman, Wagon-Lits and their traditional brands in hotels like Novotel, Sofitel, Ibis, Mercure, or in restaurants such as Churrasco, Free Time, l'Arche, Pizza del Arte). In short, the hotel trade is not as big as French tourism in general, with the exception of Accor's success story.

Table 12.3. Accommodation in France: estimate of tourism beds (millions).

Type	No. of beds (million)
Hotels with 'stars'	1.1
Camping and caravanning	2.7
Holiday villages, youth hostels	0.3
'Gites'	0.2
Second homes	14.1
Others	0.1

Source: Ministère du Tourisme (1991).

Camping and Caravaning

Camping and caravaning represent the most important field of accommodation with 2.7 million places (900,000 registered; 375,000 three or four stars). The strength of the camping or caravaning sector is well-known in some areas, and the sites located in rural areas or alongside lakes are one of the reasons why so many tourists from the north of Europe come to France.

Rented Accommodation

This word is synonymous with two different products: the old 'meublés' (self-catering flats or guest houses) and the time-sharing called in French 'parahotellerie' or 'résidences de loisir'.

According to the real estate agencies' federation (FNAIM) there were about 1.2 million beds in 'meublés' and 160,000 in time-shares in 1983. Time-sharing has been developed mainly in the new seaside and winter sport resorts during the last 25 years. The main motivating factors which lead the French to buy a time-sharing flat are the idea of investing 'in bricks and mortar' as a guarantee, or to speculate, or to provide cheap holidays for the family and finally to rent out. As a result this patrimony is not always in the tourism market, and many resort managers complain about the 'closed doors': by this is meant the flats bought by people from towns, used for 3 weeks a year and at times lent or hired even on the 'black market'. For this reason the boundaries between time-shares and second homes are very flexible and the statistics are very misleading. However some private companies, such as Maeva, Pierre et Vacances and Spie Loisirs have developed time-shares commercially with success.

In contrast to the UK, Austria or The Netherlands, bed and breakfast has only just begun to be developed. But 'Gites de France' has for many years been developing self-catering flats or houses in rural districts or small towns with a great deal of success. In 1991 Gites de France managed 52,000 'gites', i. e. around 200,000 beds.

The Social Sector

The so-called 'social sector' is relatively powerful with autonomous villages or youth hostels: as an example 'Village Vacances Famille' (VVF) manages 55,000 beds. This sector represents 300,000 beds, but the standards of the facilities are sometimes out of date and the government wants to renovate them.

Second Homes

In 1991 second homes represented some 14 million beds. They are a special French feature for many reasons: the strong migrations to the cities in the 1950s and 1960s of peasants who abandoned their houses, selling them later to the city dwellers of France, and later also gradually to the Dutch or English (with some reaction in the 1970s of people choosing to remain in the country against the invaders from the towns). They wish to invest in the stones of old farms and then in new flats or houses in winter sport resorts, marinas, golf courses, etc. This huge potential for accommodation explains partly the importance of the VFR market (Visiting Friends and Relatives), but the profitability of such an investment is doubtful.

PASSENGER TRANSPORT

Road Travel

Several methods of transport are used by French holidaymakers travelling in France in the summer. The majority travel by car (83%), others by train (10%) or by air (3%). In winter when weather conditions make travelling more difficult 16% use the train. The minority of French who travel abroad (18%) are beginning to fly in summer (18%) and prefer it in winter (50%). Between one-half and two-thirds of foreigners travelling in France also use their own cars, as the distance from the northern European countries is not as great as that for some Mediterranean countries.

It is thus clear that tourists predominantly travel by car, which results in problems of congestion on the roads. These problems are exacerbated by other factors:

- Two-thirds of the French take their holidays in July and August (Fig. 12.3).
- Holiday accommodation is let from Saturday to the following Saturday.
- People of the North-East of France travel to the South for their summer holidays. (Of 33 million stays made by French tourists in summer 1990, 5 million were in Provence/Cote d'Azur, 4 million in Languedoc, 3.3 in Rhône-Alpes, 3.2 in Britanny, 2.9 in Aquitaine.) However the concentration is not so great in winter.

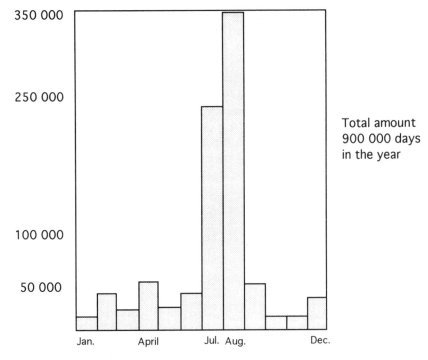

Fig. 12.3. Days of vacation in 1990 for French people. Source: Ministère du Tourisme (1991).

Rail Travel

The national railway company (SNCF) is attempting to arrest the decline in rail use. The development of the high speed train, TGV (train à grande vitesse), has been very successful during the last ten years, first for business travel, then for the mountain routes (Alps and Jura) and since 1991 for the routes to Britanny and the Atlantic coast.

The opening of the Channel Tunnel and the development of a genuine European network (see chapter 4) may also prove to be an opportunity for the railways, and thus lessen the burden on the roads and lead to a decrease in pollution.

Air Travel

Air transport was strictly controlled by the government for a number of years, and long-haul charter routes took some time to become established in France. Nouvelles Frontieres was an example of how difficult it is to develop 'against the official regulation'. It may be one of the reasons that such a small part of the population travel abroad.

As a consequence of deregulation within Europe, the largest companies are merging (Air France, UTA and Air Inter) and though faced with a great number of difficulties, tour operators are trying to develop new charter companies.

Water Transport

English tour operators have developed tours on the old, virtually abandoned network of canals. This offers great potential for rural tourism. The canals are also increasingly used by ships as a link between the North Sea and the Mediterranean.

ATTRACTIONS AND LEISURE FACILITIES

Heritage and 'Art de Vivre'

As in many other 'old' countries, France offers a large range of touristic or quasi touristic and not always commercial attractions and leisure facilities: the bustle in the streets or in the markets, visits to churches, a stroll round a village, ... walking, riding, driving, sailing through natural sites.

All of these could fit in with the idea of 'Art de vivre' which is one of the main themes of the marketing plan of the French promotion agency 'Maison de la France'. In fact the 'café', be it in Paris or in a village in Provence, is one of the strongest images abroad of tourism in France. However, this tourism-related field is progressively turning into a professional and commercial venture: concerts in the churches are no longer free; since the 'mountain law' in 1985 there is a charge on the cross country tracks; the entrance fees to museums are going up etc.

Local authorities are searching for new uses for old churches, castles, factories and citadels. Thus the baroque chapels in Savoy are restored as attractions for tourists skiing or hiking on the slopes. The revival of the old mountain life-style around the church could also be an attraction for tourists.

The spa, of which there are many scattered around France, also forms part of the heritage. Many old spa towns or facilities such as Brides les Bains, Aix or Dax, have been renovated. Unlike the last century the customers nowadays are practically all French (640,000 patients in some 100 resorts). The image of the spa is no longer one of glamour but is instead associated with the welfare-state. Some spas or 'thalassotherapie' institutions (seawater cure) are trying to create a new image with fitness centres and anti-stress treatments.

Theme Parks

For many decades the royal castles in the Loire Valley have been attracting millions of visitors. They visit the castles without creating much economic activity in the villages around them. Therefore, projects for cultural theme parks, aiming to attract the media and then the tourists, have been investigated.

In Chambord and Amboise (royal castles) local politicians, architects and experts are hesitating between 'a funfair on the terraces of the castle or a lively and attractive museum'. Some local actors think it would be possible to build a 'Chambordland' (*Le Monde*, 05 Jan 92). This refers to EuroDisney in the suburbs of Paris. The Disney company expected 11 million visitors in the first year, and it was thought that it might bring some American expertise to the French theme park industry, which has been unsuccessful until now with the relative exception of parc Asterix in the northern part of France and The Futuroscope in Poitiers.

Mountain Resorts

As an incoming country, the French tourism industry has developed a lot of facilities specifically for the tourist: spas or 'thalassotherapie' for water-cures, casinos, beaches, marinas at the seaside, golf and artificial lakes in the rural areas, and skilifts and tracks in the wintersport resorts, on such a large scale that some say that French companies could be good consultants abroad, whereas others criticize the ecological damage.

As a result France has the largest ski area in Europe with 164 Alpine ski resorts with 1.25 million bedspaces, a very good image in France and abroad for grand ski (sport ski) and the quality of the ski facilities. But in fact these facilities are not so substantial because, of the 1.25 million bedspaces 800,000 are in second homes, 200,000 to let, 120,000 in the social sector and 100,000 in hotels. Every year about 30,000 new bedspaces are built, but mainly for financial reasons (investment for the buyer, taxes for the local authorities).

The excellent ski area is no longer sufficient for the tourists, this offer being mainly concentrated on young, urban people.

The Ministry of Tourism has been trying to convince others involved to restructure the offer into a softer product. The lack of snow for three winters helped the industry to take this direction: renovation of the resorts of the 1960s or the development of fun skiing.

The Seaside

The seaside is the most frequented area: 880 municipalities are visited by

20 million French visitors and about 10 million foreigners every year. Tourism is the main activity in this area, around ten times more important than the fishing industry. In the summer of 1990, 50% of French tourists chose to go to the seaside for their holidays, and even in the winter the number is 21%. Some 25% foreign tourists go to the seaside. The pressure of tourists has caused damage to some parts of the French coast, but the great expanse of coast line has meant that most parts have been spared. The seaside is no doubt the one area where both the positive and the negative aspects of tourism are most perceptible.

Rural Tourism

About 40% of French territory has a density lower than 20 inhabitants per km^2. Trigano, Director of the Club Med, wrote in his survey for the French Parliament in 1989 that it could be an opportunity to develop a new form of tourism. In the less depressed areas, where a network of facilities is in existence, rural tourism is developing and presents a successful alternative for farmers, or small enterprises (rural guest houses or Manor House Hotels). In fact, the rural area already represents 25% of stays by French holidaymakers in summer.

Urban Life

The towns are among the big attractions for foreigners: by the beginning of the 19th century the first tourists were going to Paris, Avignon or Nice. Today 30% stay solely in the towns, and including those who tour 40% of the foreign tourists come chiefly to visit the towns. With regard to French tourists, only 7% take their summer holidays in the towns, but the number increases to 18% in the winter.

In addition to the traditional attraction of the old centres, local authorities and chambers of commerce have developed a successful line of congress tourism. With more than 750 international congresses in 1990 France is the second in the world behind the USA; Paris leads the world with the number of international congresses held in the city.

TOUR OPERATING AND TRAVEL RETAILING

In a handbook about the business of tourism in the UK (Holloway, 1989) an important part is devoted to this field. In a French handbook (Frangialli, 1991) no chapter is devoted to the same topic. This illustrates one of the major differences between the two countries. In France the inclusive tours market is relatively small for the various reasons already mentioned: a small percentage of travel abroad (18%), a very high percentage of travel by car (about 80%) and a very small one by air, the importance of second homes or visiting friends and relatives (about 50% of the stays in summer and two-thirds in winter).

The small size of the national outgoing market has prevented the development of large tour operators, with a few exceptions: the Club Med (8.1 billion FF in 1990) with a heavily integrated structure, Nouvelles Frontiers (4.5 billion FF in 1991) the symbol of travelling freedom, Fram (2 billion FF in 1990) for the middle class and Sotair (1.9 billion FF) a sister company of Air France (c.f. the German tour operators: TUI with 18 billion FF and NUR with 6.7 billion FF in the same year). Until now the large tour operators of northern Europe have failed to really enter the French market.

The package tours assembled by the tour operators are mostly sold by the travel agencies (3500 in 1988) of which there are few in comparison with other European countries (half as many as in Germany or the UK). In 1989 only 24,000 people had a job in the distribution sector, i.e. 5% of the total of people working in the whole tourism industry (510,000). Even worse, only 1% of the investment in the tourism industry is made in distribution.

Here again are the key features of French tourism: the will to structure the territory, to invest in the building industry, to create jobs in depressed areas and to preserve the power of the local authorities. Yet the marketing of products for different consumers remains of minor importance.

THE PUBLIC SECTOR

It was only in 1986 that the government took into account the potential of the tourism industry in developing jobs and attracting foreign revenue. Therefore a tourist industry department has been created (DIT). In 1987 a central agency for the marketing and promotion of French tourism abroad, which regroups older institutions (Maison de la France), was formed. It manages the promotion through specialized fairs and workshops around the world. It coordinates the actions of producers in specialized clubs to obtain the best benefit from the money invested in promotion abroad. Today tourism is at last beginning to be considered by the government as a real economic activity: in 1988 a Ministry of Tourism was created.

At regional (22 regions) and local level (95 departments) specialized agencies coordinate the development of tourism and promote the products. These agencies are: CRT (Comité Régional de Tourisme) for the regions and ADT (Association Départementale de Tourisme) for the departments. In many departments there are organizations called SLA (Service Loisirs

Accueil) which have the task of marketing the product in competition with the private travel agencies. In the resorts and in many towns information is given by OTSI (Office de tourisme et syndicat d'initiatives) to the tourist.

CONCLUSION

The image of France as a host country is not always positive; French people are sometimes critical of this activity and sometimes indifferent to their guests. But why are so many foreigners set on going to France?

Trigano (1989) provided an answer, which may still be valid. France has *strengths*:

- Paris, 'a magic town' which attracts Europeans, Japanese and Americans.
- The quality and the variety of the sites.
- Extensive facilities and accommodation.

France has weaknesses:

- Products and components originality created only for French tourists.
- A jigsaw puzzle of medium and small enterprises.
- A jigsaw puzzle of public authorities.

France has opportunities:

- A large rural area close to the major outgoing areas.
- The islands (Corsica, the West Indies, the Pacific and the Indian Ocean).

REFERENCES AND FURTHER READING

General Data
Anon. (1991) *Euroscopie*. Larousse, Paris.
Braudel, F. (1986) *L'Identité de la France*. Arthaud, Grenoble.
Credoc (1992) *L'Etat de la France*. La Decouverte, Paris.
Gravier, J.F. (1972) *Paris et le Désert Français en 1972*. Flammarion, Paris.

Tourism-specific
Cazes, G. (1989) *Le Tourisme International, Mirage ou Strategie d'Avenir*. Hatier, Paris.
Dominati, J. (1987) L'Enjeu Touristique. Debat a l'Assemblee Nationale, Paris.
Dumazedier, J. (1962) *Vers Une Civilisation des Loisirs*. Seuil, Paris.
Frangialli, F. (1991) *La France dans le Tourisme Mondial*. Economica, Paris.
Hautes Etudes Commerciales (HEC)(1962) *Le Nouveau Touriste*. HEC, Paris.

Hollier, R. and Subremon, A. (1990) *Le Tourisme dans le Communaute Euro-péenne.* Presses Universitaires de France, Paris.
Holloway, C. (1989) *The Business of Tourism.* Pitman, London.
Lanquar, R. and Raynourd, Y. (1991) *Le Tourisme Social et Associatif.* Presses Universitaires de France, Paris.
Ministere du Tourisme (1991) *Memento du Tourisme.* Paris.
Ouvry-Vial, B., Louis, R. and Pouy, J.B. (1990) *Les Vacances.* Autrement, Paris.
Pasqualini, J.P. and Jacquot, B. (1990) *Tourismes, Organisation, Economie et Action Touristiques.* Dunod, Paris.
Pasqualini, J. P. and Jacquot, B. (1992) *Tourismes en Europe.* Dunod, Paris.
Tinard, Y. (1992) *Le Tourisme, Economie et Management.* McGraw-Hill, Maiden-head.
Trigano, G. (1989) Pour Une Industrie Touristique plus competitive. In: *Problèmes Economiques,* 18/01/89. Documentation Française, Paris.

Magazines/Journals
L'Echo Touristique
Espaces
La Lettre de l'Observation Economique. Ministere du Tourisme: Paris.

13

TOURISM IN GERMANY

Richard Hill

INTRODUCTION

The reunification of East and West Germany in October 1990 brought to
an end the post-war division of the country, which had led to very different
economic and social structures in the two parts. The tourism industries of
the two Germanies also diverged in their structure, image and tourist
behaviour.

The West German part was characterized by freedom to travel, cata-
pulting the population to the top of the 'golden hordes' league, whereas in
East Germany travel abroad was restricted for political and economic
reasons so that only the privileged and pensioners could leave the country;
domestic holiday destinations were furthermore designated and directed by
the state. In the West, freedom to travel where you wished on holiday was
seen as a fundamental right in a democratic society, but in the East tourism
was seen as a basic regenerative factor for society's work-force and as a
propaganda instrument and motor of socialist domestic and foreign policy
(Godau, 1990). Whereas East Germany sought to impede entry into the
country by compulsory visas, chicanery and unrealistic official rates of
exchange West Germany set high store upon attracting large numbers of
visitors. In the West, a free business economy exists with tourism dependent upon individual freedom of choice; the East had a centrally planned
economy administered by the state with, for example, a well-developed
state system of recuperative tourism.

It is generally assumed that the post-reunification behaviour of East
Germans, as far as holiday destination areas, means of transport and length
of stay are concerned, will follow the West German patterns once this is
financially possible and the newly found freedom to indulge in VFR trips
to the West slackens. The attitude of 'the West does it best' may, however,
lead to the tourism industry of the former East Germany building into its

development the same mistakes which have been made in the West and that the golden opportunity to encourage sustainable tourism harmonizing economic, social and ecological interests will fall victim to the pressure to pull new jobs out of the hat and the urge to make a quick buck in the new economic order.

THE DEVELOPMENT OF TOURISM

Travel Patterns and Behaviour

The standard measure for holiday journeys is 'travel intensity', which in Germany means the percentage of the population over 14 years old undertaking a holiday journey of at least four bednights in a given year.

In 1954 just less than a quarter of West Germans managed to undertake a holiday journey, resulting in approx. 9.3 million trips. As a consequence of the much vaunted 'economic miracle' travel intensity rose dramatically passing the 30% mark in 1962, 40% in 1970, 50% in 1973 and 60% in 1987 (Fig. 13.1). By 1991 it had reached 66.9%, corresponding to 41.5 million holidaymakers undertaking some 45 million holiday journeys (with some taking more than one holiday). At the same time there has been an increase in short breaks of 2–4 days' duration: 70% of short breaks are to domestic destinations and 65% are by people who holiday

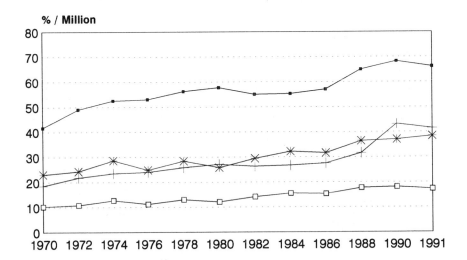

Fig. 13.1. Travel intensities: 1970–1991, West Germany. ■ Travel intensity (%); + travellers (million); ★ short breaks (%); □ short breaks (millions).
Source: Studienkreis für Tourismus (1992).

several times a year. Short breaks oil the financial wheels of the tourism industry very effectively, with short-break holidaymakers spending 1.8 times more per day than long break ones. Short breaks now account for one-third of all bednights and almost half of the estimated 82 billion DM turn-over in domestic tourism in Germany (DFV, 1991).

Travel intensity seems to have stabilized at a high level in the last few years, with only a relatively small increase in main holiday journeys. The demand potential is stable and likely to remain so, since about 45% of all travellers are regular travellers and the occasional ones are becoming regular ones. The actual number of holidays is expected to increase further because people are reducing the length of their main holidays in order to be able to set off more often.

About half of those who do not go on holiday cite money as being the main reason for their decision – in general Germans are loathe to put themselves into debt for holidays, although German law expressly insists that you spend your paid holidays recuperating and not, for example, undertaking other paid employment. Further reasons for not taking a holiday are: babies, illness and the priority of making some other more important acquisition. As far as older employees and those who have retired are concerned, the reluctance to make the effort and fear of the unknown are reasons for not travelling – the security of familiar surroundings is more important to them – and people living in rural areas find it more difficult to break away from their daily obligations than do city-dwellers.

Means of Transport

It is characteristic of modern German society that the private car has become an almost indispensable status symbol, being the main means of holiday transport for them since the mid-1960s; in 1991, 58% of holiday-makers used their cars (Fig. 13.2). Since reunification East Germans have followed in the footsteps of the West, a major priority being to acquire a

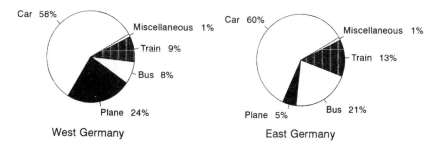

Fig. 13.2. Transport carriers, 1991. Source: Studienkreis für Tourismus (1992).

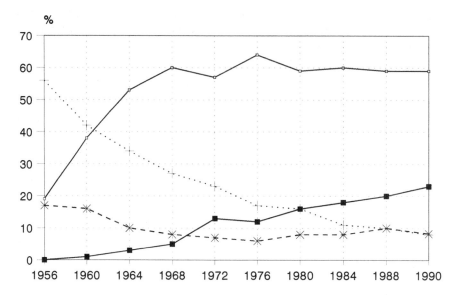

Fig. 13.3. Transport carriers, 1956–1990, West Germany. ☐ Car; + Rail; ✕ Bus; ■ Plane. Source: Studienkreis für Tourismus (1992).

high-profile 'Western' car status symbol. Despite the nationwide staggering of school holidays every holiday weekend brings huge and predictable traffic jams on the arterial roads.

The railways must be regarded as the great losers in the holiday transport market (Fig. 13.3) – their share is almost a mirror image of the private car's (from 57% in 1956 to 9% in 1991), with no sign of a significant change.

Coach transport has seen its ups and downs since the 1950s but appears to be losing out again at the beginning of the 1990s with only 8.3% of all holiday journeys (= 3.4 million trips) in 1991 being by coach. In the former East Germany the figure for 1991 was higher at 21%. The most popular destinations by coach are Italy (14.9%), France (12.3%), Austria (8.7%), Germany (8.3%) and Spain (7.8%) (DRV, 1991).

The most notable success story since the late 1960s has been the rise in air transport, accounting in 1991 for almost a quarter of holiday transport. The rapid rise in the popularity of air transport coincided with the introduction by new entrants to the market NUR and ITS of the warehouse principle charter flight (high participant numbers, low profit per person) as opposed to the previous specialist retailer principle (low participant numbers, high profit per person). Technical developments (the introduction of big jets and the expansion of airports in Mediterranean destinations) have also boosted the numbers of travellers. Increased competition through a European 'open skies' policy and the privatization of national airlines may help reduce comparative prices and increase the airlines' market in the 1990s (see also Chapter 4).

Destinations

In 1954 no more than 15% of holidays were undertaken outside Germany, but as the economy recovered and the Deutschmark gained progressively in value after the 1950s foreign holidays became increasingly attractive financially and Germans rapidly indulged in a new-found urge to travel abroad. Since 1967 foreign holidays have been more popular than domestic ones, although in this respect there are some differences between East and West Germans: in 1990 only 3% of West Germans took holidays in the East, 29% in West Germany, and 68% abroad. The comparable figures for East Germans are: 41% in East Germany, 34% in West Germany and 25% abroad (Studienkreis, 1992).

Package Tours

There is a direct correlation between package tours and holidays abroad, but foreign destinations are not the only reason for the rise in package

Fig. 13.4. Share of package tours, 1970–1991. Main holiday trips in West Germany. ☐ Package tours; + individual trips. Source: Studienkreis für Tourismus (1992).

tours – costs, convenience and security in litigation should there be any shortcomings (complaints and demands for compensation are by no means unusual in Germany) are factors which specifically appeal to the German package tourist. There is no sign of the package tour losing its importance (Fig. 13.4) – according to the Reiseanalyse 90 by the Studienkreis für Tourismus, 63% of first-time travellers book a package holiday and customers who book a partial package (e.g. charter flight or holiday accommodation) tend to be new target groups for new products. The favourite means of transport for package tourists is the plane (48.6%, threequarters of these being for charter flights) followed by the coach (27.9%) and the private car (18.4%). Only 3.9% travel by train, with even smaller percentages for boat, motor-caravan, motorcycle etc. (Studienkreis, 1992).

Changes in Holiday Motivation

Opaschowski (1988) characterized the holiday in the 1950s and 1960s as primarily a counterbalance to the everyday world of work, with the prime motives being:

- Recuperation, i.e. lazing about, lying in the sun.
- Passiveness, i.e. be spoilt and forget your worries.
- Withdrawal, i.e. switching off and being alone with the family.
- No obligations, i.e. no time constraints, being independent.
- Prosperity, i.e. enjoy your life and wealth to the full.

These values still predominate with older generations, but this 'have-a-break-from-work attitude' no longer satisfies the holiday requirements of 20–50-year-olds with their greater experience of travelling, higher educational levels and extended leisure time. For them a holiday is no longer an appendage to and reward for work; it has acquired a value of its own so that a holiday is perceived as an opportunity to make leisure time more vivid. In the 1980s and 1990s the prime motives for holidaymaking can be summed up as:

- Experience, i.e. have variety, new experiences.
- Spontaneity, i.e. not be tied down; do what you want when you want.
- Relaxation, i.e. move away from daily stress; uncouple the mind.
- Activity, i.e. be creative; join in.
- Nature, i.e. enjoy nature's presence in an unspoilt environment.

The last of these motives – nature – is seen by Germans as a particularly important motive for a holiday, and destinations are specifically selected (and marketed!) for their ecological attributes. The suspicion remains, however, that Germans often pay little more than lip-service to green tourism, succumbing to the marketing techniques of the promotional ploy – in 1992 one tour operator very publicly cancelled his first cruise-ship tour of the White Sea because 'the Russians have dumped thousands of drums of radioactive waste there'. Although destinations may change, the basic behaviour of German tourists has changed little (witness the perennial traffic jams and swarming to the Mediterranean), and the potential for greater environmental awareness and action seems to be limited to certain sections of society such as the more highly educated younger person, people from higher socioeconomic groups who prefer active holidays, and those who are involved in environmental protection in any case.

Tourism in the former German Democratic Republic

In the former East Germany there was a high travel intensity: in 1988 just over two-thirds of the adult population undertook a main holiday, giving a total of 12.5 million main holidays. Compared with West Germany there was a disproportionately high percentage of domestic holidays with only about 20% of holidays outside the country, these being mainly to COMECON states and typified by limited availability of foreign currency. The main foreign destinations according to Grossmann (1990) were the then Czeckoslovakia (74%), Hungary (12%), Poland (6%), the Soviet Union (5%) and Bulgaria (2%). As far as domestic tourism was concerned, the state was keen to promote youth tourism and recuperative holidays for company employees; there was also a high number of day trips and short breaks.

INCOMING TOURISM

The Old Federal Republic of Germany

In 1990 there were some 30 million bednight journeys to West Germany with an average duration of 2.2 days. In addition there were 10 million day trippers.

Holiday trips in the broad sense account for 65% of all bednight journeys to Germany; business trips account for 29% of all incoming visitors staying overnight, and half of these are for classical business trips – buying, selling, service – leaving 50% for special business trips to such as fairs, congresses and incentive travel (DZT, 1989).

Incoming Tourists and the Purpose of Visit

The market share of incoming holidaymakers is divided as shown in Table 13.1. The proportion of bednights by foreigners to total bednights stagnated in the 1970s at around 7–10% but rose through the 1980s to 13.6%

Table 13.1. Incoming tourists: purpose of visit.

Position	Purpose of visit	% share
1	Recuperation in rural areas	32
2	City tourism	29
3	Round trips	21
4	Recuperation on or by water	9
5	Miscellaneous	9

Source: DZT (1989).

in 1990 (= 34.8 million bednights). The increase between 1980 and 1990 amounted to 60% and the proportion of bednights by foreigners is particularly high in the city states of Hamburg (48.6%), Bremen (24.5%) and Berlin (25%) whereas it is low in the regional states such as Bavaria (12.6%) and Saarland. Total expenditure by incoming tourists amounted to 17 billion DM, i.e. some 15% of total tourism expenditure.

The countries of origin given in Fig. 13.5, show that The Netherlands (17%), the USA (14%) and the UK (9%) are the most significant as far as the number of bednights is concerned.

The picture with regard to expenditure by foreign tourists reveals marked differences – the Austrians, with a mere 3% of bednights, provided 11% of expenditure (Fig. 13.6) but the USA, with 14% of bednights, provided only 8% of expenditure in 1990. The figures for the USA vary considerably from year to year, mainly as a result of the fluctuating value of the US dollar and political events such as the Gulf War and an upsurge in terrorist activity.

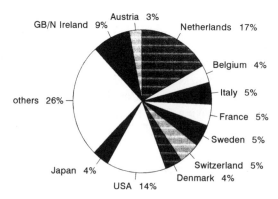

Fig. 13.5. Countries of origin, 1990: percentage of bednights.
Source: Statistisches Bundesamt (1991).

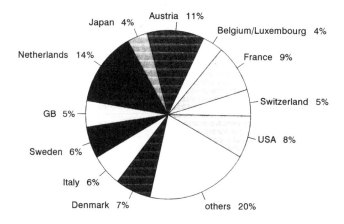

Fig. 13.6. Expenditure by foreigners, 1990. Source: Deutsche Bundesbank (1991).

The figures for bednights by incoming tourists must be treated with some caution for the following reasons:

- Accommodation units with less than eight beds are not included in the statistics.
- A reasonable guestimate indicates that up to a quarter of bednights are not communicated to the authorities (tax evasion!).
- Bednights in private households and non-commercial units such as youth hostels are not included.
- No differentiation is made according to the purpose of the visit so that it is not normally possible to separate business and holiday tourists for statistical purposes.

The German Centre for Tourism (DZT) reckons that the real number of bednights is probably four times higher than the figures published by the Federal Statistical Office.

The future may well see greater numbers of incoming tourists from the former Eastern Bloc countries than from the United Kingdom and Belgium, but financially they seem likely to make little contribution to the German economy as tourists.

The success recipe for Germany as an international tourist destination, according to DZT research, is based on the following factors:

1. castles and forts;
2. old city centres;
3. social events;
4. cleanliness;
5. scenery;

6. shopping possibilities;
7. cultural events.

According to Hank-Haase (1982) negative aspects of a holiday in Germany are:

1. the language problem;
2. the Nazi past;
3. 'unsympathetic Germans';
4. the high cost;
5. the unreliable weather.

The Former German Democratic Republic

Not counting visitors from West Germany, 8.8 million visitors entered East Germany in 1989 before reunification; 6.5 million of these originated from countries in the socialist block. In 1990 the number of incoming visitors from Socialist countries dropped to about 1 million, mainly because the introduction of the West German Deutschmark made a stay in the former East Germany dramatically more expensive. According to the Travel Monitor, foreigners spent 1.9 million bednights in the 'new states', 47% of these being for holiday journeys.

OUTGOING TOURISM

As was seen in the section on the general development of tourism, Germans now form one of the great travelling nations with West Germans in particular going abroad in large numbers, although East Germans have shown signs of following in the footsteps of their West German brothers since reunification. The percentage figures for 1991 reveal a clear picture (Studienkreis, 1992).

	Domestic holidays (%)	Foreign holidays (%)
West Germans	31	69
East Germans	55	45
Whole Country	36	64

The main feature of German outgoing tourism is the urge to stream south – to the sun (60% of Germans regard sunshine as the major factor in a successful holiday), to the easy-going, romantic atmosphere, to the great cultural cities. Over a third of German holidays are taken in Spain, Italy, Austria and France (Fig. 13.7) and interestingly more East than West

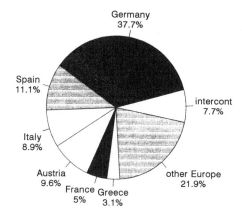

Fig. 13.7. Destinations, 1991: all Germany. Source: Studienkreis für Tourismus (1992).

Germans holidayed in Austria in 1991. The dramatic decline in holidays to the former Yugoslavia (from 3.6% in 1990 to 0.7% in 1991) is a clear indication of the sensitivity of tourists to war zones.

Expenditure by Germans in their main holiday destination countries far exceeds the receipts in Germany from incoming tourists from those countries, although Belgium, Luxemburg, Denmark, Sweden, Norway and Finland belong to the rather exclusive group whose holidaymakers spend more in Germany than the Germans do in their countries.

The notion that the constantly rising value of the Deutschmark makes holidays abroad relatively cheaper each year for Germans is illusory – in recent years years the purchasing power of the DM has dropped in many destination countries because of high price increases there, although the currency re-alignment in September 1992 may redress this. Long-haul tourism by Germans is also increasing faster than short-haul tourism, mainly due to the rapid rise in the number of backpackers, the urge of yuppies to indulge in genuinely exotic holidays, and the drop in the value of the US dollar at the beginning of the 1990s.

DOMESTIC TOURISM: WEST GERMANY

Over the last 30 years there has been a proportional increase in the number of foreign holidays – domestic holidays have stabilized at around 10 million per annum. It is still fair to say, however, that the favourite destination country of Germans is Germany itself, with over a third of all holiday-makers staying in their own country. The most popular areas are the Black

Forest, the pre-Alps, the Bavarian Forest, the Harz, the Alps and the
northern coastal resorts. Bavaria as a whole accounts for approx 9.5% of
domestic holidays, followed by Lower Saxony and Schleswig-Holstein
(5.9%) and Baden-Württemberg (5.0%).

A particular feature of West Germany's domestic tourism industry is
the 266 officially recognized spas and health resorts, which play an
important role in the tourist economy – in 1986 they accounted for 25% of
all accommodation businesses, 17.4% of bed capacity and about 45% of
bednights in West Germany's tourist trade and in 1990 they welcomed 8.9
million guests – twice as many as in 1970.

The popularity of the spas and health resorts is not just the result of a
long tradition of 'taking the waters' and a concern for healthy living; it is
also the result of state support and encouragement – the state recognizes
the value of prophylactic health care (prevention is better – and cheaper –
than cure) enabling maximum performance at work. 'Cures' fully or partly
financed by the social security systems (amounting to 5% of all social
security payments) helped to keep not only the population but also the spas
in a healthy state. In addition many people finance their own 'cure' and
there is a steady movement towards health and fitness holidays, emphasizing this aspect of tourism even further.

DOMESTIC TOURISM: THE GERMAN DEMOCRATIC REPUBLIC

Travel between the two pre-unification Germanies was characterized by
the facts that East Germans were basically not free to travel and that West
Germans had no particular inclination to visit the East. In 1989, the last
year of the two Germanies, only about 700,000 holiday trips (1.6% of all
West German holidays) were made to East Germany, most being short
second or third holidays to visit friends or relatives.

East Germany has good scenic and cultural attractions, but there are
problems with accommodation; there is not enough, it is not up to Western
standards of comfort and service, and is extremely poor value for money by
Western standards. In 1991 the number of holidaymakers from the West
fell well below expectations, and the anticipated but unrealized desire of
West Germans to 'see the other half' materialized mainly in short breaks
and day trips; only the Baltic sea coast could establish itself in the eyes of
West Germans as a tourist destination.

An image questionnaire by the Studienkreis für Tourismus gave a
negative image for East Germany; even in the holiday areas such as the
Mecklenburg Baltic Coast far away from industrial centres, most West
Germans perceived serious environmental pollution and limited holiday
quality (DRV, 1991).

STRUCTURE OF THE GERMAN TOURISM INDUSTRY

Accommodation: West Germany

In 1986 there were some 40,000 businesses with more than eight beds in the hotel, guest house, bed and breakfast, pension and holiday centre branches. A further 10,000 beds were available in youth hostels, camping sites and managed mountain huts etc.

Hotels

There were about 9000 hotels in 1989 with approx 160,000 rooms and an average occupancy of 46.6%. Between 1980 and 1990 growth averaged 5.3% but the number of hotels fell by 4% (Statistisches Bundesamt, 1991). International hotel chains with franchising and management agreements are increasing in importance and in 1992 covered 85% of the 5-star category, 40% of the 4-star, and 15% of the 3-star hotels. There is an increasing move towards the budget end of the market as evidenced by the French concerns with for example, Ibis and Formule 1. Investment in hotel building has been fuelled by the activities of such as insurance companies, pension and building funds, for whom the rising value of the building and its site is more important than the operation of the hotel itself.

Seasonality is a fact of life for the holiday hotels on the coast and in the flatlands with only one real season per year; in the mountains of central and southern Germany winter sports allow two seasons. The regional

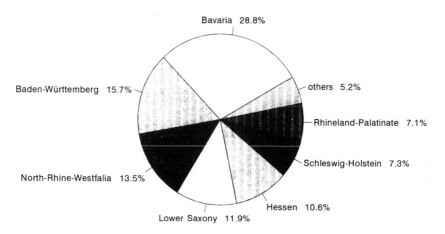

Fig. 13.8. Destinations in West Germany: bednights in hotels only.
Source: Statistisches Bundesamt (1991).

concentration of bednights in hotels is shown in Fig. 13.8.

A major problem for hotels, especially the mid-range and smaller ones, is the acquisition and retention of staff; this gap has been plugged to some extent by immigrant workers, without whom many businesses would flounder.

Accommodation: East Germany

The accommodation sector in the former East Germany is characterized by the moribund material, technical, financial and organizational legacy of the Democratic Republic times, resulting in the current spate of unprofitable businesses, inadequate maintenance investment and resistance to private investment. Many of the company and trade union rest homes, tents, caravans etc. are unsuitable for visitors from the West. Of the hotels (of which there were about 800 offering 40,000 beds at the time of reunification) almost all had been set up for business travellers and 40% of them could not be made available to guests without radical renovation.

The same qualitative inadequacies could be found in the parahotel industries – camping sites, youth hostels and youth rest homes. The influx of visitors resulting from the new freedom to enter the country could only be catered for thanks, in part, to the rapid increase in private rooms made available by people taking advantage of the new market economy (even though the influx was not as great as had been expected).

All in all, the urgent modernization of the East German tourist industry to meet the market demands and service requirements of West German and international tourists is hindered by:

- The physical lack of accommodation.
- The inadequate quality and equipment of existing capacities.
- The poor general and tourism infrastructures.
- Insufficient experience of management and staff.

Further hindrances to investment are the question of ownership of many buildings and sites – previous owners who had their property compulsorily purchased may lay claim to their former possessions – and the slow privatization of state-owned buildings. It is also not possible to turn a blind eye to the fact that some of the plans by West German investors which were received with euphoria turned out to be hollow, being no more than attempts to acquire land quickly and cheaply.

Tour Operators

The market for package tours extending to more than four nights was calculated at 36 million trips in 1991, of which some 2 million were organized by non-commercial operators such as sports clubs, churches, trades unions and evening institutes (Studienkreis, 1992).

The commercial operators can be roughly divided into three groups:

1. The 'big four' (TUI with 3.4 million package tours; NUR with 1.9 million; LTU with 1.3 million; and ITS with 0.96 million: all figures refer to 1991).
2. 12 medium-sized operators (eg. Hetzel, ADAC, Kreuzer, and Fischer).
3. Some 800 small tour operators plus about 800 travel agencies with tour operator functions.

Although the major operators are very powerful, especially in the flight package market, and especially as German law allows them to insist on exclusive trading agreements with travel agencies – ITS actually lost a court case in 1991 in which it claimed its exclusion from about 5200 of the 7000 independent travel agencies by 'sole agency' agreements with TUI or NUR was illegal – the market is not in practice dominated by any individual or group of tour operators. The reason for this is that the small companies operate in highly specialized markets (educational travel, health tourism etc., in 1992, for example there were 31 companies specializing in motor-cycle travel!) or on a strong regional basis; in either case they can present serious, if small-scale, competition to the major operators. In contrast to the situation in Great Britain, vertical concentration is unusual in German tour operators – not one of them has its own airline!

Travel Agencies

About 80% of the turnover for tour operators and scheduled flights is transacted through travel agencies and every third holiday journey is booked in a travel agency, of which there are about 7500 in total in West Germany and about 1000 in East Germany.

Travel agency chains have a significant hold on the market – 23 such chains operate 1212 outlets bringing in 27% of the travel agency turnover, and they are gradually cornering a larger share of the market by buying new offices. On the other hand there is a large number of small agencies; a quarter of all agencies are one-man operations and about 50% have two to four employees. Travel agencies in general are hardly money-spinners: profits in relation to turnover were 0.77% in 1989 and 1 17% in 1990.

Travel Agencies in East Germany

The structure in East Germany has changed radically since reunification, prior to which state agencies had a sector monopoly such as in youth tourism, trades union tourism or in company convalescence. Now almost all have been taken over by West German operators, with East German initiatives occurring in the coach sector and when a totally new agency is started up.

TOURISM POLICY IN GERMANY

There is no federal minister for tourism in Germany – matters affecting the industry are divided among a variety of ministries with the result that it is difficult to speak of a national tourism policy. Ensuring that the interests of the branch are taken care of is largely a private matter for the industry itself.

The main exception is in the advertising and representation abroad by the DZT (Deutsche Zentrale für Tourismus – German Centre for Tourism) whose activities were funded by the state to 85% of their modest 46 million DM budget in 1990. Members of the DZT are leading associations of the travel and tourism branches and large organizations such as the Federal Railways and Lufthansa. Apart from the activities of the DZT, marketing abroad is undertaken especially by regional associations and groups of cities or advertising departments. The main themes running through the advertizing are: romantic Heidelberg, Black Forest country maidens, aristocratic castles and the magnificent Alps including the Bavarian Lederhosen.

The major tourism associations are:

- Deutscher Fremdenverkehrsverband (DFV) (German Travel Association), which represents national and regional travel associations and cities. Its main task is to identify tourism needs and present them to the federal parliament and government bodies; its main interest is in encouraging more people (especially Germans) to take their main holiday in Germany.
- Deutscher Bäderverband (DBV) (German Spa Association), which has representatives of the health and spa resorts, the Association of German Spa Doctors, the Scientific Association for Balneology and Climatology, the Association for German Curative Springs. Its task is to promote and encourage spa and health resort activities and to maintain the necessary natural resources.
- Deutscher Hotel- und Gaststättenverband (DEHOGA) (German Hotel and Restaurant Association), which represents the interests of the branch to public authorities and the public in general; it is responsible for education and training in the branch and negotiates wage agreements with the relevant trade union.
- Deutscher Reisebüro-Verband (DRV) (German Travel Agencies Association), which represents the interests of travel agencies and tour

operators. It had some 2000 members in 1991.

- Bundesverband Mittelständischer Reiseunternehmen (ASR) (Federal Association of private medium-sized Travel Companies), which has some 1500 members, predominantly from private small to medium-sized companies.
- Arbeitsgemeinschaft Deutscher Luftfahrtunternehmen (ADL) (Study Group of German Air Transport Companies), which represents the interests of German charter flight companies in transport and economic matters.

A central aspect of tourism policy is the maintenance of the environment, especially at regional and local levels, and a whole range of associations has been trying – as yet without any great success – to introduce environment emblems (blue flag, green stamp, green case etc.) to enlighten the travelling public on the environment-preserving qualities of goods and services. Tourism projects are increasingly being subjected to tests of their environmental compatibility and a number of resorts are trying to introduce and market the concept of carrying capacities. The ADAC (German Automobile Club), the Alpenverein (Alps Club), the Bund Naturschutz (League for the Protection of Nature), and World Wide Fund are also active in this field.

Tour operators in particular are beginning to make a point of emphasizing their concern for nature, even if the range on offer remains largely unchanged from previous offers, and each large operator has a person responsible for environmental matters trying to exercise influence on tourist destinations (modern sewerage works, removal of waste, saving energy); catalogues are printed on chlorine-free paper and contain environmental information, and the DRV offers an annual Environment Prize. The aims are admirable, but the sudden intensity of the movement smacks of 'band-wagon mentality' and in the short term it seems to have had little influence on the destination areas (especially abroad); furthermore environment-compatible tourism products are more expensive and a slow process of education is necessary before customers are willing to pay more for what may at first sight be less.

The Economic Importance of Tourism

Turnover in German tourism is calculated to be 96 billion DM per annum (including a multiplier of 1.6). It represents 4.6% of GNP. A major economic factor in favour of the tourism industry is that it plays a significant role in helping to redress the economic imbalance between rich and poor regions of the country since tourism is generated mainly in areas such as the Black Forest, the Alps and the North Sea islands where there is little industry.

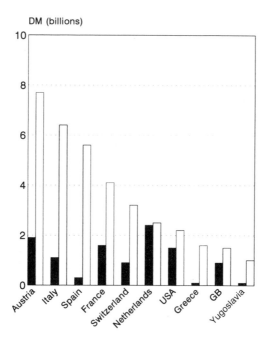

Fig. 13.9. Balance of travel expenditure: main countries, 1990; all Germany.
■ Receipts; ☐ expenditure. Source: Deutsche Bundesbank (1991).

The claims about the level of employment created by tourism reveal considerable discrepancies: the DFV gives a figure of 'at least 1.5 million; the DWIF 'at least 1.2 million' and the DRV 'around 2 million'. If a figure of 1.5 million is accepted, this would represent 6% of all employees in the former West Germany, which is more than in farming or banking and insurance. Incomes in the tourism industry tend to be low, however, when compared with the general commercial and manufacturing branches.

There is a huge deficit in the tourism balance of trade (Fig. 13.9). In 1991 German expenditure on travel abroad amounted to 51.1 billion DM (7.1% up on 1990), of which over 50% (26.1 billion DM) was in other EC countries. Austria tops the list of expenditure by Germans with 8.5 billion DM (14.5% up on 1990), followed by Italy with 7.3 billion DM (up 14% on 1990) and Spain with 6.9 billion DM (up 9.3% on 1990). By contrast receipts from incoming tourism amounted to 17.6 billion DM in 1991 (up 2.4% on 1990), of which 8.9 billion DM came from visitors from other EC countries. Receipts from countries outside Europe fell, with the exception of Japan which showed an increase of 3.6% over 1990.

This negative tourism balance of trade must be seen in the context of world trade: German international tourists make a massive financial contribution especially to the economies of countries bordering on the

Mediterranean which have large deficits in their international trade. At home, Germany's big surplus from the export of manufactured goods is to some extent balanced out by the tourism deficit. The Germans see this as bringing benefits all round – the economies of the destination countries are boosted by the inflow of German tourist money and a part of this flows directly or indirectly back to Germany in the form of export orders, which in turn strengthens Germany's export-based economy even further, allowing Germans more money in their pockets to spend abroad. It can be said that German tourists create 750,000 jobs in foreign countries and the DRV sees mutual benefit from the flow of German tourists:

> An increase in the proportion of guest workers in the Federal Republic, which would be undesirable for socioeconomic reasons, is if not prevented at least diminished by jobs (abroad) created by the tourist industry. The establishment of jobs in the native countries of the guest workers is in line with the federal government's policy.
>
> (DRV Annual Report, 1988).

THE EC AND GERMAN TOURISM

With regard to tour operators, European harmonization is likely to have little adverse effect on the German market, although there will be some changes.

The EC directive covering package tours will affect German operators insofar as it envisages the securing of customers' money in the eventuality of company insolvency; here insurance models or the establishment of funds are under consideration but the effect on prices will be insignificant. Most of the EC directive's measures to increase customer protection have been in force in Germany for over a decade, but the trade is concerned about regulations governing catalogue descriptions of products which cannot be met and the fact that non-commercially organized journeys are not included in the guidelines.

The easing of conditions for entering the market: German tour operators are giving higher priority to working on the new market in East Germany than to expansionist plans in other countries. Instead of trying to establish themselves in foreign countries or to merge with European mega operators, the big German tour operators prefer other strategic options:

- Forming wholesale cooperations to gain demand power against airlines, hotels and regional tourism organizations.
- Continue vertical diversification by acquiring hotels, incoming agencies and car rental firms in order to become 'leisure time enterprises', enabling them to profit from the values added in the different areas of tourism consumption.

- Consolidating their market position in those foreign countries where they are already well established by acquiring medium-sized operators, a strategy preferred by the leading German tour operators TUI (France, Austria, The Netherlands), NUR (Austria, Belgium, The Netherlands) and ITS (The Netherlands and Belgium).

As far as potential competition from abroad is concerned, as yet only Club Med has established itself among the big German operators. The Danish company Tjaerborg was taken over in 1981 by Allkauf/LTT. On the other hand Intasun's attempt to break into the German market was abortive and political developments have forced Yugotours out of the market. There are, however, some interesting peripheral developments; Turks, for example, who have settled in Germany have set up successful small and medium-sized tour operations specializing in travel to Turkey, and in some cases bringing additional destination countries onto the market.

With regard to spa and health resorts, there are fears that Germans may defect to foreign spas especially if it becomes possible to claim social insurance subsidies for treatment in any EC country of the planned Single European Market. By the same token, German spas could possibly attract new customers from countries such as Great Britain where there is potential for a revival of interest in health holidays but where spa facilities are sparse.

In the hotel branch Germans see a possible advantage to their competitiveness if VAT rates were to be harmonized instead of being for example 5% in France, 6% in Greece, Spain and The Netherlands, but 14% in Germany.

The DEHOGA has rejected the planned EC classification of hotels and seems prepared to resist harmonized classification on the grounds that it is unworkable and will increase costs. The fact remains that there is no national hotel classification system in Germany and there is a natural fear that clarity through classifying hotels could lead to unwelcome comparisons by clients and subsequently to reluctant price adjustments especially for the small and medium-sized hotels.

There is little evidence of German hotels trying to expand into foreign markets mainly because there are virtually no large hotel concerns (the main exception being Steigenberger). Small and mid-range hotels are neither interested in nor financially able to buy their way into foreign markets, although they may attract the interest of foreign groups wishing to move into the German market, as has already happened in some cases.

On a political level, the Bundesrat (German Upper House) has established certain policies which meet with the general approval of the trade:

- There should be no extended authority of the EC – the principles of subsidiarity and established federal structures should be respected.
- A careful watch should be kept on the use of EC funds intended to

support private investment in tourism. There are misgivings that such funds can lead to unfair competition since the subsidies go mainly to the countries on the periphery of the EC which already have natural advantages (climate, coasts) and regional advantages from being in low-wage zones.

- Rejection of the EC conducting its own tourism advertising in non-EC countries (as was envisaged in the 1991 EC tourism programme). Such advertising should remain the prerogative of private tourism operators and any supplementary promotional activities should be in the hands of municipal and regional authorities.

PROSPECTS AND TRENDS

Certain trends are already evident in the German tourism industry:

- There is a demand for higher quality, and it is likely that this will include an increasing demand for holidays in unspoilt nature.
- There will probably be a continuation of the trend towards more frequent but shorter holidays.
- There will be an increasing emphasis on active holidays and individualism.
- Holiday decisions may well be made at shorter notice, with operators having to come to terms with greater public interest in last-minute bargains (which have not been a feature of the German market). The number of last-minute bargain offers increased sharply in the summer of 1992, although only one of the 'big four' (LTU) became involved.
- Despite the trend to individualism, the bulk of German holidaymakers will continue to seek the sun and the beach.

For those in Germany concerned with incoming tourism, problems which are likely to become increasingly important are:

- The upper-age bulge which will provide a particular challenge to the industry requiring creative thinking from operators in identifying and satisfying the needs of the group.
- Some honeypot destinations have already reached their ecological breaking points and other ecologically sensitive areas must be protected, especially as tourists become sensitized to environmental issues, although this may conflict with the well-established principle of total freedom of choice as long as you can afford it.
- The private car is and looks set to remain the prime means of transport; day-trippers (who mainly use cars) to popular local destinations may find they are overburdening the very places where they seek peace and quiet;

• Accommodation capacity is increasingly being used to house the hundreds of thousands flooding into Germany as refugees and as German repatriates from the former Eastern Block countries.

CONCLUSIONS

In the medium and long terms a potentially significant reduction in German exports of manufactured goods through price and quality competition from newly emerging industrialized countries such as Korea could have serious consequences not only for the German tourism industry itself but also for the destination countries popular with Germans. In this sense it seems to be in everybody's interest to ensure the continued health of Germany's export trade.

With regard to incoming tourism, Germany must make every effort to attract those visitors in the higher socioeconomic groups who wish to experience and enjoy cultural, architectural, historical, gastronomic and scenic tourism. It will face increasingly fierce competition not only from the rapidly developing exotic resorts in Asia and Africa but also from the sun-blessed European countries which are turning away from the concrete jungles of mass seaside tourism to a more culturally based inland tourism. These higher socioeconomic tourists are discerning people and only those countries and regions which can package and promote their products imaginatively will hold their own. Germany will have to try harder.

However, success cannot depend solely on the advertising men: the professionalism, courtesy and friendliness of those who come into face-to-face contact with the tourists are ultimately the criteria of a country's image. The Germans are well-trained in their tourism professions; if they could enjoy the same reputation for their human relationships their future as tourists and as service personnel to tourists could well be assured. 'Made in Germany' is a yardstick for quality in manufactured goods; 'Welcome to Germany' has yet to achieve that status for hospitality.

REFERENCES

Deutsche Bundesbank (1991) Monatsbericht No 3 / März Frankfurt/Main.
Deutscher Fremdenverkehrs Verband (DFV) (1991) Geschäftsbericht 1990/91. Bonn.
Deutscher Reisebüro Verband (DRV) (1991) Geschäftsbericht 1991. Frankfurt.
Deutsche Zentrale für Tourismus (DZT) (1989) Die Reisen der Europäer 1988. Frankfurt/Main.
Deutsche Zentrale für Tourismus (1991) Deutschland-Tourismus: Der European Travel Monitor. Frankfurt/Main.

Economist Intelligence Unit (ed.) (1987) National Report No. 139 West Germany. The Economist Publications, London.

Godau, A. (1990) Der DDR-Tourismus nach der Umgestaltung. In: Stadtfeld, F. (ed.) *Tourismus in einem neuen Europa.* Fachhochschule Worms, Worms.

Grossmann, M. (1990) Neue Aspekte der Entwicklung der Reiseströme der DDR-Bürger. In: Stadtfeld, F. (ed.) *Tourismus in einem neuen Europa.* Fachhochschule Worms, Worms.

Hank-Haase, G. (1982) Der Ausländertourismus in der Bundesrepublik Deutschland. Der Fremdenverkehr, No. 3.

Opaschowski, H.W. (1988) Psychologie und Soziologie der Freizeit. Leske und Budrich, Opladen.

Statistisches Bundesamt (1991) Fachserie 6, Reihe 7.1 – Handel, Gastgewerbe, Reiseverkehr (monthly). Wiesbaden.

Studienkreis für Tourismus (ed.) (1992) Urlaubsreisen 1954–1991. Starnberg.

14

TOURISM IN SPAIN

Isabel Albert-Piñole

EVOLUTION AND FACTORS OF SPANISH TOURIST DEVELOPMENT

Spain is a leading tourist country worldwide, in terms both of visitors' arrivals and economic resources generated by this activity. According to the latest available data, an estimated 52 million visitors arrived in 1990 (Table 14.1.) or 34.3 million tourists, rating Spain as the third country in the world in terms of tourist arrivals.

Spanish tourism development started spontaneously, almost inevitably, in the 1950s and continued growing until 1988, except for brief inter-ruptions at the time of the 1974, 1979 and 1983 international crises. In the last three years, the rising trend seems to have stopped, with a decrease in the number of visitors (Table 14.1). Even though international events in 1991 have again favoured Spain – resulting in the recovery of 1.5 million visitors – the Spanish tourism industry has entered a transitional stage and is now aware of the need to seek new markets and to adjust to new trends in tourist demand.

The Spanish tourist tradition dates back to old times and there are plenty of books by scholars and travellers of past times describing their tours of Spain and the original and exotic customs to be found in this country. In the Middle Ages, Santiago de Compostela, the Galician town, became one of the most popular destinations for Christendom and the Pilgrims' Road to Santiago, ending in Spain, is regarded as one of the first routes of European tourist history. On the other hand, there is also in Spain an area of cold beaches on the Atlantic coast, as well as a large number of Spas, once chosen by the Royals and upper classes for their holidays and healthy treatments.

Since the Second World War, Spain has become one of the main destinations of European mass tourism; in recent years the yearly number

Table 14.1. Foreign visitors and foreign exchange earnings in Spain, 1950–1990.

Year	No. of visitors (million)	Index	Earnings ($ million)	Index
1950	0.7	100	20	100
1955	2.5	336	96	143
1960	6.1	815	296	1,439
1965	14.2	1,900	1,104	5,361
1970	24.1	3,214	1,680	8,155
1975	30.1	4,016	3,404	16,517
1980	38.0	5,070	6,967	33,807
1985	43.2	5,765	8,150	39,548
1986	47.3	6,319	12,058	58,508
1987	50.5	6,739	14,759	71,615
1988	54.1	7,224	16,686	80,962
1989	54.0	7,208	16,174	78,477
1990	52.0	6,933	18,593	90,213

Source: Secretaria General de Turismo.

of tourists has almost doubled its population, which in 1990 was 39 million, resulting in dramatic changes in its lifestyle and economics. The factors which have contributed to this mass tourism development in Spain are listed below:

1. Spain's geographical position at the southwestern end of Europe gives the country a privileged climate, with plenty of sunlight and soft temperatures, particularly on the Mediterranean coast areas where average temperatures are 12°C in winter months and 24°C in the summer. In addition there are the Canary Islands which have a subtropical climate and a year-long 'summer', with average temperatures of 18–24°C.

2. The Spanish coastline extends to almost 6000 km, of which 40% comprises beaches of varied configuration with plenty of white sand. Both factors, sunshine and seaside, proved a strong attraction for the inhabitants of the cold European cities.

3. Europe is a small continent, well equipped in terms of communications. The short distances between northern and southern countries allow fast journeys by road or plane, thus making the most of holiday time. Spain's location is an advantage which adds to the fast flow of tourist masses.

4. Until the late 1980s, prices in Spain were below average compared with those in the rest of Europe. This has enabled tour operators to offer very economical packages and to achieve significant business profits. The cost of living in Spain was also lower and visitors could enjoy high purchasing power during their holidays.

5. Spaniards are open and vital. As good Mediterraneans, they enjoy open-air life, eating outside, socializing with friends and making the most of daytime. Not without reason, Spaniards are said to be the last in Europe to go to bed. Spain's long and varied history has endowed it with a great gastronomic, folklore and artistic wealth which is displayed in its villages the whole year round. These peculiarities offer foreign visitors a varied and entertaining atmosphere during their holidays.

6. European Tour Operators found in Spain a suitable destination for the holiday needs of other Europeans and a country offering good opportunities for their investments. Spanish seashores became filled with hotels and flats financed by foreigners who could thus offer the best prices for their packages. This tourist neocolonialism allowed a mass arrival of foreigners but generated business conditions which in the long-term proved negative for Spanish companies together with a high degree of dependency from the foreign distribution channels.

GENERAL FEATURES OF FOREIGN TOURISM TRAVELLING TO SPAIN

According to the Tourist General Board (SGT: Secretaria General de Turismo, 1991a), the estimated number of tourists in 1990 (staying for more than 24 hours) amounted to 34.3 million. The remainder, up to 52 million, is made up of excursionists and North African workers in Europe who usually cross the country at the beginning and end of their annual holidays. An analysis of the data on countries of origin (Table 14.2) shows that a large percentage of visitors (41.7%) come from the neighbouring countries France and Portugal, but their length of stay in hotels is lower than that of other nationalities. Visitors from France and Portugal are mainly excursionists who return to their countries within 24 hours. Therefore the highest percentage of hotel stays belongs to Britons and Germans (57.6% of the total number), even though in the last two years their number has dropped. France and the Benelux countries follow next.

The most significant increase in visitors in recent years is that of Italians, 9.6% increase over the 1989 number of visitors, and that of Japanese, amounting to 243,413 in 1990, an increase of 12.4% over the previous year (SGT, 1991b). Tourism coming from USA has stagnated from the time of the Mediterranean crisis and tourism from Latin American is holding steady, depending on these countries' internal circumstances. Due to historic reasons, Spain is the traditional entry gate to Europe for Latin American tourism.

Table 14.2. Arrivals of visitors in Spain by country of origin, 1990.

Country	No. of visitors	% of all visitors	% of hotel overnight stays
France	11,621,206	22.3	9.1
Portugal	10,106,062	19.4	1.1
Germany	6,854,905	13.2	30.7
United Kingdom	6,285,013	12.1	26.9
Benelux	3,294,907	6.3	7.6
Italy	1,656,630	3.2	6.2
Scandinavia	1,614,515	4.0	3.5
USA	835,711	1.6	2.7
Other countries	9,766,559	17.9	12.2

Source: Secretaria General de Turismo.

The means of transport used by visitors are shown in Fig. 14.1. There is a prevailing use of road transport for the closer countries and of the plane for British, German and Scandinavian tourists, with charter flights being used by approximately 70% of the latter.

A peculiar feature of tourism in Spain is the type of accommodation chosen. Most tourists (83.5%) stay in extrahotel accommodation, either flats, villas or bungalows, as places for rent, as a second house (estimated to be more than one million) or through timesharing (over 200,000). Spain's position in this kind of extrahotel accommodation is unique in the world, and ownership by many tourists themselves accounts for a high loyalty to the country as a holiday destination. The remaining 16.5% of foreign tourists stay in hotels. Distribution according to class shows that 25% use luxury and first class hotels (five and four stars) and 75% stay at the lower classes (Table 14.3). These data, together with the estimated average expenditure, amounting to $511.7 – the world average being $581.1 – confirms that most foreign tourists belong to the middle and low middle classes.

One serious problem is the high concentration of tourism arrivals during the summer months (43%), except for the Canary Islands where the high season is in winter. Therefore recent tourism promotion is addressing those markets which might help to even out this marked summer concentration.

Favourite destinations of foreign tourists are seashores (80%), particularly the Balearic Islands and the Canary Islands, as well as the Mediter-

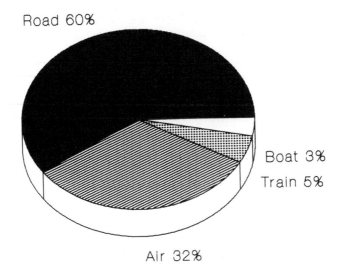

Fig. 14.1. Transportation mode used by visitors arriving in Spain.

ranean coasts of Catalonia, Andalusia and the Valencia Self-Governing Community (Fig. 14.2).

Surveys show that almost 80% of tourists visiting Spain are still attracted in the first place by its sunshine and climate. Their other main motivations are relaxation, its atmosphere, landscape and beaches, as shown in Fig. 14.3 which reflects certain differences from motivations of home tourism (Consultur Barometer, 1991). Their lack of awareness of the alternatives available in Spanish tourism (such as mountain tourism, adventure tourism, inland routes, horseback routes, cities with cultural heritage) has been clearly demonstrated in a recent survey. Current commercial efforts have focused on changing this deficiency (SGT, 1990a).

About 85% of tourists are satisfied with their holidays in Spain, which determines their loyalty to the country as holiday destination. Their main complaints are about the state of the roads, noise and cleanliness in some areas (Consultur Barometer, 1991).

GENERAL CHARACTERISTICS OF SPANIARDS AS TOURISTS

The Spanish tourism industry is increasingly paying attention to Spanish tourists, whose tendency to travel is markedly increasing as their standard of living rises. Their vital temperament makes them good customers who enjoy their holidays with a rather high level of expenses.

Their holiday customs have been regularly studied by the Tourist

Table 14.3. Overnight stays of foreign tourists in Spain in 1990 by hotel (H) and hostel (h) categories. Ranking is shown in stars, 5 stars being the highest class of hotel and 3 stars the highest for hostels (inns).

Category	Total	Percentage
4 and 5* H	16,416,930	25
2 and 3* H	37,142,450	58
1* H and 3* h	6,275,198	10
1 and 2* h	4,751,941	7

Source: Secretaria General de Turismo.

General Board and the results of the last survey (Tourist General Board, 1991a) have been used to support this section of the chapter, which should give a better understanding of their potential as travellers to other European countries.

More than half the Spanish population makes at least one holiday journey every year. The comparative survey for the last two years shows an increase in the number of annual journeys, the European trend to distribute holiday times being also confirmed in Spain (Fig. 14.4). With the last

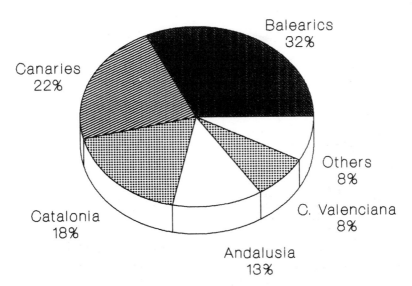

Fig. 14.2. Overnight stays by foreign tourists to Spain by region of destination, 1990.

Isabel Albert-Piñole

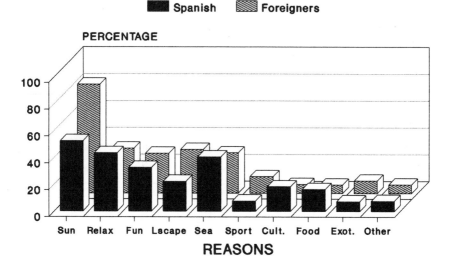

Fig. 14.3. Main reasons for choosing Spain for holidays, 1990.

survey using a reference population of 30.8 million inhabitants aged over 16, actual travellers' demand is estimated at approximately 16.5 million. For more than 80% of persons interviewed, their main holiday destination is Spain, and within the country, favourite areas are first Valencia Self Governing Community (including Benidorm) followed by Andalusia and Catalonia.

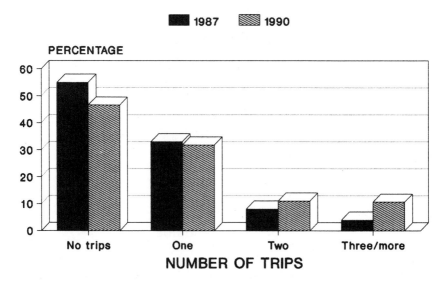

Fig. 14.4. Annual number of holiday trips by Spaniards (%), 1987 and 1990.

Table 14.4. Distribution of Spanish outgoing visitors by country of destination.

Country	%
France	16.3
Portugal	11.4
Italy	9.9
United Kingdom	8.9
USA	4.9
Switzerland	2.5
Austria	2.3
Mexico	2.3
Morocco	2.3
The Netherlands	2.1
Greece	1.9
Tunisia	1.5
Egypt	1.0
Former USSR	0.5
Venezuela	0.5
China	0.5
Other European countries	19.3
Other American countries	7.1
Other Asian countries	4.0
Other African countries	0.5
Rest of countries	0.2
No data available	0.2
Total	100.0

Source: Dirección General de Política Turística (General Department of Tourist Policy) (1991).

A total of 19% of Spaniards travelled abroad on their main holidays, which means a 7% increase over the 1987 survey. The more visited countries were France, Portugal, Italy and the United Kingdom, in Europe; USA and Mexico in America; Morocco and Tunisia in Africa and China in Asia (Table 14.4). The selection of these destinations indicates that travelling interests are itinerant and cultural.

Travel agencies are scarcely required by Spaniards, since 77.8% arrange their holidays on their own. Only 16.6% use the travel agencies, but this rate is increasing in comparison with previous studies. Average expense per person during the main journey amounts to 75,480 pesetas; however there are significant differences among the various sectors of population, average expense in the upper class being 115,000 pesetas.

As yet, no winter holidays have been officially recognized in Spain, which results in a marked seasonality, as shown by 41.6% of the travelling population having their main holidays in August, 24.2% in July and 11.3% in September.

Spaniards' travelling motivations are also shown in Fig. 14.3, with cultural and gastronomic interests playing a greater role than with foreign tourists. The most recent survey shows that walking, photography, eating in restaurants, shopping, monument sightseeing and socializing with friends and relatives are the most popular holiday activities.

THE CURRENT SPANISH TOURIST OFFERINGS

The prevailing motivations of sunshine and beach are the reasons for the Mediterranean coast areas being the most popular tourist regions. Mass tourism resorts have developed in these areas, some known worldwide,

Fig. 14.5. Main tourist resources in Spain.

Table 14.5. Tourist lodgings (beds) in Spain, 1990.

Type of lodging	No. of beds
Hotels	929,533
Pensions	173,658
Camp sites	571,278
Apartments (Registered beds)	384,904
Apartments (Non registered beds)[a]	7,170,900
Apartments (Potential touristic use)[a]	16,302,049

Source: Secretaria General de Turismo.
[a]Estimation 1989.

such as Benidorm in the province of Alicante, Torremolinos in Malaga, or the municipality of Calviá in Mallorca, with more accommodations than the whole of Greece (Fig. 14.5). These tourist resorts often have an urban structure which consists of a main street, almost always the Waterfront Walk, lined by hotels and apartment buildings, as well as lots of restaurants and coffee houses with terraces, shops and discos which provide these locations with a lively and popular atmosphere. The pleasant climate of Benidorm in the Costa Blanca, Marbella in the Costa del Sol, Maspalomas in Gran Canaria or Puerto de la Cruz in Tenerife attract tourism in winter, particularly European pensioners who own a second house or who periodically travel there to enjoy the sunshine.

There are other tourist resorts with distinguishing features, such as Ibiza island, a regular resort destination for the hippies in the 1960s and today for a frivolous and cosmopolitan tourism flow and Lanzarote island with an exotic volcanic landscape. Bohemian Cadaqués in the Costa Brava or Fuerteventura on the Atlantic coast with its desert landscapes, a paradise for windsurf lovers, are other examples of coastal attractions.

Throughout these years, high standing tourist resorts have also developed in Spain. Aiming at a minority tourism group, they are less well known. Their structure is different, including villas and luxury hotels spreading over hills close to the sea, often with a small yachting port. The best known are Aiguablava and S'Agaro in the Costa Brava, the latter having a great musical tradition. Cala D'or and Formentor in Mallorca; Marbella in Malaga, known as 'the golden mile' due to the number of Rolls Royces which can be seen nearby Puerto Banús; Costa Teguise in Lanzarote, where vegetation has been protected branch by branch, or Sotogrande in Cadiz where golf alternates with polo, horse riding and sherry.

The accommodation in 1990 amounted to more than two million beds, distributed as follows: 929,533 in hotels, 173,658 in boarding houses, 571,278 in camping grounds and 384,904 in apartments (Table 14.5). Outstanding among them is the Network of State Hotels ('Paradores'),

Table 14.6. Number of hotels by region and star rating, 1991.

Region	Hotels by star rating					Pensions			Total
	5	4	3	2	1	1	2	3	
Andalucia	14	61	186	168	114	15	284	2	844
Aragon	3	7	38	59	63	4	90	123	387
Asturias	2	9	26	34	43	1	88	37	240
Baleares	6	48	345	203	190	18	180	410	1400
Canarias	11	71	98	52	23	2	48	7	312
Cantabria	1	4	24	30	45	7	80	67	258
Cast./Mancha	–	7	28	45	32	1	114	119	346
Cast./Leon	2	15	64	66	67	6	245	266	731
Cataluña	11	70	255	260	316	20	469	595	1996
Ceuta	–	2	1	–	–	–	2	–	5
Comun. Valenc.	4	22	101	120	117	9	122	218	713
Extremadura	–	5	12	18	26	1	51	75	188
Galicia	3	16	42	61	114	4	195	333	768
La Rioja	–	3	10	6	5	1	12	12	49
Madrid	13	39	51	24	15	39	211	355	747
Melilla	–	–	1	2	1	1	4	2	11
Murcia	–	8	11	32	10	–	34	50	145
Navarra	–	2	15	14	9	5	37	32	114
Pais Vasco	2	11	22	27	20	2	66	31	181
Total	72	400	1330	1221	1210	136	2332	2734	9435

Source: Federacion Española de Hospedaje; Turespaña.

with 86 extremely comfortable residences, mostly situated in castles, palaces and old monasteries. This initiative dates back to 1928, its purpose being the preservation of buildings of an artistic and monumental value, the creation of stable jobs in generally less developed areas and the promotion of home and cultural tourism. The territorial distribution of the Network of State Hotels is shown in Fig. 14.5, being the starting or stability point for a large part of the alternative offer.

As regards hotels distributed throughout the country, 20% are upper class (five and four stars); 43% are three star hotels and the rest are lower class hotels (SGT, 1990b). The territorial distribution of these establishments is shown in Table 14.6 (Travel and Tourist Analyst Database, 1991). The increasing concentration of proprietary interests has originated 65 hotel networks, 25% of which are participated in through foreign capital (SGT, 1989).

There are also about 7 million places in apartments which are not legally recorded. This over-development of the extra-hotel offer has taken place mainly in the 1980s resulting in an offer surplus illegally competing with hotels and a marginal and uncontrolled tourist congestion. According to SGT (1987a) the provinces of Gerona, Alicante, Valencia and Palma de Mallorca have the most of this kind of establishment.

As regards Spanish transport infrastructure, there is a wide network of national and local roads, but an insufficient number of motorways and highways. This is particularly evident during the summer months where there is the increase in traffic due to tourism. However, the Second Road Plan is being completed, which will expand the current network of motorways and highways from 3100 km to 3785 km.

In Spain there are 39 airports connected to more than 50 countries by the leading air company Iberia. One of these airports, Palma de Mallorca, has the highest volume of traffic in Europe during the summer. In addition, there are home and regional air companies and over 15 charter flight companies.

The railway network is equipped with modern vehicles but its radial layout emanating from Madrid, and its wider gauge of the rails are disadvantages for connections with other European countries. In recent years, high investments have been made in this sector and a High Speed network is being opened in 1992 along the Madrid–Seville route. Tourist trains such as Al-Andalus, an old luxury train, or the 'Transcantabrico', a modern train with narrow gauge track, offer tourist circuits lasting several days throughout Andalusia, the Road to Santiago and the Northern Coast.

Sea transport for passengers is mostly by the ferries linking the peninsula with the Balearic Islands, the Canary Islands and northern Africa. There are also ferries between the Spanish northern coast and southern England. After a period of recession, tourist cruises are being increasingly promoted; and there are a large number of yachting ports all along the coast.

Tourist marketing is performed by 4500 Travel Agencies which are legally recorded as wholesalers, not selling directly to the public, wholesalers–retailers and retailers. Of these 56.9% deal with Spanish outgoing traffic and only 18.1% deal with incoming tourism (SGT, 1987b). Most incoming tourism is organized by foreign tour operators, 50% of whose business is situated in Spain, according to the SGT (1991c).

SOCIOECONOMIC IMPACT OF TOURISM IN SPAIN

Tourism has played and is still playing a major role in the Spanish social and economic development. Foreign currency income in the 1960s and 1970s significantly helped to finance the industrial development plans

(Cals Joan, 1974), and tourism is at present the main economic activity for regions such as the Balearic and Canary Islands.

Worries over this sector are justified since it is currently one of the main national industries, as shown by the economic variables which are discussed below.

Tourist activity has accounted for approximately 9% of the Gross National Product (GNP) up to the end of the 1980s, when it dropped, amounting to 8.09% in 1990. The services sector as a whole accounts for 54.5% of GNP whereas the industrial sector accounts for 25.5% and the agricultural sector 4.5% (SGT, 1991a).

Total tourist consumption dramatically increased up to the last three years, when it became stabilized due to a stagnation in foreign tourist consumption. However, numbers are still rising as they are compensated by an increasing rise in home tourist consumption (SGT, 1990b).

The Spanish balance of payments has been traditionally characterized by a deficit in the balance of trade, which is compensated by tourism revenues of 57.4%. The tourism balance of payments has always yielded a large positive result. Final accounts in 1990 were as follows:

Income	$18,593.0 million
Payments	$ 4,253.5 million
Balance	$14,339.5 million

The tourist sector employed 1.4 million persons in 1990, which accounts for 11.2% of the Spanish working population. Almost 60% of these jobs are regarded as directly related to the tourist sector and 40% as indirectly related. This rate could be increased if employment induced in other activities such as construction or food was included.

The main problem of Spanish tourist employment is its seasonal and geographical concentration, together with the abandoning of traditional productive sectors such as fishing or farming. The transfer of working population to the tourist resorts has resulted in dramatic population increases during the last 25 years in provinces such as Gerona (260%), Alicante (170%) or Malaga (150%) (Valenzuela Manuel, 1991a).

Tourism has also been responsible for the rise in the standard of living in most tourist provinces. This is so with the Balearic Islands and Gerona, rated as first and second respectively when assessing the Spanish per capita income.

Tourism business in Spain was originally structured around small and medium-size companies, resulting in a highly fragmented sector. In recent years there is a clear trend towards concentration; it is worth noticing the sudden investment of Spanish banks in this sector.

However, tourism has also had some negative impact on the country which should be corrected in the future. The improvised growth of the tourism industry was not accompanied by suitable territorial planning;

some areas suffered aesthetical degradation due to the excessive urban concentration. High buildings on the seashore front replaced the local architecture, which was much more picturesque, thus making some fishing towns into tourist resorts lacking personality.

Notwithstanding the early incorporation of Spain into the movement for environmental preservation (1916), in the last decades there has been a significant delay in this field, which within the context of fast economic growth, rural depopulation, intensive urbanization and marked tourist specialization, has resulted in irreparable damage to the environment. However, Spain still has a remarkable legacy in terms of its quantity, variety and peculiarity. In the 1980s, there are hopes of novel approaches and initiatives from the various Public Administrations (Cals and Riera, 1989).

In many tourist municipalities, the requirements for public services infrastructures exceed the local financing resources, this being one of the serious problems which the Spanish tourist development will have to face in the future (Official Gazette of Spanish Parliament, 1991). On the other hand, a commercial overdependence on foreign tour operators and their pressure to keep prices low have decapitalized some companies established on the coast, leading them to deal only with groups with the lowest purchasing power.

The excessive seasonal and space concentration has resulted in serious human and traffic congestion with the subsequent environmental degradation in areas with mass tourism.

PUBLIC ORGANIZATION OF TOURISM

In view of the significant role played by the tourism industry in Spain, governments have promoted its development making foreign investments easier, granting credits and even establishing a tourist insurance protecting travellers. Activities of any tourism-related business, such as accommodation, restaurants and travel agencies, have been regulated through strict legal regulations establishing categories and protecting consumers by demanding guarantees and endorsements. Tourism has been incorporated into the government bodies with a high status even though not achieving the status of a separate Ministry. Throughout the years it has been linked to the Ministries of Information, Trade, Transport and at present, Industry.

This lack of definition together with the different levels of decision making at Public Administrations resulted in a lack of general planning and coordination among the bodies concerned, which in turn has prevented a more harmonious development in this industry.

In 1978 the new Spanish Constitution was enacted, dividing the State into 17 Self-Governing Communities (see Fig. 14.5). Thereafter most tourism-related capacities were transferred to each Community, the Central Government keeping its capacity as coordinator of the tourism general policy and promotion abroad, as well as education, credit and research, by itself or together with the other governments (Ferreiro, 1990). The highest body in the central government is the Tourist General Board, to which Turespaña is subjected as well, the latter dealing with promotion.

Tourism promotion is assigned a major budget share from the Central Government, which in 1992 will exceed 5000 million pesetas. Campaigns include advertising in newspapers, magazines and TV, brochures, videotapes, newspaper articles, participation in international tourism fairs, special celebrations, and a permanent presence in 21 countries through 28 Spanish Tourist Offices.

Many of these campaigns, particularly those requiring attendance at Fairs and Workshops, are arranged in close cooperation with the General Departments of Tourism Promotion of the Self-Governing Communities and the Tourist Municipal Boards and urban Convention Bureaus, as well as the private tourist sector.

The 17 Self-Governing Communities have been give the responsibility to regulate tourist business and activities, to inspect and supervise them and to develop their own promotion campaigns locally and abroad, emphasizing the peculiarities of each area e.g. Asturias, a Natural Paradise; art and history of Castile-Leon; hunting, wines and Don Quixote's itineraries in Castile La Mancha, etc.

The third level of tourist responsibility is assigned to the Town Councils, which are responsible for infrastructures and services as well as promotion and social tourism.

The Central Public Administration through a state holding, the National Institute for Industry (INI), keeps ownership of basic public transport such as international, national and local air transport (Iberia Air Lines, Aviaco, Binter Canarias and Mediterraneo and Viva charter flight company); rail transport (RENFE and FEVE), sea transport (Transmediterranea), and at times financing certain regular coach lines and one travel agency (Viajes Marsans).

Relations with the EEC culminated on 1 January 1986 with the incorporation into the European Community. Thereafter previous laws had to be adjusted to those of the EC. The tourism sector was particularly affected by the introduction of VAT, which increased consumer prices by 6%, to 33%. The new economic requirements for charter companies also affected tourist companies due to the significant increase in the paid up capital.

Tourism regulations, such as Combined Travel, have not had a noticeable impact on travel agencies, since they were already partly included in the Spanish regulations for these companies.

The 1993 Single European Market will ease the exchange of capital and manpower even more. After recent amalgamations and mergers of various kinds, Spanish companies are getting ready to increase their contacts and involvements with other European companies.

PROSPECTS FOR TOURISM IN SPAIN

Spain's main attraction has traditionally been its climate and coasts, as well as certain topics such as flamenco, bullfighting and dark-haired women. These topics have created a single picture of Spain abroad, over shadowing other attractions discovered only by a minority of tourists. Over the last two years, this mass tourism in search of sunshine and seaside has diminished. This decrease is attributed to the following factors:

1. Tastes are changing and foreign tourists' traditional loyalty to Spain has been tempted by new tourist resorts in the eastern Mediterranean, northern Africa and the Caribbean Islands. These places have become accessible by a decrease in air fares and they have been included as new destinations in the programmes of the tour operators.
2. Customers are presently more varied and demanding; Spain should offer a wider variety and improve the quality of service in certain areas.
3. Prices at home have increased, due to social and labour reasons, the entry into the EC and the subsequent implementation of new taxes such as VAT, and the monetary policy keeps a strong peseta in terms of international rates of exchange.
4. The excessive concentration of countries generating tourists causes a significant decrease in the total number of arrivals due to those countries' internal situation, particularly the United Kingdom and Germany.

Even though it is not thought that the Spanish tourist model is declining, it would be convenient to renew the offer and to change the business criteria, to try to capture other markets with a higher purchasing power and to promote the unknown touristic potential in Spain.

For these purposes, the following measures have been taken:

1. National and local Marketing Plans have been implemented in order to plan and coordinate actions related to tourism. The new 1992 promotional campaigns aim at showing the entire Spanish alternative offer, which fulfils today's tourism requirements (sports, history, culture, excellent facilities for meetings and conferences, art, music, painting, spas, mountain sports, etc.). The new motto for this offer is: 'Spain, passion for life', plus the emblem with a sun designed by the Catalonian painter Joan Miro (Fig. 14.6).
2. Updating business structures through a Competitivity Plan announced by the Central Public Administration. This Plan applies industrial recovery

Fig. 14.6. The promotional campaign for Spain showing a sun designed by the painter Joan Miro. Source: Secretaria General de Turismo.

programmes to a sector traditionally related to services, offering tax deductions and subsidies. It also includes state aids to improve training and introduce new technologies. Its purpose is to improve the negotiating position of Spanish tourist companies faced with foreign Tour Operators and to improve quality of services.

3. As regards new products, there is a policy aimed at capturing new market niches with a higher purchasing power, and helping to overcome seasonalness. This is being done on two action lines:

Improving the complementary offer

Without renouncing the traditional sunshine and seaside offer, which is still valid, facilities are renewed and a wide complementary offer is added in order to satisfy a new kind of tourist, more active and with a higher purchasing power. To this effect, 104 golf courses have already been built, most of them linked to luxury hotels or private clubs, since Spain offers the advantage of long sunlight hours to practise this sport. Further, 326 water facilities have been opened, for the coastal traffic of sport vessels all along the Spanish coast, and sailing schools and nautical charter hiring.

To provide for tourists' spare time in the evenings, there are 31 aquatic parks, 20 casinos, six fun fairs and over 50,000 restaurants, bars and pubs, as well as a wide range of exhibitions, festivals, sports tournaments and concerts. Night life can be enjoyed at thousands of discos, nightclubs and dance halls, in addition to the typical Flamenco shows.

Promoting the Spanish alternative offer

The alternative offer focuses on culture, nature and the market of meetings' organizing. In contrast to other countries, these three are focused on the remarkable variety of landscapes in a small territory.

Cultural Spain displays its long and troubled history through its various tourist routes, i.e. Prehistoric, Greek, Roman, Jewish, Visigothic, Arab, Romanesque, Gothic, Baroque …; itineraries through Monasteries or 1500 castles. In addition to these historical routes, there are other popular ones, such as The White Villages, Don Quixote's, Alpujarras or Food Routes, as well as Saint Patron festivities in villages, the whole year round. This cultural legacy can be enjoyed by staying at the 'Paradores', where decorations and architecture date back to old times.

Natural Spain can be experienced through 13 National Parks and 33 Natural Parks with programmed routes on horseback, on foot or bycicle (see Fig. 14.5). Spain's southern position at one end of Europe has made this country into a great hunting reserve with unique species, e.g. *Capra hispanica* or red partridge. Spain preserves special kinds of big game hunting, such as venery, and small game, such as beating, which may be practised in 41 Reserves and Game Preserves and in 3600 private game preserves which are offered to tourists by specialized companies. In fact, hunting attracts some 100,000 foreigners every year and more than 1.3 million Spaniards are holders of a hunting licence (Romero, 1985).

Another largely unknown aspect of Spain is the number of mountains where a wide variety of sports, such as trekking, rafting, 'parapente', mountain-climbing, delta wing, etc. can be practised. Spain is the second most mountainous country in Europe, after Switzerland, and in recent years 27 skiing resorts have been developed, with modern facilities and varied and lively après-ski facilities (see Fig. 14.5 above).

Health tourism has turned into beauty and healthy-life tourism. There are 95 spas in Spain, whose facilities are being restored to provide for these new tourist trends. The increasing age of the European population allows for the revival of these kind of resorts.

The most recent tourist boom has already occurred in the market of meetings organization, where Spain has moved up from 20th place to ninth place, in terms of numbers of international meetings held, with Madrid being ranked seventh in the world ranking of conference cities (UIA, 1990). The rapid development of this market can be accounted for by the suitable hotel infrastructure, together with the 15 conference halls, 17 fair sites and 19 convention bureaus which have been opened in Spanish towns.

The major events of 1992 provided a springboard for the new Spanish tourist model, highlighting its three main features: sports tourism at the Olympic Games in Barcelona; cultural tourism at Madrid, appointed 'Europe's Cultural Capital', and progress and science tourism at the Seville World Fair.

Spain's challenge during the next decades is not just to offer more but also to consolidate this broader offer, aiming at stable figures, and better promotion and marketing.

REFERENCES AND FURTHER READING

Albert-Piñole, I. (1991) *Gestión y Técnicas de agencias de viajes.* Sintesis, Madrid.
Cals, J. (1974) *Turismo y Política Turística en España: Una aproximación.* Ariel, Barcelona.
Cals, J. and Riera, P. (1989) La protección de los espacios naturales y su aportación a la oferta turística recreativa. *Estudios Turísticos* 103, 47–83.
Chamber of Deputies, IVth Legislature (1991) Análisis de la actual situación turística en España. *Parliament's Official Gazette,* 16 October 1991, Series E 172.
Consultur Barometer (1991) Análisis de la satisfacción de la demanda turística en España en 1990. *Editur* 1616.
Ferreiro, J.A. (1990) Las Administraciones Turísticas de las Comunidades Autónomas en la década de los 90. *Spic.*
General Department of Tourist Policy (1991) Las vacaciones de los españoles en 1990. *Estudios Turísticos* 109, 65–96.
International Union of Associations (UIA) (1990) *Bulletin on Statistics from International Meetings.* Brussels.
National Institute of Statistics (1990) *Anuario.* Madrid.
Romero, J.M. (1985) Adecuación y desarrollo de la oferta de caza mayor a la demanda turístico-cinegética. *IInd Symposium on Cynegetic Tourism.* 11–13 November, Cordoba.
Tourist General Board (1987a) Estudio de la demanda extrahotelera en España. *Estudios Turísticos* 96, 19–51.
Tourist General Board (SGT) (1987b) *Estructura Económica Financiera de las Agencias de Viajes.* Madrid.

Tourist General Board (1989) Concentración y asociacionismo empresarial en el sector turístico. *Estudios Turísticos* 103, 3–33.

Tourist General Board (1990a) *Estudio sobre el grado de satisfacción de la demanda turística nacional y extranjera en relación con el producto turístico español.* Madrid.

Tourist General Board (1990b) *Libro Blanco del turismo español.* Madrid.

Tourist General Board (1991a) General Department of Tourist Policy. El Turismo Español en cifras 1991. *Estudios Turísticos* 111, 85–94.

Tourist General Board (1991b) *Movimiento Turístico.* December 1990.

Tourist General Board (1991c) El precio de los packages turísticos. Temporada 1990–91. *Estudios Turísticos* 109, 3–64.

Travel and Tourist Analyst Database (1991) The travel and tourism industry in Spain. *The Economist Intelligence Unit* 5, 90–94.

Valenzuela, M. (1991) Spain: the phenomenon of mass tourism, 3. In: Williams, A. and Shaw, G. (eds) *Tourism & Economic Development: Western European Experiences*, 2nd edn. Belhaven Press, London, pp. 40–60.

15

TOURISM IN PORTUGAL

Jonathan Edwards and Francisco Sampaio

INTRODUCTION

Over the last 30 years tourism has become established as an industry of major importance to the Portuguese economy, being second only to textile and garment manufacturing and having a value of receipts over expenditure in excess of £1500m (375,000 million escuedos or 2000 million ECU (European Currency Units) in 1990. This is approximately equal to £150 (200 ECU)/head of the Portuguese population. Thus the significance of tourism, particularly when the remittances from emigrants, for many years a mainstay of the country's economy, are continuing to decline to below 20% of the current account, cannot be over emphasized. Consequently, although major efforts are being made both to modernize the textile industries in order to retain their competitiveness as labour costs rise and to diversify the manufacturing sector, the service industries (particularly tourism) are likely to remain as one of the cornerstones of the Portuguese economy in the forseeable future.

The development and establishment of the present structures of the Portuguese tourism industry have to be placed in the context of political events in Portugal in the 20th Century. The Portuguese monarchy was overthrown in 1910 and the First Republic inaugurated. The next 20 years were marked by political instability which ended when Salazar assumed the premiership in 1932. Under his rule Portugal adopted a policy of focusing her attention internally and upon her African colonies.

While Marcelo Caetano, who succeeded Salazar in 1968, attempted to reverse some of these attitudes Portugal re-emerged as a democracy in 1974 at a considerable economic disadvantage when compared with the majority of countries of western Europe. Economic recovery has been significantly assisted by Portugal's application for (1976) and subsequent membership of (1986) the European Community in that community funds

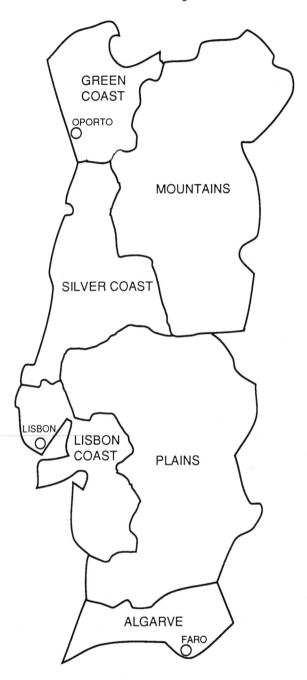

Fig. 15.1. The tourist regions of mainland Portugal.

have been made available for a wide range of development and modernization programmes from the late 1970s onwards.

To many people, tourism in Portugal is synonymous with the development of package holidays in the last 30 years. Portugal's attractions are
thought of as being 'sun, sea and sand' and the main location as the
southern coastal Algarve (Fig. 15.1). This perception reflects the facts that
of the 19 million visitors to Portugal in 1991 over 8 million were tourists,
90% of whom were there for holiday purposes and of these, 40% were
staying in the Algarve, a further 20% in and around Lisbon and 14% on
the Island of Madeira (DGT, 1992).

Although this widespread view is perfectly understandable it is
important to realize that Portugal has a long history of domestic and
international tourism. Although not on the 'Grand tour' circuit it received
a good many foreign travellers over the centuries (Macaulay, 1946, 1991),
and the British in particular had established the practice of taking several
weeks vacation on Madeira on their way back home from India and the Far
East by the end of the 18th century (Hudson, 1986). Domestically, beach
tourism was also underway in the late 18th century (Mapplebeck, 1992)
and well-developed adjacent to the larger coastal towns by the late 19th
century (Ortigao, 1876). In addition, spa tourism was also developed for
both the domestic and international market in the 19th century (Cavaco,
1979).

DEVELOPMENTS PRIOR TO 1940

In the late 19th and early 20th centuries the importance and potential of
tourism to Portugal was recognized and the natural landscapes and sun
were perceived to be the major attractions. The inauguration of the 'Sud
Express' train linking Paris to Madrid and then Lisbon in 1887 was a
considerable boost to Portugal's tourism particularly in the area around
Lisbon Cascais and Estoril (Pina, 1988).

Both private individuals and the government of the first republic,
established in 1911 after the overthrow of the monarchy, recognized the
potential importance of tourism and with this the need actively to promote
Portugal to an international audience. The appointment of a government
minister in 1911 gave added impetus to promotion, and despite considerable
political instability, this was maintained with the result that by 1930
overseas tourism offices had been established in London, Paris, New York
and Amsterdam.

Subsequently the government came forward with proposals for
developing the Portuguese 'Costa del Sol' along the Estoril–Cascais coast,
immediately to the west of the capital Lisbon. The Estoril–Cascais develop-

ment can claim to be the first major planned tourist development in Portugal, although the importance of tourism to the development of various Portuguese coastal towns had already been recognized – Ortigao in 1876 described the northern resort of Povoa de Varzim as 'one enormous Inn'. Most development had previously been confined to the provision of hotel accommodation, for example the hotels associated with thermal spas such as the Palace hotels at Bussaco and Vidago. Partly as a result of the award of the Estoril design contract to the French architect Henry Martinet and despite interruptions due to Portuguese involvement in the First World War, publicity material in the 1920s was proclaiming this area the Portuguese Riviera. The development of the area was further secured through the building of one of the first electric train services linking Cascais to Lisbon in 1927, the establishment of a permanent Casino at Estoril and the opening of the Hotel Pálacio in 1931. These developments and the rapid acceptance of the miraculous appearance at Fatima in central Portugal resulted in Estoril and Fatima being the major foci of Portuguese tourism in the early 1930s and led to a situation where annual international arrivals throughout the 1930s averaged around 36,000 (Lewis and Williams, 1988).

In 1933 the Estado Novo, the 'new state' was introduced by Salazar and the promotion of tourism was brought, together with the promotion of all of Portugal, under the direction of the SPN (Secretariado de Propaganda Nacional) and its associated IPN (Instituto Promocao Nacionais). Although the dictatorial regime of the Estado Novo affected many aspects of Portuguese life, it does not appear to have restricted the development of the country's tourism. There is considerable evidence (Pina, 1988) that the SPN under dynamic leadership continued to promote Portugal effectively to an international audience and, in January 1936, at the first National Congress of Tourism which was held in Lisbon. The organizers intended that this congress should increase awareness of the significance of tourism and the final communique sought to establish appropriate fiscal structures to support a tourism information infrastructure, appropriate travel agency services and to develop the general standards of hotel management.

FROM 1940 TO 1990

Portugal's relative isolation from the rest of Europe was turned to advantage in the 1940s when her neutrality resulted in there being a large influx of refugees seeking the protection of a neutral state. The influx of thousands of refugees, principally to the Lisbon–Estoril area, led to considerable discussions about the short and long-term effects of these refugees on the development of the country's tourism. Another outcome of

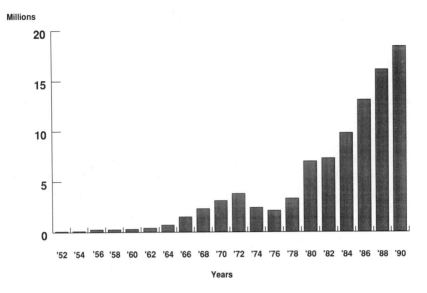

Fig. 15.2. Total visitor arrivals, 1952–1990. Source: Customs.

the demand the refugees generated for hotel accommodation, was the decision by the state in 1942 to follow the Spanish example and to provide and assume direct responsibility for a number of high quality, state run hotels or Pousadas.

The 1950s were a period of active growth in Portugal's tourism industry partly due to the interest shown by Marcello Caetano who was later to succeed Salazar. This decade also saw the production of the first, in what were to become a series, of 'Planos de Fomentos' (Plans to facilitate, encourage and promote development) for all Portugal. The first two of these, covering the years 1953–1958 and 1959–1964, placed particular emphasis on primary industry, water resources and communications. Although tourism itself was not referred to in these first National plans the origins of many of the current governmental agencies of Tourism were established in the period 1955–1960. For example, the 'Fundo Turismo', providing low interest development loans, and craft-based training schools run by the Tourism, as opposed to Education, ministry were established in 1956. The same year saw the creation of a few 'Regiões de Turismo' (Tourism Regions) although they had a very restricted remit. These developments in the 1950s were rewarded not only by the opening of more prestigious hotels, such as the Ritz in Lisbon in 1959, but also by a rise in international vistor arrivals from 150,000 in 1953 to 250,000 in 1958. Despite the rapidly escalating colonial wars in her African colonies, which were not only a considerable financial burden but also fuelled large-scale

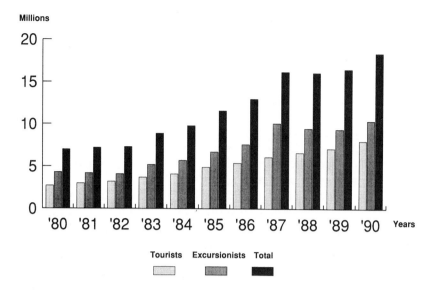

Fig. 15.3. Visitor arrivals: total, tourists and excursionists, 1980–1990.
Source: DGT/INE.

illegal (and some legal) migration, Portugal's popularity as a tourist destination increased sharply in the period 1958–1964 (Fig. 15.2), a period in which a number of hotels opened on previously undeveloped coastal locations both in the Algarve and on the Western Atlantic coast.

The early 1960s saw an increasing realization of the economic importance of tourism to the Portuguese economy. It was recognized then that while the remittances from emigrants were a vital contribution these would not last for ever and it was not long before earnings from tourism were being cited as the saviour of the Portuguese economy. This recognition of the increasingly important role of tourism led the national government to sponsor a report on tourism development by the Swiss consultant Kurt Krapf in order to identify the major lines of future development. This concern with the country's tourism industry coincided with the recording of one million visitor arrivals in 1964, and with the end of the second five-year plan.

As with many other destinations the mid 1960s was characterized by the emergence and rapid development of the package holiday market. This was particularly the case in the Algarve where development was stimulated by the opening of an international airport at Faro in 1965. Prior to this there had been very little tourism development, due largely to the very poor road and rail links with the rest of Portugal and Europe. A distinguishing feature of the early years of tourism in the Algarve was the successful policy of providing for and attracting the relatively high-spending sector of the international tourist market.

The rapid development of the summer sun package holiday resulted in a doubling of tourist arrivals in the four year period 1964–1968 (see Fig. 15.2) and these events led to a decision in 1968 to rationalize the national tourism agencies which were brought together in a new body responsible for all aspects of tourism activity, the 'Direcção Geral do Turismo' or DGT. It was perhaps inevitable that in compiling the third plan (1968–1973) tourism was recognized as a 'vital strategic sector' and this recognition of the economic importance of tourism was also reflected in the fourth and last of these national plans drawn up in 1974.

As with many other countries Portugal's tourism development was curtailed in the late 1960s and early 1970s by a world recession and then in 1973 by the sharp rise in oil prices. Additionally the 'quiet' revolution of 25 April 1974 had a major impact upon the country's tourism, effects which are clearly seen in the number of international tourist arrivals which had risen to 2.3 million in 1973 but which fell to 888,000 in 1975 and did not exceed 2.3 million again until 1979. Events were further complicated by the return of 800,000 military personnel and Portuguese nationals to mainland Portugal. The most immediate need of many of these 'retornados' was accommodation and as a result many of the country's hotels particularly in the Lisbon area were taken over to accommodate the 50,000 who had been made homeless. Additionally, the uncertainty surrounding the political changes and the nationalization of many companies all contributed to disturb the development process. Some projects begun before the revolution are still awaiting completion.

Following the turbulent period of the 1970s the period from 1978 to 1987 was one of significant growth in Portugal's tourism industry when visitor arrivals rose from 3.2 million to 16.2 million (10.1 million excursionists and 6.1 million tourists) (Fig. 15.3).

In the next two years growth slowed to a total of 16.5 million in 1989 but increased again to 18.4 million in 1990 and 19.5 million in 1991. The pattern of tourist arrivals maintaining a more even growth than that of the more volatile excursionist market (Fig. 15.3), dominated by Spanish visitors, reflecting the relative strength of the Spanish economy.

The four most important nationalities for Portugal's tourism industry are Spanish, British, German and French (see Table 15.1). Whereas Spain accounts for almost half of all arrivals, visitors from the United Kingdom and Germany both account for a higher percentage of total bednights. Although there has been a consistent and rapid rise in the numbers of tourist arrivals this has to some extent been offset by a significant reduction in the average length of stay which has fallen steadily from an average of 12 days in 1975 to 7.4 days in 1990 (DGT, 1991).

If we exclude the Spanish market, over 98% of whom travel by road,

Table 15.1. Tourist arrivals by nationality 1989/1990 and bednights by nationality 1990.

Nationality	1989 (1000's)	1990 (1000's)	% change 1989–90	% of 1990 total	Bednights % of total
Spain	3264.8	3924.3	+20.9	48.9	7.3
United Kingdom	1027.3	1061.1	+3.3	13.2	22.1
Germany	564.7	621.4	+10.0	7.8	9.9
France[a]	610.8	617.8	+1.1	7.7	3.5
The Netherlands	316.7	298.9	−5.6	3.7	6.0
Italy	167.2	189.4	+13.3	2.4	1.9
USA	186.7	183.8	−1.5	2.3	2.8
Belgium	146.4	168.3	+14.9	2.1	1.7
Brazil	97.2	112.4	+15.7	1.4	n.a.
Denmark	83.9	100.7	+20.0	1.2	1.7
Canada	83.1	83.2	+0.2	1.0	1.6
Switzerland	81.8	88.2	+7.8	1.1	2.3
Others	503.2	570.4	+13.4	7.2	8.1
Portugal					29.8
Total	7133.8	8019.9	+12.7	100.0	

Source: DGT (1991).
[a]The figures for French nationals include dependents of the many Portuguese migrants who moved to France in the 1960s and 1970s.

two-thirds of all other visitors in 1990 arrived by air, half of these (48.5%) with the state-owned airline TAP or with a Portuguese owned charter company. The great majority of these visitors travelled to Portugal for their holidays (92.2%), others came for religious reasons (3.1%), principally to visit the shrine at Fatima, some were on business (144,000; 1.8%) and the remainder gave reasons of sport, culture and visiting friends and relatives (DGT, 1991).

As with other Southern European destinations, arrivals to Portugal show a marked seasonality. The three peak months of July, August and September accounted for 47% of all arrivals in 1990 (DGT, 1990). The seasonality figure has remained more or less constant in the 1980s with a slight increase over the 44% figure recorded in 1972. This seasonality of the international market coincides with that discussed below in connection with Portuguese domestic tourism.

DOMESTIC TOURISM

Over the last decade the numbers of Portuguese, over the age of 15, taking a holiday away from home fell from 30% in 1980 to 20% in 1989, although the 1990 figure of 22% suggests this trend may be stabilizing. A further 10% of the population take their holidays at home. The three principal reasons given by those who took a holiday in 1990 were for rest and recuperation (71%), beach activities (28%), visiting the countryside (21%) and travel to other regions for cultural reasons (20%). The principal reasons given by those who did not take a holiday were, not surprisingly, lack of money, professional commitments and personal health, age and constraints of the family.

Holidays tend to be taken at one time and to average three to four weeks duration and to be very much concentrated in the summer months particularly August when over 50% of holidays are taken. This seasonality is apparently dictated by employment constraints as over 70% of those questionned indicated that they were not able to take their holidays at their preferred time. This constraint is of course particularly relevant to those working in the tourism industry who are generally constrained to taking their holidays in the low season periods, traditionally in the autumn. Relatively few people (14%) take a second holiday and only 1% take a third (DGT, 1991).

The majority (90%) of Portuguese who take a holiday stay in Portugal; of those who go abroad 40% travel to France, a reflection of the many thousands of Portuguese who have migrated to France, often illegally, over the last 30 years. Others go to Germany, again a reflection of patterns of outmigration, with Spain the third most popular destination, being the destination of 10% of all those leaving Portugal. Regional differences may be discerned in terms of destination choice, for example the majority of residents of Porto holiday at home with approximately equal numbers of those travelling going abroad as those who visit the Algarve, 8–12% of those taking holidays. This compares with the greater Lisbon area where the majority who take holidays leave the city with the Algarve being the most popular destination (22%) compared with the 8–10% who go abroad and the 1–3% who travel to either Madeira or the Azores. In fact travel to these autonomous Atlantic Island locations accounts for less than 2% of all holidays taken by the Portuguese, most of the those who choose these locations coming from the Lisbon area.

It is not possible to determine the contribution that domestic tourism makes to the overall tourism related revenue. What is known is that the average expenses per day for those holidaying in Portugal away from home in 1990 was 2603 escuedos (£10.60) as compared to the 8872 escuedos (£36) per day spent by those travelling abroad. Within Portugal expenditure per day varies regionally, being least in coastal areas (1300–1600 escuedos, £5–£6) and greatest in the inland mountain areas 2086 escuedos (£8.50) and in the Azores 2887 escuedos (£11.80) and Madeira 4616 escuedos (£18.80) (DGT, 1991).

ACCOMMODATION

Portugal offers a wide range of accommodation types (Table 15.2), including traditional hotels which provide a little under 40% of the available beds. The other forms of serviced accommodation are motels, the state-run Pousadas and private sector Estalagem and Albergaria together with the large numbers of Residencials and Pensoes, and the recent emergence of 'Turismo Habitação' or ManorHouse accommodation Estalagem are in general the private equivalent of the state-owned Pousadas and may extend to several buildings (a hotel in Portugal must be confined to a single integral building). Albergeria can best be described as originating from the old concept of a coaching inn and are smaller (usually less than 20 rooms), but with a high level of service. The self-catering sector is officially recognized as representing approximately one-quarter of all accommodation, although various estimates suggest that the true figure

Table 15.2. Accommodation: type and distribution (beds).

Accommodation	1989	1990	1991	% of 1991 total	% occupancy (1991)
Hotels 5*	14,518	15,187	14,576	7.7	45.7
Hotels 4*	19,344	21,869	23,230	12.3	51.7
Hotels 3*	20,884	22,091	24,659	13.1	41.7
Hotels 2*	7,641	7,241	8,073	4.2	n.a.
Hotels 1*	2,219	1,657	1,345	<1.0	n.a.
Total Hotels	64,606	68,045	71,883	38.0	
Aparthotels	16,555	20,290	22,412	11.9	46.3
Motels	1,155	1,400	1,486	<1.0	35.7
Pousadas	1,159	1,237	1,199	<1.0	64.2
Estalagem	2,876	2,862	2,730	1.4	36.0
Residencial/pensoes	44,784	45,879	46,316	24.6	25.6
Self-catering	22,213	24,124	24,981	13.2	41.1
Tourist villages	15,089	15,500	17,494	9.2	37.1
Turismo de Habitação				n.a.	
Total	168,437	179,337	188,501		

Table 15.3. Regional distribution of accommodation (beds) and occupancy (bednights).

Region	1989	1990	% ∧	1991	% ∧	Regional beds	% (1991) bednights
Costa Verde	19,108	20,715	+5.5	21,495	+3.8	11.4	8.9
Costa de Prata	19,189	19,896	+3.6	21,257	+16.8	11.2	6.8
Costa de Lisboa	32,732	34,116	+4.2	34,962	+2.4	18.5	22.4
Mountains	11,686	11,904	+1.8	12,087	+1.5	6.4	3.5
Plains	5,287	5,638	+6.6	5,794	+2.7	3.1	2.3
Algarve	64,921	70,159	+8.6	76,007	+8.3	40.3	40.5
Madeira	12,749	13,419	+5.2	13,610	+1.4	7.2	14.0
Azores	2,765	3,490	+26.0	3,289	−5.7	1.7	1.6
Total	168,437	179,337	+6.5	188,501	+5.1		

of available beds in this sector may be up to three times the number officially registered.

The data in Table 15.3 shows the regional distribution of accommodation and some of the discrepancies that characterize different locations, e.g. Madeira and Lisbon, where occupancy measured in terms of bednights is disproportionately high when viewed against availability whereas the reverse relationship exists in the Coste Verde and particularly the Costa de Prata. The data also demonstrate clearly the regional disparities of the Portuguese tourism product with the heavy reliance on three locations, the Algarve, Lisbon and its surroundings and the Island of Madeira. Such a simplistic analysis not only depends upon the dependability of the occupancy returns but also raises the question as to whether the correct type of accommodation is being provided in the appropriate locations. Lewis and Williams (1988) draw attention to the regional nature of Portugal's tourism product which has evolved due to a combination of climatic and other natural resources and accessibility. Portuguese nationals traditionally use established family property (35%) supplemented to some degree over recent years by recently purchased second homes (9%). Camping and hotels are equally popular being used by 10% of those holidaying, and there has been a recent increase in the use of purpose built tourist accommodation including timeshare purchase.

THE PUBLIC SECTOR

As we have seen a range of public sector agencies concerned with tourism have developed during the 20th century. National involvement, although beginning in 1911, is currently organized as shown in Fig. 15.4. The long-established National Council, comprising a range of experienced individuals, advises the Secretary of State on relevant issues. The Ministry maintains a major interest in essentially craft-based training both for the hotel and tourism industry and in the administration of gambling. ENATUR, best known for its work in developing and managing the Pousada chain, may well be a candidate for privatization as the current centre-right government moves into its second period of majority rule. The principal functions of the office of the DGT concern project approval, hotel and restaurant classification, encouragement of international investment, internal promotion and work with the regional tourism boards. From 1986 to mid-1992, international promotion of Portugal's tourism was the responsibility of the Institute of Tourism Promotion (IPT) but a recent decision has been made to combine tourism promotion with other international promotional activity under the auspices of the Portuguese Foreign Trade Institute (ICEP).

The organization of tourism at a local level has effectively developed on an area by area basis. The tier immediately below central government is represented by the 17 Regional Tourist Boards. Some of these, most noticeably the Algarve RTA (Regional Tourism Board of the Algarve)

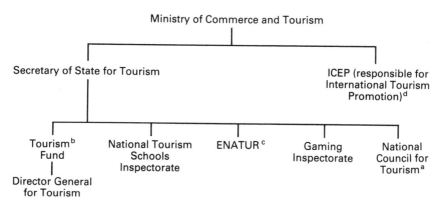

Fig. 15.4. The structure of public sector tourism in Portugal at the national level.
[a]The National Council for Tourism comprises a range of nominated individuals who advise the Secretary of State. [b]The Tourism Fund effectively acts as the government funding agency for tourism, more recently it has taken on the role of administering some of the European Community funding which has been made available for tourism. [c]ENATUR (Empressa Nacional de Turismo) was formed in 1976 as the agent responsible for the planning and development of government-owned and -managed hotels and restaurants. It takes particular interest in developing and renovating historic properties which are so characteristic of the Pousada network. [d]ICEP (Portugese Foreign Trade Institute) from October 1992 assumed responsibility for promoting all Portuguese products, including tourism, to the international market.

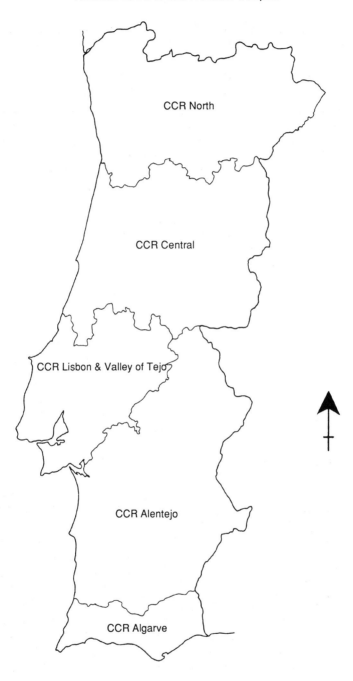

Fig. 15.5. The five coordinated planning regions, CCRS.

which, not surprisingly, has by far the largest budget, corresponds well with other administrative and spatial boundaries. However, this is not the case with the majority of the regional Tourist Boards. The reason for this lies in the fact that Regional Boards are proposed by groupings of Concelhos (Municipalities) of which there are over 300 in mainland Portugal. Such groupings evolve and are maintained due to a considerable measure of local politics and an individual Concelho may withdraw from a Region or join another. Equally the majority of Concelhos are not currently and never have been affiliated to a Tourist Board.

While some of these regional boards were recognized in the late 1950s the majority have developed in the years following the revolution. The associated legislation dating from 1978 to the present time has sought to allow these regional boards increasing funds and responsibilities. Operating, in a sense, at the local rather than regional level many Concelhos assume direct responsibility for their own tourism activities including promotion to the international market. Finally there are Juntas de Turismo, which in many cases date back to the 1920s. These represent very local interests, the village or Parish (Fregusia) and are either associated with the early spa or coastal resorts. For historical reasons these Juntas may still endeavour to represent these local tourism interests with little if any coordination with regional or national interests.

The present situation regarding the organization of the public sector at regional and local levels does not in all cases fit the major promotional areas that have traditionally been used to promote Portugal's tourism product. Again the Algarve is an exception as are Madeira, Azores and to a large measure Lisbon and its surrounding area. For example the promotional area the 'North' or 'Coste Verde' encompasses, at least in part, five regional tourist boards, a number of Concelhos and Juntas and the metropolitan area of Porto. Complex bureaucracy such as this is not confined to the tourism industry and can be seen in many other aspects of the public sector. In an attempt to rationalize many public sector services, a regional planning strategy recognizing five coordinated planning Commissions or regional coordinating committees (CCRs) (Fig. 15.5) has been put in place over the last 20 years. These Commissions are, however, largely advisory and the detailed implementation of their proposals remains the responsibility of the appropriate agency. For example in the Algarve the need for a coordinated planning policy has been apparent for several years, not least because of the overdevelopment in the tourism sector. The regional Coordinating Commission for the Algarve (Fig. 15.5), published in 1990 its proposals in PROTAL, which is in essence, a sophisticated land use plan, and these were formally adopted by government. The responsibility now passes to the regional and national tourist boards to work together with the Concelhos to draw up and implement a plan for the tourism sector.

A major factor in the development of public sector tourism agencies and in development terms generally, since 1974, relates to the very considerable autonomy in development and planning matters that were seized on by the Concelhos following the overthrow of dictatorship and the return to democracy. The Concelho is administered by an elected body, the Camara, and this highly politicized assembly and the elected leader, or mayor can, and does, play a decisive role in local development opportunities. This, for example, emerges clearly when comparing the style and speed of tourism developments in neighbouring Concelhos in the Algarve.

INCOME AND INVESTMENT

The result of this period of growth in the tourism economy resulted in 1990 in the income from tourist receipts of 506 billion escuedos (£2023 million, 2850 million ECU) compared to the 1984 figure of 140.5 billion escuedos and a 1974 figure of about 13 billion escuedos. The positive balance of tourism income in 1990 of 384.3 billion escuedos (£1537 million, 2165 million ECU) represented a growth rate in excess of 40% compared with 1988 values and showed that on average each tourist contributes 8500 escuedos (£34, 48 ECU) for each day spent in Portugal.

Hotel investment in the ten years 1979–1988 was 153 billion escuedos (£612 million, 860 million ECU), with annual growth rates in investment increasing year on year between 10 and 80% (see Table 15.4).

Throughout the period 1985–1988, 4 and 5 star hotels continued to attract the bulk of the investment in Portuguese tourism, 43.5 billion escuedos. During the same period investment in Apart hotels totalled some 18.4 billion escuedos, that in holiday villages and apartments 16.5 billion and Pensoes 13.2 billion escuedos. In 1988 the bulk of the investment was in the Algarve (40%) with 22.4% in the Lisbon area, 10% in Madeira and the Costa Prata, 6.7% in the Coste Verde, 4.9% in the interior mountain region, 2.9% in the Azores and 2.7% in the Plains of the Alentejo.

What is very evident is the minimal investment in the non-accommodation sector which was above 4% of the total only in 1988. This highlights the industry's dependence on natural attractions particularly the country's beaches. In the southern Algarve, golf has traditionally attracted the majority of the non-accommodation investment and recently there have been developments in the 'attraction' sector, most noticeably in the development of casinos and water parks. In the rural areas there has been considerable interest in the development of tourist hunting areas although as yet these have attracted relatively little investment.

Government commitment to tourism took an important step in 1956 with the establishment of the Tourism Fund (Fundo Tourismo) which was established to assist tourism projects. This scheme has been modified a

Table 15.4. Total tourism investment (billions of escuedos), sources and projects.

Year	Total	% international	% 4 and 5 star hotels	% other hotels	% in construction	% existing	% non-accommodation
1985	14.9	3.4	37.2	16.0	n.a.	n.a.	3.1
1986	26.9	12.6	45.0	6.5	49.5	50.5	3.1
1987	29.8	8.6	49.1	7.9	30.5	69.5	3.5
1988	36.4	7.2	30.8	16.3	32.4	67.6	4.6

number of times and is currently concentrated on a number of specified lines of investment, namely hotel and restaurant renovation and reconstruction, provision of rural, agri-tourism and camping facilities and support for sporting, cultural and animation projects. In practice, different lines of investment benefit from a combination of initial, interest only, repayment periods and rates of interest that are significantly below the commercial bank rate. In the five year period, 1986–1990, projects with an investment of in excess of 41 billion escuedos were facilitated by this means (DGT, 1990).

As a consequence of Portugal's application to and subsequent membership of the European Community considerable development funds have been made available to Portugal through the regional development policy. Funds earmarked for tourism development in the period 1982–1988 were administered under the System for Incentives for Investment in Tourism (SIIT) and over this seven-year period these amounted to 46.6 billion escuedos involving 157 different projects, with the majority of the investment occurring in Lisbon, Porto and Faro districts. Unlike investment from the Tourism Fund, European regional development funds take the form of grants estimated as a percentage of the total project costs and may exceed 60% of the investment in particular areas. It has been estimated that the savings on interest payments on these SIIT-supported projects over the period 1982–1988 exceeds 5.5 billion escuedos.

In 1988 the SIIT scheme was replaced by the SIFIT (System for Incentives for the Financial Investment in Tourism). This scheme related to the philosophy of tourism planning then being pursued, namely to encourage the development of tourism in the largely rural interior as opposed to the traditional coastal locations. To achieve this Regions Especially Approved for Tourism (REATs) and Axis for the Development of Tourism (EDTs) (Fig. 15.6) were designated and within these locations projects could potentially receive up to 65% grant aid reliant upon their economic forecast and employment potential.

In the three years 1988–1990 28.5 billion escuedos (£114 million/160 million ECU) were invested through this SIFIT scheme, the majority going to the interior of mainland Portugal, Faro district for example received 4.3% of the available funding, Porto 2.3% and Lisbon 1.7%, whereas interior areas such as those north of Lisbon around Leiria received 6.7% and Evora district, in the largely undeveloped Alentejo, received 6.1%, 1.7 billion escuedos (DGT, 1991). The northern 'Coste Verde' having failed to attract development designation, and hence beneficial access to these particular Community funds, has subsequently been assisted by a national government initiative which adopts the criteria of the SIFIT scheme but draws upon the tax revenue of the area's casinos.

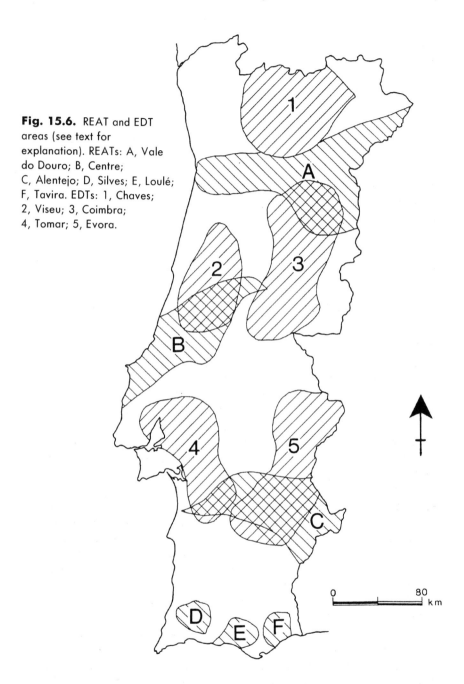

Fig. 15.6. REAT and EDT areas (see text for explanation). REATs: A, Vale do Douro; B, Centre; C, Alentejo; D, Silves; E, Loulé; F, Tavira. EDTs: 1, Chaves; 2, Viseu; 3, Coimbra; 4, Tomar; 5, Evora.

THE PRIVATE SECTOR

The private sector in Portugal is represented in a variety of ways. The 700 or so travel agent outlets are all privately owned and there are also a number of privately owned coach and airline companies, although the transport sector is at the moment largely dominated by state ownership. In the accommodation sector there are a number of Portuguese hotel groups such as Dom Pedro and Tivoli Hotel groups. Other companies such as Sopete and Torralta are expanding from a hotel/accommodation base into golf, casinos and other-leisure based operations. In addition there are a number of Portuguese controlled investment groups developing interests in tourism such as SONAE and a group headed by the Amorim family whose strength is based upon their major role in the cork industry. International investment is most apparent in the Algarve where many of the golf village and timeshare developments are funded by international groups with a preponderance of British and other northern European companies. In addition to these large organizations there are many small accommodation units, cafes and restaurants striving to capitalize upon the rapid growth in visitor arrivals.

TOURISM PLANNING

The ten years following the return to democracy in 1974 was a period of rapid political adjustment during which there was no definitive strategic or operational tourism planning other than the legacy of the previous Planos de Fomentos. The reason for this was the succession of relatively short-lived minority governments who were probably not in a position to implement a national plan on a rapidly expanding and apparently highly profitable industry. However, in 1984 when a centre right political philosophy was gaining ground, a team was drawn together to report on the principle and desirability of a National Tourism Plan. Nevertheless, at the time of its publication in 1985 the authors doubted that the then, or indeed, any future minority government would be able to implement a national tourism strategy despite their assertion that a national strategic plan was essential, not least because of the emphasis being given to the developmental role of the private sector. The report considered many of the problems associated with the rapid expansion of tourism in terms of human and natural resources. It pointed out that there was a lack of necessary and relevant data and that also there were many deficiencies in the existing infrastrucure with inappropriate development and illegal building having already ruined some of the best sites. Having assembled and then audited mainly qualitative data the report concluded by setting out proposed goals and measures for a national tourism policy as follows:

1. Increase employment.
2. Attract and improve foreign investment.
3. Prioritize the development of areas that are attractive to international tourists.
4. Raise general standards, particularly the transport infrastructure.
5. Promote tourism development in less favoured areas as an agent of regional development (it was recognized that these areas had yet to be designated in terms of being less favoured for tourism).
6. Reduce and curb pollution.
7. Protect and enhance the natural and cultural heritage.
8. Renovate and reinstate traditional spa resorts.
9. Provide more efficient medical support.
10. Promote tourism to both the international and domestic market; in particular to promote 'Country or Manor House' tourism (as early indications of this scheme, at that time 5 years old, were described as very encouraging).

In order to achieve many of these aims the report called for detailed environmental and planning policies. Pinho (1989), in providing a review of environmental planning and management in Portugal, demonstrates that whereas in some areas (e.g. water pollution), there has been legislation for 100 years it has not been economically possible to implement it. Equally in many areas of environmental policy, the lead of the European Commission has been a vital stimulus but few of the measures had, until then, been translated into the appropriate Portuguese legislation. With regard to planning the report calls for this to begin by establishing basic points of reference, for example, to define optimal capacity, recognize tourism saturated zones, impose architectural standards and set out clear building consent guidelines.

THE NATIONAL TOURISM PLAN 1986-1989

The National Tourism Plan, introduced in 1986, reflects in some measure the proposals of the Report, the stated strategies being to assist in the revival of the Portuguese economy and to alleviate regional disparities. The overall economic benefit of tourism was argued to be its ability to reduce the country's foreign exchange debt by stimulating economic activity that increases the input of externally generated income.

The objectives of the National Tourism Plan (1986–1989) were as follows:

Objective 1. To contribute to the reduction of the country's foreign exchange debt. Proposed measures:

1. Increase externally generated revenue.
2. Reduce the import component of tourism related expenses.
3. Increase external investment.

Objective 2. To contribute to alleviating regional differences. Proposed measures:

1. Territorial division of the country including the creation of priority areas.
2. Selection of spas with potential in both the short and medium term for renovation.
3. The implementation of steps to encourage regional development.

Objective 3. To improve the quality of life of the Portuguese. (In saying this the plan recognizes the need for local participation in development and their receipt of a significant part of the benefits.) Proposed measures:

1. Increase domestic tourism.
2. Promote rural tourism.
3. Increase Manor/Country House Tourism (Turismo de Habitação).
4. Support the development of social tourism.

Objective 4. To contribute to the protection of the natural environment and to enhance the country's cultural assets. Proposed measures:

1. Well planned spatial organization.
2. Protection of the natural environment, particularly the coastline.
3. The definition of optimal tourism carrying capacity.
4. The protection of local architecture.
5. Preservation of monuments and the protection of open areas.
6. Development of handicraft skills, support for the artisans and support for the country's rich legacy of folklore.

In laying emphasis upon tourism as an agent of regional development Portugal was following the lead of the European Commission which was itself in the mid-1980s giving serious attention to tourism for the first time. The main thrust of the plan can be seen to be the encouragement of the development of non-coastal locations deemed to have tourism potential by chanelling the majority of the European Community development funds, allocated to tourism projects, to the development areas discussed above (Fig. 15.6).

Although many of the initiatives of the 1986–1989 plan were carried well beyond this three-year period there was no attempt to introduce an immediate successor. However, in 1990 the Secretary of State for Tourism initiated a review of Portugal's tourism with the assistance of consultants Horwath and Horwath, under the coordination of the Office of the Director General of Tourism. The results were published in 1991 as the 'Livro Branco do Turismo', the 'White Book' of Tourism. A number of other

Government Ministries also produced similar studies. In all cases these were legitimate attempts to produce a complete appraisal of an industry or topic and in the case of tourism the study was subtitled 'Eighty Years of Tourism in Portugal'.

In the autumn of 1991 Prime Minister Cavaco Silva's Social Democrats were returned to power for a second period of majority government. There have been a number of changes relating to tourism as a result of this, perhaps most noticeably the abolition of the Institute of Tourism Promotion and the merging of international tourism promotion with the other activities of the Portuguese Foreign Trade Institute. As regards planning, the National Council for Tourism was charged with drawing up a National Plan for Tourism for the period 1993–1996 and in the vitally important Algarve the regional tourist board working with the office of the Director General for Tourism indicated that a plan for this region would be published in late 1992.

REFERENCES AND FURTHER READING

Barrett, F. (1989) On the Algarve's road to ruin. *Independent* 22 July, pp. 45–46. London.

Cavaco, C. (1979) *O turismo em Portugal: aspectos evolutivos e espaciais.* University of Lisbon Estudos de Geografia Humana e Regional, Lisbon.

Comissão de Coordenação da região do Algarve PROT Algarve (1990) Ministerio do Planeamento e da Administracão do Território CCR Algarve Faro Portugal.

Direção-Geral do Turismo/Fundo de Turismo (1991) *Ferias dos Portugues em 1990.* DGT, Lisbon.

Direccao-Geral do Turismo (1991) *Livro Branco do Turismo* (compiled by Horwath and Horwath, ed. Direccao-Geral do Turismo) Ministry of Commerce and Tourism, Lisbon. The *Livro Branco* represents a 'one off' publication but the annual *Turismo em 19--*, a collection of many tourism statistics, has been published for the last ten years, and there are in addition a number of occasional statistical summaries dealing with topics such as the domestic holiday market.

Hudson, M. (1986) Basic resources. In: Cabral, M. (ed.), *1386–1986 Portugal: Business Partners in Europe.* De Montfort, London.

Lewis, J. and Williams, A.M. (1988) Portugal: market segmentation and regional specialisation. In: Williams, A.M. and Shaw, G. (eds) (1991) *Tourism and Economic Development: Western European Experiences*, 2nd edn. Belhaven Press, London and New York.

Macaulay, R. (1946) *They Came to Portugal.* Jonathan Cape, London.

Macaulay, R. (ed. Taylor, L.C.) (1991) *They Came to Portugal Too.* Carcanet, Manchester, UK.

Mapplebeck, P. (1992) 'Povoa de Varzim Past Present and Future.' Unpublished graduate thesis, Department of Tourism, Bournemouth University, England.

Ortigao, R. (1876) *As Praias de Portugal.* Magalhaes e Moniz, Lisbon.

Pina, P. (1988) *Portugal O Turismo no Seculo XX*. Lucidus, Lisbon.
Pinho, P. (1989) Environmental planning in Portugal. Unpublished paper presented
   to the American Portuguese Studies group, Durham, USA.
Which Magazine (1991) '*The worst resorts in the world.*'

16

TOURISM IN GREECE

Helen Briassoulis

HISTORICAL DEVELOPMENT OF TOURISM SINCE THE 1950S

In ancient Greece, foreigners were considered sacred and as they did not have political rights a god protected them: Xenius Zeus, the father of gods and god of hospitality. In modern times, the tradition continues but now tourists, no longer called foreigners, travel to Greece to enjoy her sun and mild climate in the more than 3000 islands and 30,000 beaches scattered along 15,000 km of coastline, as well as to see the Acropolis and the remnants of a glorious historical and cultural past.

Although past records reveal a considerable number of foreign visitors to Greece, mostly artists and men of the letters, tourism, as an organized and systematically pursued economic activity, developed after the Second World War and specifically after 1950. This year marks the establishment of the National Tourism Organization of Greece (NTOG) and the direct intervention of the government to promote tourism development as tourism was viewed as a main source of foreign exchange, a cure for the country's balance of payments problem and as a generator of employment. Tourism has grown at a very fast pace since that time, as changes in the number of tourist arrivals, beds and tourist exchange over time reveal (Table 16.1).

Governmental support for tourism has taken several forms throughout the years. In the 1948–1952 period, the state intervened directly by building infrastructure in tourist centres well known before the war (Athens, Delphi, Rhodes, Corfu) and introducing a short-term credit policy for renewal and modernization of hotel units which had been damaged during the war (Konsolas and Zacharatos, 1992). Between 1953 and 1966, NTOG began an extensive programme of public investment in tourist superstructure (hotels, motels and organized beaches) in various regions of the country in order to offer building and management models

Table 16.1. Tourist arrivals, number of beds and tourist exchange, 1956–1990.

Year	Arrivals	Number of beds	Tourist exchange ($ 000s)
1956	210,301	–	–
1957	261,738	–	–
1958	276,000	–	–
1960	400,000	–	–
1968	1,018,000	–	–
1970	1,454,629	118,869	193.6
1971	2,058,277	–	305.3
1972	2,529,414	–	392.7
1973	2,951,236	–	514.9
1974	1,998,001	–	484.3
1975	2,975,487	185,275	699.4
1976	4,070,411	–	901.1
1977	4,461,084	–	1081.1
1978	5,081,033	–	1473.3
1979	5,798,360	265,552	1859.7
1980	5,271,115	276,498	1978.9
1981	5,577,109	286,020	2100.2
1982	5,463,860	311,089	1712.6
1983	5,258,372	318,515	1381.3
1984	6,027,266	333,816	1499.0
1985	7,039,428	348,171	1653.5
1986	7,339,015	359,377	2132.2
1987	8,053,052	375,367	2835.8
1988	8,351,182	395,812	3059.8
1989	8,540,962	423,790	2722.0
1990	9,310,492	438,355	3707.8

Source: KEPE (1984);Tsartas (1989); AGTE (1992).

for further tourism development and to encourage private investment in these areas by undertaking the cost of 'first opening' them to tourism development. Initially, public investment in commercial facilities covered 100% of the total public funds allocated to tourism. In 1966, this percentage had dropped to 27% and it continued to decrease until the beginning of the 1980s, with a parallel increase in the contribution of the private sector in the creation of fixed tourist capital (Konsolas and Zacharatos, 1992). Public investments for the improvement of the trans-portation and telecommunication infrastructure of the country also indi-rectly benefited tourism development. After the mid-1960s, state tourism development policy shifted from direct investment in tourism infrastructure and superstructure towards the formulation of favourable bank credit policy for hotel building and the legislation of incentives for private investments by dividing the country into three tourist incentive zones initially (1967–1982 period) and later (after 1982) into four general industrial development zones (Tsartas, 1989). The trend of the 1990s is towards the provision of favourable tax incentives and amortization rates for the development of facilities such as marinas, golf courses, convention centres, sport-related, medical and winter facilities.

ORIGIN AND DESTINATION OF TOURISTS

The majority of visitors to Greece come from Europe, especially the countries of the EEC, and North America. Table 16.2 shows the percentages of tourist arrivals by region of origin between 1970 and 1990 and Table 16.3 gives a more detailed picture of arrivals, by country of origin, for the years 1988 to 1990. Recently, the numbers of North American tourists have declined whereas those from the EEC countries are increasing. Naturally, geographical proximity is the major reason for the observed composition of tourist nationalities.

Until the early 1970s, traditional tourist destinations were Attica (mainly the Greater Athens Area), with the most important cultural/archaeological tourist resources and ancillary facilities and services, and the islands of Rhodes (Rodos) and Corfu (Kerkyra) (Fig. 16.1). Since then two new regions have gained in importance as tourist attractions: Chalkidiki and the island of Crete (Kriti) (especially Heraklion and Lassithi). Several smaller geographical areas have also attracted a considerable share of tourists such as the Cyclades islands (especially Myconos and Santorini) and the Sporades islands. Table 16.4 shows the distribution of tourist nights among the principal tourist places for selected years between 1982 and 1990. Most tourist destinations are located by the sea. In 1973, 95% of international and 80% of domestic tourists visited coastal resorts.

Table 16.2. Tourist arrivals by region of origin, 1970–1990 (%).

Regions	1970	1980	1988	1989	1990
Europe	60.7	79.9	89.2	88.5	90.1
EC	46.3	49.9	67.9	67.3	67.1
North America	28.5	8.6	4.8	4.6	4.0
Other	10.8	11.5	6.0	6.9	5.9

Source: AGTE (1992).

Table 16.3. Tourist arrivals by country of origin, 1988–1990.

Countries	1988	1989	1990
Belgium-Luxembourg	138,171	162,901	201,807
France	466,769	478,031	565,407
W. Germany	1,597,019	1,655,277	1,922,029
Denmark	281,759	315,660	281,598
Ireland	66,114	62,685	67,835
Spain	83,189	103,435	127,516
Italy	556,600	569,345	620,766
Great Britain	1,811,296	1,632,582	1,647,361
The Netherlands	357,344	428,573	495,699
Portugal	25,371	37,180	27,408
EC total	5,383,632	5,445,669	5,957,426
Austria	269,660	267,939	286,525
Switzerland	132,949	139,502	151,695
Scandinavian countries	574,825	586,602	589,444
Yugoslavia	398,549	369,161	580,733
Other	308,589	344,264	426,892
All Europe total	7,068,204	7,153,137	7,992,715
USA	274,720	278,856	273,849
Canada	71,330	78,933	74,218
Other America	37,289	42,013	34,556
America total	383,339	399,802	382,623
Asia	267,893	321,138	316,826
Africa	90,267	80,531	67,056
Oceania	113,764	127,243	114,090

Source: AGTE (1992).

MARKET SEGMENTATION AND REGIONAL SPECIALIZATION

Two broad tourist markets exist in Greece: the domestic and the international, the latter being the most significant and well developed. Data on domestic tourism are scarce because, frequently, Greeks visit their home towns and villages and stay with relatives or own homes, hence their movements cannot be easily registered. Also, most tourist accommodation facilities cater for international tourists and are not widely used by domestic tourists.

Fig. 16.1. Main tourist destinations in Greece.

Based on a 1990 survey of Greek hotels conducted by Howarth Consulting, six main market segments were identified: groups representing 61.3% of hotel guests, businessmen (14%), vacationists (7%), congress participants (6.8%), public servants (0.7%) and others (10.2%) (AGTE, 1992). These figures reveal the dominance of group tourism in Greece, a phenomenon attributed mainly to the influence of tour operators who have comparative advantages and control the tourist market since they are more organized and can offer 'tourist packages' at low prices to tourists in the countries of origin. In tourist destination countries like Greece, with less organized tourist enterpreneurs and tourism subject to the influence of international events, tour operators, with a secure clientele, act as oligopsonists achieving low rates and thus reinforcing further their position.

Sea-based tourism is an important component of the Greek tourist market, being associated with high income tourism and bringing direct and

Table 16.4. Distribution of tourist nights in the principal tourist areas in Greece, 1982–1990 (in thousands).

	1982		1985		1989		1990	
Region	(1)	(2)	(1)	(2)	(1)	(2)	(1)	(2)
Attiki	6,011	7,686	6,331	7,912	5,606	8,029	5,703	8,276
Thessaloniki	601	1,514	598	1,469	466	1,398	535	1,413
Chalkidiki	821	1,096	1,271	1,618	1,228	1,480	1,119	1,333
Corfu	3,017	3,298	3,487	3,787	2,617	2,989	2,678	3,094
Crete	5,426	5,947	7,490	8,090	7,846	8,498	8,836	9,436
Rhodes	5,747	6,005	6,709	7,118	7,135	7,602	7,543	8,004
Cyclades	544	757	658	902	675	902	642	921
Rest of Greece	7,788	14,219	9,073	16,014	7,365	13,380	7,957	13,881
Total	29,955	40,522	35,617	46,910	32,938	44,278	35,013	46,358

Source: AGTE (1992).
(1) International tourist nights.
(2) Total tourist nights.

indirect benefits to the economy as it sets in motion a whole series of other economic activities necessary to support it. In the 1980–1990 period, the number of international tourists who entered the country on cruise boats ranged between 450,000 and 500,000 (AGTE, 1992). Alternative forms of tourism are currently being promoted, namely, agrotourism, cultural tourism, third-age tourism in response to initiatives offered by the EC, changes in consumer preferences and as a means for the achievement of rural and cultural in addition to tourism development.

Tourist demand has a particular spatial pattern due to preferences of certain nationalities for specific tourist regions. The island of Rhodes (Rodos) has attracted mostly Swedes, the island of Corfu (Kerkyra) British, the Ionian islands attract Italian and French, Crete Germans and Dutch, Chalkidiki Germans (Komilis, 1986; Chiotis and Coccossis, 1992). Also, until recently, Yugoslavian tourists frequented Northern Greece. Greek tourists have a less distinct pattern of regional preferences although Skiathos (Northern Sporades), Peloponnese (Peloponissos), Pilion and the Saronicos islands have been traditional domestic tourist centres. Of course, the regional pattern of tourist demand changes over time under the influence of exogenous factors and events.

STRUCTURE OF THE TOURIST INDUSTRY

The Greek tourist industry consists of the usual mix of interdependent and mutually supporting economic sectors – accommodation, catering, transportation, services, and entertainment – which are briefly described below.

The accommodation sector is the most developed given the extensive direct and indirect government support already mentioned. The total number of beds in the various types of tourist accommodation (hotels, motels, furnished hotel apartments, pensions, rented rooms) grew by 123% in the 1970–1979 period and by 49% in the 1980–1989 period reaching a total of 438,355 in 1990. It is estimated that an additional 15,000 beds were added in 1991. Until 1970, the majority of the hotels (55%) were of the third to fifth classes but after 1980 this percentage dropped and the share of luxury, first and second class hotels has increased (46% in 1990 compared to 34% in 1970). The hotel occupancy rate in Greece is among the highest in the EEC ranging between 54 and 57% recently (beginning of the 1990s) but exhibits considerable fluctuation among tourist regions with a 1989–1990 low in the island of Chios and a 1989–1990 high in Heraklion (on the island of Crete). The number of furnished apartments has also increased considerably between 1970 and 1990 from 0.4% in 1970 to 7.9% in 1990 as this type of accommodation is preferred by domestic and international tourists. Moreover, there are about 250 camping sites and their number is increasing because a preference has been expressed by tourists (especially Greeks). Finally, international interest has been expressed for timesharing units which are promoted as a partial solution to the seasonality problems of the tourist market. In 1986, a law addressing legal and other issues for the operation of timesharing units was passed (Tourism and the Economy, 1987).

Catering facilities (restaurants, tavernas) are privately owned and usually frequented by locals and tourists so there is no information pertaining exclusively to tourism. Because of the popularity of eating places in Greece, they are in abundant supply especially in tourist regions where they have grown considerably in recent years.

Greece is connected by air to all major cities around the world and this is one of the reasons why most tourists arrive by air – 67.7% in 1990 compared to 60.5% in 1975. Other transport modes include private car, boat and rail but the shares of these are changing over time. In 1975 14% of tourists entered the country by car compared to 25% in 1990. Rail use was always very low and dropped from 5.3% in 1975 to 3% in 1990. The percentage of tourists arriving by boat increased from 9.3% in 1975 to 15.1% in 1990. Greece has the largest fleet of all types of commercial ships in Europe; a total of 430 ships in 1990 with a capacity of 737,000 registered tonnes. Eleven marinas with a total of 4668 moorings operate in

Greece currently and many more are planned. Moreover, 65 cruiseboat refuelling stations operate in various places.

Domestic transport is mainly by road, ship and air, the two latter modes being used mostly by international tourists. Service is adequate and satisfactory although congestion is always a problem during the peak tourist months of July and August.

Services include a variety of enterprises used either by tourists exclusively, e.g. souvenir shops, or by both tourists and locals, e.g. banks, petrol stations, car and boat rentals, etc. The car rental sector is quite important in Greece where there are more than 2000 car rental businesses owning about 30,000 cars and employing 4000 persons; 90% of their customers are international tourists (AGTE, 1992).

Privately owned entertainment services and facilities are numerous especially in the highly touristic places operating mostly during the tourist season. NTOG, the Ministry of Culture and local government play significant roles specifically in organizing events. There are numerous beaches along the 15,000 km of the Greek coastline but most of them do not offer a variety of facilities since they are used mostly for sunbathing. Sixteen beaches are managed by NTOG and several others are managed by seaside hotels. Water-based sport facilities (water skiing, wind surfing, scuba diving, sailing) are available in most managed beaches. Winter sport facilities (basically skiing) are also available in several mountainous areas used mainly by domestic tourists since Greece is mostly known as a summer holiday destination.

MARKETING THE COUNTRY AS A TOURIST DESTINATION

Until recently, Greek tourism suffered from a lack of promotion for various reasons. Greece was always renowned for its antiquities and fabulous coastline, islands and beaches, qualifications considered in the past to provide 'self-advertising' and to offer the country a competitive advantage in the tourist market. In addition, public resources available for promotion by NTOG were (and are) usually limited. Finally, Greek tourist entrepreneurs lacked professional management experience and, thus, attributed less importance to promotion than was required.

Promotion of Greek tourism is undertaken primarily by NTOG although the private sector has been making serious efforts recently. Advertising by NTOG has been directed primarily to four countries, i.e. USA, United Kingdom, West Germany and France, through the mass media, brochures, posters, fairs and exhibitions (JICA, 1989). The sales promotion activities of NTOG include: tourism promotion assistance to public and private agencies abroad; assistance to travel missions of the Greek tourist sector; participation in trade and consumer travel shows;

liaison with journalists, travel writers, photographers; cooperation with and assistance to mass media during their visits to Greece; organization of study tours for travel agents; seminars and workshops for the tourist industry; provision of incentives for tourist agents; participation in tourist exhibitions. In addition, NTOG organizes several important festivals like the Athens, the Epidavros and the Lycabettus festivals featuring ancient tragedies, Greek dances, etc.

NTOG offices abroad are located in 24 cities in 17 countries, which compares well with Italy and Spain which have 24 and 26 offices respectively in 19 countries.

Tourism promotion by the private sector includes the Greek Hoteliers Association's activities (mainly participation in tourist exhibitions in Greece and abroad) and efforts of individual hotels to attract tourists by participating in exhibitions and workshops, distributing promotional materials, sales to travel agents in Greece and foreign countries, approaching organizers of international congresses, conventions and exhibitions. Given the recent trend internationally towards congress tourism, Greek hotels are active in attracting congresses and conventions to counteract the low occupancy during the off-tourist seasons.

SOCIOECONOMIC IMPACTS OF TOURISM

Tourism development in Greece has had a variety of positive and negative economic and social impacts which are presented below.

Economic Impacts

Tourism has been and is promoted in Greece primarily because of its supposedly beneficial economic impacts. Tourism receipts increased sixfold in the 1971–1980 period. In 1982 and 1983 the growth rate declined but the upward trend resumed in 1984 and receipts were 3.7 billion dollars in 1990 (AGTE, 1992). Tourism receipts covered more than 20% of the country's trade deficit in the 1975–1986 period with a high of 40.8% in 1981 (JICA, 1989). In the 1981–1991 period this percentage was 30% on the average. The importance of tourism receipts for the national economy is more obvious when they are compared to 'invisible receipts' and to export receipts. Table 16.5 which shows the percentage contributions of the various categories of 'invisible receipts' over time reveals the growing importance of tourism receipts over all other categories. In 1990 tourism receipts represented 58% of all export receipts and in the January–November 1991 period 61.2%. Also in 1990, tourism receipts were greater than the sum of all types of industrial exports and much greater than the

Table 16.5. Percentage contributions of the various categories of 'invisible receipts', 1975–1990.

Year	Tourism	Nautical	Emigrants	Other	Total
1970	20.4	29.1	36.2	14.3	100
1975	24.5	29.6	27.4	18.5	100
1980	32.1	29.5	17.6	20.8	100
1985	37.6	23.6	18.2	20.6	100
1986	41.6	19.5	19.2	19.7	100
1987	41.1	17.3	20.0	21.6	100
1988	37.5	16.9	21.2	24.4	100
1989	35.4	17.9	18.2	28.5	100
1990	36.6	17.4	18.0	28.0	100

Source: AGTE (1992).

sum of all categories of food and beverages exports (AGTE, 1992). Compared to the GNP, the contribution of tourism receipts increased from 2.3% of the GNP in 1970 to 6.4% in 1990. On the contrary, the percentage of export receipts remained rather constant, 10–11%, in the 1980s.

Average per capita tourist spending is rather low in Greece compared to other tourist countries and fluctuates considerably; in 1970 it was $133, in 1980 it increased to $375, it dropped to $219 in 1985 and rose again to $398 in 1990. Low average per capita tourist spending is attributed to the lack of many first and second class hotel and other accommodation facilities which attract high income tourists, the relatively weak tourism promotion efforts and certain structural problems of the Greek economy.

Tourism is an important generator of direct and indirect employment in Greece although the available data do not reflect the actual number of jobs generated because: (i) many jobs are not reported; (ii) several represent second jobs; (iii) female labour is not always counted as employment and, thus, is not reported. Assessment of indirect employment impacts is even more problematic. Direct employment in tourism recorded an impressive growth in the post-1966 period starting from an estimated 23,500 employed persons in 1966 (Tsartas, 1989) and reaching an estimated 335,000 in 1988 which represented 7.2% of total national employment (AGTE, 1992). It has been estimated that direct employment grew by 265% and indirect employment by 270% between 1970 and 1980 (KEPE, 1984a). A 1984 study by KEPE (National Center for Planning and Research) estimated tourism-related employment at 210,000 persons (145,000 directly and 65,000 indirectly employed) and tourism-induced employment at 100,000 (KEPE, 1984a).

From the national economy point of view, it has been estimated that international tourist demand represents 30% of the national total (the corresponding figure for domestic demand being 34%). The general production tourist multiplier (direct and indirect demand) has been estimated to be 1.52 whereas the corresponding domestic figure is 1.62 (KEPE, 1984a).

From the regional development perspective, tourism generates jobs (most of them seasonal, however), provides income to persons and enterprises, and contributes to population retention especially in areas suffering from population decline. Moreover, infrastructure built to serve the purposes of tourism development has opened up many previously isolated areas and has helped them improve their economic situation and quality of life. In recent years, governmental policy has explicitly used tourism as a regional development tool to assist development in relatively undeveloped regions (possessing the necessary tourism resources, of course) and discourage further development of congested tourist areas (Konsolas and Zacharatos, 1992).

However, the positive economic impacts of tourism mentioned above are partially offset by certain negative, not directly visible, impacts, which draw mainly from particular structural problems of the Greek economy. Domestic production of tourist final consumer goods requires imports whose value represents 13.5% of actual tourist consumption. Exchange outlays for annual capital formation in the tourist sector reach 9.3% of actual tourist consumption. Other government spending and royalties paid in relation to tourism promotion represent another 0.8–0.9% of actual annual tourist consumption. Moreover, tourist consumption activates an additional domestic consumption which requires imports representing 28% of actual tourist consumption (KEPE, 1984a). In sum, the lack of vertical integration among the productive sectors of the Greek economy, their strong dependence on imports, and the lack of promotion of Greek products reduce the real value of the tourist exchange flowing into the country.

Another serious negative impact, related also to the structural problems of the Greek economy, is the significant degree of 'underground' tourist economy. This is mainly manifested by the considerable number of tourist accommodation units (basically, rented rooms) which are not declared and thus evade taxation as well as the required quality control by NTOG. In 1983, a conservative estimate of the number of undeclared tourist beds was 200,000–250,000 (Tsartas, 1989) and the associated revenues 8–10 billion drachmas. In 1990, undeclared beds were estimated to be 400,000 and the associated foreign exchange 68 billion drachmas (Tourism and the Economy, 1990). A serious effort is currently trying to control this phenomenon which impacts negatively not only on the economy but also on the tourist image of the country.

Finally, because of the high degree of dependence of Greek tourist enterprises on tour operators, the actual amount of tourist spending remaining in the country was only 40–50% of total tourist spending in 1983. In other words, although a tourist was paying on average $625 for the Greek 'tourist package', the Greek share was only $250–300 (KEPE, 1984b).

Social Impacts

Assessment of the social impacts of tourism in Greece is mostly qualitative because, frequently, they take several, not always quantifiable, forms and very little related research has so far been done. A notable exception is the systematic analysis of the (negative) social impacts of tourism, with a special focus on the islands of Ios and Serifos (Tsartas, 1989). The following list of the social impacts of tourism draws mainly from this work.

1. Increased crime rate during the tourist season as more thefts, rapes, drug trafficking and other similar crimes occur in tourist areas.
2. Creation of a fake 'authenticity' in tourist places. Traditional ornaments, tools, cultural artifacts, etc. are used in a non-functional, purely decorative manner to convey a sense of the 'original' local culture.
3. Commercialization of the Greek historic, religious and cultural tradition. Traditional feasts become tourist attractions, cultural stereotypes are created (e.g. bouzouki as the traditional musical instrument and syrtaki as the traditional Greek dance), 'Greek art' souvenirs are marketed, etc.
4. Erosion of the mores, a serious multifaceted impact, manifested in the commercialization of human relations (the well-known summer lovers), the loss of the sense of hospitality for which Greece was renowned worldwide, the breaking of the ties of solidarity and cooperation among locals since they become competitors in the tourist market.
5. Impacts on the attitudes and personalities especially of the young in tourist areas who adopt foreign life styles, speak a mixture of Greek and English (or French or German) and behave like the tourists.
6. The demonstration effect among the general population who try to 'keep up with the foreign tourists' imitating their eating, dressing, consumption and life styles.
7. Creation of a peculiar parasitic group of tourist entrepreneurs operating tourist-serving enterprises, like tavernas, cafeterias, etc., the principal characteristics of which are high profits and tax evasion. Consequently, a particular personality type is created: the 'successful' entrepreneur who earns a lot with little work, has a rich erotic life and is professionally independent (in contrast to public and private employees). This model is followed by many young people who abandon other productive, year-round, occupations, 'work' only during the tourist season, stay idle for the

rest of the year and, eventually, suffer from the volatility of the tourist market.

ENVIRONMENTAL IMPACTS OF TOURISM

Among the unfortunate impacts of tourism in Greece have been those on the natural and manmade environment of many tourist places. Most of these impacts have not been quantified as this is a difficult undertaking in general and interest in them is rather recent (Briassoulis, 1992).

Coastal areas, being important tourist attractions, have been affected most by the negative impacts of tourism, such as: water pollution, water shortages, solid waste disposal, traffic congestion, noise pollution and aesthetic pollution. Water pollution of coastal waters is occurring because, until recently, most hotels have been discharging their sewage untreated into the sea. The problem is further compounded by the presence of many small-scale accommodation units which are difficult to control. Water shortages are very common in the arid islands of the Aegean sea for which water is always in short supply. However, the problem impacts on all tourist areas whose water supply systems are designed to serve a much smaller human population. Solid waste disposal is another 'headache' for most tourist areas as disproportionate amounts of wastes are generated during the tourist season and the existing garbage collection systems have limited capacity to cope with them. Some localities schedule extra collection shifts to overcome this problem. However, uncontrolled disposal of solid wastes, especially in remote areas, is very common and detracts significantly from the beauty of the landscape. Traffic congestion is a problem caused by the uneven concentration of tourists in popular tourist places which are, naturally, unprepared to accommodate the resulting traffic volumes. Curfew measures are used to control the problem but with limited success. Noise pollution affects popular tourist resorts due to the presence of numerous tourists, traffic and entertainment places. Finally, aesthetic pollution has resulted from the uncontrolled and haphazard development of accommodation and other tourist-serving facilities next to places of natural and/or cultural interest. To date, limited action has been taken to control these impacts, given the difficulties (the political costs), to demolish already built structures, and to prevent new ones from developing. Aesthetic pollution has also occurred in traditional settlements during the 1960s and 1970s, the era of high tourism growth and intense urbanization of the country, as the style of the newly built structures was totally incompatible with the local physiognomy and architectural style. Since the mid-1970s, NTOG has provided grants to property owners who wish to refurbish their old houses in the traditional parts of touristic towns and villages with the requirement to use local materials (wood and stone) and follow the architectural style of the locale. Moreover, architectural control of proposed touristic facilities is exercised, as far as possible, to ensure conformance to their surroundings.

Other environmental impacts of a more local character are air pollution and destruction of certain rare species habitats. Air pollution is a problem mainly in the big cities and it is difficult to assert that it is caused by tourism only. Destruction of rare species habitats is partially caused by tourists frequenting these places, building construction and, of course, the lack of effective controls. Recently, the sea turtle (*Caretta caretta*) and the Mediterranean monk seal (*Monachus monachus*) have been declared protected species and their habitats are under control although public opposition and boycotting are problems being faced by the local authorities.

RELATIONSHIPS WITH THE EUROPEAN COMMUNITY

At EC level, policies aiming at European integration have had various positive direct and indirect effects on Greek tourism. A full blown community tourism policy has not appeared yet and, thus, it is not possible to evaluate its impact on Greek tourism.

General community policies – the transport policy (especially the deregulation of airlines and related measures; see chapter 4), the abolition of the tax frontiers, and business law – facilitate the free movement of people and capital and eliminate obstacles such as exchange allowances and taxation thus increasing tourist flows to the country and demand for more tourist facilities of diverse types. The free movement of businesses, however, is expected to create conditions of intense competition between Greek and European tourist enterprises because the former are relatively small and less organized, already depend on tour operators, and in general, are in an inferior position in terms of capital and other resources, compared to their European counterparts.

Specific sectoral community policies concerning regional development (especially for regions lagging behind in development), rural development, cultural development, consumer protection, environmental protection, education and training, have brought diverse benefits to Greek tourism. The European Community Fund has supported educational programmes of the School of Tourist Professions as well as training programmes for women consultants on tourist development and tourist guides specialized in environmental issues (Tourism and Economy, 1985). The European Regional Development Fund (FEDER) supports special 'small scale tourism' programmes for the Aegean islands concerning the improvement of tourist infrastructure and superstructure, transportation, communications and tourist services. In the framework of the Integrated Mediterranean Plans, several programmes have received funding for the development of regions possessing special natural and cultural resources as well as for environmental and cultural protection purposes such as construction of wastewater treatment facilities, preservation of traditional houses and other monuments, etc. Special financial support is available for the development of agrotourism. Moreover, Integrated Activity Complexes are promoted providing for the creation of leisure harbours, health tourism and ski centres.

Finally, various activities undertaken during 1990, the European Year of Tourism, helped Greek tourism as useful information and experience were exchanged with other tourist countries, ties between national organizations, administrations and agencies were developed and common actions were decided. Moreover, impetus has been provided for the development of rural and cultural tourism as well as for protecting environmental quality.

The Community tourism policy currently under development is expected to complement national policies adopted for the promotion of the industry and to reinforce activities already under way.

FUTURE ISSUES AND CHALLENGES FACING TOURISM DEVELOPMENT IN GREECE

Greece, like most Mediterranean countries, is expected to face increased tourist demand in the future which will put heavy pressures on its natural, physical and human resources in addition to those from population growth and industrial development. Coastal areas will face the greatest pressures since most activities and population will seek to locate along and take advantage of the coast as they do at present. At the same time, the volatility of tourist demand is an issue of particular importance in Greece. Whether the Greek tourist market will be able to meet and take advantage of this increased demand will depend on how the whole complex of the constituent enterprises as well as the competent public agencies are going to cope with the problems of the present and take the necessary steps to meet the challenges of the future. The public and private actions needed for successful future tourism development in Greece are briefly outlined here.

The public sector will still have to intervene dynamically in the tourism development process but not on the basis of the models of the past. Public policy should offer the broad frame of action for the private sector, the coordination needed for the smooth functioning of the several interdependent and sometimes conflicting tourism-related activities, and the infrastructure necessary for regional and tourism development. More specifically, cohesive, consistent and comprehensive tourism policy is needed for: (i) the coordinated development of tourism and all other activities with which it necessarily interacts and the resolution of the unavoidable conflicts arising out of their demand for common property resources (land, air, water); (ii) a balanced distribution of tourism's costs and benefits over space and time; (iii) diversification of the industry in order to be able to withstand exogenously induced changes in tourist demand. More general public policy concerning environmental protection, industrial development, exports, trade, taxation, etc., must also provide for the needs of tourism in terms of improving the quality of the tourist product offered and contributing to the retention of tourist exchange. Provision of infrastructure (transportation, telecommunications, water supply, solid and liquid wastes disposal) will serve the dual goal of tourism and regional development of the country. Finally, the role of the government in taking advantage of the benefits of European integration will be instrumental for the development of tourist services suitable to meet a more varied future demand.

The private sector, on the other hand, needs to concentrate its efforts on improving the competitiveness of the Greek tourist enterprises which still lack managerial competence, quality of services provided, aggressive marketing and coordination. The last requirement is particularly important since tourist enterprises, unlike other economic entities, depend critically on one another with respect to the product they 'sell' and the share of the tourist market they can capture. Promotion activities will be indispensable in the future if Greek tourism is to survive the keen competition of established and emerging tourist-receiving countries and in a market as volatile as the tourist one is.

Sustainable tourism development and promotion of quality versus quantity are two recently advanced international goals which Greek tourism should pursue by means of long-range tourism policy and active participation and cooperation of the private sector.

REFERENCES

AGTE (1992) *The Place of Tourism and its Contribution to the National Economy.* Association of Greek Tourist Enterprises, Athens (in Greek).

Briassoulis, H. (1992) Environmental Impacts of Tourism: A framework for analysis and evaluation. In: van der Straaten, J. and Briassoulis, H. (eds) *Tourism and the Environment: Regional, Economic and Policy Issues.* Kluwer Academic Publishers, Dordrecht.

Chiotis, G. and Coccossis, H. (1992) Tourist development and environmental protection in Greece. In: van der Straaten, J. and Briassoulis, H. (eds) *Tourism and the Environment: Regional, Economic and Policy Issues.* Kluwer Academic Publishers, Dordrecht.

JICA (1989) *The Study of Tourism Promotion.* Interim Report. Japan International Cooperation Agency, Hellenic Republic.

KEPE (1984a) KEPE: Tourism does not participate in the formation of the GNP, *Tourism and the Economy* 62, 24–25 (in Greek).

KEPE (1984b) KEPE: The structural and long-term problems of tourism, *Tourism and the Economy* 63, 23–25 (in Greek).

Komilis, P. (1986) *Tourism Activities.* Athens (in Greek).

Konsolas, N. and Zacharatos, G. (1992) Regionalization of tourism activity in Greece: problems and policies. In: van der Straaten, J. and Briassoulis, H. (eds), *Tourism and the Environment: Regional, Economic and Policy Issues.* Kluwer Academic Publishers, Dordrecht.

Tourism and the Economy (1985) 79, 27–28.

Tourism and the Economy (1987) 104.

Tourism and the Economy (1990) 135, 28.

Tsartas, P. (1989) *Social and Economic Impacts of Tourist Development in the Prefecture of Kyklades and Particularly in the Islands of Ios and Serifos for the 1950–80 Period.* National Centre for Social Research, Athens (in Greek).

17

TOURISM IN ITALY

Aureliano Bonini

THE LEADING TOURISM AREAS

Italy remains one of the leading tourist destinations in the world. In contrast with other countries it can count not only on its geographical position, climate and natural beauty but also on the fact that at least 40% of the world's wealth of monumental, historical and artistic works is distributed throughout its territory. The Vatican in Rome (seat of one of the most authoritative world religions), the Alps (a paradise for winter sports), and romantic and picturesque lakes (for health resorts and spas, one of the leaders in Europe) are among the other reasons for Italy's great attractiveness. For a full understanding of Italian tourism it is necessary to examine the types of tourist facilities it offers. Unlike other nations that offer only one type of tourism or are considered by tourists the goal for this or that type of vacation, Italy is prismatic. It is perceived by millions of tourist all over the world as the destination for at least five types of tourism:

1. Art, culture, religion (and business).
2. Seaside tourism (sun, sand and sea).
3. Mountain tourism (nature, health resorts, climbing, snow and winter sports).
4. Hot springs and spas (fitness, therapy, beauty).
5. Other tourist attractions (lakes, natural parks, theme parks).

Art, Culture, Religion (and Business)

In the 19th century Italy's cultural, artistic and historical heritage was the great beacon for European artists, aristocrats and intellectuals. Travel experiences, such as those narrated by Goethe, Stendhal or Poe, became

Fig. 17.1. Areas of art, culture, religion (and business) tourism in Italy.

one of the bases of scholarly education for generations of Europeans. Italy was one of the principal stops in the first form of modern tourism, 'the Grand Tour', the trip across the paradises of classic history which was recommended to young aristocrats and the offspring of the wealthy European bourgeoisie. In the 20th century this 'bath of art and culture', although still valid, underwent certain transformations and changes from the end of the 1970s that made Italy less important as a tourist mecca. The new generations preferred study trips to the United States to classical culture.

In addition to tourism dedicated to art, culture and religion, Italy has today become increasingly important for business trips and summer holidays, although the three classic destinations are still Rome, Venice and Florence. Until the mid-1970s the Naples–Pompei–Capri area was still one of the most important tourist stops, but increasing social problems, pollution and degradation in this area have led to its exclusion as one of the basic stops on the tour market and today, for tourists everywhere, it is but 'a second choice' along with the tour of Sicily.

There are instead some smaller destinations gaining in popularity that appeal to the more discerning tourist, namely the 'minor cities' (Siena, Pisa, Spoleto, Assisi, Verona, Padua). Concentrated in the central and northern areas of Italy they benefit from tourist routes between Rome, Venice and Florence. These towns preserve outstanding artistic treasures and in many cases are also associated with myths (the Leaning Tower, the Palio), celebrated love stories (Romeo and Juliet), miracles (St Francis of Assisi), etc. (Fig. 17.1).

The problems related to this type of tourism are common and evident; day-time trips and excursions cause an excessive tourist overload, but the tourist traffic remains seasonal (April–October) and causes extensive urban degradation.

The attraction of the three great 'classic' destinations is decreasing while there is growing interest in the 'minor cities'. What are the reasons for this change? The research and marketing surveys affirm that ancient cities decrease in popularity because their hotels are old, lacking in comfort and overly expensive. Tourists also report that restaurant prices are excessive, that transportation is inefficient and, last but not least, the general short-sightedness of local authorities in closing museums, exhibitions, art galleries on Sundays and during holidays.

Seaside Tourism (Fig. 17.2)

About 50% of Italian tourism comes under the heading 'seaside holidays'. Italian tourist services and hotels, generally small and family operated, are concentrated along the coast and near the beaches. The history of seaside

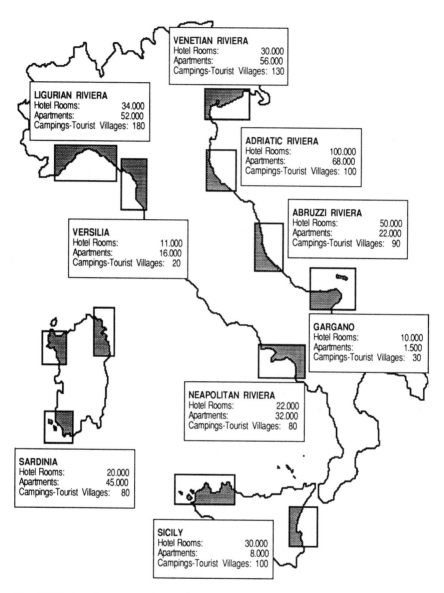

VENETIAN RIVIERA
Hotel Rooms: 30.000
Apartments: 56.000
Campings-Tourist Villages: 130

LIGURIAN RIVIERA
Hotel Rooms: 34.000
Apartments: 52.000
Campings-Tourist Villages: 180

ADRIATIC RIVIERA
Hotel Rooms: 100.000
Apartments: 68.000
Campings-Tourist Villages: 100

ABRUZZI RIVIERA
Hotel Rooms: 50.000
Apartments: 22.000
Campings-Tourist Villages: 90

VERSILIA
Hotel Rooms: 11.000
Apartments: 16.000
Campings-Tourist Villages: 20

GARGANO
Hotel Rooms: 10.000
Apartments: 1.500
Campings-Tourist Villages: 30

NEAPOLITAN RIVIERA
Hotel Rooms: 22.000
Apartments: 32.000
Campings-Tourist Villages: 80

SARDINIA
Hotel Rooms: 20.000
Apartments: 45.000
Campings-Tourist Villages: 80

SICILY
Hotel Rooms: 30.000
Apartments: 8.000
Campings-Tourist Villages: 100

Fig. 17.2. Leading areas of seaside tourism in Italy.

tourism is recent, since before the 1960s only a small number of well-to-do Italians went on holiday. In those years tourism was concentrated in five areas: Versilia in Tuscany, the Amalfi and Sorrento coast (Neapolitan Riviera), the Venetian lidos, the Riviera of Romagna (Cesenatico, Rimini, Riccione) and the Ligurian Riviera.

The first large concentration of hotels and tourist infrastructures was started in Liguria (toward the middle of the 1950s) reflecting the success of the French Riviera. The Riviera Adriatica of Emilia-Romagna, a large area specializing in mass tourism, became popular in the late 1950s. Now, over thirty years later, the Adriatic Riviera of Emilia Romagna represents the largest market for tourism in Italy with more than 100,000 hotel rooms, 68,000 apartments and 100 camping grounds.

Hotels and tourist infrastructure rapidly expanded in the 1960s to meet the boom in European demand. Hotels grew by political permissiveness and from the efforts of self-made operators and small investors. Both tourists and hospitality operators appeared overnight, converted villas and private homes and started building new hotels on small lots of land. Lack of space and poor management are the main reasons why many of the seaside hotels are largely incomplete and unable to meet modern European demand: when hotels have a garden, they have no parking lot, when they have a parking lot they have no swimming-pool. Generally speaking hotel rooms are small, bathrooms not up to standard and most of the facilities are spartan. Italian hospitality in the 1990s fails to reach the minimum standards to compete with international hotels.

Italian tourists too have been discouraged by this situation. Since their relative poverty in the 1960s they have become as prosperous and demanding as their European counterparts who require a standard of comfort at least similar to that which they have at home when they go on holiday. In the 1990s the number of foreign tourists is decreasing while the domestic market continues to prefer island resorts. The scenario is bleak but not for every destination; the Italian islands continue to be successful (the Aeolians, Lipari, Ponza, Elba, Tremiti, while Sardinia is always the Mediterranean leader), because tourists seem more adaptable and willing to accept the inconveniences of hotel accommodation there.

Today, even though the Riviera Adriatica has lost a large share of its market among tourists from northern European countries and signs of development along its seaside are weak, Rimini, the leading destination of seaside tourism in Italy, continues to surpass its competitor, Palma de Majorca (Baleares, Spain) in terms of available accommodation. The most exclusive and luxurious Italian beaches (and seaside hotels) are those on the Costa Smeralda in Sardinia.

There is an enormous annual concentration of demand during July and August which overloads all types of accommodation, transportation and entertainment available. Excessive demand causes both prices and poor service to enter a vicious circle.

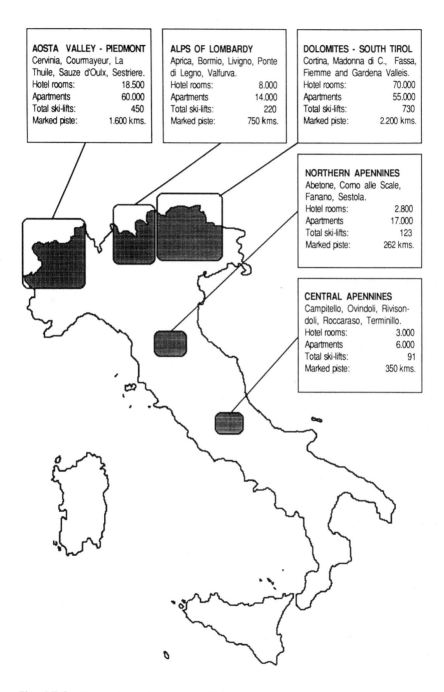

AOSTA VALLEY - PIEDMONT
Cervinia, Courmayeur, La
Thuile, Sauze d'Oulx, Sestriere.
Hotel rooms: 18.500
Apartments 60.000
Total ski-lifts: 450
Marked piste: 1.600 kms.

ALPS OF LOMBARDY
Aprica, Bormio, Livigno, Ponte
di Legno, Valfurva.
Hotel rooms: 8.000
Apartments 14.000
Total ski-lifts: 220
Marked piste: 750 kms.

DOLOMITES - SOUTH TIROL
Cortina, Madonna di C., Fassa,
Fiemme and Gardena Valleis.
Hotel rooms: 70.000
Apartments 55.000
Total ski-lifts: 730
Marked piste: 2.200 kms.

NORTHERN APENNINES
Abetone, Corno alle Scale,
Fanano, Sestola.
Hotel rooms: 2.800
Apartments 17.000
Total ski-lifts: 123
Marked piste: 262 kms.

CENTRAL APENNINES
Campitello, Ovindoli, Rivison-
doli, Roccaraso, Terminillo.
Hotel rooms: 3.000
Apartments 6.000
Total ski-lifts: 91
Marked piste: 350 kms.

Fig. 17.3. Mountain tourism areas in Italy.

Mountain Tourism (Fig. 17.3)

Mountain travel (about 15% of the total holiday market), is distributed over two tourist seasons: (i) 'summer holiday' (experts call it 'climatismo montano') and (ii) 'winter sports, snow and skiing'.

The development of mountain travel and the fame of top destinations started in Switzerland, attracting quality tourists for summer walks and healthy vacations. Initially tourism was concentrated in the Eastern Alps, in particular in the area of the Dolomites, and in the Western Alps near the great peaks of Mont Blanc, Monte Rosa and the Matterhorn. From the end of the 1960s through the 1970s, Italian prosperity and the general growth of the holiday market brought about an enormous increase in the number of tourists and mountain resorts. Today the leading Italian ski localities are: Cortina d'Ampezzo, Courmayeur – Val d'Aosta, Madonna di Campiglio, Canazei – Val di Fassa, Selva and Valgardena, Corvara and Val Badia, and Brunico and Val Pusteria. In the 1970s a few areas in the Apennines were developed (Cimone, Abetone and Abruzzo) but for winter sports they are still fighting for second place because of the lower altitudes and more temperate climate.

The most important mountain vacation areas enjoy double seasons: *summer vacation* and *winter sports*. Their major income comes from Italian guests (domestic tourism counts for over 85%) and since 1989 most places do their best to guarantee snow even in dry years (using 'artificial snow' equipment on ski trails).

Today many mountain areas claim to be overloaded and try to limit traffic during week-ends and national holidays. Indeed tourists in the summer season are also nearing the point of overload. Trends in the 1990s indicate that mountain destinations below 1200 m above sea level are more vulnerable economically during winter but more successful in the summer.

Hot Springs and Spas (Fig. 17.4)

The origin of 'hot-spring holidays', the use of waters and mud baths for therapy or fitness, dates back to Roman times. The golden age of hot springs and spas has passed, when such tourism meant luxury holidays in prestigious hotels frequented by aristocratic clients and rich tourists; in the 1990s spas seem to be entering a slow decline as their share of the market gradually contracts. After the Second World War, Italian hot springs and spas failed to modernize and gradually deteriorated. To replace the aristocratic clients, 'state-run hot springs and spas' were gradually developed which offered more therapy treatments but less tourism opportunity. Many famous spas were characterized by a massive inflow of clients assisted by the National Health System who were accommodated in hotels

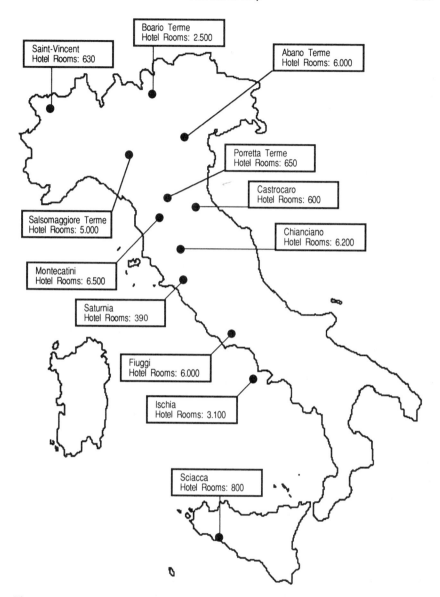

Fig. 17.4. Leading hot springs and spas in Italy.

where they received services similar to those offered in hospitals. The question in Italy is still controversial. Public managers continue to discuss the question: more holidays and less medical treatment or more medical attention and less tourism, pleasure and entertainment? Currently, the Italian hot springs and spas concentrate on meeting domestic demand. Abano,

Ischia, Merano and Montecatini are the leading health resorts in Italy, but Fiuggi and Salsomaggiore are also striving to keep their position as prestigious therapeutic centres.

The first Italian examples of an American style resort (self-sufficient hotels with health centres, fitness and beauty farms) are operating in Tuscany, Saturnia being a clear example of these advanced and new 'health resorts'. There is an emerging, distinct separation between this new type of health tourism and the traditional Italian spa. The few foreign guests of the spas market come almost exclusively from Germany. The different resorts have a limited, constantly narrowing radius of attraction.

Other Tourist Attractions

The lakes

This type of tourism continues to be considered a secondary attraction in Italy even though millions of vacationers spend their holidays in the lake areas every year (lakes attract around 6% of the total number of tourists). Tourists concentrate around the famous and picturesque waters of Northern and Central Italy. The leading destination is Lake Garda which comprises around 32% of the total lakes market. Other well known locations include: Lake Maggiore, Lake Como, Lake Iseo, Lake Trasimeno, Lake Bracciano and Lake Bolsena.

The natural parks

The attraction of the protected nature areas and national parks as tourist destinations is still limited. Only rarely has the relationship between environmental protection and the development of tourist facilities resulted in advantages for holiday makers. The famed, international parks are: 'Gran Paradiso' (Val d'Aosta), 'Stelvio' (South Tyrol), 'Parco d'Abruzzo' and the marine park at 'Circeo' (Lazio).

Although every region tries to institute, organize and develop its own parks as protected oases, they are still a long way from realizing holiday paradises similar to those founded in the United States many years ago. Rules, access, organizations are rigid, and service and accommodation models are only occasionally capable of attracting holiday makers.

The amusement parks

This type of attraction is very important for tourism and leisure time, but it is still too recent to meet full demand. The existing structures are often compact 'miniatures' compared to the large US and French parks, which can generally count on enormous spaces. The currently operating parks are: 'Gardaland' on the shores of Lake Garda, 'Italia in Miniatura' on the Riviera Adriatica and 'MinItalia' in Lombardia (near Milan). Projects for new parks are growing and, among these, worthy of note are 'Mirabilandia' and 'Millenium', which will be built on the Riviera Adriatica. Following the example of Aquafan (created in Riccione in 1987) many leading seaside resorts, cities and areas have created a medium size aquatic park. Larger projects are expected during the 1990s both on the Adriatic and the Versilian Coasts.

ECONOMIC DIMENSION OF THE SECTOR

In 1991 tourists in Italy spent about 61,000 billion lire for travel, accommodation, food, entertainment, recreation, and shopping but the overall figure stimulated by the vacation market amounted to 140,000 billion lire. Tourism turnover means direct purchases of products and services plus added market shares (employees' wages and salaries, hospitality income, investments, bank interest, taxes, etc.). Tourism therefore is a consistently significant factor in the GNP (Gross National Product), but Italy is still dominated by mentalities that give exclusive importance to agriculture and manufacturing industry: the government is oriented towards industrial development and fails to acknowledge the significance of tourism. Thus, even though the hospitality industry is economically and socially more important than many industrial sectors (that are constantly in crisis, subsidized or supported by the State), Italy struggles to keep pace with the five great world powers, neglecting its important tourist role and failing to make tourism a priority.

The Italian economic and industrial infrastructure is based on small and very small companies which may be independent, self-contained and creative, but frequently have no overall view of the market and its development. Fragmentation is extremely high and the concept that 'small is beautiful' prevails over the idea that concentration–association is worthwhile.

While Italy dreams of an industrial future, the average size of its hotels is 27 rooms, one of the smallest in the world. France is becoming the strongest European competitor for Italy and in terms of quantity and quality, French hospitality is largely the winner. The new wave of entertainment imported by EuroDisney, the quality of hotels available and the efficiency of the Disney organization will modify European holiday habits and will attract a substantial share of the tourist trade from all over Europe to France. France has perceived the importance of hospitality and French

Table 17.1. Hotel chains in Italy.

Company	Nationality	Rooms	Properties
Jolly Hotels	Italy	5200	32
Atahotels/Interhotels	Italy	5100	20
Ciga Hotels	Italy	3300	23
Semi Granturismo	Italy	2500	46
Starhotels	Italy	2304	15
Accor/Wagon Lits	France	2100	11
ITT Sheraton	USA	1300	4
Cogeta Palace Hotels	Italy	1200	12
Holiday Inns	GB	1200	5
Trust House Forte	GB	1200	4

Source: Trademark Italia from Kleinwort Benson Securities, NEO Magazine, Horwath International (1991).

hotel chains have also penetrated Italy, replacing some small domestic hotel companies. Domestic hotel chains are generally controlled and managed by families that operate them mostly by instinct and through poorly qualified management. Table 17.1 provides an overview of hotel chains in Italy.

Tourism in Italy is often underrated. The Italian automobile and chemical industries together provide 600,000 jobs, whereas the tourism and hospitality industry, according to the WTTC Report (1991), account for over 2.5 millions jobs (one Italian job holder in nine receives income from the hospitality industry in general). Furthermore, national official data collectors do not have accurate statistical references. Trade unions probably do not take into account unreported jobs and occasional employment, and official statistics cannot or do not want to include them. Actual official figures speak of only 867,000 employed in the 'travel and tourism' sector (of which almost 70% are in the hotel, café and restaurant sector). Table 17.2 shows the official distribution of jobs by type of activity. One remarkable aspect of these figures is that 467,000 workers are employees (56.6%) whereas 400,000 are independent operators and/or self-employed workers (43.4%). The presence of so many independent operators is due to three structural characteristics of the hospitality industry:

1. Supply is markedly deconcentrated.
2. The companies are family organized so that it is often the same person who gives the orders and carries them out.
3. Employment is mainly seasonal.

Table 17.2. Distribution of jobs.

Sector	Number	%
Hotels, Restaurants, Cafes, Catering	603,000	69.5
Transport and Communications	120,000	13.9
Travel operations	87,000	10.0
Other services	57,000	6.6
Total employees	867,000	100.0

Source: Fourth National Report of Tourism Ministry.

THE STRUCTURE OF TOURISM IN ITALY

Hotel Accommodation

Hotels in Italy are classified by the star system (1 to 5 stars). Table 17.3 briefly summarizes Italy's tourism potential:

Table 17.3. Hotels in Italy from 1980–1990.

Rating	1980	1987	1990	Difference 1980–1990
5 stars	53	82	105	+52
4 stars	715	1,240	1,520	+805
3 stars	4,528	6,668	7,380	+2,852
2 stars	9,614	11,404	11,410	+1,796
1 star	26,787	17,765	15,100	−11,687
Total	41,697	37,159	35,515	−6,182

Sources: Trademark Italia/OMT/Istat/Faiat/CEI.

In the last ten years the number of hotels (but not overall accommodation capacity) has declined considerably. From the beginning of the 1980s to today the number of hotels has decreased about 15%. Almost 6200 small pensiones have closed down whereas the number of 4 and 5 star units has practically doubled (in percentage terms the biggest increase concerns the 4 and 5 stars hotels). However, the total number of hotel

Table 17.4. Hotel rooms from 1980–1990.

Rating	1980	1987	1990	Difference 1980–1990
5 stars	7,744	13,175	16,600	+8,856
4 stars	62,971	112,365	139,500	+76,529
3 stars	227,690	269,104	312,200	+84,510
2 stars	264,946	311,136	311,500	+46,554
1 star	320,315	214,956	187,200	−133,115
Total	883,666	920,736	967,000	+83,334

Sources: Trademark Italia/OMT/Istat/Faiat/CEI.

rooms has grown (+ 83.334 rooms, + 9.5%), largely due to restructuring and enlargement of existing hotels (Table 17.4).

The 3 and 4 star hotels are those that expanded the most in terms of rooms, and today the 3 star category accounts for 32% of Italian hotel accommodation. In short, Italy has about 470,000 hotel rooms (48% of its total) with adequate standard to satisfy an international clientele and roughly 500,000 rooms below the international standard of accommodation. Table 17.5 shows the average size of Italian hotels with reference to the number of rooms.

Non-hotel Accommodation in Italy

At the beginning of 1990, non-hotel accommodation ('extralberghiero'), where capacity is officially rated by the number of beds, was as follows:

- 2300 campings and tourist villages; 1.2 million available beds.
- 3200 student inns, vacation homes and typical mountain cabins; 190,000 available beds.
- 460,000 tourist apartments and tourist condominiums; 2.2 million available beds.

Italy on the whole offers about 4.6 million beds for holiday makers. Obviously the supply of beds meeting the standards of frequent travellers and international business clientele is limited to only 470,000 units (out of the country's 976,000 total hotel capacity). Basically, 4 million beds are suitable more for domestic than international tourism, by failing to guarantee minimum European comfort standards.

Table 17.5. Average hotel size (no. of rooms) 1980–1990.

Rating	1980	1987	1990
5 stars	146.1	160.7	158.1
4 stars	88.1	90.6	91.8
3 stars	50.3	40.4	42.3
2 stars	27.6	27.3	27.3
1 star	12.0	12.1	12.4
Total	21.2	24.8	27.2

Sources: Trademark Italia/OMT/Istat/Faiat/CEI.

HIGHLIGHTS OF THE TOURISM MARKET IN ITALY

Official tourism sources (Istat) declare 246.5 million overnight stays in 1989, but this figure, as well as most of the data concerning tourist flows, is more an estimate than an authentic statistical reference. Moreover, in Italy, as in the rest of the OCSE countries, statistical data are often flawed or unreliable; however, they are useful as indicators of the deviations or progression of the domestic components of the market. Most tourists coming to Italy visit the northern part of the country in the regions of Val d'Aosta, Piemonte, Liguria, Lombardia, Trentino–Alto Adige, Friuli, Veneto and Emilia-Romagna. About two-thirds of the seaside accommodation is found in this area together with almost all the mountain and lake tourist facilities. Three tourist towns (Venice, Verona and Rimini), together with the leading business towns (Milan and Bologna), attract most of the international and domestic tourism. This explains why 58.3% of the 246.5 million officially recorded overnight stays occur in the north.

Central Italy (consisting of the regions of Tuscany, Umbria, Marche and Lazio), in relation to the size of its territory, receives a high proportion of visitors. The most popular destinations in this area are Rome, Florence and all of Tuscany. Southern Italy receives fewer tourists in proportion to the size of its territory, because of its general lack of development. Table 17.6 shows the distribution in 1989 of tourists in the various facilities.

About three-quarters of all tourists registered in Italy are accommodated in hotels classified 1 to 5 stars. Hotels in the lowest categories (1–2 stars), although having 51.5% of the total number of rooms, accommodate 78 million visitors, only 41.5% of the total (official data). In these categories of hotels the number of registered guests has been declining 5%

Table 17.6. Distribution of tourists in various facilities, 1989.

Type of accommodation	Overnight stays (million)	Percentage
Hotels	187.3	76.1
Camping grounds and villages	40.5	16.4
Tourist apartments	9.2	3.7
Other accommodation	9.5	3.8
Total	246.5	100.0

annually. The 3 and 4 star hotels accommodate 107 million visitor-nights. Their share is now 57.2% and rising continuously.

More caution is required in evaluating non-hotel accommodation ('extralberghiero') since the number of beds available in flats and apartments is largely underestimated. There is greater fluctuation in demand in tourist resorts than in hotels and overnight stays are not controlled.

A complex tourist destination such as Italy with its five types of tourism can rely on a year round tourist traffic. However, even if winter is an important tourist season for the trade, the busiest time is summer. Peak months of the year are July and August, accounting for one-third of all accommodation nights distributed in hotels and non-hotel accommodation (Table 17.7).

The flow of foreign travellers in Italy changes throughout the year and the 1989 borders and customs movement shows that 77.8% of the tourists arrive in Italy by car or bus (Table 17.8). This table illustrates the unreliability of Italian tourist statistic figures and in particular the method for collecting data. A calculation of border traffic gives only random, questionable figures; and there is enough daily commuter traffic back and forth between Italy and its border countries to reduce any credibility the annual surveys might have. For instance the over 10 million 'Swiss tourists' (Switzerland's total population is 8.3 million), arrivals in Italy of more than 62,776 Swiss tourists by sea and the figure for the Yugoslavs who apparently outnumber the English three times. Excluding the data on Switzerland, it is nevertheless apparent that first in importance among foreign tourists are the Germans (40.4%) with 35 million (the historical maximum for German tourists was reached in 1982 with 43.8 million visitors). The English are definitely second with 6.5 million (7.5% of foreign tourists). In 1982 they were 7.2 million but today the English are sixth in the classification of arrivals. This type of data indicates that the volume of foreign tourism in Italy is continually decreasing with the excep-

Table 17.7. Overnight stays in hotels (bi-monthly).

Months	Italians	Foreigners	Total
January–February	11,541,556	4,731,284	16,272,840
March–April	15,604,724	9,469,487	25,074,211
May–June	18,169,453	15,753,583	33,923,036
July–August	43,449,812	18,668,835	62,118,647
September–October	19,360,772	15,294,600	34,655,372
November–December	11,035,233	4,221,284	15,256,517
Total	119,161,550	68,139,073	187,600,623

tion of tourists from Japan who have almost doubled in number to 1.5 million.

In general the decline in interest towards Italy by citizens from those foreign countries whose people travel most, began in 1983 but rapidly accelerated in 1989 because of the algae bloom on the Adriatic coast and in 1990/1 because of the war in the Persian Gulf. The decline was slowed in late 1991 because of the civil war in Yugoslavia which caused German tourists to travel to Italy and other countries in the Mediterranean basin.

There were certain specific problems in 1991 which affected the Italian tourist market:

1. A decline in Italy's competitiveness as a tourist attraction worldwide due:

    a) to the poor quality/price ratio of its transportation, restaurant and entertainment system;

    b) second, to the failure of Italian hotels to adjust to international models;

    c) third, to social disorder, news of strikes, and environmental crises, all of which discouraged international tourism.

2. A change in the demands of foreign tourists, for whom the *sun-sand-sea* formula no longer seems to work. Europeans enjoy better education and growing prosperity and therefore trips to exotic places are more 'appealing'. This means long-haul holidays and consequently fewer high-income visitors to Italy and less foreign exchange.

3. A change in the habits of Europeans: there is a trend towards taking shorter vacations at different times of the year. Shorter and more frequent travelling means more hotel reservations and fewer bookings of flats and apartments on a long-term basis.

Table 17.8. Foreign travellers entering Italy at borders.

Nationality	Border traffic				Total
	Train	Road	Air	Sea	
Switzerland	1,225,190	8,710,549	192,044	62,776	10,190,559
West Germany	727,963	8,345,180	686,404	374,666	10,134,213
France	980,002	7,648,877	655,273	106,000	9,390,152
Austria	371,550	5,540,647	124,446	46,727	6,083,370
Yugoslavia	316,815	5,506,718	37,344	48,864	5,909,741
Great Britain	110,835	746,990	953,846	94,565	1,906,236
The Netherlands	106,855	1,497,378	205,275	31,336	1,840,844
United States of America	171,651	546,178	557,194	81,639	1,356,662
Belgium	48,419	820,445	161,050	19,016	1,048,930
Spain	42,257	376,598	266,948	14,806	700,609
Denmark	56,950	484,402	95,504	9,479	646,335
Sweden	56,568	379,013	144,365	17,158	597,104
Greece	26,477	175,387	157,331	149,643	508,838
Japan	58,545	65,289	329,373	3,493	456,700
Canada	71,830	150,472	177,232	23,405	422,939
Other European countries	260,722	1,114,944	529,123	65,811	1,970,600
Other non-European countries	181,979	736,452	859,098	149,930	1,927,459
Total	4,814,608	42,845,519	6,131,850	1,299,314	55,091,291

Sources: Trademark Italia/Istat (1989).

4. The trend, especially among tourists under 45 years old, to look for an exclusive and unique travel experience. Thus anything related to mass, group, or collective tourism is less attractive, causing a sharp decline in the demand for tours and package holidays organized by tour operators.

For these reasons and because of the economic and social crises in the countries from which most foreign tourists to Italy come, the overall foreign expenditure is continuing to decrease. Now it is about 16,500 billion lire (according to Bankitalia). In comparison with 1987 the number of overnight stays by foreign visitors in 1991 has declined by 10.3%.

The domestic holiday habits of Italians have also substantially changed and now most Italian tourists come from the northern regions of Italy. Six regions (two of them southern) account for 67% of Italian tourists: Lombardia, 23%; Piemonte, 10%; Veneto, 7%; Emilia Romagna, 7%; Lazio, 11%; Campania, 9%. The number of Italians who annually go on holiday has risen from 49% in 1985 to 56% in 1990. Specifically 25.9 million Italians take a long vacation (average two weeks) during the year. More than two-thirds of Italian tourists choose July and August for their holidays but the number of Italians who break up their holiday time is increasing. The types of accommodation used are shown in Table 17.9.

Italian tourists' overnight stays are shared between regions. Figures show a concentration in six leading areas (Table 17.10).

In 1990 4.4 million Italians spent at least one holiday period abroad, and in 1991 this figured increased to 14%. Italian tourist habits are becoming more European and several market researchers predict that by the end of the millenium, Italians as a whole will account for 25 million trips a year (against 15 million today). The Banca d'Italia predicts that from now to the year 2000 spending by Italians for trips abroad will increase at an average rate of 5% per year.

Table 17.9. Accommodation make-up % 1985–1990.

Type	1985	1988	1990	Trend
Hotels and hotel villages	27	34	35	upward
Flats and apartments	19	18	21	upward
Friends and relatives	26	22	21	strong decline
Own homes	17	16	15	downward
Camping and caravaning	11	10	8	downward
Total	100	100	100	

Source: Trademark Italia on Doxa data 1991.

Table 17.10. Popular holiday regions.

Region	Tourists (%)
Emilia Romagna	13.1
Tuscany	11.8
Veneto	9.4
Trentino-Alto Adige	9.1
Lombardia	8.6
Liguria	8.0
Lazio	5.9
Campania	4.9
Sicily	3.8
Puglia	3.5
Piemonte	3.5
Marche	3.5
Sardinia	3.4
Abruzzo	2.7
Friuli Venezia Giulia	2.2
Calabria	2.1
Umbria	1.7
Val d'Aosta	1.7
Basilicata	0.5
Molise	0.2

Sources: Trademark Italia/Istat/Faiat/CEI.

THE TRAVEL AGENCIES SECTOR

From 1980 to 1990, the number of travel agencies in Italy more than doubled from 2383 to 4825. In 1981, 16,267 people were employed in this sector, whereas at the end of 1990, including permanent and seasonal jobs, there were about 28,000 workers involved in the travelling trade.

In Italy each travel agency serves 11,900 residents but the Italian Federation of Travel Agencies (FIAVET) estimates that the appropriate ratio is one agency per 9000/10,000 residents. The travel agencies system is simple and fragmented; from the management point of view it seems almost similar to the hotel system, built up with no real strategy and often with seasonal goals. Thousands of independent agents employ only one or two people; often their principal activity is selling package holidays from catalogues or arranging excursions and local assistance for larger tour operators. Italian tour operators are also small. Average size businesses are markedly smaller than their Northern European counterparts (Table 17.11).

Table 17.11. Sales by leading operators in 1990.

Tour operators	Lire (millions)
Alpitour	379,584
Francorosso International	145,092
Aviatour	117,269
Comitours	93,508
I Grandi Viaggi	92,657
I Viaggi del Ventaglio	54,253
Vacanze	49,991
Hotelplan Italia	41,523
Teorema	36,696
Viaggi Kuoni	34,886

Sources: Trademark Italia/TTG Italia.

Most agencies operate like newstands, passing out catalogues of package tours rather than planning special holidays to suit individual customers. In future years the Italian travel agencies will face an unfavourable market situation, even if not as unfavourable as that in countries such as Great Britain or Germany. Indeed, two positive trends may favour travel operators: Italians' increasing reliance on travel agencies and their increasing interest in travelling and vacationing abroad.

THE ORGANIZATION OF TOURISM IN ITALY

Italy enjoys a wealth of natural and artistic beauty and this wealth has produced an almost spontaneous growth of its tourist and hospitality system. The public organization of tourism has therefore served as no more than a framework with no proper managerial structure and has remained, in its personnel and facilities, an expression of a preindustrial system (Fig. 17.5).

It is unclear who is actually in charge, who has the responsibility for enhancing the tourism system and who effectively runs the Hospitality Industry. Almost everybody in Italy perceives tourism as an unproductive sector, in common with sport, cinema, circus and theatre. The Ministry of Tourism was in fact in charge of all leisure activities and over the years it had never had a separate tourism portfolio. In the hierarchy of public administration, coming below the Ministry was the Ente Nazionale Italiano del Turismo (ENIT) (Italian National Tourism Board) which was theoretically the Ministry's operative branch both in Italy and abroad. In fact, ENIT is scarcely significant and its delegates abroad, assimilated with

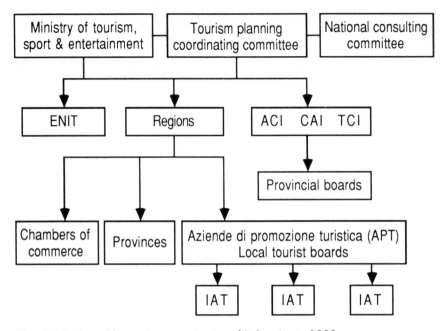

Fig. 17.5 The public tourism organization of Italy prior to 1993.

diplomatic personnel, are generally experts in public relations instead of promotion.

Locally, in the different tourist areas, a network of local tourist and promotion boards sustain the burden of tourist promotion: Aziende di Soggiorno and Pro Loco frequently dominated by political parties can hardly determine promotion investments and what is to be promoted. In the late 1980s the Aziende di Soggiorno changed their name (but not the management organization) and became APT (Tourist Promotion Agencies). In 1992 the Ministry of Tourism was expected to promulgate a new law for tourism which would change the rules and partly the organization of tourism in Italy. However, the Ministry was cancelled on 8 April 1993 by a national referendum and it is hard to predict the effects on any future administration.

SUMMARY

Tourism in Italy is in a stage of maturity and tending towards decline. Official national data on tourism and employment have little connection with the real economy and effective labour market. In spite of the recurring crises in tourism, trade unions have never acknowledged declines in employment nor staff cuts in the tourism sector.

The Government is scarcely concerned with tourism and the lack of an academic authority (Italy has no Tourism or Hospitality University faculty), plus the general situation of Italian accommodation – which remain obsolete and dispersive with no effective managerial structure – discourages an improvement of the situation over the short term. It is difficult to predict development of the structures of hospitality: hotels, restaurants, managerial mentality and the public tourist system will probably face a further decline of quality. Consumer loyalty is also destined to decrease because of the rise in prices and the decline in overall accommodation comfort.

The European tourists' buying power will decline and lower quality will aim foreign visitors towards more competitive destinations. Italian tourism will thus tend to be increasingly domestic and less international. There may be some positive trend for small 1 and 2 star hotels on the market of tourists coming from the Eastern European countries (Poland, the Czech Republic, Slovakia and Hungary). However, that tourism will be infrequent, temporary, and is unlikely to improve the image of the country.

BIBLIOGRAPHY

Ministero del Turismo e dello Spettacolo (1991) *Quarto Rapporto sul Turismo Italiano.* Mercury, Firenze.

Hotel & Restaurant Marketing (1991) Publistampa, Milano.

Censis (1990) *La Sfida dell'Offerta*, Roma.

Economist Intelligence Unit (1991) *Travel and Tourism Analyst* No 4–5, The Economist, London.

WTTC Report (1991) *Travel & Tourism in the World Economy.* World Travel and Tourism Council, Brussels.

18

TOURISM IN NON-EC COUNTRIES: THE CASE OF SWITZERLAND AND AUSTRIA

Claude Kaspar and Christian Laesser

INTRODUCTION

The Single European Market, 1993 and its impacts are excitingly awaited by non-EC countries. Still, opinions in those countries on the question, 'will it be possible to participate in this market without being a member of the Community', are very much divided, whether they intend to join the EC as soon as possible or not. The degree of international economic interlocking (in this case between the EC and the EFTA) has reached a point where a national stand-aside has become impossible. Economic legislation in the Community affects all of Europe, with non-members having to adjust to a different order sooner or later, too.

As competition in a more and more unified Europe becomes tougher, most businesses in non-member countries have tried to prepare for this challenge. This is especially important in countries with a small domestic market, dependent on the exportation of their products. Companies offering touristic products are not different. Available capacities are too big and can therefore not be sold solely on the domestic market. That fact is of special importance for countries, where tourism plays a significant economic role, such as in Austria or Switzerland (neither being members of EC). This chapter will therefore show some specific trends and structures of tourism in non-EC countries, i.e. special features will be described which might make a difference for a non-member of the EC, treating Austria and Switzerland as case studies. As future choice of destination of tourists is of particular interest, we shall confine the focus of this chapter to incoming domestic and international tourism and will not discuss the issue of transportation.

ECONOMIC IMPORTANCE OF TOURISM

The GDP-share of tourism can be taken as a practical measure of the economic importance of tourism in a country or a community of countries such as the EC. Table 18.1 shows the direct ratio of the 'Travel' account receipts to the GDP; the non-direct, induced share (emerging by multiplier-effects), is not taken into consideration. The direct share not surprisingly varies significantly from country to country (Table 18.1). It should be noted that of all non-EC countries in Western Europe, only Austria and Switzerland show a higher GDP-rate than the European average. In the EC, only Greece (4.6%), Portugal (5.8%), Spain (4.9%) and Ireland (3.1%) have comparable shares. The rates of all other members are considerably lower than the European average.

Austria and Switzerland depend to a considerable extent on exports of touristic products, i.e. foreigners visiting or touring those countries. In most countries, that rate has been more or less stable (Austria and Switzerland included), except in those non-EC countries, where that number is currently below the European average (Table 18.2).

In the group of non-EC countries, only Austria and Switzerland gain a

Table 18.1. Ratio of the 'Travel' account receipts to the gross domestic product (GDP).

	GDP-share (%)	
	1986	1988
EFTA		
Austria	7.5	7.9
Switzerland	4.0	3.9
Iceland	1.5	1.8
Norway	1.5	1.7
Sweden	1.2	1.3
Finland	0.9	0.8
Europe[a]		
All countries average	1.8	1.8
OECD		
All countries average	0.9	1.0

Source: OECD (1990), 60.
[a]Western Europe (Europe except countries belonging to the former Warsaw Pact, Yugoslavia and Albania).

Table 18.2. Share of 'Travel' account receipts in exports of goods and services.

	Exportation-share (%)	
	1986	1988
EFTA		
Austria	18.1	18.9
Switzerland	8.4	8.1
Iceland	3.8	5.5
Norway	3.7	4.1
Sweden	3.3	3.7
Finland	3.1	3.6
Europe		
All countries average	5.4	5.5
OECD		
All countries average	4.8	4.9

Source: OECD (1990), 60.

Table 18.3. International tourist receipts and expenditure in billion current US$ (1988).

	Income	Expenditures	Surplus/deficit
EFTA			
Austria	10.094	6.309	+3.788
Switzerland	5.738	5.034	+0.704
Iceland	0.107	0.199	−0.092
Norway	2.872	3.443	−0.571
Sweden	2.346	4.559	−2.213
Finland	0.984	1.843	−0.859
Total EFTA	22.141	21.387	+0.754
Europe			
All countries	99.991	96.200	+3.791
OECD			
All countries	140.725	158.529	−17.804

Source: OECD (1990), 61.

(a)

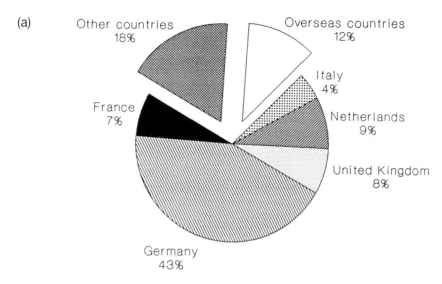

(b)

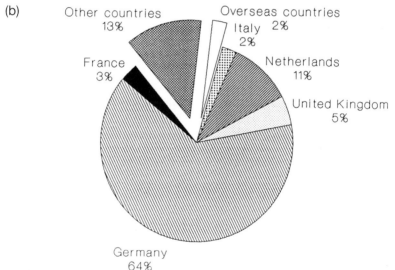

Fig. 18.1. Incoming tourism from the five strongest EC countries compared to the rest of the world, expressed as bed-nights. (a) Annual rates for Switzerland; (b) annual rates for Austria.

surplus from tourism for the balance of payments (Table 18.3). The surplus in Europe as a whole is mainly created by 'classy' tourism areas like Italy and Spain. There, the income and surplus numbers are even higher than in Austria and Switzerland. But in two 'EFTA-stars' the per capita income from tourism is of much greater significance than that in the two 'EC-stars'. The remainder of this chapter will take a closer look at Austria and Switzerland. If there is likely to be any significant impact from the simple European market, it will be most apparent in the latter two countries. The question remains however whether it would be of greater advantage for these two countries to pursue different goals regarding their touristic structure and development than the rest of Europe.

In comparison with Europe as a whole, both Switzerland and Austria depend more than average on incoming tourism from the five strongest EC countries (Fig. 18.1). Whereas in all of Europe only a little more than 56% of all nights are spent by persons of that 'group of five', in Switzerland (and Austria) 70% (84%) of all nights are spent by people coming from those countries (Table 18.4). As that group of five is part of the EC, and as the EC will increasingly influence the economic and social development of those countries, that kind of dependency needs to be seriously taken into account.

The role of tourism in the national economies is significant in Austria and Switzerland. Even if the domestic arrival rate is high (in Switzerland: about 50% of all overnight stays), international tourism in both countries will remain a very important factor in the generation of foreign currencies and improving their traditionally negative balance of trade. As tourism

Table 18.4. Annual rates of nights spent in the various means of accommodation from main generation countries expressed in percentage terms.

From (Country of residence):	Switzerland	Austria	Europe
France	7.2[a]	3.0	6.2
Germany	43.0	64.0	25.4
United Kingdom	7.5	4.8	12.8
Netherlands	8.6	10.6	7.0
Italy	4.4	2.4	4.9
Five European countries	70.7	84.8	56.3
United States	6.6	1.8	8.4
Canada	0.7	0.3	2.2
Japan	4.4	0.4	1.6
Three main overseas countries	11.7	2.4	12.2
Other countries	17.6	12.8	31.5

Source: OECD (1990), 48–49.
[a] 7.2% of nights spent in Switzerland are nights spent by persons coming from France (country of residence).

structures and trends in Austria and Switzerland are similar in many ways, we shall now examine tourism in Switzerland to try to analyse some specific aspects.

TOURISM IN SWITZERLAND

Business Structures in General

The main share of accommodation facilities in Switzerland can be found in apartments (32%). Concerning capacities, the number of beds in hotels ranks 2nd (see Table 18.5).

Hotels are the preferred type of accommodation for foreign visitors, while other means of accommodation are preferred by domestic tourists and Germans (Table 18.6). Although the number of beds in hotels amounts to only about a quarter of all available beds, they are still the 'backbone' of Swiss tourism, because most guests from foreign countries prefer hotels as accommodation while staying in Switzerland. More than 80% of foreign touristic income is generated by persons staying in hotels.

The largest share of international overnight guests arrives from EC countries, of which Germany plays a very important role: over the past 10 years, the share of tourists arriving from Germany has been continuously decreasing, but the number of nights spent by Germans still maintains a very high level (1990: 14.8 million; 40% of all nights spent by foreigners).

The division between countries of residence with regard to overnight stays in hotels has been better than in other types of accommodation. Although in hotels, the EC-share is 'only' 65% of all nights spent by foreigners (Table 18.7), the dependency of other means of accommodation

Table 18.5. Number of beds, 1990.

	Number	%
Hotels	269,400	23.79
Apartments	362,460	32.01
Camping	267,530	23.62
Group-accommodation	224,380	19.81
Youth-hostel	8,630	0.77
Other means of accommodation	863,000	76.21

Source: Tourismus in Zahlen, 7, 13.

Table 18.6. Overnight stays, 1990.

	Domestic		International	
	Number (million)	%	Number (million)	%
Hotels	14.7	41	21.1	59
Other means of accommodation	23.9	61	15.5	39

Source: Tourismus in Zahlen, 10, 14.

on tourists from the EC is, as Table 18.8 shows, much more significant. This indicates that 90% of international overnight visits comes from EC countries.

Hotels

Even in 1912 – before the First World War – there were more than 200,000 beds available in hotels in Switzerland. That number had risen to about 270,000 by 1990. Although the change in quantity has been very small, the quality has been more and more adjusted to international standards. In Switzerland, most hotels are still small or middle-sized businesses and are still run by families or other private individuals: 78% of all hotels have only 50 or fewer rooms. Only a few belong to national or international chains or are part of a larger corporation. As voluntary chains are also not very common, most hotels rely on their own ability to manage. This results in high costs per room available and toughens the competition.

Table 18.7. Hotels.

Generating countries 1990	Number (million)	%
European Community	13.7	65
United States	2.5	12
Japan	0.8	4
Others	4.0	19

Source: Tourismus in Zahlen, 10.

Table 18.8. Other forms of accommodation.

Generating countries 1990	Number (million)	%
European Community	14.0	90
Others	1.5	10

Source: Tourismus in Zahlen, 14.

So, during the 1980s, increased national and international competition has led to a contraction in the number of businesses, while the average size of business has grown. While the number of business has decreased by 12% to 6700, the number of beds has decreased by only 2.2% to 269,800; thus the average size of hotels has grown. Between 1980 and 1990, the quality of hotel rooms has been continuously improving: the increase of rooms with showers or baths was more than 28,700, whereas the number of rooms without has decreased by more than 34,000. The share of rooms with shower/bath has increased from 54% (1980) to 77% (1990).

Other Means of Accommodation

Other means of accommodation (holiday apartments, camping, group accommodations, youth hostels) are mostly preferred by Swiss and German tourists. The economic importance of these types is not very great, because the daily spending by a tourist in that category of accommodation is only about one quarter of that by guests staying in hotels.

Environmental issues have been increasingly affecting the construction of new capacities in those categories. It is therefore not surprising that the relative number of some capacity categories have been continuously decreasing over the years.

Conclusion

Because of the central location of Switzerland, it is not surprising that most tourists visiting that country originate in Europe and especially in the EC. Although the share of overseas visitors may be remarkable, it should be remembered that visitors from overseas are normally visiting more than one European country. As most countries in central Europe will be part of a unified Europe, Switzerland (and Austria, too!) will become the only additional 'foreign country' left in Europe. One cannot say what effect borders will have in a borderless Europe. But as a consequence of the dependency from EC countries, both Switzerland and Austria will have to try to attract more foreign visitors from outside the EC area.

SPECIAL FEATURES OF TOURISM FOR A NON-EC COUNTRY LIKE SWITZERLAND

After the rejection in the referendum held in late 1992 on Switzerland's closer participation in the European Economic Space, that country will remain some sort of 'a European special case'. With the rejection in the referendum, a package of adapted laws also failed to find the nation's support. To match the EES's requirements, the laws would have laid the foundation of deregulating the Swiss markets to a significant extent.

Yet, this (somehow discouraging) development in Switzerland will not mean no change in economic legislation. Currently, a discussion on passing the majority of the EES-induced laws regularly through national legislation, is under way. An example is the fourth (!) attempt to pass the law (and eventually the referendum) on the replacment of the current one-phase consumer tax by a 6–7% VAT. Other examples are on their way. In the long run, deregulation and liberalization of the economy and its factor-markets will be very important for tourism in Switzerland. In addition, the autonomous harmonization of the Swiss economy by the standards of the EC will help to reduce disadvantages to a certain extent.

But, as the following remarks show, the potentials for either a negative or positive development remain great. Time will tell, if the negative ones will result in real problems for tourism in Switzerland.

Dangers/Fears

Although not belonging to the EC, Switzerland depends heavily on visitors coming from the Community. Fears of a 'stay at home' campaign inside the EC are becoming quite accurate. Especially the promotion of Europe in a 1989 campaign turned out to be a hidden, though obvious, recommendation to take especially Europe (in the sense Europe = EC) into consideration when making travel-plans (Schelbert, 1990, p. 184).

The workforce for the tourism sector will have to be recruited from a mainly small domestic market. To retain a good image as a quality destination, Swiss tourism businesses rely on a large number of well-educated employees. By not being a member of the EC and therefore not part of the liberalization of the factor-markets, the potential pool of workers will be very limited by national laws and therefore quite costly. Because of a never-ending increase in prices due to burgeoning personnel costs, it will become harder to compete with other European destinations and there is a serious danger of worsening even further the image of high prices.

The protection of the rural economy in Switzerland results in the second highest prices for agricultural products in all of Europe (Finland as a non-EC country has the highest). The EC prices for animal products are 40% lower than in Switzerland; for grain the price difference is even 60% (Keller, 1990, p. 21). That situation, due to the Swiss agricultural policy, makes an important part of value-added chain's preliminary steps quite expensive and leaves hardly any flexibility in the creation of the price of a final product in the food sector.

The tourism branch in Switzerland is not protected as much by financial aid and fiscal legislation as that of the EC. Subsidies very often affect prices of tourism products in the EC. Greece for example received subsidies for the development of tourism infrastructure by the 'Cohesion-program' of the EC (Keller, 1988, p. 15). That was intended to be a financial compensation for branches of industry ruined by too much competition inside the EC.

In a unified Europe, Switzerland will remain one of the very few 'foreign' countries. For security reasons, one has to assume that checks at the community borders will continue to be enforced (Kommission der EG, 1985, Part 29), or even be intensified. The long-lasting delays which could thus be caused might deter potential visitors from the Community who are no longer used to border-checks.

Cooperation between the EC and non-EC countries regarding social security, health care, legal aid and judicial assistance leaves something to be desired: this also affects tourism. Foreign visitors, like those from the Community, who are involved in accidents of any kind, will have problems obtaining compensation from their community-insurance, because most of them will not be willing to pay the high costs of medicare in Switzerland. After they had paid for those costs in any EC-country, a potential visitor might think twice about a journey to a non-EC country.

Even if it does not become a member of the EC, Switzerland has to adjust many economy-affecting policies (also affecting tourism) because of economic pressure from the EC, without being able to participate in the process of decision making. That might include the undermining of the currently strict environmental legislation (example: emission-regulation), which now provides one of the possible legal means for quality-tourism in this country.

Opportunities

The EC-Tourism-industry is (or will be) exposed to a 15% VAT. After the third(!) failed national referendum in 1991, discussions on the introduction of VAT have started again. The proposed tax-level is somewhere between

6 and 7%. Thus, Switzerland's sales tax would be very much lower than that in the Community. Yet, due to low financial margins in the Swiss tourism sector, a newly introduced tax might result in higher tourist prices, because accommodation has been tax-free so far. Nevertheless, the harm will be less than that caused by a very high-level of 15% VAT.

Tourism in the EC will remain national. According to the German Minister of Economy, Tourism Policy should remain national (Bundes-ministerium für Wirtschaft, 1989) to allow more efficient solutions for smaller regional units. But as the autonomy in the EC to shape legislation on a national level is decreasing, there is a better possibility for a small non-EC country like Switzerland to shape and promote its own tourism environment.

It will be easier for a non-EC country to create effective general conditions for tourism, because the (aforementioned) smaller units can more or less directly influence policies on a high (mostly national) level. That means keeping bureaucracy as low as possible, and trying to play a leading role in certain fields of legislation which affect tourism such as in the protection of the environment (Keller, 1992, p. 22). This might also promote the image of a destination country.

There is still no supranational tourism authority with considerable centralized competence. Although there are several programmes of the EC which will influence the development of tourism, there is still no supranational authority with centralized competence. The Commission considered becoming active, and therefore a tourism department has been set up in the Brussels administration receiving funds from the EC budget. However, up to now, the member states have only planned on consulting and cooperating in questions of tourism.

POSSIBLE TRENDS

(based on Muller *et al.*, 1991, and Kaspar, 1990)

Macrotrends and Microtrends Influencing the Demand in Tourism

The aims of those macrotrends are to give an overall view of the general development of tourism and, in this case, Switzerland in particular.

There are four main macrotrends which will positively affect tourism in Switzerland. Factors like the increase in free time, and therefore the time for leisure activities, the demographical development in favour of senior citizens, the increase in available income and a better standard of education will have a positive impact on tourism in Switzerland.

There are three main macrotrends which will negatively affect tourism in Switzerland. Certain circumstances will have negative side effects on tourism in this country, such as a decreasing number of young people, an unstable US dollar and nationalism, which leads to a hostility towards foreigners.

The four following microtrends will affect behaviour regarding holidays and vacations: besides general developments, the behaviour of tourists will change in the long run, too. Behaviour such as the need for information, the use of airplanes for transportation, the requirement for quality and the trend towards active holidays have to be met by corresponding tourism products.

General Conditions

Aspects of quantity

Arrivals in international tourism will grow by about 50% by 2010. The global growth of international tourism will continue, although the time needed to double the number is getting longer. An earlier poll, taken in 1977, guessed the number of international arrivals in the year 2000 at around 440 million. The latest statistics show that in 1990 415 million international arrivals were recorded (Muller *et al.*, 1991, p. 10). Switzerland will have to try to attract at least part of that growing number to improve the use of the current capacity. However there will not be any attempt to increase that capacity to host more guests during peak seasons. Mass tourism would be contradictory to the promotion of quality tourism.

In the future, Switzerland will be confronted by diminishing market shares. The main reasons for a potential future loss of market shares are as follows (Smeral, 1990). First, Switzerland has significant scarcities of inhabitable areas, natural and human resources. Growth will be mainly restricted by the environment. Apart from that, the current and future price/quality standard will make it impossible to attract large shares of low-income customers from eastern Europe. The last reason for the loss of market shares is a latent, growing hostility towards foreigners; a tendency observed not only in Switzerland. The combination of hostility and tourism naturally cannot work and will therefore pose a sizeable problem in the future.

However, due to the absolute growth of international tourism, an absolute growth of nights spent in Switzerland can be expected.

By the year 2000, the number of nights spent in Switzerland will increase by about 17%. The expectations for hotels and the other means of accommodation are not equal. Nights spent in hotels are expected to increase by about 15% whereas lodging numbers of other kinds of accommodation will increase by 19%. So, due to a strict market segmentation in favour of the quality-conscious tourist, the national rate of growth will be somewhat smaller than the international (global) one.

The tourists' countries of origin will hardly vary. The current rate of 53%/47% of domestic/international tourists in Switzerland will more or less remain stable around the rate of 50/50. The share of German visitors to Switzerland is expected to decline slightly to about 40%. Therefore, other countries of origin will gain in importance as providers of visitors to Switzerland. The dependency on visitors from the EC will remain high, however.

Aspects of quality

As the price is not a variable parameter, the only aspect in Swiss tourism which can always be improved is the quality of the product. As each country will have to rely on its home-made strengths, Switzerland will have to try to attract more and more environment- and quality-conscious tourists. As it cannot and will never be a 'low price destination', it will have to try to guarantee a high level of quality without making compromises. That means specifically protecting the currently unharmed landscape and making sure that the visitor is aware of those efforts and behave the same way.

As a small country with a great cultural diversity, Switzerland will rely more and more on natural and traditional strengths. Those strengths are (besides the scenic landscape) a more or less intact environment and a proverbial cleanness, stability and precision. A very attractive public transportation system might become another unique selling proposition for the country.

In favour of public transportation, individual transportation by car will lose significance. As road capacities are not endlessly enlargeable and as the demand for transportation will grow at least by the rate of the global growth-rate of tourism, other means of transportation, especially public transport, need to be developed. With the project 'Rail 2000', Switzerland will create improved conditions for public transport, which then will hopefully become a unique selling proposition (USP) in the long term.

Type of Tourism

The significance of certain forms of tourism will grow in the future. Some of them will positively affect tourism in Switzerland.

1. Holidays in the mountains during the summer: The expected rate of growth can be defined as medium to strong. There are a number of reasons for the expected growth of that form of tourism. First, Switzerland is centrally located in the heart of Europe, has a landscape which is still relatively intact and is in an environmentally rather comfortable condition. The abovementioned demographic trend (growth in the proportion of senior citizens) also favours that kind of tourism. The fact that senior citizens prefer summer holidays in the mountains has been empirically proven several times. The 'ecological horror' in the Mediterranean area (pollution by algae) has also led to a shift in consumer preferences. And last but not least, in the long run, there will be the urge to travel, always keeping in mind ecological problems. If Switzerland is able to keep up its high ecological standards, it will be able to meet those demands.

2. Excursion tourism: the expected rate of growth can be defined as medium to strong. The reasons for the expected growth of excursion tourism are a continuous increase in the urge to spend shorter, but more, holidays and the possibilities for excursions due to the increase in leisure time.

3. The significance of other forms of tourism will be important for future decisions in the Swiss tourism business. Besides the forms of tourism already mentioned, there are some additional kinds of tourism which are expected to grow moderately such as individual tourism, congress/business tourism and city tourism. Although all of these are expected to be of significant importance for Swiss tourism, they will hardly reach the importance of the previous forms.

Some forms of tourism are growing at a rate which might negatively affect tourism-demand for Switzerland, one of these is the taking of holidays in sun-belt areas during winter time. The future growth-rate of that form of tourism is estimated somewhere between medium to strong and this is directly affecting the whole traditional winter holiday business in the mountains: an expected decline in the latter form of tourism is therefore not surprising.

There are manifold reasons for that development. First, the over-crowding of traditional sun-belt areas in the summer favours a change in consumer behaviour. The alternative of taking a sun break in winter (to evade the overcrowding) is therefore becoming quite attractive. In addition the developments of new tourist areas bring about new capacities, which are, in many cases, oversized. That development has serious consequences. The level of prices is very much in favour of the tourist, and the market is therefore a demand-market. It was and will be impossible for a country like Switzerland to participate in a substantial price war. And the last reason, and probably the most serious, is the fact that in the life cycle of vacations participating in wintersports is in the phase of downturn. There are no means to change that trend and adapting to it will be very difficult.

Tourism Infrastructure

The share of large hotels will grow, to the disadvantages of small and medium hotels. Increasing competition and cost-cutting goals force the accommodation industry to work together as much as possible. The last consequence of that development is that larger hotels will be able to survive and smaller ones will have problems maintaining the service demanded. The main reason for that development is the increasing costs; larger hotels have better chances of cost cutting. In addition, only large hotels can offer the extensive service demanded by today's tourists. Further, the trend to part-operation leads to the formation of large businesses and a hotel needs to be fairly large to profit from technical developments in telecommunications.

The significance of both types of hotel (full service/reduced service) will gain importance, even if only to a small degree. The reasons for this are to be found in the markets. For the positive development of full service (traditional) hotels factors like cosiness (rooms) and friendliness (service) will become more and more important. Furthermore, the segment of young senior citizens with great purchasing power is increasing. On the other hand, the reasons for the positive development of reduced service hotels are a possible serious shortage of labour willing to work in traditional hotels, a promising future for reduced service hotels in cities, more freedom to create market-oriented prices (price differentiation), and an increased consciousness toward prices of tourist products.

The profitability and willingness to invest in the branch of tourism businesses (accommodation and transportation) will decrease slightly. City hotels are the only branch where the profitability and willingness to invest are expected to grow. The main reason for this is the expected increase in demand for that category of accommodation. With regard to those two factors for all other tourist business branches a decrease is expected because of insufficient to poor build-up of financial reserves as a result of very small margins, a hardly controllable increase in operational costs, a stagnation of quantitive demand in general, and the massive explosion of personnel and capital costs.

REMARKS ABOUT FEDERALISM IN TOURISM

Both politically and economically, Switzerland is very federalistic. The consequence is a strong regionalization in the tourism sector. Especially in times when money is short, a greater degree of cooperation is needed. Although not much effort towards centralization of the tourism sector is expected in the EC, small countries like Switzerland as a whole will have to concentrate their efforts (for example: towards marketing) to survive in times of strong and possibly hostile competition. Current actions aim for greater competence on a national level (not politically!) and to reorganize the assignments on regional and local levels.

CONCLUSION

For non-EC countries it will be important to adjust to a different economic environment as smoothly as possible and it seems, in the case of Switzerland, that all efforts are being directed that way. It would be wrong, though, simply to adjust blindly and autonomously to new rules and to overthrow national defined goals, regardless of what kind they are. To deal with European integration is not just a matter of federal legislation and regulation. To deal with the challenge of the EC is mainly or at least to the same extent a task for businesses. The greater the degree of liberalization, the greater and more important the role of enterprises and private households.

For the tourism sector, it will be necessary to find market niches. This implies 'greater efforts in education, performance, imagination, qualities of leadership and hospitality' (Keller, 1988, p. 23). Although prices and costs are high, the quality is still high, too. It will be important to remain 'qualitatively something special'. Perhaps then, the country will be able to retain its eighth position in the world tourism market.

REFERENCES

Bundesministerium für Wirtschaft (1989) Bericht über die tourismuspolitischen Vorstellungun der Bundesregierung. In: Aktuelle Beiträge zur Virtschafts- und Finanzpolitik, no. 5.

Kaspar, C. (1990) Touristische Entwicklung unter schweizerischen Rahmenbedingungen. In: *Tourismuspolitik der 90er Jahre*, Die Volkswirtschaft no. 12/90. Bern.

Keller P. (1988) Europäische Integration und Schweizer Tourismus. Manuskript. Zwischenbericht des Bundesamtes für Industrie, Gewerbe und Arbeit BIGA. Bern.

Keller, P. (1990) Tourismus im europäischen Integrationsprozess. In: Kaspar, C. (ed.) *1992: Standort und Chancen des Tourismus*. Verlag Haupt, Ben.

Kommission der EG (1985) Weissbuch zur Vollendung des Binnenmarktes. Mailand/Luxemburg: AfV, 28/29. Juni. (English language edition: *EC Commission*: White Paper on the Completion of the Internal Market (June 1985.)

Müller, H.R., Kaspar, C. and Schmidhauser, H.P. (1991) Tourismus 2010. Delphi-Umfrage 1991 zur Zukunft des Schweizer Tourismus. Eigenverlag Forschungsinstitut für Freizeit und Tourismus an der Universität Bern (FIF) / Eigenverlag Institut für Tourismus und Verkehrswirtschaft an der Hochschule St. Gallen (ITV HSG).

OECD (1990) Tourism policy and international Tourism in OECD member countries. Paris.

Schelbert, R.W. (1990) Folgen der EG 92 für die Schweizerische Hotellerie. In:

Kaspar, C. (ed.) *1992: Standort und Chancen des Tourismus.* Verlag Haupt, Bern.

Smeral, E. (1990) Schweiz 2000: Eine Modellprognose für den Tourismus. Wien internal paper, unpublished.

Schweizer Tourismus Verband STV (1991) *Schweizer Tourismus in Zahlen* Ausgabe 1991. Verlag STV, Bern.

19

TOURISM IN EASTERN EUROPE*

Derek R. Hall

INTRODUCTION

This chapter discusses the characteristics of international tourism development in Eastern Europe. Although trends during the last years of state socialism are discussed, the main body of the chapter will address the industry's problems and possibilities during the transitional, post-communist period. The focus is placed specifically on the international dimension: tourism data for the region present the usual range of analytical problems (Hall, 1991b), but domestic tourism statistics in particular are limited and unreliable. For the short to medium term, the focus of international tourism marketing will remain on the hard currency source countries of the 'West', Japan and the Middle East. While the region's economies remain crippled and their currencies inconvertible, its citizens as tourists will not play a significant economic role although cross-border movement between neighbouring countries is now considerable.

POST-WAR TOURISM TRENDS IN EASTERN EUROPE

Under the region's post-war communist regimes, international tourism could have been employed to help achieve such 'socialist' objectives as spatially equalizing employment opportunities and instilling a positive image of the socialist system into visitors (Hall, 1984, 1990a,b,c, 1991b). However, the bureaucratic inflexibility and early economic priorities of state socialism, together with the, at best, indifference shown towards 'capitalist' visitors, postponed the flowering of international tourism

---

*Eastern European countries in this chapter are referred to by their socialist state names.

Table 19.1. Eastern Europe: international tourist arrivals 1970–1990 (millions).

	1970	1980	1985	1986	1987	1988	1989	1990	% change		
									1985–1988	1988–1989	1989–1990
Albania	nd	nd	nd	nd	nd	nd	nd	nd		nd	
Bulgaria	2.5	5.5	3.4	3.5	3.6	4.0	4.3	4.5	15.8	8.8	4.3
Czechoslovakia	3.5	5.1	4.9	5.3	6.1	6.9	8.0	8.1	41.4	16.7	0.8
GDR	nd	1.5	1.6	2.0	2.1	2.2	3.1	–	43.5	39.0	–
Hungary	4.0	9.4	9.7	10.6	11.8	10.6	14.5	20.5	8.6	37.2	41.5
Poland	1.9	5.7	2.7	2.5	2.5	2.5	3.3	3.4	–9.2	32.0	3.2
Romania	2.3	6.7	4.8	4.5	5.1	5.5	4.9	6.5	15.5	–12.0	34.6
USSR	nd	nd	4.3	4.3	5.2	6.0	7.8	7.2	38.4	29.0	–7.1
Yugoslavia	4.7	6.4	8.4	8.5	8.9	9.0	8.6	7.9	6.9	–4.1	–8.8

Sources: WTO *Yearbook* (1991) 1, 104; (1992) 1, 103; author's calculations.
Notes: nd = no data.

programmes aimed at Western markets until relatively late in the socialist period. The region was certainly ill-equipped to respond to the demands of package-holiday growth in the 1960s. International tourism was character-ized by planned and often symmetrical patterns of movement between Soviet bloc members. Currency inconvertibility, a low ceiling on disposable income and personal mobility, coupled to the stringency of exit visa policies, imposed severe limitations on outbound tourism development.

Emerging from their Stalinist torpor at varying rates, noticeably different approaches to tourism development were taken by the region's regimes. Yugoslavia's pragmatic attitude from the mid-1960s encouraged a rapid growth in the arrival of Western tourists, stimulated further by aid and investment in hotel construction and highway development along the Adriatic coast. International tourist numbers to Yugoslavia were not substantially greater than to several other East European countries (and had been overtaken by those to Hungary and Czechoslovakia by the late 1980s) (Table 19.1). The predominance of Western tourists, however, generated substantially greater income for Yugoslavia, which was equiva-lent to the total for the rest of the region by the late 1980s.

PROBLEMS OF THE POST-COMMUNIST TRANSITION

The quality of the region's tourist services has often been low and very variable by accepted Western standards. Decades of neglect have resulted from a reluctance to upgrade infrastructure for the benefit of ideologically alien foreigners. Accommodation represents one of the most obvious bottlenecks. Much more modest to medium-grade accommodation is required in the region, together with selected investment in top quality hotels to cater for the requirements of high spending conference and business tourism. A freeing of private initiative has seen bed and breakfast become a booming industry in Czechoslovakia and in Hungary, where the private sector had already secured a significant foothold. In the latter, however, with only an estimated 40% of tourist spending actually reaching state coffers and the rest being diverted into the local population's pockets through stays in private homes and unofficial currency exchange, tensions between the industry's public and private sectors have been generated in the period of transition.

There is a considerable requirement for staff training throughout the tourism industry, most notably in hotel management, catering and travel agenting, for skills in computing, telecommunications and foreign languages. One response has seen American Express launching a $500,000 fund to develop tourism personnel skills in Czechoslovakia, Hungary and Poland (Hamilton, 1991). Subsequently, Poland was to receive 4.5 million

ECU from the European Community's Phare Programme to help form an international task force of Spanish, Dutch, German and British consultants to help the Polish authorities draw up a master plan for tourism development. Together with the provision of training for about 5000 industry employees, the programme was to begin in October 1992 (BBC, 1992). Both the World Bank and the European Bank for Reconstruction and Development have also been instrumental in funding tourism training and development in the region.

The way in which many of the former communist *nomenklatura* have managed to hold on to positions of economic power, legal or otherwise, while ostensibly relinquishing political power is a continuing source of concern. Tensions between government departments involved in tourism, between the public and emerging private sectors, and between old and new

Table 19.2. North Americans' repulsion from Eastern Europe (with Western European comparisons) in 1986.

Country	Arrivals of US citizens			Arrivals of Canadian citizens		
	% of total tourist arrivals		% change	% of total tourist arrivals		% change
	1985	1986		1985	1986	
Albania	nd			nd		
Bulgaria	0.24	0.13	−45.0	nd		
Czechoslovakia[a]	1.72	1.32	−11.8	nd		
GDR	nd			nd		
Hungary	1.08	0.65	−34.3	0.23	0.18	−13.6
Poland	nd			nd		
Romania	0.51	0.29	−45.1	0.08	0.05	−38.9
Soviet Union	nd			nd		
Yugoslavia	2.83	1.74	−38.3	0.47	0.41	−12.8
Austria	6.51	3.38	−48.4	0.62	0.51	−19.2
FR Germany	20.74	15.16	−29.6	1.62	1.44	−14.3
Switzerland	20.73	12.99	−41.2	1.94	1.65	−20.1
United Kingdom	21.91	16.53	−27.7	4.37	4.01	−12.1

Source: WTO *Yearbook* (1987).
Notes: [a]Figures for all non-European arrivals.
nd = no data.

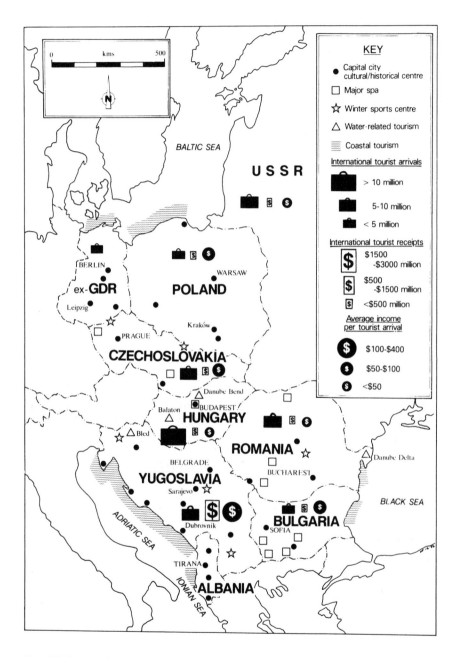

Fig. 19.1. Key features of tourism in Eastern Europe.

public sector organizations may often reflect this problem.

Most of the region's currencies remain inconvertible. In a number of cases, notably in Poland, where inflation has been excessive, successive devaluations have brought official exchange rates into line with previous black market levels. But with continuing fiscal instability, constraints are placed on investment, joint venture development and such practical requirements as pricing future holiday programmes are rendered less secure. Particularly for potential foreign investors, legislative and regulatory frameworks appropriate for a restructured industry may appear slow in taking shape.

How tourism administration will survive or re-emerge out of the Balkan centres of conflict is a matter of some speculation. Uncertainty, instability and conflict in host regions will usually repel tourism activities. Yugotours, Yugoslavia's largest tour operator, was forced to abandon its 1991 programme in the face of mounting conflict in the tourist republic of Croatia. The company then forsook its home 'country' to promote Mediterranean sailing holidays and packages to Malta, Greece and Turkey for 1992, at which point Yugoslavia disintegrated.

In Albania, Albturist, the state tourism administration which hitherto maintained a centralized tourism monopoly within the country, began implementing a decentralization programme in 1991 for a second tier of 'tourist agencies' in all of the country's tourist centres. But only in Tirana was such a body set in motion, before political upheaval curtailed progress, and even here no plans or programmes were able to be formulated for 1992 (Shilegu, 1991). By contrast, the plan devised by the Romanian authorities for the 1990–1992 period was overly optimistic (RMTT, 1990).

PATTERNS OF TOURIST NUMBERS

Just as the processes of post-communist economic restructuring and social change now characterizing Eastern Europe have yet to attain stability, so patterns of tourism development appear far from coherent. The picture is further clouded by data inconsistencies (Buckley and Witt, 1990; Hall, 1991b), and by the fact that although some annual national tourism statistics for the previous year and some unconfirmed details for the current year are available, the most recently available comparative international compilation (WTO, 1992, at the time of writing) employs data which are at least two years old.

During the last years of state socialism, considerable growth in tourist (as opposed to all types of visitor) arrivals was experienced in the region (Table 19.1; Fig. 19.1) despite the short-term deterrent effects, particularly for North American tourists, of the Chernobyl disaster and US bombing of Libya in the spring of 1986 (Table 19.2). Growth was particularly notable for the non-beach holiday states of Central Europe: Czechoslovakia (41.4% increase 1985–1988, 16.7% rise 1988–1989), the German Democratic Republic (43.5 and 39.0% respectively), and Hungary (8.6 and 37.2% respectively) together with the Soviet Union (38.4 and 29.0% respectively). Poland fared less well (−9.2% 1985–1988), but recovered in 1989 (32.0% up). The beach holiday destinations – Yugoslavia, Bulgaria and Romania – showed modest growth up to 1988, but both Yugoslavia and Romania saw downturns in 1989, a trend to be continued subsequently in the former, but arrivals in Romania in 1990 showed a 34.6% increase, albeit in large part because of a cross-border influx of low-spending Soviet citizens from Moldova.

In the early transition period, the most spectacular growth in tourist arrival numbers came about in Hungary, with increases of 37.2% for 1989 and 41.5% for 1990. Apart from Romania and Hungary, the region witnessed a considerable reduction in the growth of tourist arrivals for 1990, and in the case of the Soviet Union and Yugoslavia an absolute reduction in numbers of arrivals. With troubles looming fast, Yugoslavia experienced the greater decline, of 8.8%, following a 4.1% reduction for 1989. By contrast, the Soviet Union's 7.1% decline in 1990 followed an increase of 29.0% for the previous year.

PATTERNS OF TOURIST RECEIPTS

Under state socialism, with the exception of Yugoslavia, the economic impact of international tourism remained relatively small, certainly by comparison with Western Europe: in 1988, the last full year of state socialism in the region, Bulgaria's tourist income was just 2.2% of that of Spain, Czechoslovakia earned just 10.3% of that of Switzerland, and Romania's tourist income was the equivalent of just 7.3% of that earned by Greece (WTO, 1990). That Turkey could raise its level of tourism receipts by more than 600% between 1980 and 1988 was a salutary example for the region. By contrast, receipts declined substantially in Romania, largely due to the deteriorating image of the country's domestic conditions, and they fell dramatically in Poland in the early 1980s only later to recover somewhat. In Bulgaria and Czechoslovakia, however, receipts increased at rates comparable to the major Western tourist economies, in Hungary even more rapidly, and in Yugoslavia fastest of all.

The second half of the 1980s up to 1988 witnessed increases in tourism receipts for all countries of the region except Romania (Table 19.3). Considerable increases over the 1985–1988 period in particular countries – 90.8% for Yugoslavia and 98.0% for Czechoslovakia – reflected the role of high-spending tourists from the West: substantial for the former and rapidly increasing for the latter. Romania by contrast experienced a 6.0%

Table 19.3. Eastern Europe: international tourist receipts, 1980–1990 (US$ millions).

	1980		1985		1988		1989		1990	
	a	b	a	b	a	b	a	b	a	b
Albania	nd	nd	nd	nd	nd	nd	nd	nd	nd	nd
Bulgaria	260	47.3	343	100.1	359	90.5	362	83.9	394	87.6
Czechoslovakia	338	66.3	307	63.1	608	88.3	581	72.3	470	58.0
GDR	nd	nd	nd	nd	nd	nd	nd	nd	nd	nd
Hungary	504	53.6	512	52.7	758	71.8	798	55.1	1000	48.8
Poland	282	49.5	118	42.9	206	82.6	202	61.3	266	78.2
Romania	324	57.9	182	38.1	171	31.0	167	34.4	106	16.2
USSR	nd	nd	163	37.6	216	36.0	250	32.2	270	37.5
Yugoslavia	1115	174.2	1061	125.8	2024	224.9	2230	258.0	2774	352.0

% change

	1980–1988		1985–1988		1988–1989		1989–1990	
	a	b	a	b	a	b	a	b
Albania	nd	nd	nd	nd	nd	nd	nd	nd
Bulgaria	38.1	−8.5	4.7	−9.6	0.8	−7.3	8.8	4.4
Czechoslovakia	29.0	−53.1	98.0	39.9	−4.4	−18.1	−19.1	−19.8
GDR	nd	nd	nd	nd	nd	nd	nd	nd
Hungary	50.6	33.6	48.0	36.2	5.3	−23.3	25.3	−11.5
Poland	−31.6	56.0	74.6	92.5	−1.9	−25.8	31.7	−27.5
Romania	−45.7	−44.7	−6.0	−18.6	−2.3	11.0	−36.5	16.2
USSR	nd	nd	32.5	−4.3	15.7	−10.6	8.0	16.3
Yugoslavia	81.5	29.1	90.8	78.8	10.2	11.2	24.4	36.5

Sources: WTO *Yearbook* (1991) 1, 104; (1992) 1, 103; author's calculations.
Notes: nd = no data.
a, receipts (US$ million).
b, average income per tourist arrival (US$).

decrease, and for the longer 1980–1988 period a 47.2% downturn. In terms of growth of receipts per tourist, Poland recorded the best performance for 1985–1988 with an increase of 92.5% whereas Romania, along with Bulgaria and the USSR, experienced decreases.

During the early stages of transition, as tourist numbers increased, and particularly day trippers responded to the easing of cross-border movement, receipts increased less than proportionately, such that for 1989, all countries of the region except Romania and the USSR saw a decrease in receipts per tourist, and for 1990 only Bulgaria, Yugoslavia and again the Soviet Union recorded per capita increases, in the latter two cases reflecting declining rather than increasing tourist numbers.

CENTRAL EUROPE – BALKAN CONTRASTS

Despite the division of Czechoslovakia (Hall, 1992a), relative stability, more advanced economies, a concentration of international funding (Hamilton, 1991; Michalak and Gibb, 1993) and initial advantage, point to Central Europe, and particularly the landlocked states of Czechoslovakia and Hungary, making advances in international tourism development which the troubled Balkan societies are now poorly placed to pursue.

A sample of more recent figures for Hungary can exemplify that country's position as the region's leading tourist destination in terms of numbers, and, since the Yugoslav upheavals, also in terms of tourist receipts. Hungary derived a tourism income surplus of $170 million for the first seven months of 1991, a 30% increase on the previous year's figure. The industry became the country's largest balance of payments contributor. For the first six months of 1992, despite a 6% decrease in tourism income, Hungarians travelling abroad spent 21% less than incoming tourists, resulting in a surplus of $202.1 million, an increase of $30 million.

The Balkan countries, despite possessing the most favourable climatic and coastal conditions for mass tourism, have experienced stagnation or even decline in tourist numbers, reflecting an initial lack of clarity of political change, continuing instability, and a generally lower degree of road transport accessibility from major West European markets. Further, tourists from the northern part of the region, no longer restricted to Soviet bloc vacation destinations, started to abandon their post-war Black Sea coast holiday playgrounds for more enticing Western venues. However, in Bulgaria at least, preliminary figures for the first half of 1992 were showing an increase of 23–25% in foreign visitors compared to the previous disastrous year, perhaps the result of deflection from the former Yugoslavia.

Beset by internal conflict and long-term uncertainty, the former

Yugoslav lands, previously unique in the region with their predominance of Western tourists (Allcock, 1991), experienced a decrease in tourism earnings of 69% during the first seven months of 1991, with 62% fewer foreign visitors and 68% per cent fewer overnight stays. The decline in numbers had begun in 1989, and a 40% reduction in 'domestic' tourists on the Adriatic riviera was recorded during the first six months of 1990, reflecting an unwillingness of Serbs to return to Croatian coastal resorts. Pegging the dinar rate to the Deutschmark meant that Yugoslavia's once inexpensive resorts became relatively costly for foreigners. A $2 million publicity campaign aimed at the Austrian and German markets to redress the situation was soon overtaken by domestic events. In neighbouring Albania, international tourism activity, never excessive, had come to a virtual halt by 1992 (Hall, 1991b, 1992b).

MODAL SPLIT OF INTERNATIONAL VISITOR ARRIVALS

The relationship between patterns of tourism development and transport use in the region is complex (Hall, 1993). Unfortunately, most transport mode data available on a comparative basis relate to all visitor arrivals and usually fail to distinguish tourist figures separately.

In the late 1980s, road transport was the predominant mode for visitor arrivals in the region, ranging from 56% of all arrivals in Romania (1988) to 88% in Yugoslavia (1988) (Table 19.4). The figures for several countries, but notably Yugoslavia and Bulgaria, are distorted by high levels of transit traffic, predominantly by road. Romania had a high proportion of arrivals by rail (36%), reflecting its dependence on the regional market in 1988. Western 'packages' accounted for most of the air arrivals in Yugoslavia, Romania and Bulgaria, although the overall proportion of arrivals by air (between 1 and 12%), was far lower than for major West European package holiday host countries such as Spain (31.6%) and Turkey (50.6%) (Hall, 1991b, p. 70).

Although subsequent data available from the WTO (1991, 1992) are more limited, for Bulgaria and Hungary at least, the political and economic changes of 1989–1990 appear to have had at least three significant effects on patterns of visitor arrivals:

1. A substantial increase in overall numbers of arrivals: to Bulgaria by over 25% between 1989 and 1990, and to Hungary by over 51%.
2. An increase in the proportion as well as absolute numbers of arrivals by road: to Bulgaria by over 36%, to Hungary by over 60%.
3. Stimulating a decrease in arrivals by air both proportionately, and perhaps a little surprisingly, in absolute terms, with Bulgarian air arrivals down nearly 28% and those to Hungary by 12%.

Of the other two recorded modes of arrival, rail-borne travellers increased in number to both Bulgaria and Hungary although they decreased in relative terms. The small water-borne sector recorded both absolute and relative declines at the turn of the decade.

The relationship between road and air arrivals in Bulgaria and Hungary for 1990 is noteworthy (Table 19.5). Although both countries experienced significant proportional decreases of air arrivals from Eastern Europe (with the notable exception of newly freed citizens of Romania, although the 147.5% increase in visitor arrivals to Bulgaria from that country represented only an additional 2000), the pattern of arrivals from Western Europe was far less uniform, with Bulgaria recording mostly losses but Hungary making some notable gains.

For arrivals by road, much greater numbers of Romanians, and for Bulgaria, also Soviet citizens, distort the picture for incoming East Europeans. The number of Romanians entering neighbouring Bulgaria by road increased from a 1989 figure of 181,921 to 1.56 million for 1990, raising their share of all road arrivals to Bulgaria from 2.88 to 18.13%. For Hungary the change was even more dramatic, with the relative freedom of movement now afforded to Romanian ethnic Hungarians and with Hungary being viewed by many Romanians as a gateway to the West: numbers increased from 0.10 to 7.04 million, raising the Romanian share of road arrivals in Hungary from 0.52 to 22.92%. In respect of this latter consideration, Romanians arriving in Hungary by rail in 1990 increased by 403.1% compared to the previous year, again by far the largest increase of any source country.

The arrival figures for Hungary (aside from the Romanian skewing, and the increase in Yugoslavs – presumably Serbs turning away from the Croatian coast) saw the strengthening of a number of West European markets for overland travel boosted significantly.

MOBILITY CONSTRAINTS

Most of the region's border-crossing facilities require modernization to speed up often tiresome formalities. Progress is being made in Hungary, for example, where 5000 professional border guards are to replace 22,000 soldiers by the mid-1990s, and a computerization of border checks at all of the country's 723 crossing points is being undertaken to ease handling of the coded EC passport. Although the need for entry visas has been mutually abolished between various of the region's countries and the outside world, progress in this direction, particularly involving the Balkan states, has been hampered by Western governments' fear of large influxes of impoverished refugees, migrant workers and organized crime.

Table 19.4. Central and Eastern Europe: visitor arrivals by mode of transport, 1988–1990.

(i) Visitor arrivals by mode of transport, 1988–1990 (%).

Countries	Air			Rail			Road			Sea/river		
	a	b	c	a	b	c	a	b	c	a	b	c
Albania	nd	nd	nd	nd	nd	nd	nd	nd	nd	nd	nd	nd
Bulgaria	12.2	12.1	7.0	7.8	10.0	8.9	79.1	76.8	83.4	0.9	1.1	0.8
Czechoslovakia	1.7	1.4	nd	24.0	25.1	nd	74.1	73.3	nd	0.2	0.2	nd
GDR	3.0	nd	nd	28.8	nd	nd	67.4	nd	nd	0.8	nd	nd
Hungary	3.6	2.7	1.6	20.5	20.2	16.6	75.4	76.6	81.6	0.6	0.5	0.3
Poland	nd	nd	nd	nd	nd	nd	nd	nd	nd	nd	nd	nd
Romania	5.5	nd	nd	36.2	nd	nd	55.9	nd	nd	2.3	nd	nd
Yugoslavia	5.3	nd	nd	4.2	nd	nd	88.3	nd	nd	2.2	nd	nd

(ii) Visitor arrivals by mode of transport 1989–1990 (millions).

Countries	Air			Rail			Road			Sea/river			Totals		
	b	c	d	b	c	d	b	c	d	b	c	d	b	c	d
Bulgaria	0.99	0.72	−27.7	0.82	0.92	12.5	6.32	8.61	36.3	0.09	0.08	−14.4	8.22	10.33	25.65
Hungary	0.68	0.60	−12.1	5.03	6.24	24.0	19.10	30.70	60.7	0.11	0.10	−9.5	24.92	37.63	51.02

Source: WTO Yearbooks, Vol. 2, 1990, 1991, 1992.
Notes: a, 1988; b, 1989; c, 1990; d, 1989–90 % change; nd = no data.
The data in this table refer to all 'visitor arrivals', the only statistics broken down by transport mode in WTO Yearbooks. By contrast, data in Tables 19.2 and 19.3 refer specifically to the more narrowly defined 'tourist arrivals'.

Table 19.5. Bulgaria and Hungary: major changes in visitor arrivals by mode of transport, 1989–1990 (%).

Source	Bulgaria	Hungary
(i) Major changes in arrivals by air, 1989–1990.		
'Eastern Europe'	−38.3	−65.8
Czechoslovakia	−27.3	−53.7
Poland	−40.6	−55.0
Austria		−34.9
Finland	−31.8	
Hungary	−30.6	−
All Europe	−29.9	
Soviet Union		−29.7
The Netherlands		+18.2
Turkey	+33.0	
USA	(−5.6)	+35.0
UK		+36.0
France		+42.1
Romania	+147.5	+400.0
(ii) Major changes in arrivals by road, 1989–1990		
'Eastern Europe'	+73.5	+75.5
Romania	+758.5	+936.0
The Netherlands		+329.4
Soviet Union	+235.2	(−1.3)
France		+200.0
Yugoslavia	+13.1	+90.4
UK		+56.7
Turkey	+32.7	
Czechoslovakia	−28.9	
Austria	−39.4	
Hungary	−44.6	−

Source: WTO *Yearbook* (1992) Vol. 2.

Thus, although since the events of 1989 exit visa requirements for East Europeans have been abolished, administrative and financial constraints on their movement have been imposed or extended by Western governments replacing the 'iron curtain' with a 'dollar curtain'. In Britain, for example, although visa-free agreements with the region's governments have largely focused on Central Europe, Romanians wishing to visit the UK still require visas costing two weeks' average income, and need to provide letters of invitation from their host and confirmation from their employer that they are actually on leave during their visit. UK visa requirements have been reimposed on visitors from all parts of the former Yugoslavia except Slovenia and Croatia, after decades of visa-free travel. At the time of writing, something of a constitutional crisis had arisen in Germany concerning the need to modify the country's relatively liberal approach to refugees and asylum seekers.

'Sustainable' Tourism

The extent to which the often poor environmental image of the region (Carter and Turnock, 1993) has acted as a force of repulsion against tourism development, and the environmental impacts of tourism activities in their turn, remain to be assessed. While official recognition is now being extended to the need for 'sustainable', 'green' and 'eco' tourism, as in the Romanian national tourism programme (RMTT, 1990, 3), and in the UK Environmental 'Know How Fund' for the region, there may be little conceptual discussion and analysis of the appropriateness of adopting what may be little more than fashionable buzz-words. This can result in contradictory and conflicting policy statements. Further, a newly unleashed entrepreneurial sector may have neither the resources nor the inclination to take a longer-term view of tourism's environmental impacts, particularly where environmental considerations may impact upon such local economic activities as hunting, fishing and smuggling.

Attempts to involve local communities in tourism development processes are inhibited by the lack of experience of bottom-up development on which citizens can draw. For example, researchers from the Danube Delta Institute have been breaking new ground by surveying local populations on their attitudes towards accommodating tourists and on other ways of being drawn into 'ecotourism' processes in the Delta (DDITRG, 1991). Yet such crucial questions as defining and recognizing tourism-carrying capacities and 'saturation levels' have barely begun to be addressed, and may be neglected because of skill shortages, inadequate resources and political in-fighting (Hall, 1991a).

CONCLUSIONS

Eastern Europe is vulnerable to tourism fashion changes, which are themselves sensitive to the instability and myriad problems besetting the region. The euphoria of 1989/90 was short-lived. The repulsion effects of the region's image of instability and conflict, particularly in the Balkans, may have long-term, if not permanent damaging consequences. Further, the impact of socioeconomic change has witnessed rapidly rising crime and accident rates, although the relationship with tourism development is far from easy to evaluate.

Yet the region's cultural and environmental diversity provides the potential for substantial market segmentation. Targeting niche markets – ideally high spending groups with minimal adverse impacts and season-extending activities – should emphasize the significance of conference/ business tourism and exploitation of both West European and North American incentive travel. The region's substantial heritage potential, varied health resorts and natural protected areas can be employed to supplement such activities. With a heightened awareness of nationality, ethnic tourism can increase in importance (Ostrowski, 1991). Gender issues in tourism marketing also need to be addressed (Kinnaird and Hall, 1993).

But tourism development is not a short cut to employment and income generation for hard-pressed governments. The danger of Eastern Europe falling into a dependency relationship with the West is a real one, becoming dominated by transnational, vertically and horizontally integrated tourism and travel conglomerates and financial institutions. The proportion of tourists to the region concentrating in a few specific locations may well be increased as more package holidays are organized, as accommodation and transport economies of scale for host countries are realized, and as disparities in service levels and tourist investment in the region grow. The widening gulf between Central Europe and the Balkans is likely to be exacerbated, with considerable implications for tourism development patterns and policies. A number of localities in Central Europe are already rapidly reaching saturation level, with increased overcrowding, infrastructural strains, environmental deterioration, cultural degradation and consequent host antagonism.

Underscored by potential threats to fragile cultural and physical environments, the question of the nature, speed and quality of international tourism development in Eastern Europe is likely to be one of the more critical components of the region's precarious post-communist pathway. For tourism development to be successful and acceptable, sensitivity of implementation and sustainability must be more than just clichés in national or corporate plans. Yet for the foreseeable future, the governments, companies and institutions of the region are unlikely to have sufficient resources to put into practice and evaluate such requirements. Unless such management is forthcoming, however, longer-term tourism development in Eastern Europe is likely to pose more problems than it solves.

REFERENCES

Allcock, J.B. (1991) Yugoslavia. In: Hall, D.R. (ed.), *Tourism and Economic Development in Eastern Europe and the Soviet Union.* Belhaven, London and Halstead, New York, pp. 236–258.

BBC (1992) Poland: EC: finance for development of tourism; Spanish consultancy to advise. *Summary of World Broadcasts: Eastern Europe* SWB EE/WO253 A/3.

Buckley, P.J. and Witt, S.F. (1990) Tourism in the centrally-planned economies of Europe. *Annals of Tourism Research* 17(1), 7–18.

Carter, F.W. and Turnock, D. (eds) (1993) *Environmental Problems in Eastern Europe.* Routledge, London.

DDITRG (Danube Delta Institute Tourism Research Group) (1991) *Researches to Achieve a Tourism Based on the Support Capacity of Deltaic Ecosystems.* Danube Delta Institute, Tulcea.

Hall, D.R. (1984) Foreign tourism under socialism: the Albanian 'Stalinist' model. *Annals of Tourism Research* 11(4), 539–555.

Hall, D.R. (1990a) Eastern Europe opens its doors. *Geographical Magazine* 62(4), 10–15.

Hall, D.R. (1990b) Stalinism and tourism: a study of Albania and North Korea. *Annals of Tourism Research* 17(1), 36–54.

Hall, D.R. (1990c) The changing face of tourism in Eastern Europe. *Town & Country Planning* 59(12), 348–351.

Hall, D.R. (1991a) New hope for the Danube Delta. *Town & Country Planning* 60(9), 251–252.

Hall, D.R. (ed.) (1991b) *Tourism and Economic Development in Eastern Europe and the Soviet Union.* Belhaven, London and Halstead, New York.

Hall, D.R. (1992a) Czech mates no more? *Town & Country Planning* 61(9), 250–251.

Hall, D.R. (1992b) Skills transfer for appropriate development. *Town & Country Planning* 61(3), 87–89.

Hall, D.R. (1993) Transport implications of tourism development. In: Hall, D.R. (ed.) *Transport and Economic Development in the New Central and Eastern Europe.* Belhaven, London.

Hamilton, G. (1991) Amex sets initiative for EE tourism development. *Business Eastern Europe* 20(46), 412.

Kinnaird, V.H. and Hall, D.R. (eds) (1993) *Tourism Development: the Gender Dimension.* Belhaven, London.

Michalak, W. and Gibb, R. (1993) Development of the transport system: prospects for East/West integration. In: Hall, D.R. (ed.) *Transport and Economic Development in the New Central and Eastern Europe.* Belhaven, London.

Ostrowski, S. (1991) Ethnic tourism – focus on Poland. *Tourism Management* 12(2), 125–131.

RMTT (Romania Ministry of Trade and Tourism) (1990) *The Programme of Modernization and Development of the Romanian Tourism in 1990–1992.* Ministry of Trade and Tourism, Bucharest.

Shilegu, H. (1991) *Personal Interview.* Managing Director, Tirana Tourist Agency, Tirana.

World Tourism Organization (WTO) (Annual) *Yearbook of Tourism Statistics.* WTO, Madrid.

INDEX